EXODUS

This commentary views Exodus as a cultural document, preserving the collective memories of the Israelites and relating them to the major institutions and beliefs that emerged by the end of the period of the Hebrew Bible. It is intended to help the reader follow the story line of Exodus, understand its sociocultural context, appreciate its literary features, recognize its major themes and values, and note its interpretive and moral problems. It explains important concepts and terms as expressed in the Hebrew original so that both people who know Hebrew and those who do not will be able to follow the discussion.

Carol Meyers is the Mary Grace Wilson Professor in the Department of Religion at Duke University. Meyers has authored, co-authored, or edited such books as *Haggai and Zechariah 1–8* and *Zechariah 9–14*, *The Excavations of the Ancient Synagogue at Gush Halav*, *Discovering Eve: Ancient Israelite Women in Context*, and *Women in Scripture: A Dictionary of the Named and Unnamed Women in the Hebrew Bible, the Apocryphal/Deuterocanonical Books, and the New Testament*.

NEW CAMBRIDGE BIBLE COMMENTARY

GENERAL EDITOR: Ben Witherington III

HEBREW BIBLE/OLD TESTAMENT EDITOR: Bill T. Arnold

The *New Cambridge Bible Commentary* (NCBC) aims to elucidate the Hebrew and Christian Scriptures for a wide range of intellectually curious individuals. While building on the work and reputation of the *Cambridge Bible Commentary* popular in the 1960s and 1970s, the NCBC takes advantage of many of the rewards provided by scholarly research over the last four decades. Volumes utilize recent gains in rhetorical criticism, social scientific study of the Scriptures, narrative criticism, and other developing disciplines to exploit advances in biblical studies. Accessible, jargon-free commentary, an annotated "Suggested Reading" list, and the entire New Revised Standard Version (NRSV) text under discussion are the hallmarks of all volumes in the series.

Exodus

Carol Meyers

Duke University

CAMBRIDGE
UNIVERSITY PRESS

CAMBRIDGE UNIVERSITY PRESS
Cambridge, New York, Melbourne, Madrid, Cape Town, Singapore, São Paulo

Cambridge University Press
40 West 20th Street, New York, NY 10011-4211, USA

www.cambridge.org
Information on this title: www.cambridge.org/9780521807814

First published 2005

Printed in the United States of America

A catalog record for this publication is available from the British Library.

Library of Congress Cataloging in Publication Data

Meyers, Carol L.
Exodus / Carol Meyers.
     p.   cm. – (New Cambridge Bible Commentary)
Includes bibliographical references and index.
ISBN 0-521-80781-6 (hardcover) – ISBN 0-521-00291-5 (pbk.)
1. Bible. O.T. Exodus – Commentaries.   I. Title   II. Series.
BS1245.53.M49   2005
222′.12077 – dc22   2004027721

ISBN-13   978-0-521-80781-4 hardback
ISBN-10   0-521-80781-6 hardback

ISBN-13   978-0-521-00291-2 paperback
ISBN-10   0-521-00291-5 paperback

*T*o Baruch A. Levine and Nahum M. Sarna

Contents

Tables

Supplementary Sections

Preface

Of all the books in the Hebrew Bible, Exodus perhaps has had the greatest impact beyond the ancient community in which it took shape. The account of escape from oppression has become a great narrative of hope for peoples all over the world. The tale of courageous prophetic activity often has served as a model for struggling community leaders. The values embodied in the legal traditions are reflected in the law codes of many countries. The attention to the physical setting as well as the moral issues involved in the service of God reverberates in houses of worship everywhere. The establishment of a final form of Exodus as part of Hebrew scripture was both the end product of a long process of tradition formation and, at the same time, part of the beginning of the book's profound and enduring role in Christianity and Islam as well as Judaism.

Although it is not the first book in the Bible, Exodus arguably is the most important. It presents the defining features of Israel's identity, as it took shape by the late biblical period. First and foremost are memories of a past marked by persecution and hard-won, if not miraculous, escape. As it is recounted in Exodus, this past is inextricably linked with a theophany on a national level at Sinai, the initiation of a binding covenant with the god whose name is revealed to Moses, and the establishment of community life and guidelines for sustaining it. In addition, Exodus connects central characteristics of ancient Israel's spiritual and religious life as well as its defining cultural practices, as they are known from texts that were formed centuries after Israel first emerges in the land of Canaan, with the story of freedom. The forty chapters of this biblical book give vivid reality and texture to the paradigm of divine communication through prophets, the existence of a national shrine with priestly officials and sacrificial offerings, the celebration of festivals such as the weekly Sabbath and the annual Passover, and the practice of ancient customs such as circumcision and the redemption of the firstborn. And perhaps most significant, ideas about the nature of the divine in relation to humanity are given specificity through the role of one god, Yahweh, in the unfolding drama of what is reported in Exodus.

The dramatic flow of the narrative, however, belies the diversity of its literary genres as well as the complexity of the text and the problem of its relation to the emergence of the people of Israel in the eastern Mediterranean thousands of years ago. The appealing universality of many of its themes masks the moral ambiguities of an account that celebrates the freedom of one people amidst the suffering of others. And its canonical authority tends to privilege social constructs that were pioneering in the Iron Age but are less compelling in the twenty-first century. Moreover, so well known are the outlines of this master narrative of escape to freedom and establishment of community that the various shadings and nuances of the dramatic picture are overlooked. And many of the ideas about God and God's manifestation in the world so often are accepted as unique that their origins in or relation to the wider culture of the ancient Near East go unnoticed.

Exodus demands close attention. Too few people outside the academy are aware of how scholars and students of the Bible since antiquity have puzzled over the form and function of its contents while at the same time drawing inspiration from its story. In each generation, new insights have become available from developments in the wider intellectual world of its interpreters. This commentary thus attempts to examine afresh the historical, social, literary, and religious dimensions of Exodus in light of the tools and insights available at the beginning of the twenty-first century. While remaining mindful of the long tradition of scholarly and theological exegesis, it takes into account the contributions of approaches that have developed in recent decades, in which scholars have become more attuned to the particular social settings of the shapers, as well as of the subjects, of the text and have learned much about how to understand the literary artistry of the Bible. Although they are not explicitly labeled as such, various methodologies have been incorporated into this commentary. I have sought to combine sociocultural perspectives with attention to the design of the completed text as well as to the cumulative wisdom of centuries of biblical scholarship in the hope that a multiplicity of resources allows for a balanced and comprehensible reading of the text.

Many people have played a role in bringing this project to completion. I am grateful to the editors of the *New Cambridge Bible Commentary* series for inviting me to participate in this enterprise and, especially, to the Hebrew Bible/Old Testament editor, Professor Bill T. Arnold, for his many helpful editorial comments. I am greatly appreciative of the guidance of Andrew Beck of Cambridge University Press at every step of the way and of the expertise of Michie Shaw of TechBooks in seeing this book through production. I am deeply thankful for the cheerful and competent assistance of graduate students Ingrid Moen and Erin Kuhns at Duke University. I am indebted to the many Duke undergraduates whose interests and questions over the years have contributed to my endeavors to understand Exodus. And I am incredibly fortunate to have had the abiding patience and understanding of my husband Eric, especially when my absorption with Exodus affected our weekends and holidays.

In my first semester of graduate school, I found myself enrolled in a course called "Priestly Documents of the Pentateuch"; the instructor was Professor Baruch A. Levine. Not long afterward, I was in a class, taught by Professor Nahum M. Sarna, in which considerable attention was given to the exodus narrative. As a result of these two experiences early in my doctoral program, I wrote a dissertation focusing on aspects of the tabernacle texts of Exodus. I then moved away from such research interests, drawn to other aspects of biblical studies by my extensive responsibilities in field archaeology as well as my growing awareness of gender issues in ancient societies. It has thus been a special pleasure, in immersing myself in this Exodus project, to return to some of my earliest academic pursuits while drawing upon the fruits of subsequent ones. It is with profound gratitude to them for introducing me to the richness and complexity of the second book of the Bible that I dedicate this commentary to my Exodus mentors, Professors Levine and Sarna. The directions I have taken in this book represent my own navigation of a path they showed to me decades ago.

A Word about Citations

All volumes in the *New Cambridge Bible Commentary* (NCBC) include foot-notes, with full bibliographical citations included in the note when a source text is first mentioned. Subsequent citations include the author's initial or initials, full last name, abbreviated title for the work, and date of publication. Most readers prefer this citation system to endnotes that require searching through pages at the back of the book.

The Suggested Reading lists, also included in all NCBC volumes after the Introduction, are not a part of this citation apparatus. Annotated and organized by publication type, the self-contained Suggested Reading list is intended to introduce and briefly review some of the most well-known and helpful literature on the biblical text under discussion.

Abbreviations

AASOR	Annual of the American Schools of Oriental Research
AB	Anchor Bible
ABD	*Anchor Bible Dictionary* (6 vols.), ed. David Noel Freedman (New York: Doubleday, 1992)
ABRL	Anchor Bible Research Library
AnBib	Analecta Biblica
ANEP	*The Ancient Near East in Pictures Relating to the Old Testament*, ed. James B. Pritchard (Princeton: Princeton University Press, 1954)
ANET	*Ancient Near Eastern Texts Relating to the Old Testament*, ed. James B. Pritchard (2nd edition; Princeton: Princeton University Press, 1955)
ASOR	American Schools of Oriental Research
AUSS	*Andrews University Seminary Studies*
BA	*Biblical Archaeologist/Archeologist*
BAR	*Biblical Archaeology Review*
BASOR	*Bulletin of the American Schools of Oriental Research*
Bib	*Biblica*
BR	*Bible Review*
BZAW	Beihefte zur *ZAW*
CBC	Cambridge Bible Commentary
CBQ	*Catholic Biblical Quarterly*
COS	*The Context of Scripture* (3 vols), ed. William W. Hallo and K. Lawson Younger, Jr. (Leiden: Brill, 1997–2002)
CR:BS	*Currents in Research: Biblical Studies*
DOTP	*Dictionary of the Old Testament: Pentateuch*, ed. T. Desmond Alexander and David W. Baker (Downer's Grove, Ill.: InterVarsity Press, 2003)
EA	El Amarna (tablets)

EDB	*Eerdmans Dictionary of the Bible*, ed. David Noel Freedman (Grand Rapids, Mich.: Eerdmans, 2000)
EJ	*Encyclopaedia Judaica* (16 vols; Jerusalem: Keter, 1972)
HBD	*Harper's Bible Dictionary*, ed. Paul J. Achtemeier (San Francisco: HarperSanFrancisco, 1996)
HCOT	Historical Commentary to the Old Testament
HSM	Harvard Semitic Monographs
HUCA	*Hebrew Union College Annual*
IBC	Interpretation: A Bible Commentary for Preaching and Teaching
IDB	*Interpreter's Dictionary of the Bible* (4 vols. and supplement), ed. George A. Buttrick and Keith Crim (Nashville, Tenn.: Abingdon, 1962 and 1976)
IEJ	*Israel Exploration Journal*
Int	*Interpretation*
JANES	*Journal of the Ancient Near East Society*
JAOS	*Journal of the American Oriental Society*
JBL	*Journal of Biblical Literature*
JEA	*Journal of Egyptian Archaeology*
JJS	*Journal of Jewish Studies*
JLA	*Jewish Law Annual*
JQR	*Jewish Quarterly Review*
JLR	*Journal of Law and Religion*
JNES	*Journal of Near Eastern Studies*
JPS	Jewish Publication Society
JRS	*Journal of Religion & Society*
JSJ	*Journal for the Study of Judaism*
JSOT	*Journal for the Study of the Old Testament*
JSOTS	Journal for the Study of the Old Testament Supplement
KJV	King James Version
LXX	Septuagint
NAB	New American Bible
NCB	New Century Bible
NEA	*Near Eastern Archaeology*
NIB	*New Interpreter's Bible* (12 vols.), ed. Leander Keck et al. (Nashville, Tenn.: Abingdon, 1994–2002)
NIDOTTE	*New International Dictionary of Old Testament Theology and Exegesis* (5 vols.), ed. Willem A. Van Gemeren (Grand Rapids, Mich.: Zondervan, 1997)
NIV	New International Version
NJPS	New Jewish Publication Society version (*Tanakh: A New Translation of the Holy Scriptures*; Philadelphia: JPS, 1985)

OCB	*Oxford Companion to the Bible*, ed. Bruce M. Metzger and Michael D. Coogan (New York: Oxford University Press, 1993)
OEANE	*Oxford Encyclopedia of Archaeology in the Near East* (5 vols.), ed. Eric M. Meyers et al. (New York: Oxford University Press, 1997)
OTG	Old Testament Guides
OTL	Old Testament Library
OTS	*Oudtestamentishe Studiën*
RS	field numbers of tablets excavated at Ras Shamra
RSV	Revised Standard Version
RSR	*Religious Studies Review*
SBL	Society of Biblical Literature
SBLDS	Society of Biblical Literature Dissertation Series
SBLMS	Society of Biblical Literature Monograph Series
TAD	*Textbook of Aramaic Documents from Ancient Egypt* (4 vols.), ed. Bezalel Porten and Ada Yardeni (Jerusalem: Hebrew University Press, 1986–99)
TDOT	*Theological Dictionary of the Old Testament* (14 + vols.), ed. G. Johannes Botterweck, Helmer Ringgren, and Heinz-Josef Fabry (trans. J. T. Willis, G. W. Bromley, David E. Green, Douglas W. Stott; Grand Rapids, Mich.: Eerdmans, 1974–)
TOTC	Tyndale Old Testament Commentary
TynBul	*Tyndale Bulletin*
UBS	United Bible Societies
VT	*Vetus Testamentum*
VTS	Vetus Testamentum Supplement
WBC	Word Bible Commentary
WIS	*Women in Scripture: A Dictionary of Named and Unnamed Women in the Hebrew Bible, the Apocryphal/Deuterocanonical Books, and the New Testament*, ed. Carol Meyers, Toni Craven, and Ross S. Kraemer (Boston: Houghton Mifflin, 2000; Grand Rapids, Mich.: Eerdmans, 2001)
ZAW	*Zeitschrift für die alttestamenliche Wissenschaft*

I. Introduction

*T*he English name of the second book of the Bible is "Exodus," a term that comes to us, via the Latin, as an abbreviation of the Greek title *exodos aigyptou* ("Road out from Egypt"). This title focuses the reader's attention on the narrative in the first fourteen chapters of the book, which tell the story of Israelites departing from Egypt. The remaining thirty-six chapters of the book recount the journey to Sinai and then the revelation there of the covenant and its stipulations; and they conclude with a description of a tabernacle and an account of its construction. The Hebrew title of the book follows ancient Semitic practice of naming a work by its opening words, in this case *wĕʾēllê šĕmôt* ("And these are the names"), which is usually shortened to *šĕmôt*, Names. This title, which refers to the "names" of the sons of Jacob whose descendents are now in Egypt, conveys the connection of Exodus with the preceding biblical book, Genesis, which ends with the story of their descent to Egypt. In so doing, it indicates that Exodus is part of the larger literary unit known as the Torah, or Pentateuch.

According to Exodus, a group of people is oppressed in Egypt, manages to escape, and then journeys through the wilderness to a mountain where God reveals through Moses community guidelines and instructions for a national shrine, which they construct. It begins with the Israelites subjected to enforced service to a human ruler; and it ends with their willing service to a divine sovereign. The first part of the narrative, about the sojourn in and exodus from Egypt, reverberates throughout other parts of the Hebrew Bible – in psalms, prophecy, and narrative. Just as importantly, it becomes the grounding for the second part of Exodus, presenting the covenant and the tabernacle. It also integrates major Israelite rituals into the story of departure. And it has long been the focus of popular and scholarly attention, especially as it relates to the issue of historicity.

1

EXODUS, THE EXODUS, AND THE PAST

A generation ago, most biblical scholars accepted the story line of Exodus un-critically, assuming that the account of oppression and deliverance, of wilder-ness journey, and of theophany and covenant at Sinai was historical fact. It was believed that the transmission of that story among different groups of Israelites led to the formation of separate narratives or sources that over time were com-bined into the master narrative as we have it in Exodus; and the attachment of the tabernacle texts to the exodus–Sinai account by priestly groups seemed likely. But the underlying veracity of most, if not all, of the events reported was never seriously doubted. Even by the 1970s and 1980s, when most schol-ars ceased to consider the ancestral narratives of Genesis as a record of life in the early second millennium BCE, assumptions about an exodus experience in the Late Bronze Age, sometime between 1500 and 1200 BCE, survived in many quarters of academia. Using what is known broadly as the historical–critical, or diachronic, approach scholars tried to understand what happened in biblical times by reconstructing the historical, social, and religious realities that were thought to underlie the text.

Changes, however, were in the offing. Frustration with the long-standing tra-dition of approaching Exodus as a compendium of sources, with concomitant neglect of overall themes, had already led by the 1970s to the emergence of studies that focus on the final product.[1] Such approaches are sometimes labeled canon-ical criticism. While not ignoring the likelihood that the text as it now stands has a complex history, they emphasize the importance of the canonical whole and are often explicitly theological as they seek to understand what its constituent sections contribute to that whole. At about the same time, trends in modern literary studies began to have an impact on biblical studies.[2] Like canonical studies, literary analyses of various kinds (such as rhetorical criticism, narrative criticism or narratology, reader-response criticism, and ideological criticism) are synchronic in approach. Concerned with the existing text and not its compo-nent parts, literary studies examine the existing structure, artistry, and themes of the biblical texts as communicative compositions. Whether intentional or not, such approaches have tended to assume, if not conclude, that the bibli-cal materials are invented and that their authors have exercised consummate and imaginative creativity in their carefully arranged and rhetorically powerful discourse.

The emergence of these newer approaches late in the twentieth century has led to radical changes in traditional ways of understanding the relationship of the Hebrew Bible to the past. Two extreme positions, with respect to the veracity of

---

[1] Epitomized by Brevard S. Childs, *The Book of Exodus: A Critical Theological Commentary* (OTL; Philadelphia: Westminster, 1974).

[2] Robert Alter's book (*The Art of Biblical Narrative* [New York: Basic Books, 1980]) is an early example of the outpouring of such studies.

events and people mentioned in the Bible, can be identified. One, sometimes labeled revisionist or minimalist, dates virtually all biblical writings to the Persian period (sixth to fourth centuries BCE) or later and sees no value in them for understanding earlier centuries.[3] In its extreme, this approach has tended to negate the existence of an Israel that bears even the slightest resemblance to the monarchies of Samuel and Kings, let alone to the tribal groups of Joshua and Judges or the people experiencing escape from Egypt and nation-formation at Sinai. Biblical "Israel" is said to be a literary invention, or fictional construction, produced by Jewish groups of the sixth–fourth or third–first centuries BCE in order to stave off assimilation and create an identity in the face of imperial domination. Indeed, the exodus itself is said to be "without any plausible historical basis or other nonhistorical explanation."[4]

Some minimalist scholars do allow that Israel existed in the Iron Age (twelfth to sixth centuries BCE) but insist that evidence for its existence and for what sort of society it was can come only from archaeology or extrabiblical written sources. The Bible itself cannot be used; only written or material remains contemporary with the purported existence of a monarchy and a premonarchic group of affiliated tribes constitute legitimate witness to a preexilic past for Israel. Yet in their writings, scholars skeptical of the value of biblical materials also tend to malign or misuse archaeology and thus to find no extrabiblical evidence for Israel's preexilic past.[5]

This nihilistic view is often contrasted with what has been termed a maximalist perspective, which accepts the basic picture of Israel's past as related in the Bible as essentially reliable. Ironically, such positions likewise look to archaeology as well as to documents from the ancient Near East. But they attempt to use the results of excavations and surveys, along with written remains, to illuminate and perhaps even to "prove" what is reported in the biblical text, much as modern archaeology and Near Eastern studies set out to do at their inception in the nineteenth century.[6] In giving considerable weight to the assertions in Exodus, such approaches deal with its narrative in several ways. They attempt to show that the catastrophes that befell the Egyptians or the splitting of the sea could have happened as depicted in the narrative; they endeavor to establish a precise date for the birth of Moses and the escape of Israelites from Egypt; and they seek to trace the route of the exodus and establish the location of Mount Sinai.

---

[3] E.g., Thomas L. Thompson, *The Mythic Past: Biblical Archaeology and the Myth of Israel* (London: Basic Books, 1999), and Giovanni Garbini, *Myth and History in the Bible* (JSOTS 362; Sheffield: Sheffield Academic Press, 2003).

[4] Philip R. Davies, *In Search of 'Ancient Israel'* (JSOTS 148; Sheffield: Sheffield Academic Press, 1992), 119.

[5] Pointed out by archaeologist William G. Dever, "Histories and Nonhistories of Ancient Israel," *BASOR* 316 (1999): 89–105.

[6] E.g., Kenneth A. Kitchen, *On the Reliability of the Old Testament* (Grand Rapids, Mich.: Eerdmans, 2003).

Between the relatively few revisionists and the somewhat more numerous scholars with allegiance to the general if not complete veracity of the information in the biblical record lie mainstream scholars who occupy a middle ground.[7] They reject the binary notions represented by the minimalist–maximalist opposition. As most biblical scholars have done for more than a century, they recognize that biblical narratives cannot be read as straightforward history. They seek to understand the relationship between the textual narrative and the real experience of human beings in the biblical past. And they realize that no two of us will see the biblical story in quite the same way, that we all read it with our own individual interests, training, and worldviews.

But let us go back to the revisionists again. However disturbing their perspective may seem in its complete rejection of the biblical account of Israel's beginnings and nationhood, their insistence that the Bible contains no history – and that there can never be a "history" of Israel or of any people, for that matter[8] – has done a service in causing mainstream scholars to reevaluate their own concepts of what history is and how it relates to biblical materials. Postmodern critiques of the very project of writing history have challenged traditional ways of using written sources to reconstruct the past. Realizing that it is often difficult or impossible to know what "really" is happening even in our own world, we "centrists" have let go of the notion that we can recover what "really" happened" thousands of years ago. And we are far more sensitive to the ways that the world in which historiographers of any generation live colors their view of the past. Moreover, we are finally letting go of the modes of thought conditioned by European historicism, whereby we have tended to separate all written sources into categories of historical and true or not historical and therefore fiction.[9]

To be sure, the results of generations of source criticism and redaction criticism, which have sought to discover the component parts of the Pentateuch and to recover the process by which they were edited and joined, have shown that the Hebrew Bible is hardly a straightforward and factual telling of Israel's past. Awareness of what is involved in the construction of history now has helped us realize that, at least when it comes to Exodus, it is not even appropriate to think of its constituent materials as historiography. That is, the authors and redactors of Exodus were not writing about the events and peoples of the past in a way that involved the critical examination of sources and the attempt to use reliable materials. Literary analyses have shown Exodus to be a carefully

---

[7] John R. Bartlett, "Between Scylla and Charybdis: The Problem of Israelite Historiography," in *Biblical and Near Eastern Essays: Studies in Honour of Kevin J. Cathcart*, eds. Carmel McCarthy and John F. Healey (JSOTS 375; London: T&T Clark International, 2004), 180–94.

[8] Such is the opinion of many of the essays in Lester L. Grabbe, ed., *Can a "History of Israel" Be Written?* (JSOTS 245; European Seminar in Historical Methodology 1; Sheffield: Sheffield Academic Press, 1997).

[9] Hans Barstad, "History and the Hebrew Bible," in ibid., 39–53.

organized and artistic work. It has its own logic and plan that have no relation to the concerns of modern history writing. It draws on an unrecoverable array of traditions and materials; it incorporates legends, folklore, archival materials, institutional records, and legal collections. It does so not to preserve a record of the past but rather to demonstrate God's purposes and deeds with respect to one people, Israel, especially in light of conditions at the time in which an early draft of the preexilic biblical books was compiled, probably in the era of national catastrophe in the sixth century BCE. Like the Hebrew Bible as a whole, Exodus is meant to teach, not to record. It may look like a history book, and it is its appearance as history that has led to much investigation of the period about which it purports to tell us; but it is no longer useful to think of Exodus in such terms.

How then should we conceptualize what this literature is and what it achieves? At the outset of the twenty-first century, we are more willing than ever to look at other modes for understanding how it was formed and what connection it may have to real-time processes and events. Before suggesting what such new perspectives for examining the exodus traditions may be, the traditional historical–critical approaches that sought to locate the exodus in relation to Egypt and Sinai in the late second millennium BCE must be reviewed for two reasons. One is to indicate why the specific information in the narratives of exodus and Sinai remain outside the realm of verifiable history. The second is to show how the broad strokes of the exodus narrative might nevertheless reflect the past that can be recovered from primary sources other than the Hebrew Bible. Archaeology in its most inclusive terms – as a way to recover both artifactual and written remains – is the tool for this enterprise. Such remains constitute independent primary sources from the period the text seems to describe.

Archaeology has been enormously valuable in establishing the convergences between references in the biblical text and what can be recovered from the sites and documents of the biblical world.[10] Beginning with the Merneptah Stela, a late thirteenth-century BCE Egyptian inscription that contains the earliest extrabiblical reference to ancient Israel,[11] a wide range of artifacts, occupation levels, and epigraphic remains connect us to the Israel of the Promised Land. However, for the period before that, the era of the supposed departure from Egypt and journey through the Sinai Peninsula, archaeology is of little value. After more than a century of research and the massive efforts of generations of archaeologists and Egyptologists, nothing has been recovered that relates directly to the account in Exodus of an Egyptian sojourn and escape or of a large-scale migration through Sinai.[12]

---

[10] See William G. Dever, *What Did the Biblical Writers Know and When Did They Know It? What Archaeology Can Tell Us about the Reality of Ancient Israel* (Grand Rapids, Mich.: Eerdmans, 2001).

[11] Michael G. Hasel, "Israel in the Merneptah Stela," *BASOR* 296 (1994): 45–61.

[12] James Weinstein, "Exodus and Archaeological Reality," in *Exodus: The Egyptian Evidence*, eds. Ernest S. Frerichs and Leonard H. Lesko (Winona Lake, Ind.: Eisenbrauns, 1997), 87.

A few examples of this failure of archaeology to substantiate the narratives in Exodus will suffice. For one thing, no texts ever discovered in Egypt mention Moses or Aaron, their struggles with the political and religious leaders of the land, and the departure of a sizable number of Asiatics who had been forced to work on large-scale state projects. Another problem is that, despite extensive surveys and excavations throughout the 23,000 square miles of the Sinai Peninsula for more than a century, no trace of the movement of a group of people from the eastern Delta of Egypt to the southern Levant has been recovered. Indeed, although there are remains of way stations or strongholds in northern Sinai along the coast of the Mediterranean, the remote areas in central and southern Sinai that are presumably the setting for the wilderness narratives have no traces of human presence in the Middle and Late Bronze Ages. Moreover, virtually all of the toponyms (place names) mentioned in the exodus account, including the land of Goshen, the store cities of Pithom and Rameses, the Red (or Reed) Sea, and even Sinai itself (for which as many as sixteen different possibilities have been proposed) escape positive identification despite the best efforts of generations of explorers.[13] Even one of the few sites that can be identified – Kadesh Barnea, the largest oasis in northern Sinai and an important staging ground for the Israelites before their entry into the land of Canaan, according to various passages in Numbers – does not appear in Exodus and in any case turns out to have been constructed in the tenth century BCE and to have no remains dating to the era (the Late Bronze Age, fourteenth–thirteenth centuries BCE) postulated to be the period of the exodus.[14] The archaeological evidence from Egypt and Sinai is all negative.

Archaeological research in the land of Israel itself, with accompanying theories of Israel's beginnings, has done nothing to help with the exodus problem. If anything, the opposite has occurred. Hundreds of new village sites in the highlands dating to the Iron I period (twelfth–eleventh centuries BCE) were discovered in the 1960s and 1970s. Built in areas left largely unoccupied by the Canaanites, who lived mainly in urban sites, city-states really, along the coast and in the larger valleys, these settlements have been identified as Israelite and linked with the biblical traditions of Israel's occupation of the land, which is generally dated to Iron I. These would be precisely the people to whom the Merneptah Stela refers.

But who were these settlers? For one thing, the biblical tales of conquest by tribal groups coming out of Egypt are not borne out by excavations. Of the thirty-one sites conquered by the Israelites according to Joshua, only one

---

[13] John Van Seters, "The Geography of the Exodus," in *The Land that I Will Show You: Essays on the History and Archaeology of the Ancient Near East in Honour of J. Maxwell Miller*, eds. J. Andrew Dearman and M. Patrick Graham (JSOTS 343; Sheffield: Sheffield Academic Press, 2001), 255–76.

[14] Carol Meyers, "Kadesh Barnea: Judah's Last Outpost," *BA* 39 (1976): 148–51.

(Bethel) fits the criteria that could link it with the biblical narrative.[15] A mass invasion cannot be supported by the archaeological evidence. In addition, the material culture in the new settlements marks their inhabitants as heirs to much of the material culture of the indigenous Canaanites.[16] In addition, the language found on inscriptions of subsequent periods, and of course in the Hebrew Bible, is closely related to the language of the Canaanites.

Many archaeologists and biblical scholars thus identify the occupants of the new settlements as Canaanites who left their urban centers to strike out on their own in the hill country. Such movements of people apparently were the result of the profound turmoil at the end of the thirteenth century BCE because of collapse of the Late Bronze Age urban culture and the disintegration of Egyptian imperial control over the Levant, to say nothing of extensive drought, famine, and disease. Joined by other similarly affected groups from the coast and the north and perhaps also by some pastoral elements from the east, they became known as Israelites. The relatively isolated villages of the highlands provided a congenial environment for the emergence of a new ethnic identity, with an ideological component acknowledging Yahweh as their god.[17]

This compelling and widely accepted hypothesis is the substantial refinement of a theory called the *peasant revolt* model, which was first generated in the 1960s as a replacement for the *conquest* and *peaceful infiltration* models that were then vying for position as the way to understand Israelite origins. It has the unintended consequence of casting doubt upon the biblical account of the settlers of Canaan all being outsiders whose parents or grandparents had escaped from Egyptian servitude. If many of the new villages were really founded by displaced or disaffected Canaanites among others, the exodus account appears to be little more than a tale developed to dramatize their new settlements and justify their eventual displacement and absorption of the Canaanites still living in urban centers and strategic towns. Even those who contest this hypothesis do not claim an Egyptian origin for newcomers.[18]

The vigorous attempts to show historicity for the exodus narrative at best can show plausibility, as even those who have made such efforts concede.[19] Yet, as both conservative scholars and centrists are quick to point out, the lack of

[15] Lawrence E. Stager, "Forging an Identity: The Emergence of Ancient Israel," in *The Oxford History of the Biblical World*, ed. Michael D. Coogan (New York: Oxford University Press, 1998), 131–4 and Table 3.1.

[16] Elizabeth Bloch-Smith and Beth Alpert Nakhai, "A Landscape Comes to Life: The Iron Age," *NEA* 62 (1999): 62–92, 101–27.

[17] Beth Alpert Nakhai, "Israel on the Horizon: The Iron I Settlement of the Galilee," in *The Near East in the Southwest: Essays in Honor of William G. Dever*, ed. Beth Alpert Nakhai (AASOR 58; Boston: ASOR, 2003), 140–2.

[18] Ziony Zevit, *The Religions of Ancient Israel: A Synthesis of Parallactic Approaches* (London: Continuum, 2001), 84–121.

[19] James K. Hoffmeier, *Israel in Egypt: The Evidence for the Authenticity of the Exodus Tradition* (New York: Oxford University Press, 1999).

direct evidence – from the land of Canaan as well as from Egypt and Sinai – does not mean that the exodus and Sinai are pure inventions. What is presented as a series of momentous events, which would spawn religious cultures eventually affecting millions of people, would in their own time have been little more than a tiny blip in the shifting movements of peoples in the east Mediterranean, unlikely to be noticed or noted by the superpowers of the day and leaving no mark on ancient monuments or in the ruins of desert outposts. But although the specific events, leaders, and masses of people dominating the narrative thread of the first part of Exodus cannot be verified by historical research, the overall story line and many of its colorful details are open to verification by archaeology and Egyptology.

The first problem is establishing the era in Egyptian history to which one should look for materials that may relate to the narratives in Exodus. Attempts to use the Bible's own chronology to "date" the exodus is an exercise in futility. This is evident in the fact that there are strong proponents, with no consensus or prospects for resolution, of dates ranging from the sixteenth to the early twelfth centuries BCE.[20] But if one eschews the need to find an exact date in the highly schematic biblical data, such as the numbers in Exod 12:40–41 and 1 Kgs 6:1, the suggested range provides an adequate framework for examining germane materials. In other words, we can look to Egypt and Sinai of the Late Bronze Age, the period of the Eighteenth and Nineteenth Dynasties, for circumstantial evidence relevant to the exodus narrative. Indeed, the general historical parallels or analogues to the three main components of the narrative – the descent of non-Egyptians from western Asia into Egypt, their sojourn there, and their departure – are found uniquely in this era of the Egyptian past.[21]

Information about intermittent movements by Asiatics into Egypt is plentiful for nearly all periods of Egyptian history, from the fourth millennium onward. However, in the second half of the second millennium BCE, when Egypt exercised hegemonic control of Syria–Palestine, substantial numbers of people from western Asia found themselves in Egypt. Many were brought there as slaves, captured by Egypt's frequent military expeditions into the southern Levant and beyond. For example, a late fifteenth-century BCE expedition into Syria–Palestine yielded "550 Maryanu [charioteers]; 240 of their wives; 640 Canaanites; 232 sons of chieftains; 323 daughters of chieftains; 270 concubines" in addition to great quantities of nonhuman booty.[22] Another Asiatic campaign brought astronomical and perhaps hyperbolic numbers of human booty, including "33,600 Apiru, 15,200 live Shasu [desert dwellers], 36,000 Syrians, . . . [and others] totaling

[20] John H. Walton, "Exodus, Date of," *DOTP*, 258–72.

[21] The Egyptian information about these three parts of the narrative are collected in Carol Redmount, "Bitter Lives: Israel in and out of Egypt," in *The Oxford History of the Biblical World*, ed. Michael D. Coogan (New York: Oxford University Press, 1998), 98–103.

[22] "The Memphis and Karnak Stelae of Amenhotep II," translated by James K. Hoffmeier (*COS* 2.3), 21.

89,600."[23] The term *Apiru,* probably a social rather than an ethnic designation, is thought by some to be related to the Hebrews of the Bible.[24]

During this period, other Asiatics were sent to Egypt as tribute from vassal states. A fourteenth-century BCE letter from the pharaoh to the ruler of Gezer mentions that forty beautiful female cupbearers are to be transported to the royal court, and letters from the ruler of Jerusalem refer to people being sent as gifts to the pharaoh.[25] Still others entered Egypt as part of commercial ventures, with special residential quarters established in port cities for these foreign traders. Syrian merchants are depicted in tomb paintings from Thebes of the New Kingdom and were so prominent that the Egyptian term "to bargain" seems to have been synonymous with "to speak Syrian."[26] In addition, small groups of western Asiatics who were experiencing hardships in their own territories apparently migrated into Egypt, notably the eastern Nile Delta, in search of economic security. A late thirteenth- or early twelfth-century BCE letter refers to tribal groups from areas east, and perhaps west, of the Jordan River entering Egypt at its northern Sinai border to find relief for themselves and their flocks.[27] All these patterns of migration clearly indicate that in the fifteenth to twelfth centuries BCE, the descent of people to Egypt from western Asia would not be unusual.

Other sources attest to the sojourn of Asiatics in Egypt, especially in the New Kingdom in the second half of the second millennium BCE. Of particular interest in light of the story of Moses' childhood is the Egyptian practice of taking children of vassal rulers as hostage and raising them in elite Egyptian households, as if they were Egyptian children. Some of the Asiatics in Egypt held important positions – as scribes, overseers of building operations, palace butlers, and heralds – in the government, and those with technical skills were valued in artisans' workshops. But most of the immigrants, especially those brought into Egypt as captive or tribute, worked as menial laborers in state or temple projects. A thirteenth-century BCE text, for example, refers to Apiru used in building operations.[28] Foreigners in Egypt were generally dispersed among the general populace or served in its institutions and became assimilated into the local culture. However, sometimes groups of foreigners were settled in enclaves, especially in the Delta in the late thirteenth or early twelfth centuries BCE, and provide a reasonable parallel to the sojourn depicted in Exodus.[29]

---

[23] Ibid., 22. The math in the document is wrong; the actual total is 101, 128!
[24] See the discussion of Exod 1:15.
[25] *The Amarna Letters*, edited and translated by William L. Moran (Baltimore: The Johns Hopkins University Press, 1992), 366 (letter 369), 326–8 (letters 286, 287).
[26] C. Redmount, "Bitter Lives," in *Oxford History* (1998), 99.
[27] "A Report of Bedouin," translated by James P. Allen (*COS* 3.5), 16–17.
[28] Cited by William Johnstone, *Exodus* (OTG 2; Sheffield: JSOT Press, 1990), 19.
[29] C. Redmount, "Bitter Lives," in *Oxford History* (1998), 102–3.

Information about foreigners departing from Egypt is less abundant, no doubt because most foreigners were absorbed into Egyptian society and made no attempt to leave. Also, Egyptians were less apt to record their failure to retain foreign workers than their success in acquiring them. Still, a papyrus letter records that two laborers fled from Egypt into Sinai, apparently headed to Canaan, and resisted efforts to capture them.[30]

In sum, the sporadic movement, whether coerced or voluntary, of Semites from southern Syria into Egypt is particularly intense in the Eighteenth and Nineteenth Dynasties, when Egyptian rulers were determined to maintain a firm grip on their imperial holdings in western Asia. This fits the vague biblical chronology. It does not constitute concrete documentation of what Exodus reports, but it does mean that the broad outlines of the biblical narrative are within the realm of the possible. Indeed, the general turmoil at the end of the Nineteenth Dynasty created precisely the kind of weakened Egyptian power that would have occasioned attempts of foreigners to leave Egypt. Moreover, the folklore and local Egyptian color embedded in the narrative imply familiarity with conditions of this period.[31]

Although there is no specific historical grounding for the biblical account of descent, sojourn, and departure, these analogues suggest a core of reality. But how was the experience of Semites, in and out of Egypt, transformed into the biblical story? If historicity ceases to be an issue, as perhaps it should lest the uniqueness of the themes of the overall story be compromised, how can we understand the narrative that links an account of escape from forced servitude with theophany, community regulations, and sacral institutions?

A fresh perspective is provided by bringing the category of *memory* into the analysis. Both Judaism and Christianity are communities for which memory of the past is central to present beliefs and identity. The same is arguably true for the biblical communities from which they emerged. Yet most debates about history and historiography have paid scant attention to the role of memory in the formation of tradition when, in fact, the consideration of memory is an approach that can transcend the pitfalls and shortcomings of historical analysis.[32] The term *mnemohistory* represents this kind of thinking, in which the biblical traditions of national origin are understood as phenomena of collective cultural memory rather than as historical record.[33] Moses and the exodus thereby become figures of memory rather than history. By replacing a positivistic investigation of the past with an analysis of how the past is remembered, mnemohistory allows

---

[30] "A Report of Escaped Laborers," translated by James P. Allen (*COS* 3.4), 16.

[31] Baruch Halpern, "The Exodus and the Israelite Historians," *Eretz Israel* 24: 89*–96*.

[32] Michael A. Signer, "Introduction: Memory and History in the Jewish and Christian Traditions," in *Memory and History in Christianity and Judaism*, ed. Michael A. Signer (Notre Dame, Ind.: University of Notre Dame Press, 2001).

[33] The term has been coined and explained by Jan Assman, *Moses the Egyptian: The Memory of Egypt in Western Monotheism* (Cambridge, Mass.: Harvard University Press, 1997), 8–22.

historical research to merge with the perspectives of literary studies and the sophistication of ideological and reader-reception theories.

Unlike the everyday family memories with which all of us are familiar and which rarely endure for more than several generations, collective or cultural memory forms around intense group experiences, which are organized, transformed, expanded, and ritualized to serve an evolving present. Collective memories create identity; their truth represents the actuality rather than the factuality of the past.[34] To put it another way, the truth of the past encoded in memory lies in the identity it shapes.[35] The Merneptah Stela provides textual evidence of a group called Israel in the Canaanite highlands by the late thirteenth century BCE; and various aspects of their material culture, in relation to biblical texts, also indicate that the origins of a people self-identified as Israelites can be legitimately placed in the early Iron Age (thirteenth to eleventh centuries BCE).[36] The exodus story would be the kind of narrative that would help form the identity of an emerging people. The mnemohistory in Exodus is evidence of just the kind of intense experience around which collective memory forms in the process of the formation of a new *ethnos*. This emerging people is biblical Israel, struggling to differentiate itself from its Canaanite forebears or neighbors.

In considering the exodus and the other traditions in Exodus, we are studying the commemoration of the past, with all its multifaceted developments. The canonical book is a result of how the past was remembered and shaped in ways that served its community of origin, many subsequent communities of Israelites, and many factions within those communities.[37] Indeed, the text of Exodus is punctuated with explicit references to memory and commemoration. The entire body of Sinai materials, for example, attributes to hoary Israelite antiquity the values and programs developed over time and in later times, making them part of a single eternal unity.[38] The festivals and rituals (the Passover, among others) that give Israelites identity as a community and bind them into what anthropologists call a "communitas"[39] (people who share an intense sense of commonality) are integrated into and derive meaning from the account of liberation. The account of exodus becomes celebrated and augmented into a master narrative that includes covenant, community norms, rituals, priesthood, and a national shrine. The richness and complexity of the end result is a tribute to the imagination and creativity of those nameless people who, probably over

---

34 See Maurice Halbwachs, *The Collective Memory* (trans. Francis J. Ditter, Jr., and Vida Y. Ditter; New York: Harper & Row, 1980).

35 J. Assman, *Moses the Egyptian* (1997), 14–15.

36 Elizabeth Bloch-Smith, "Israelite Ethnicity in Iron I: Archaeology Preserves What Is Remembered and What Is Forgotten in Israel's History," *JBL* 122 (2003): 401–25.

37 Ronald S. Hendel, "The Exodus in Biblical Memory," *JBL* 120 (2001): 601–4.

38 Mark S. Smith, *The Memoirs of God* (Minneapolis: Fortress, 2004), 131–50.

39 Victor Turner's term; see Edith Turner, "Rites of Communitas in *Encyclopedia of Religious Rites, Rituals, and Festivals*, ed. Frank A. Salamone (Religions and Society 6; New York: Routledge, 2004), 97–101.

the course of many centuries, made the experiences of some the foundational stories of all.

MOSES, GOD, AND MIDIAN

The story of Moses, which begins in the opening chapters of Exodus and ends at the close of Deuteronomy, frames the exodus–Sinai account. He is the extraordinary mediating human character in the memory of this foundational part of Israel's larger national epic.[40] He is a heroic, larger-than-life figure, as will become clear in this discussion and in the commentary. He is portrayed as the founder of a nation, enabling his people to escape from Egypt and become a covenanted community at Sinai. In the process he interacts with Israelites and Egyptians. And he has an unparalleled relationship with God, whom he first meets in Midian.

The origin of Israel's national deity, through the revelation to Moses at the bush, is remarkable in that it occurs outside Israel's territory – not what one would expect were this story a pure invention. Does the narrative of Moses in Midian commemorate another kind of intense experience, one that deserves special scrutiny with respect to the leadership of Moses and the origins of Yahwism (the worship of a god named Yahweh)? Is there a core of authentic experience in this account that is elaborated and made memorable to serve later generations?

Several features of the Midian connection are striking. Although Moses is the leader par excellence throughout Exodus, in two episodes, both with ritual components, he falters or accedes to two others, both Midianites. One is his wife Zipporah, who shows ritual competence when she rescues him (or his son) in an incident that remains inscrutable (4:24–26). The other is his father-in-law, the priest Jethro, who guides Moses in arranging for adjudication and offers the first sacrifice in the exodus account. These highly unusual and positive features of the Midianite connection, especially in light of the genealogical connection between Israel and Midian (Gen 25:1–4), suggest a note of validity for a formative Midianite role in Israel's past. That it would have had to come in at some point early in Israel's experience is indicated by the hostility toward Midian in some biblical texts (e.g., Judges 6) dealing with later periods.

This possibility that the origins of Israel's god are authentically reflected in these Midianite narratives is sometimes called the "Midianite hypothesis." First formulated in the early twentieth century, it has since been updated and re-argued using archaeological as well as textual data.[41] The archaeological evidence for the existence of the Midianites in Sinai in the era commemorated in Exodus is striking. A particular kind of painted ceramics, called "Midianite ware" or

---

[40] R. S. Hendel, "Exodus in Biblical Memory," *JBL* 120 (2001): 615–20.
[41] Summarized by L. E. Stager, "Forging an Identity," in Coogan, *Oxford History* (1998), 142–9.

"Hijaz pottery," appears from northern Arabia (Midian) to the Negev in the late thirteenth and early twelfth centuries BCE. The distribution patterns link it with the great caravaneers, the Midianites, who controlled the highly profitable aromatics trade in the Late Bronze Age. In other words, Midianites flourished in the area associated with Moses and the Israelites in the period just before or coinciding with the first mention of Israelites in the highlands of Canaan. There is textual evidence too. They were one of the groups of desert tent dwellers called "Shasu" by the Egyptians of the New Kingdom (mentioned in one of the texts quoted previously). Two of their territories appear in geographic lists of the fourteenth-thirteenth centuries BCE: "the Shasu of S^{c}rr," probably referring to people located at Mount Seir, a name associated with Sinai in the archaic poetry of Deut 33:2; and "the Shasu of *ya-h-wa*," referring to a people of Yahweh.[42] The *ya-h-wa* element in this and other inscriptions is likely the YHWH (Yahweh) of the Hebrew Bible.[43]

The vivid tales of Moses, his intimate relationship with a priestly Midianite family, and the first revelation of Yahweh's name at a mountain in Midian are collective memories supported by the documented information about a people in this area with a deity whose name becomes the name of Israel's deity. But questions arise. Why is this link so powerful that it becomes part of Israel's master narrative? How does it relate to the prominence of Moses in Exodus and the Pentateuch?

An overview of Moses' prominence is instructive. Beginning with his dramatic birth story, Moses is the most important human figure in the unfolding story of the Israelites, from oppression in Egypt to witnessing God's presence at Sinai. Role after role accrues to his characterization. Early in his life he experiences a prophetic call and continues throughout as a prophet – as the mediator of God's word to the people. He functions as a diplomat and political leader. He performs priestly rites. He brings about a military victory against the Amalekites. He adjudicates disputes among the people. He transmits the covenant. And of course he is a family man, with parents, siblings, a wife, in-laws, and children. Yet, despite the humanity portrayed in these family relationships, he transcends ordinary humanity in the astonishing variety of his roles and the success, often despite the resistance of friend and enemy alike, with which he exercises leadership in all areas of national life. It is not an understatement to call him super-human. Moses is a larger-than-life figure, if not a demi-god.

Such culture heroes tend to emerge in situations of rupture in cultural flow. Constructing a mythic founder–leader creates security amidst the chaos and instability of change and provides unity for disparate groups. It is useful to

---

[42] Frank Moore Cross, *From Epic to Canon: History and Literature in Ancient Israel* (Baltimore: The Johns Hopkins University Press, 1998), 67.

[43] David Noel Freedman, Michael Patrick O'Conner, and Helmer Ringgren, "*YHWH*," *TDOT* 5:510. The name for God in the Hebrew Bible is discussed in relation to Exod 3:13–15 and in A Closer Look: The Name of God, pp. 57–9.

note, by way of analogy from American history, that the crucial and multi-faceted leadership role of George Washington took on mythic proportions in the early literature of the new republic. During his lifetime and for genera-tions to come, the first president and founding father par excellence became imbued with divinity. Even while some criticized aspects of his leadership, a national myth emerged in which Washington truly transcended ordinary hu-manity in collective popular acclaim. The extraordinary growth of what has been called the "Washington legend" signaled that the diverse groups that were to constitute the new nation had chosen to risk revolution and to unite in pur-suing a new way of life, committed to ideals different from those of the English overlords.[44]

Perhaps the mythic and multifaceted characterization of Moses served simi-lar purposes in establishing and maintaining a collective Israelite identity for the amalgam of peoples settling in the highlands in the Iron I period. Whether the rupture and disunity resolved by his heroic stature and intimacy with God was that of the foundational period of ancient Israel or of the trauma of destruction and exile many centuries later cannot be determined. It is more likely that both are involved, for traditions in collective memory serve the present in their rec-ollections of the past. Similarly, rituals and rules as well as sacred accounts are typically generated among people who have shared traumatic transitions and attempt to capture their experience in normative expressions.[45] They form the basis for the shared institutions that maintain group identity.[46]

A core of reality underlying Moses' biblical prominence, in fact, can solve one of the problems regarding Israelite beginnings. The various theories about the new settlers in the highlands becoming the Israelites identified as such in the Merneptah Stela and perhaps in archaeological remains do not account for the dynamics of this transformation or for the emergence of ethnic identity. If the experience of freedom was the "what" that motivated this process, Moses would have been the "who." It is not atypical for legendary figures to be part of the "revolution" of new national self-awareness among disparate groups such as would have been part of ancient Israel's beginnings in the premonarchic and early monarchic periods (cf. "mixed crowd," the ethnically diverse group of 12:38[47]). Such figures are typically the catalysts of some sort of radical cultural change that is sometimes religious, sometimes political, or sometimes both, as in the case with Moses. Can one imagine Christianity without Jesus? Islam without Mohammed? The mystery of how highland farmers began considering

---

[44] Catherine L. Albanese, *Sons of the Fathers: The Civil Religion of the American Revolution* (Philadelphia: Temple University Press, 1976), 143–81.

[45] E. Turner, "Rites of Communitas," in *Encyclopedia of Religious Rites* (2004), 98.

[46] Paul Spikard and W. Jeffrey Burroughs, "We Are a People," in *We Are a People: Narrative and Multiplicity in Constructing Ethnic Identity,* eds. Paul Spikard and W. Jeffrey Burroughs (Philadelphia: Temple University Press, 2000), 10–11.

[47] Heinz-Josef Fabry and Hedwig Lamberty-Zielinski, "II/III ʿrb II/III," *TDOT* 11:332.

themselves Israelites may lie in their acceptance of a new god, brought in by a small group of refugees from Egypt, led by a charismatic figure convinced that the escape was the result of the will of this new deity who had been encountered in Midian. A new deity with a new narrative of journey and a commitment to freedom would spread among the highlanders, creating a new collective identity and signifying a distinction from certain aspects of the surrounding culture. Journey, after all, represents a movement away, a transformation, a new way of life. And the seeds of cultic practices to memorialize and celebrate the narrative would be planted by Moses' closest family. Moses is portrayed as coming from a priestly family, the tribe of Levi; and it is striking that the several biblical figures with Egyptian names (Moses himself, Hophni, Phineas, and Pashhur) are Levites. Indeed, it may be that the Levites were the people who sojourned in and departed from Egypt, becoming dispersed among the highland communities of Canaan without territories of their own, and functioning as guardians, transmitters, and shapers of the past.

And there may be more, if one considers the Moses–covenant connection that is the culmination of the journey to freedom in Exodus. The highland communities seem to be independent sociopolitical entities, loosely connected with each other in small chiefdoms and manifesting a quasi-egalitarian material culture. Guidelines for the stability of the communities may well have been influenced by the insistence of a charismatic founding figure (Moses) or his followers on certain standards of behavior grounded in the experience of freedom. It is characteristic of founding fathers to be connected with community standards, whether informal stipulations or formal law.[48] Prophetic or religious figures of communities with a new identity are typically considered lawgivers for their groups. Think, for example, of how Jesus was seen by some as a Mosaic figure who transcended him; and the prophet Mohammed is a prophetic founder of a community in which religion and behavioral precepts are merged.[49] The fact that the Israelite and Judean kings of the books of Samuel and Kings are never depicted as lawgivers may well be grounded in the memory of and commitment to a theistic basis for human behavior promulgated by the followers of the prophetic figure of Moses.[50] The collective past shaped in the mnemohistory of Exodus would one day, toward the end of the first millennium BCE, become canonical. But in the interim, according to the narratives of Judges through Kings and the oracles of the prophets, the beliefs, values, and practices

---

[48] David Noel Freedman, "The Formation of the Canon of the Old Testament," in *Religion and Law: Biblical-Judaic and Islamic Perspectives*, eds. Erwin B. Firmage, Bernard G. Weiss, and John W. Welch (Winona Lake, Ind.: Eisenbrauns, 1990), 328–9.

[49] E. P. Sanders, "When Is a Law a Law? The Case of Jesus and Paul," pp. 139–58, and Bernard G. Weiss, "Covenant and Law in Islam," pp. 49–83, both in *Religion and Law: Biblical-Judaic and Islamic Perspectives*, eds. Edwin B. Firmage, Bernard G. Weiss, and John W. Welch (Winona Lake, Ind.: Eisenbrauns, 1990).

[50] A possible exception is David, another founding father figure, in 1 Sam 30:25.

embedded in Israel's recollection of exodus, including the notion of the worship
of one god, did not become all pervasive. It took another impending and then
actual rupture, that of destruction and exile, to revive the importance of the
exodus story as a unifying force in the struggle to maintain identity.[51]

FORMATION AND STRUCTURE

In the late monarchic and early postmonarchic periods, when various traditions
were organized into the emerging canon of the Pentateuch, Moses emerges as
the authoritative figure for those combined traditions. The first five books of the
Bible all become attributed to Moses, as in the references to the "Torah [NRSV,
law] of Moses" in Ezra and Nehemiah (e.g., Ezra 3:2; Neh 8:1). As is often the
case in traditional societies, the major culture hero in the collective memory of
the past gives status and truth to many subsequent traditions.[52]

Theories about the formation of the book of Exodus are thus subsumed into
considerations of the formation of the Pentateuch as a whole. By the end of
the nineteenth century, the difficulties of seeing one man, Moses, as the author
of these five books and the awareness of blatant discrepancies, repetitions, and
inconsistencies, among other problems, in this corpus led scholars to posit that
the Pentateuch is an amalgam of at least four distinctive sources. Given its most
eloquent and extensive expression by a German scholar named Wellhausen,
this "documentary hypothesis" labeled the sources J, E, D, and P. The first two
labels, which are abbreviations of the name used for God in different passages of
the Pentateuch, denote the supposed authors of many of its narratives: *J* for the
author or tradition, dating to early in the monarchy (tenth or ninth century BCE)
using "Yahweh" (Jahweh in German; hence the designation *J*); and *E*, dating
to about the same period or slightly later, for those using "Elohim." *D* denotes
the Deuteronomist, the putative seventh-century BCE author of Deuteronomy,
an influential voice in the "historical" books of Judges through 2 Kings, and also
a major redactor of Exodus in the exilic period.[53] *P* designates a priestly writer,
dating either to the late monarchy (a minority view) or to the exilic or postexilic
period, responsible for all the priestly matters in the Pentateuch as well as some
passages in the narrative sections. According to this scheme, the book of Exodus
contains combined JE narratives, with the emphasis on E, and large sections of
P material, in chapters 25–40 as well as interspersed in other chapters. D may
also have had a hand in the book's formation.

---

[51] F. Volker Greifenhagen, "Ethnicity In, With, and Under the Pentateuch," *JRS* 3 (2001):
     1–17; http://moses.creighton.edu/JRS/2001/2001-1.html
[52] David Lowenthal, *The Past Is a Foreign Country* (Cambridge, Mass.: Harvard University
     Press, 1985), 235.
[53] W. Johnstone, *Exodus* (1990), 76–86.

The compelling nature of this hypothesis gave it extraordinary longevity, despite the controversial nature of its theological underpinnings. The concept of a complex text with at least four discrete components masterfully merged into the Pentateuch by P in the mid–first millennium BCE provided a viable model in Pentateuchal studies for all but the most conservative, who hold to Mosaic authorship. The impact since the 1970s of the literary and other approaches noted previously has led to serious challenges to the foundational role of the documentary hypothesis in biblical studies. What was once taken for granted by all has now been discarded by some and seriously revised by others.[54]

The documentary hypothesis may no longer dominate biblical studies, but recent overviews show that little consensus has emerged about the formation of the Pentateuch as a whole or of its component books.[55] Virtually no one doubts that there are layers of material produced by multiple authors in Exodus, but identifying and dating them and suggesting how and when they were organized into a coherent whole is an ongoing process that may never achieve results as generally accepted as was the documentary hypothesis. Meanwhile, J, E, D, and P remain convenient symbols for some of the components of Exodus. In this commentary the dominant hand of P in many of the materials will be mentioned, and the vestiges of other sources occasionally will be noted.

Just as resistant to scholarly agreement about the formation of Exodus are views about its structure. The Hebrew manuscripts from which modern translations are made lack the familiar division of the text into chapters and verses, which were not inserted until ca. 1200 CE, let alone a division into thematic or literary units. Imposing an outline on the lengthy contents of the book is thus an accommodation to contemporary needs to comprehend the flow of the narrative as well as to acknowledge the diversity of its constituent materials. Yet many scholars believe that there is an internal logic to the organization of materials.

One strong possibility is that Exodus is a diptych. The first half would end at the beginning of freedom with the poetic celebration of the crossing of the sea in chapter 15, and the second half would be the Sinai experience.[56] Another consideration is that the Midian–Jethro episodes in the opening chapters and in chapter 18 frame the first half, with the second half beginning at chapter 19 and consisting of the theophany at Sinai.[57] Somewhat different bipartite

---

[54] Richard E. Friedman, *The Bible with Sources Revealed: A New View into the Five Books of Moses* (San Francisco: HarperSanFrancisco, 2003), 1–31.

[55] Rolf Rendtorff, "Directions in Pentateuchal Studies," *CR:BS* 5 (1997): 43–65; David M. Carr, "Controversy and Convergence in Recent Studies of the Formation of the Pentateuch," *RSR* 23 (1997): 22–9.

[56] Mark S. Smith, "The Literary Arrangement of the Priestly Redaction of Exodus: A Preliminary Investigation," *CBQ* 58 (1996): 25–50.

[57] Eugene Carpenter, "Exodus 18: Its Structure, Style, Motifs and Function in the Book of Exodus," in *A Biblical Itinerary: In Search of Method, Form and Content: Essays in Honor*

arrangements have merit, as does the notion of Exodus as a theme of interlocking concentric circles with God's presence as the radiating centerpiece.[58] Using various spatial, temporal, literary, or theological considerations, others suggest dividing it into three, four, or even five sections.[59] It is clear that there is no single organization of the materials that captures all the possible features that one could take into account.

Another consideration is that Exodus as we have it may be a by-product of the size limitations of the scrolls that were used for writing and not an intentional construct as a self-standing "book."[60] After all, although Exodus can surely stand alone, it is also part of the larger narrative of the Pentateuch. Many of its details and motifs are linked to the preceding Genesis narrative, the tabernacle materials continue into the succeeding book of Leviticus, and the account of the wilderness journey begins in Exodus and proceeds in Numbers. In the final analysis, perhaps it is better not to subdivide but rather to think of it as a long, coherent part of the Pentateuchal whole. The tripartite division of this commentary is meant to facilitate reading Exodus and does not claim to represent an arrangement intrinsic to the ancient Hebrew text.

NOTE TO READERS

Exodus is essentially a narrative – a connected series of episodes with characters and a plot. This masterpiece of ancient Hebrew literature reached its final form thousands of years ago. Thus a contemporary audience cannot always recognize its literary conventions, some of which are not accessible to those reading in translation. Moreover, many of its cultural allusions seem vague or incomprehensible across the time and distance that separate us from the biblical world. As a companion to reading Exodus, this commentary is meant to help the reader in several ways:

1.   to follow the story line,
2.   to understand the sociocultural context – the relevant cultural, economic, religious, institutional, and social structures of ancient Israel and its world,
3.   to appreciate its literary features and rhetorical strategies,
4.   to identify its themes, values, and innovations,
5.   to note the interpretive and moral problems it poses.

of George W. Coats, ed. Eugene E. Carpenter (JSOTS 240; Sheffield: Sheffield Academic Press, 1997), 91–108.

[58]   John I. Durham, *Exodus* (WBC 3; Waco, Tex.: Word Publishers, 1987), xxi–xxii.

[59]   Summarized in William H. C. Propp, *Exodus 1–18* (AB 2; New York: Doubleday, 1998), 37–8.

[60]   See Menahem Haran, "Book-Scrolls at the Beginning of the Second Temple Period: The Transition from Papyrus to Skins," *HUCA* 14 (1983): 11–22.

In addition to the full NRSV text of Exodus, which has been divided into three main sections and a number of subsections, and the commentary on these parts in succession, several additional kinds of information are provided:

1. tables that show the organization of certain groups of passages,
2. inserted sections, called "A Closer Look," that provide additional consideration of the sociocultural context, and
3. inserted sections, called "Bridging the Horizons," that describe the survival of certain customs or features into the post–Hebrew Bible periods until the present.

Two other conventions of the commentary should be noted. One is that, although in the NRSV translation the name of God is generally represented by LORD,[61] the deity will generally be referred to as "God" unless the discussion requires particular attention to the divine name. The second is that the "children of Israel," who – along with God and Moses – are one of the three major protagonists of Exodus, will ususally be referred to as "Israelites" even though the use of that term has multiple meanings and may not be historically accurate for the people who depart Egypt. That is, as a religio-ethnic designation, it may come from a period later than that which the text purports to describe. In the Hebrew Bible, "Israel" sometimes denotes the northern kingdom of the late tenth to late eighth centuries BCE and sometimes a larger ethno-political entity. It can be a political, ethnic, and theological term – an abstract concept as well as the designation of a nation or people.

The reader should also be aware that this commentary will not repeat the explanatory discussions of passages that appear, in virtually the same form, in each of the two sets of texts presenting the tabernacle (Exodus 25–31 and 35–40), although differences in the two presentations will be noted. Comments will appear in the discussion of the first set of tabernacle materials, Exodus 25–31; and chapter and verse references will be given in **bold** print, in the discussion of Exodus 35–40, to indicate the relevant parallel passages.

Some readers might expect that a commentary on Exodus would have maps to illustrate the so-called "route of the Exodus" and also plans and drawings to illustrate the tabernacle and some of its appurtenances. Such materials have been omitted because they would give the impression of reality to those features as they appear in the narrative of the departure from Egypt and in the instructions for building and furnishing the tabernacle. Analysis of the Israelite journey and of the sacred structure indicates that, despite the impression of precision, the various places on the itinerary and the specifications for the tabernacle and its furnishings are sometimes incomplete, often the result of literary arrangement, and at times the result of the conflation of sources that can no longer be disentangled. Although there well may have been a real route of emigrants from Egypt

---

[61] The divine name is explained in the discussion of Exod 3:1–4:17.

and a real portable shrine, the collective memory of ancient Israel has left us textual versions that are one or more steps removed from that reality. To supply maps and graphics would be to provide a false sense of historical accuracy to the information that appears in the biblical text.

Finally, cross-references to other relevant passages have been kept to a minimum to avoid frequent interruptions of the discussion. It is hoped that use of the index will compensate.

II. Suggested Readings on Exodus

*T*he literature on Exodus is voluminous. Perhaps more has been written on the second book of the Bible than on any other biblical book, except possibly the first one (Genesis). For centuries, scholars have been drawn to the major features of Exodus – the compelling and dramatic story of freedom from oppression, the foundational statements of community values in the Decalogue and covenant materials, and the richly textured depiction of a national shrine and its personnel. The abundance of materials appearing in journals and produced by publishing houses specializing in religion and biblical studies makes it impossible for even the most dutiful scholar to keep up with the publications on Exodus. Clearly this survey of the literature cannot be comprehensive. Rather, it is intended to provide the reader, especially those unfamiliar with the variety and complexity of biblical scholarship, with a small sample of accessible and useful resources. Most of the works in these suggested readings represent the scholarship of recent decades, although an occasional older classic may be noted. Virtually all of them are in English, including some translated to English from other languages.

Many of the books, essays, and articles mentioned here have extensive bibliographies. Those seeking further resources should consult them, along with the works cited in the notes to this volume. Another worthwhile resource is Kenton L. Sparks, *The Pentateuch: An Annotated Bibliography* (Grand Rapids, Mich.: Baker Academic, 2002). Sparks has selected relatively recent works, written in English or appearing in English translation, that have made major contributions or that provide promising new approaches. The chapter on "Prolegomena to Exodus-Deuteronomy" provides brief comments on studies of specific themes, features, and genres relating to Exodus within its pentateuchal context (Moses, biblical and Near Eastern law, composition and tradition history, biblical cult, the Decalogue, treaty and covenant, the priesthood, and the wilderness tradition). The chapter on Exodus contains short summaries of works on various aspects of the book of Exodus (such as authorship and composition, history, the narratives of chapters 1–18, the Sinai pericope, the tabernacle, and the golden calf incident).

Among the early modern commentaries of the twentieth century, the one by Driver is worth mentioning because of the author's special expertise with texts and versions as well as his attention to pioneering source–literary analysis and his consideration of geographical and historical matters. Subsequent commentaries generally have followed that approach, attempting to take into account sources, redaction, and context. Noth's mid-century volume epitomizes that approach, although Noth is somewhat less interested in external historical matters and especially focused on unraveling the "prehistory" (i.e., the component documents) of the present text.

More recent approaches are skeptical about the value of unraveling the sources and instead concentrate on the final or canonical shape of Exodus. Childs' landmark volume, which I frequently consulted, is especially noteworthy among all commentaries to date. Although not ignoring the contributions of earlier works concerned with sources and tradition history, Childs also strives to understand the text of Exodus as we have it as well as its place in subsequent Christian and Jewish tradition. For each of the twenty-four sections into which he divides the text, he provides textual and philological notes, a discussion of literary and tradition–historical problems, an exposition of the biblical text, and then a history of the exegesis of that section followed by Christian or New Testament interpretations as well as theological reflections. The emphasis on Exodus as a unified work and on the rhetorical features of the text as a whole also characterizes Cassuto's earlier detailed, although precritical, commentary, which I found especially helpful in identifying literary patterns and allusions. Greenberg's commentary, unfortunately never completed, also provides perceptive comments about the themes of the early chapters, and makes suggestions about the redaction history of the text.

Surprisingly few commentaries, no matter how detailed, provide close attention to specific words and phrases. Sarna's book is thus especially useful in its insightful exegesis of individual terms as well as in its attention to Near Eastern context, although the overall orientation is conservative in its attempt to find historical explanations for or veracity in many features of the narrative and is often somewhat apologetic in tone. I kept his commentary open in front of me at virtually every stage of my work. I did the same with Propp's compendious work, which is probably the most significant addition to the genre of Exodus commentaries since Childs'. Propp provides textual notes, which use Qumran (Dead Sea Scrolls) materials not available to earlier text-critical studies, and traditional source and redactional analysis as well as general notes and comments. His detailed expositions engage previous treatments and are noteworthy for bringing more recent works in anthropology (especially folklore studies) and comparative religion, parallels from Near Eastern cultures, and even his own speculations into the discussion. Propp covers only Exodus 1–18, but a volume on Exodus 19–40 (AB 2A), with the same format and with five appendices, is to be published soon.

In terms of sheer detail, Houtman's four-volume work, recently translated from the Dutch, is also worth consulting, especially as a source for European scholarship. Eschewing the disinterest in history of many contemporary studies, Houtman is concerned not only with internal historical issues but also with the history of traditional exegesis of each pericope by Jews, Christians, and occasionally even Muslims. He presents extensive scholarly exposition, including analyses of all significant Hebrew words and phrases, and also less technical exegetical summaries suitable for the general reader who may have little or no knowledge of biblical languages. The fourth volume is actually a supplement, containing indices facilitating access to the contents of the first three volumes.

A number of commentaries pay less attention to traditional scholarly exegesis and instead provide more discussion of the theological issues that might concern many contemporary readers. Among such works, which are often extended essays more than commentaries in the traditional sense, I found Fretheim's book to be useful, grounded as it is in careful attention to scholarship; he offers many insights into literary aspects of Exodus in the process of providing hermeneutical reflections meant to be helpful for teaching or preaching.

One other book, which is not a commentary in the traditional sense, may be of value to readers who have little or no knowledge of Hebrew. Osborn and Hatton's handbook is prepared for translators of the Bible from English into a foreign language. Because such translators often do not know Semitic languages, Osborn and Hatton provide exegetical, historical, and linguistic information about many individual words and phrases, explaining the different nuances of the Hebrew so that translators can make informed decisions as they render the text into language that best communicates the Hebrew original.

Cassuto, Umberto. *Commentary on the Book of Exodus*, trans. Israel Abraham. Jerusalem: Magnes Press, the Hebrew University, 1983 (1st Hebrew edition, 1953).

Childs, Brevard S. *The Book of Exodus: A Critical, Theological Commentary*. OTL. Philadelphia: Westminster, 1974.

Clements, Ronald E. *Exodus*. CBC. Cambridge: Cambridge University Press, 1972.

Coggins, Richard. *The Book of Exodus*. Epworth Commentaries. Peterborough: Epworth, 2000.

Cole, R. Alan. *Exodus: An Introduction and Commentary*. TOTC. Downers Grove, Ill.: InterVarsity Press, 1973.

Davies, G. Henton. *Exodus*. Torch Bible Commentaries. London: SCM, 1967.

Driver, Samuel R. *The Book of Exodus*. Cambridge: Cambridge University Press, 1911.

Durham, John I. *Exodus*. WBC 3. Waco, Tex.: Word, 1987.

Enns, Peter. *Exodus*. The NIV Application Bible. Grand Rapids, Mich.: Zondervan, 2000.

Fretheim, Terence E. *Exodus*. IBC. Louisville, Ky.: John Knox, 1991.

Greenberg, Moshe. *Understanding Exodus*. New York: Behrman House, 1969.

Houtman, Cornelis. *Exodus*. HCOT, 4 vols. Leuven: Peeters, 1993–2002.

Hyatt, James P. *Commentary on Exodus*. NCB. London, Oliphants, 1971.

Janzen, J. Gerald. *Exodus*. Westminster Bible Companion. Louisville, Ky.: Westminster John Knox, 1997.

Noth, Martin. *Exodus: A Commentary*. OTL. Philadelphia: Westminster, 1962 (German edition, 1959).

Osborn, Noel D. and Howard A. Hatton. *A Handbook on Exodus*. UBS Handbook Series. New York: United Bible Societies, 1999.

Propp, William H. C. *Exodus 1–18*. AB2. New York: Doubleday, 1998.

Exodus 19–40. AB 2A. New York: Doubleday, forthcoming.

Sarna, Nahum M. *Exodus*. JPS Torah Commentary. Philadelphia: JPS, 1991.

In the past decade and a half, a number of one-volume – or multi-volume in the case of the *NIB* – Bible commentaries have appeared. These briefer treatments by leading scholars are all to be recommended for their explanatory summaries of the text as well as for their helpful expositions, each with different emphasis. Brueggemann's commentary, for example, is the longest and most theological. Johnstone's book is particularly interested in redactional history. I found the most recent, that of Tigay, to be especially helpful in explaining and contextualizing many important phrases and passages of Exodus.

Brueggemann, Walter. "Book of Exodus." Pages 676–981 in Vol. 2 of *The New Interpreter's Bible* (*NIB*), 12 vols., ed. Leander Keck et al. Nashville, Tenn.: Abingdon, 1994–2002.

Clifford, Richard J., SJ "Exodus." Pages 44–60 in *The New Jerome Biblical Commentary*, ed. Raymond E. Brown, Joseph A. Fitzmeyer, and Roland E. Murphy. Englewood Cliffs, N.J.: Prentice Hall, 1990.

Dozeman, Thomas B. "Exodus." Pages 85–144 in *The New Interpreter's Study Bible*, ed. Walter Harrelson et al. Nashville, Tenn.: Abingdon, 2003.

Johnstone, William D. "Exodus." Pages 72–100 in *Eerdmans Commentary on the Bible*, ed. James D. G. Dunn and John W. Rogerson. Grand Rapids, Mich.: Eerdmans, 2003.

Houston, Walter. "Exodus." Pages 67–91 in *The Oxford Bible Commentary*, ed. John Barton and John Muddiman. Oxford: Oxford University Press, 2001.

Tigay, Jeffrey H. "Exodus." Pages 102–202 in *The Jewish Study Bible*, ed. Adele Berlin and Marc Zvi Brettler. Oxford: Oxford University Press, 2004.

REFERENCE WORKS[1]

A generation ago, the four-volume *Interpreter's Dictionary of the Bible* (*IDB*), with its supplementary volume, was virtually the only reference work in English for those wanting further information, provided by scholars, about a specific place, theme, concept, institution, deity, or person referred to in the biblical text.

---

[1] Full bibliographical information about these reference works is found in the list of abbreviations.

Now an abundance of fine reference works, notably dictionaries of the Bible and the biblical world, are available. I frequently have consulted one or more of these volumes. The many individual entries on a wide range of topics that have been helpful to me are too numerous to list individually; instead, I will mention the dictionaries to which I turned most often.

Perhaps the most extensive such work is the encyclopedic six-volume *Anchor Bible Dictionary* (*ABD*), which presents technical but readable information utilizing relevant disciplines – archaeology, philology, social sciences, Near Eastern studies, and literary analysis – and also provides bibliographical resources. Less useful because of brevity but nonetheless handy are several one-volume Bible dictionaries, such as *Harper's Bible Dictionary* (*HBD*), *The Oxford Companion to the Bible* (*OCB*), and, most recently, *Eerdmans Dictionary of the Bible* (*EDB*). In addition, the first volume, *Dictionary of the Old Testament: Pentateuch* (*DOTP*), of a projected four-volume series covering the entire Hebrew Bible, offers clear and comprehensive discussions, from a conservative Christian perspective, of the major themes and issues of the Pentateuch in light of recent scholarship. Another work with theological interests but also with strong linguistic analysis and cultural information is the multivolume *New International Dictionary of Old Testament Theology and Exegesis* (*NIDOTTE*). A reference work that includes Jewish perspectives, the *Encyclopedia Judaica* (*EJ*), is a multivolume work, with yearbooks, dealing with all of Jewish culture and history, including of course, Jewish scripture.

Two other references works were extremely helpful to me. One is the massive *Theological Dictionary of the Old Testament* (*TDOT*), which consists now of fourteen volumes, with at least one more to come. The entries contain detailed etymological and semantic analyses, involving comparative Semitics and Septuagint, Qumran, and New Testament usage, of terms in the Hebrew Bible to help the readers comprehend the fundamental concepts they represent. Each entry has an extensive bibliography that favors European biblical scholarship, as would be expected for a work that is a translation from the German (*Theologisches Wörterbuch zum Alten Testament*). Because the entries are Hebrew words, arranged alphabetically, and because the content of the entries is often quite technical, some knowledge of biblical languages is necessary to access the information about specific words. Those with even a little facility in Hebrew will find it well worth the effort to consult relevant articles.

The other is *Women in Scripture: A Dictionary of Named and Unnamed Women in the Hebrew Bible, the Apocryphal/Deuterocanonical Books, and the New Testament* (*WIS*), which provides entries for all the women mentioned in Jewish and Christian scripture. Only six women (Elisheba, Jochebed, Miriam, Puah, Shiphrah, and Zipporah) are mentioned by name in the book of Exodus. But many more are referred to in the narratives, especially in chapters 1–3; and generic women are mentioned in the Decalogue and community regulations of chapters 20–23. *WIS* has entries, drawing on current feminist scholarship, for all of these, and bibliographies are provided for the longer entries.

NEAR EASTERN LITERATURE

Understanding biblical literature is not possible without looking at the rich assortment of documents produced by other peoples of the biblical world and discovered in excavations. For more than half a century, students and scholars without expertise in ancient languages had access to such texts largely through the outstanding collection first published in 1950 by James B. Pritchard. His edited volume, *Ancient Near Eastern Texts Relating to the Old Testament* (*ANET*), contains translations by distinguished scholars of all kinds of documents from Anatolia, Egypt, Mesopotamia, and Canaan, including extrabiblical Hebrew texts. I referred to it occasionally; but its translations are so text-oriented and stilted that in citing materials for the readers of this commentary, I more often turned to the more readable translations in the extensive new work – with one volume each dedicated to canonical, monumental, and archival materials, many of which have been discovered in the decades since *ANET* first appeared – edited by Hallo and Younger: *The Context of Scripture* (*COS*). "Context" refers not only to the selection of texts that illumine the biblical world and the inclusion of references to relevant biblical texts but also to the fact that the translators provide information about the context of each document. In addition, in several instances in which I have quoted extensively from an ancient document, I have used the less literal and more reader-oriented translations of Matthews and Benjamin.

Hallo, William W. and K. Lawson Younger, eds. *The Context of Scripture: Canonical Compositions from the Biblical World* (vol. 1); *Monumental Inscriptions from the Biblical World* (vol. 2); *Archival Documents from the Biblical World* (vol. 3). Leiden: Brill, 1997, 2000, 2002.

Mathews, Victor H. and Don C. Benjamin. *Old Testament Parallels: Laws and Stories from the Ancient Near East.* Rev. edition. New York: Paulist Press, 1997.

Pritchard, James A., ed. *Ancient Near Eastern Texts Relating to the Old Testament.* 2nd edition. Princeton: Princeton University Press, 1955.

SPECIAL STUDIES 1: EXODUS, MOSES, SINAI

The diversity in these works is mind-boggling. For example, the essays in Frerichs and Lesko's book represent historical approaches that find no factual evidence for the exodus; in contrast, Hoffmeier's book provides an example of attempts to establish plausible historicity. Hendel's study is noteworthy in exploring the way cultural memories are formed and become situated in narrative. Virtually all of these studies, even the explicitly theological, grapple in some way with the complex literary traditions combined in the first nineteen chapters of Exodus.

Coats, George W. *Moses: Heroic Man, Man of God.* JSOTS 57. Sheffield: JSOT Press, 1987. *The Moses Tradition.* JSOTS 161. Sheffield: Sheffield Academic Press, 1993.

Davies, Gordon F. *Israel in Egypt: Reading Exodus 1–2*. JSOTS 135. Sheffield: JSOT Press, 1992.

Frerichs, Ernest S. and Leonard H. Lesko, eds. *Exodus: The Egyptian Evidence*. Winona Lake, Ind.: Eisenbrauns, 1997.

Halpern, Baruch. "The Exodus and the Israelite Historian." *Eretz Israel* 24 (1993): 89*–96* (Malamat volume).

Hauge, Martin R. *The Descent from the Mountain: Narrative Patterns in Exodus 19–40*. JSOTS 323. Sheffield: Sheffield Academic Press, 2003.

Hendel, Ronald S. "The Exodus in Biblical Memory." *JBL* 120 (2001): 601–22.

Hoffmeier, James K. *Israel in Egypt: The Evidence for the Authenticity of the Exodus Tradition*. Oxford: Oxford University Press, 1997.

Levenson, Jon D. *Sinai and Zion: An Entry into the Jewish Bible*. Minneapolis: Winston, 1985.

Na'aman, Nadav. "Ḫabiru and Hebrews: The Transfer of a Social Term to the Literary Sphere." *JNES* 43 (1986): 271–88.

Nicholson, Ernest W. *Exodus and Sinai in History and Tradition*. Oxford: Basil Blackwell, 1973.

Phillips, Anthony. "A Fresh Look at the Sinai Pericope – Part 1." *VT* 34 (1984): 39–53. "A Fresh Look at the Sinai Pericope – Part 2." *VT* 34 (1984): 282–94.

Rainey, Anson F., ed. *Egypt, Israel, and Sinai: Archaeological and Historical Relationships in the Biblical Period*. Tel Aviv: Tel Aviv University Press, 1987.

Redmount, Carol A. "Bitter Lives: Israel in and out of Egypt." Pages 78–121 in *The Oxford History of the Biblical World*, ed. Michael D. Coogan. New York: Oxford University Press, 1998.

SPECIAL STUDIES 2: TREATY AND COVENANT

All of these authors have made significant contributions to our understanding of the origins of the covenant idea in the Bible and its specific formulations in Exodus.

Friedman, Richard E. "Torah and Covenant." Pages 154–63 in *The Oxford Study Bible*, ed. M. Jack Suggs, Katherine D. Sakenfeld, and James R. Mueller. New York: Oxford University Press, 1992.

Haran, Menahem. "The *bĕrith* 'Covenant': Its Nature and Ceremonial Background." Pages 203–19 in *Tehilah le-Moshe: Biblical and Judaic Studies in Honor of Moshe Greenberg*, ed. Mordecai Cogan, Barry L. Eichler, and Jeffrey H. Tigay. Winona Lake, Ind.: Eisenbrauns, 1997.

Hillers, Delbert R. "Rite: Ceremonies of Law and Treaty in the Ancient Near East." Pages 351–64 in *Religion and Law: Biblical-Judaic and Islamic Perspectives*, ed. Edwin B. Firmage, Bernard G. Weiss, and John W. Welch. Winona Lake, Ind.: Eisenbrauns, 1990.

Covenant: The History of a Biblical Idea. Baltimore: The Johns Hopkins Press, 1965.

McCarthy, Dennis J. *Treaty and Covenant*. AnBib 21A. Rome: Biblical Institute Press, 1978.

Mendenhall, George E. "Covenant Forms in Israelite Tradition." *BA* 17 (1954): 50–76.

"The Suzerainty Treaty Structure: Thirty Years Later." Pages 85–100 in *Religion and Law: Biblical-Judaic and Islamic Perspectives*, ed. Edwin B. Firmage, Bernard G. Weiss, and John W. Welch. Winona Lake, Ind.: Eisenbrauns, 1990.

Nicholson, Ernest W. *God and His People: Covenant and Theology in the Old Testament.* Oxford: Clarendon Press, 1986.

Niehaus, Jeffrey J. *God at Sinai: Covenant and Theophany in the Bible and the Ancient Near East.* Grand Rapids, Mich.: Zondervan, 1995.

SPECIAL STUDIES 3: DECALOGUE AND LAW

Some of these items, such as the works by Greenberg, Mendenhall, Paul, Patrick, and Phillips, are classic studies. Others are important, more recent contributions. Several of the edited volumes contain many essays that I read and reread; see especially the contributions by Weinfeld, Mendenhall, Greenberg, Jackson, Paul, and Hillers in Firmage et al. as well as the wide-ranging essays in Segal and Levi.

Brin, Gershon. *Studies in Biblical Law: From the Hebrew Bible to the Dead Sea Scrolls.* JSOTS 176. Sheffield: Sheffield Academic Press, 1994.

Firmage, Edwin B., Bernard G. Weiss, and John W. Welch, eds. *Religion and Law: Biblical-Judaic and Islamic Perspectives.* Winona Lake, Ind.: Eisenbrauns, 1990.

Gemser, Berend. "The Importance of the Motive Clause in Old Testament Law." Pages 50–66 in *Congress Volume Copenhagen 1953.* VTS 1. Leiden: Brill, 1953.

Greenberg, Moshe. "Some Postulates of Biblical Criminal Law." Pages 5–28 in *Yehezkel Kaufmann Jubilee Volume*, ed. Menaham Haran. Jerusalem: Magnes Press, 1960.

Hiers, Richard H. "Biblical Social Welfare Legislation: Protected Classes and Provisions for Persons in Need." *JLR* 17 (2002): 49–96.

Jackson, Bernard S. "Reflections on Biblical Criminal Law." Pages 25–63 in *Essays in Jewish and Comparative Legal History.* Leiden: Brill, 1975.

 Studies in the Semiotics of Biblical Law. JSOTS 314. Sheffield: Sheffield Academic Press, 2002.

Levinson, Bernard M. *Theory and Method in Biblical and Cuneiform Law: Revision, Interpolation, and Development.* JSOTS 181. Sheffield: Sheffield Academic Press, 1994.

Marshall, Jay W. *Israel and the Book of the Covenant: An Anthropological Approach to Biblical Law.* SBLDS 140. Atlanta: Scholars Press, 1993.

Matthews, Victor H., Bernard M. Levinson, and Tikva Frymer-Kensky, eds. *Gender and Law in the Hebrew Bible and the Ancient Near East.* JSOTS 262. Sheffield: Sheffield Academic Press, 1998.

Mendenhall, George E. "Ancient Oriental and Biblical Law." *BA* 17 (1954): 26–46.

Miller, Patrick D. "The Place of the Decalogue in the Old Testament and Its Law." *Int* 43 (1989): 229–42.

Nicholson, Ernest. "The Decalogue as the Direct Address of God." *VT* 27 (1977): 422–33.

Patrick, Dale. "The Covenant Code Source." *VT* 27 (1977): 145–57.

 Old Testament Law. Atlanta: John Knox Press, 1985.

Paul, Shalom. *Studies in the Book of the Covenant in Light of Biblical and Cuneiform Law.* VTS 18. Leiden: Brill, 1970.

Phillips, Anthony. *Ancient Israelite's Criminal Law: A New Approach to the Decalogue* Oxford: Basil Blackwell, 1970.

Essays on Biblical Law. JSOTS 344. Sheffield: Sheffield Academic Press, 2002.

Segal, Ben-Tsiyon and Gershon Levi, eds. *The Ten Commandments in Tradition and History.* Jerusalem: Magnes Press, 1990 (Hebrew edition, 1985).

Sonsino, Rifat. *Motive Clauses in Hebrew Law: Biblical Forms and Near Eastern Parallels.* SBLDS 45. Chico, Calif.: Scholars Press, 1980.

Sprinkle, Joe M. *The Book of the Covenant: A Literary Approach.* JSOTS 174. Sheffield: JSOT Press, 1994.

Stamm, Johann J. *The Ten Commandments in Recent Research,* trans. M. E. Andrews London: SCM Press, 1967 (German edition, 1962).

Watts, James W. *Reading Law: The Rhetorical Shaping of the Pentateuch.* Biblical Seminar 59. Sheffield: Sheffield Academic Press, 1999.

Weinfeld, Moshe. "The Origin of the Apodictic Law: An Overlooked Source." *VT* 23 (1973): 63–7.

The Place of the Law in the Religion of Ancient Israel. VTS 100. Leiden: Brill, 2004.

Westbrook, Raymond. *Studies in Biblical and Cuneiform Law.* Paris: Garabalda, 1988.

Wright, Christopher J. H. "The Israelite Household and the Decalogue: The Social Background and Significance of Some Commandments." *TynBul* 30 (1979): 101–24.

SPECIAL STUDIES 4: SANCTUARIES, CULT, AND PRIESTHOOD

This list includes classic studies, such as the works by Cross, Haran, Levine, and Milgrom. Among the more recent publications, I found the contributions of Fleming, Hendel, Homan, and Hurowitz to be enlightening. In addition to the works on this list, I frequently turned to the Anchor Bible and Jewish Publication Society commentaries on Leviticus and Numbers, in which the priestly themes of Exodus are continued.

Anderson, Gary A. *Sacrifices and Offerings in Ancient Israel: Studies in Their Social and Political Importance.* HSM 41. Atlanta: Scholars Press, 1987.

Cross, Frank M., Jr. "The Priestly Tabernacle in the Light of Recent Research." Pages 91–105 in *The Temple in Antiquity: Ancient Records and Modern Perspectives,* ed. Truman G. Madsen. Religious Studies Monograph 9. Provo, Utah: Brigham Young University, 1984.

Fleming, Daniel. "Mari's Large Public Tent and the Priestly Tent Shrine." *VT* 50 (2000): 484–98.

Haran, Menahem. *Temples and Temple Service in Ancient Israel.* Oxford: Clarendon Press, 1978.

Hendel, Ronald S. "Sacrifice as a Cultural System: The Ritual Symbolism of Exodus 24, 3–8." *ZAW* 101 (1989): 366–90.

Hendrix, Ralph E. "*Miškān* and *'ōhel mô'ēd*: Etymology, Lexical Definitions, and Extrabiblical Usage." *AUSS* 29 (1990): 213–23; 30 (1992): 3–13, 123–38.

Homan, Michael M. *To Your Tents, O Israel! The Terminology, Function, Form and Symbolism of Tents in the Hebrew Bible and the Ancient Near East.* Culture and History of the Ancient Near East 12. Leiden: Brill, 2002.

Hurowitz, Victor (Avigdor). "The Priestly Account of Building the Tabernacle." *JAOS* 105: 221–30.

I Have Built You an Exalted House: Temple Building in the Bible in Light of Mesopotamian and Northwest Semitic Writings. JSOTS 115. Sheffield: JSOT Press, 1992.

Jenson, Philip P. *Graded Holiness: A Key to the Priestly Conception of the World.* JSOTS 106. Sheffield: JSOT, 1992.

Koester, Craig R. *The Dwelling of God: The Tabernacle in the Old Testament, Intertestamental Jewish Literature, and the New Testament.* Washington, D.C.: Catholic Biblical Association of America, 1989.

Levine, Baruch A. "The Descriptive Tabernacle Texts of the Pentateuch." *JAOS* 85 (1965): 307–18.

In the Presence of the Lord: A Study of Cult and Some Cultic Terms in Ancient Israel. Leiden: Brill, 1974.

Milgrom, Jacob. *Studies in Cultic Terminology and Theology.* Studies in Judaism in Late Antiquity 36. Leiden: Brill, 1983.

ADDITIONAL RESOURCES

This list is just a tiny selection of the many worthwhile monographs or collections of essays, part or all of which deal with some aspect of Exodus. When I typed "exodus" into the keyword search engine of the online catalogue of my university library, a list of 913 items appeared. Although many of them are books dealing with other episodes of mass departure, often using the term "exodus" in the title to evoke resonance with the biblical exodus, many others are works that investigate or expand on some aspect of the exodus and the traditions that have emerged from it over the millennia. If there are nearly a thousand books dealing with Exodus, the number of articles, dictionary entries, and other such shorter treatments must be in the many thousands. Finding it impossible to compile a brief list of selections from that vast number, I instead urge the reader to consult the bibliographies in the commentaries, the appropriate entries in the reference works mentioned previously and in many of the other suggested readings, and, of course, the references cited in this commentary.

Among the monographs, of particular note is Blenkinsopp's book, which helps readers understand the role of Exodus in its canonical place within the Pentateuch. Another worthwhile book is that of Dozeman, who uses tradition–critical and literary–critical approaches to struggle with the seemingly manipulative character of God. Johnstone's book is not a commentary but rather a brief and balanced introduction to the major approaches to the study of Exodus, with special attention to deuteronomic redaction. Burns and several of the essays in Brenner represent scholarship that attends to the gender of the human actors, especially Miriam, in the Exodus story. The rest deal with some theme or special characteristic of Exodus, other than those noted in the "Special Studies" suggestions given previously. I have also included two examples (van Iersel and Weiler, and Walzer) of the plethora of works in which the exodus serves as the paradigm for liberation and revolution.

Alter, Robert B. *The Art of Biblical Narrative.* New York: Basic Books, 1981.

Blenkinsopp, Joseph. *The Pentateuch: An Introduction to the First Five Books of the Bible.* ABRL 1. New York: Doubleday, 1992.

Bloom, Harold, ed. *Exodus: Modern Critical Interpretations.* New York: Chelsea House, 1987.

Brenner, Athalya, ed. *A Feminist Companion to Exodus to Deuteronomy.* Feminist Companion to the Bible 6. Sheffield: Sheffield Academic Press, 1994.

Burns, Rita J. *Has the Lord Spoken Only through Moses.* SBLDS 84. Atlanta: Scholars Press, 1987.

Chirichigno, Gregory. *Debt-Slavery in Israel and the Ancient Near East.* JSOTS 141. Sheffield: JSOT Press, 1992.

Dozeman, Thomas B. *God at War: A Study of Power in the Exodus Tradition.* Oxford: Oxford University Press, 1996.

Gowan, Donald E. *Theology in Exodus: Biblical Theology in the Form of a Commentary.* Louisville, Ky.: Westminster/John Knox, 1994.

Johnstone, William. *Exodus.* OTG 3. Sheffield: Sheffield Academic Press, 1990.

Loewenstamm, Samuel E. *The Evolution of the Exodus Tradition,* trans. Baruch A. Schwartz. Jerusalem: Magnes Press, 1992 (Hebrew edition, 1965).

Meyers, Carol. *The Tabernacle Menorah: A Synthetic Study of a Symbol from the Biblical Cult.* Repr. edition. Piscataway, N.J.: Gorgias, 2003.

Moberly, R. W. L. *At the Mountain of God: Story and Theology in Exodus 32–34.* JSOTS 22. Sheffield: JSOT Press, 1983.

Sarna, Nahum M. *Exploring Exodus: The Heritage of Biblical Israel.* New York: Schocken, 1986.

Smith, Mark S. *The Pilgrimage Pattern in Exodus.* JSOTS 239. Sheffield: Sheffield Academic Press, 1997.

The Memoirs of God: History, Memory, and the Experience of the Divine in Ancient Israel. Minneapolis: Fortress, 2004.

Van Iersel, Bastiaan, Anton Weiler, and Marcus Lefébure, eds. *Exodus – A Lasting Paradigm.* Concilium 189. Edinburgh: T&T Clark, 1987.

Vervenne, Mark, ed. *Studies in the Book of Exodus: Redaction – Reception – Interpretation.* Leuven: University Press, 1999.

Walzer, Michael. *Exodus and Revolution.* New York: Basic Books, 1985.

III. Commentary Part I. Israel in Egypt – Exodus 1–15:21

THE OPPRESSION – EXODUS 1

NRSV 1 These are the names of the sons of Israel who came to Egypt with Jacob, each with his household: ²Reuben, Simeon, Levi, and Judah, ³Issachar, Zebulun, and Benjamin, ⁴Dan and Naphtali, Gad and Asher. ⁵The total number of people born to Jacob was seventy. Joseph was already in Egypt. ⁶Then Joseph died, and all his brothers, and that whole generation. ⁷But the Israelites were fruitful and prolific; they multiplied and grew exceedingly strong, so that the land was filled with them.

8 Now a new king arose over Egypt, who did not know Joseph. ⁹He said to his people, "Look, the Israelite people are more numerous and more powerful than we. ¹⁰Come, let us deal shrewdly with them, or they will increase and, in the event of war, join our enemies and fight against us and escape from the land." ¹¹Therefore they set taskmasters over them to oppress them with forced labor. They built supply cities, Pithom and Rameses, for Pharaoh. ¹²But the more they were oppressed, the more they multiplied and spread, so that the Egyptians came to dread the Israelites. ¹³The Egyptians became ruthless in imposing tasks on the Israelites, ¹⁴and made their lives bitter with hard service in mortar and brick and in every kind of field labor. They were ruthless in all the tasks that they imposed on them.

15 The king of Egypt said to the Hebrew midwives, one of whom was named Shiphrah and the other Puah, ¹⁶"When you act as midwives to the Hebrew women, and see them on the birthstool, if it is a boy, kill him; but if it is a girl, she shall live." ¹⁷But the midwives feared God; they did not do as the king of Egypt commanded them, but they let the boys live. ¹⁸So the king of Egypt summoned the midwives and said to them, "Why have you done this, and allowed the boys to live?" ¹⁹The midwives said to Pharaoh, "Because the Hebrew women are not like the Egyptian women; for they are vigorous and give birth before the midwife comes to them." ²⁰So God dealt well with the midwives; and the people multiplied and became very strong. ²¹And because the midwives feared God, he gave them families. ²²Then Pharaoh commanded all his people, "Every boy that is

born to the Hebrews you shall throw into the Nile, but you shall let every girl live."

One of the most gripping narratives in the Hebrew Bible – the account of the escape of an oppressed people from bondage to freedom – begins with a rather mundane listing of the Israelite tribes. Echoing the frequent lists and genealogies of Genesis as well as providing narrative continuity with the first book of the Bible,[1] verses 2–4 list the names of Jacob's sons. These eponymous ancestors and their households are *seventy* in all (v. 5), a number that emphatically proclaims the totality of the Israelites in Egypt, just as it does Gen 46: 8–27. Seventy is a symbolic number; seven and its multiples represent comprehensive completeness in the ancient Semitic world.[2] The tale about to be told concerns an entire people, rhetorically represented by the seventy ancestors of all of them. Whatever small group or groups actually participated in a sojourn in and departure from a foreign land, the collective memory shaping Exodus has all Israelites experiencing that formative event.

Another echo of Genesis appears in verse 7. The fertility of the Israelites is expressed in language ("fruitful" and "multiplied") reminiscent of the fertility of humanity at creation (Gen 1:28) and at the new creation after the flood (Gen 9:1, 7). But the wording of the Genesis passages is augmented with "prolific" and "grew exceedingly strong," emphasizing Israelite obedience to the divine imperative. Now, in fulfilling the commandment for demographic expansion, the Israelites in Egypt become another creation, the beginnings of a people. But that beginning is hardly like the mythic or glorious origins often told in national foundation stories. In this case, as the narrative immediately discloses, Israel's origin is inextricably linked with the oppressive policies of a superpower.

After its introduction in verse 7, the language of population growth punctuates the rest of the chapter. The pivotal Hebrew verb *râbâ* ("to be/become great, numerous"), translated "multiplied" in verse 7, reappears in verse 9 (as part of the phrase "more numerous"), verse 10 ("increase"), verse 12 ("multiplied"), and verse 20 ("multiplied"). This repetition, less clear in English translations that vary the vocabulary, is a characteristic literary device of Hebrew narrative.[3] Repetition establishes a theme, in this case the increase of Israelites and the concomitant escalation of the Egyptians' strategies to deal with the perceived threat.

The idea that the sojourners in Egypt were relatively comfortable until this point is conveyed by the description of the pharaoh of the exodus as one who

---

[1] Especially Gen 46: 8–27, which the narrator reshapes; see Moshe Greenberg, *Understanding Exodus* (Heritage of Biblical Israel Series, Vol. II, Part I; New York: Behrman, 1969), 18–19. Note too that the first verse begins with the connective "and," thus providing narrative continuity with the end of Genesis.

[2] Eckart Otto, "*šebaʿ; šābûʿôṯ*," *TDOT* 14:336–67.

[3] R. Alter, *Art of Biblical Narrative* (1980), 88–113.

"knew not Joseph" (v. 8). Again, a link is made with the narratives of the ancestors in this allusion to the Joseph story in Genesis. In contrast, by mentioning an Egyptian king but not providing his name, a link with Egyptian history is rendered problematic. Who was this ruler? The Bible does not always shy away from identifying foreign kings, and in later biblical books names of several pharaohs (Shishak and Neco) appear. The absence of the name of this king, who may or may not be the same pharaoh as the ones mentioned in subsequent episodes of the exodus account, gives an ahistorical quality to the narrative. If the story of the exodus indeed has a historical core, could the historical memory of the people have suppressed the name of the oppressor? Or did the narrator have no access to records that would provide the identity of this pharaoh? It is more likely that the pharaoh is intentionally unnamed. The anonymity of key figures in biblical narratives can serve rhetorical purposes.[4] By not having a specific name, the pharaoh who subjugates the Israelites can represent all such oppressors. At the very least, denying him a name may serve to demean him.[5]

The oppressive policies originate with the pharaoh. In a brief speech, addressed to his people and also designating the Israelites as a "people" – this is the first use of "people" for the Israelites in the Bible[6] – the Egyptian monarch gives an order that will allow his officials to assign the Israelites to work camps. The bondage prescribed for them is not slavery, in the sense of the ownership of persons by individuals. Rather it is "forced labor" (v. 11), which probably denotes what is known as corvée labor,[7] in which groups of people were conscripted for large public works projects, in this case the construction of massive Egyptian storage facilities at Pithom and Rameses, cities that elude identification. The ancient audience would probably understand them to be in the eastern Nile Delta. Because of its physical proximity to Asia and because two major routes between Egypt and Syria–Palestine passed through it, this area served as a haven for Asiatic immigrants.[8]

Although the word "slavery" does not appear in English translations, the Hebrew text of verses 13 and 14 contain repeated uses of its root ('*bd*), which means "to serve, work"; and the root is used five times in these verses (in "imposing tasks," "service," "labor," "tasks," and "imposed"). This frequent repetition intensifies the impression of suffering; the "serve" words in Hebrew

---

[4] Adele Reinhartz, '*Why Ask My Name?' Anonymity and Identity in Biblical Narrative* (New York: Oxford University Press, 1998).

[5] Richard E. Friedman, *Commentary on the Torah: With a New English Translation and the Hebrew Text* (San Francisco: HarperSanFrancisco, 2001), 169–70.

[6] "People" ('*am*) is a kinship term, as distinct from the political term *goy*, "nation."

[7] See Isaac Mendelsohn, "On Corvée Labor in Ancient Canaan and Israel," *BASOR* 167 (1962): 31–5.

[8] C. Redmount, "Bitter Lives," in *Oxford History* (1998), 100.

come like hammer blows, making the Israelite agony palpable to the audience of the story.[9]

A CLOSER LOOK: BONDAGE, SERVITUDE, AND SLAVERY

Liberation from bondage characterizes the exodus story and becomes a paradigmatic theme in the Hebrew Bible. The word "slavery" is often used to refer to the status of the Israelites in Egypt, but in fact the NRSV of the exodus narrative rarely translates any of the frequent uses of the root *'bd* as "slave," "slavery," or "enslave." The reader encounters "slave" mainly in the legal sections, especially Exodus 21. That root actually has a broad range of meanings, some technical in reference to some form of bondage, as when it designates household "slaves." But it can often mean servitude more generally or figuratively. A subordinate person in the governmental bureaucracy would be the *'ebed* ("servant") of a higher official, and any human would be considered the servant of God, with the worship of God and the performance of sacrifices considered forms of service to the deity. Biblical Hebrew does not have a vocabulary that accounts for the different kinds and conditions of servitude that we recognize in the language of various genres of biblical literature, and the specific kind of labor must generally be discerned from context.

Aside from these general or figurative uses, three kinds of commodified labor can be identified for the ancient Near Eastern world of which Israel was a part. It first is important to recognize that no form of slavery mentioned in the Hebrew Bible was the same as the race-based slavery most familiar to us from eighteenth- and nineteenth-century American history. That system of large-scale coerced labor was a mode of production that apparently originated with the Greeks and Romans.[10] This is not to say that the commodification of individuals for the economic benefit of their masters did not exist in the ancient Near East. The institution of slavery was certainly integral to the functioning of the state societies surrounding ancient Israel.[11] The Israelites, too, assume that the holding of slaves was part of their way of life.

Forced labor could be organized by the state or exist as a feature of individual households. The bondage of the Israelites in Egypt would be one form of compulsory state labor. Foreigners, whether prisoners-of-war or destitute immigrants, or even groups of local residents could be placed in work companies to carry out building projects or to serve in other labor-intensive industries.

---

[9] Umberto Cassuto, *Commentary on the Book of Exodus* (trans. Israel Abrahams; Jerusalem: Magnes Press at the Hebrew University, 1983; odp 1951), 12.

[10] Moses I. Finley (*Ancient Slavery and Modern Ideology* [New York: Viking, 1980], 67–92) describes the emergence of slave societies, to be distinguished from societies in which there were slaves.

[11] Muhammed A. Dandamayev, "Slavery. Ancient Near East," *ABD* 6:58–62.

Indeed, such oppressive behavior is attributed to King Solomon in 1 Kgs 5:13–14 and arouses such ire that the taskmaster over the corvée is stoned to death (1 Kgs 12:18.)

On the household level, compulsory service in ancient Israel could involve the labor of non-Israelite chattel, perhaps obtained as spoils of war. In addition, servitude might be the result of the temporary indenture of an indebted person, or a member of that person's family, in order to pay the debt through labor.[12] This servitude did not normally involve permanent ownership and was not technically forced – it was the voluntary decision of an indebted individual or that person's parent. Although their legal position may have had some features in common with that of slaves, such persons are better considered indentured servants rather than slaves, because the latter term has connotations that do not fit the status of such persons. The laws concerning the manumission of "Hebrew slaves" in Exod 21:2–11 concern debt servitude.

The Egyptian strategy of trying to deplete the Israelite population by subjecting them to intolerable working conditions fails, for they continue to multiply and are still perceived as a threat to the regime. The pharaoh intended to act shrewdly, but the futility of his policy calls that into question.[13] The audience of the story is now aware of Egyptian ineptitude even as the assigned tasks become more oppressive, with the Israelites forced to toil in both construction and agriculture (v. 14). At this point, another tactic, which will lead to the introduction of the figure of Moses, is added to the repertoire of strategies for population control – namely, selective infanticide. Approaching two midwives, the king instructs them to kill any male child that they deliver but to let every girl live. This directive echoes Abraham's words, expressing his fear of being killed by the pharaoh yet being certain that Sarah, the female, would be allowed to live (Gen 12:12). Once again, a link with the ancestor narratives is made.

The midwives are identified as Hebrews.[14] Scholars have long debated whether the term "Hebrew" is related to 'apīru (or ḫabiru), a designation for marginal groups – outcasts, bandits, refugees, mercenaries, or fugitives – mentioned in a variety of ancient Near Eastern documents of the second millennium BCE.[15] This designation fits the social location of the women in this text as well as the status of the ancestors in Genesis, but the philological link between the biblical word

---

[12] Gregory C. Chirichigno, *Debt-Slavery in Israel and the Ancient Near East* (JSOTS 141; Sheffield: JSOT Press, 1993).

[13] Gordon F. Davies, *Israel in Egypt: Reading Exodus 1–2* (JSOTS 135; Sheffield: Sheffield Academic Press, 1992), 53–4.

[14] According to the Hebrew text. The Greek translation (LXX) and other traditions take the text to mean "[Egyptian] midwives to the Hebrews," a reading that contradicts the Semitic roots of both their names.

[15] Niels Peter Lemche, "Ḫabiru, Hapiru," *ABD* 3:6–10, and idem, "Hebrew," *ABD* 3:95.

and that of extrabiblical texts is problematic. What does seem clear, however, is the nonethnic character of both Hebrew and *'apīru*. In calling the midwives Hebrews, the narrator acknowledges their marginal social status in Egypt and also connects them to the ancestors of Genesis.

Moses may be the major Israelite figure in the book of Exodus, but the first individual Israelites mentioned in the narrative are two women, Shiphrah and Puah. Two female members of an outcast group are conferred the dignity of names, in contrast to the namelessness of the powerful king. Moreover, they are the first of a series of twelve women who appear in the opening chapters of Exodus. As an aggregate, those twelve women are rhetorical counterparts to the twelve tribes whose freedom depends on the women's deeds as well as on the leadership of Moses.[16] Their collective and often heroic contributions to the exodus narrative begin with the resistance of the midwives to the directives of the political regime. Divine authority seems to be more important than the word of the powerful pharaoh; because they "feared God," they refuse to do the king's bidding. In not killing male newborns, they engage in what might be termed civil disobedience.[17] They are courageous, unlike the Egyptians who "dread" the Israelites (v. 12); and God rewards them for their stance, apparently with the same fertility that continues to characterize the rest of the Israelites. Perhaps childless themselves, they now will be given "families" (v. 21).[18] The Hebrew word translated "families" actually means "house" or "households." As such, in this female-centered text, the identification of households is with women, as it is in several other female-centered biblical texts, rather than with men.[19] The midwives – the first in a series of female professionals who appear in the narratives, laws, and sanctuary texts of Exodus – are exemplary figures (see A Closer Look: Musicians and Midwives as Professionals, pp. 117–9).

Foiled again in the attempt to reduce the Israelite population, the pharaoh calls the midwives to task for violating his command. They exonerate themselves

---

16 Jopie Siebert-Hommes, "But if She Be a Daughter . . . She May Live! 'Daughters' and 'Sons' in Exodus 1–2," in *A Feminist Companion to Exodus and Deuteronomy,* ed. Athalya Brenner (The Feminist Companion to the Bible 6; Sheffield: Sheffield Academic Press, 1994), 62–74. This positive evaluation is disputed, unfairly in my opinion, by some feminist scholars; see, for example, Cheryl Exum, "Second Thoughts about Secondary Characters: Women in Exodus 1.8–2.10," in *A Feminist Companion to Exodus and Deuteronomy,* ed. Athalya Brenner (Feminist Companion to the Bible 6; Sheffield: Sheffield Academic Press, 1994), 75–87.

17 While acknowledging the legendary nature of the account, David Daube (*Civil Disobedience in Antiquity* [Edinburgh: Edinburgh University Press, 1972], 5, 7) calls the midwives' refusal "the oldest record in world literature of the spurning of a governmental decree."

18 Shalom M. Paul, "Exodus 1:21: "'To Found a Family.' A Biblical and Akkadian Idiom," *Maarav* 8 (1992): 139–42.

19 Carol Meyers, "'To Her Mother's House': Considering a Counterpart to the Israelite *Bêt 'āb,*" in *The Bible and the Politics of Exegesis: Essays in Honor of Norman Gottwald on His Sixty-Fifth Birthday,* eds. David Jobling, Peggy L. Day, and Gerald T. Shepard (Cleveland: Pilgrim, 1991), 39–51.

by deception, a theme that appears frequently in the Hebrew Bible; the needs of a subordinate group or individual are achieved against the will of a more powerful figure by wiliness rather than force. Accepting their explanation – that the Hebrew women give birth so easily that the midwives never manage to assist the delivery – he orders his own people to solve the Israelite problem by casting all male progeny into the Nile. The thread of violence running through the account of the exodus, with people against people, is initiated with the pharaoh's mandate for quasi-genocidal slaughter of newborn sons. This mandate is puzzling, however, in that it would probably have been an inadequate policy for his stated goals of population control and would also have limited the availability of corvée laborers. Implausible as a reasonable though reprehensible political strategy, its role in the exodus story may best be understood on a literary, not literal, level.[20] The literary aspect of this final mandate is also manifest in the fact that it is the fourth in a series of increasingly harsh measures. Such a progression is an example of a rhetorical device used by biblical authors to heighten the tension leading to an ultimate situation, in this instance the utter hopelessness of the circumstances of the Israelites.[21]

The first chapter of Exodus serves as a prologue, setting the stage for what comes next – the birth of the person who will be God's partner in the liberation of the Israelites from their plight. The pharaoh's attention to male Hebrew offspring anticipates the narrowing of the story's focus from the endangered people as a whole to the one person, a male, who will bring them to safety. The increasingly oppressive tactics of the Egyptians now have reached their culmination, and the story of liberation can begin with the appearance of the liberator.

THE EMERGENCE OF MOSES – EXODUS 2:1–25

NRSV 1 Now a man from the house of Levi went and married a Levite woman. [2]The woman conceived and bore a son; and when she saw that he was a fine baby, she hid him three months. [3]When she could hide him no longer she got a papyrus basket for him, and plastered it with bitumen and pitch; she put the child in it and placed it among the reeds on the bank of the river. [4]His sister stood at a distance, to see what would happen to him.

5 The daughter of Pharaoh came down to bathe at the river, while her attendants walked beside the river. She saw the basket among the reeds and sent her maid to bring it. [6]When she opened it, she saw the child. He was crying, and she took pity on him. "This must be one of the Hebrews' children," she said. [7]Then his sister said to Pharaoh's daughter, "Shall I go and get you a nurse from the Hebrew women

---

[20] M. Greenberg, *Understanding Exodus* (1969), 29–30.
[21] Yairah Amit, "Progression as a Rhetorical Device in Biblical Literature," *JSOT* 28 (2003): 20–2.

to nurse the child for you?" ⁸Pharaoh's daughter said to her, "Yes." So the girl went and called the child's mother. ⁹Pharaoh's daughter said to her, "Take this child and nurse it for me, and I will give you your wages." So the woman took the child and nursed it. ¹⁰When the child grew up, she brought him to Pharaoh's daughter, and she took him as her son. She named him Moses, "because," she said, "I drew him out of the water."

11 One day, after Moses had grown up, he went out to his people and saw their forced labor. He saw an Egyptian beating a Hebrew, one of his kinsfolk. ¹²He looked this way and that, and seeing no one he killed the Egyptian and hid him in the sand. ¹³When he went out the next day, he saw two Hebrews fighting; and he said to the one who was in the wrong, "Why do you strike your fellow Hebrew?" ¹⁴He answered, "Who made you a ruler and judge over us? Do you mean to kill me as you killed the Egyptian?" Then Moses was afraid and thought, "Surely the thing is known." ¹⁵When Pharaoh heard of it, he sought to kill Moses.

But Moses fled from Pharaoh. He settled in the land of Midian, and sat down by a well. ¹⁶The priest of Midian had seven daughters. They came to draw water, and filled the troughs to water their father's flock. ¹⁷But some shepherds came and drove them away. Moses got up and came to their defense and watered their flock. ¹⁸When they returned to their father Reuel, he said, "How is it that you have come back so soon today?" ¹⁹They said, "An Egyptian helped us against the shepherds; he even drew water for us and watered the flock." ²⁰He said to his daughters, "Where is he? Why did you leave the man? Invite him to break bread." ²¹Moses agreed to stay with the man, and he gave Moses his daughter Zipporah in marriage. ²²She bore a son, and he named him Gershom; for he said, "I have been an alien residing in a foreign land."

23 After a long time the king of Egypt died. The Israelites groaned under their slavery, and cried out. Out of the slavery their cry for help rose up to God. ²⁴God heard their groaning, and God remembered his covenant with Abraham, Isaac, and Jacob. ²⁵God looked upon the Israelites, and God took notice of them.

*M*oses is the most important human figure in the account of the exodus, in the book of Exodus, and in the Pentateuch as a whole. Indeed, his name appears hundreds of times throughout the Hebrew Bible and dozens of times in the New Testament. He is a partner with God in the unfolding story of how Israel gains its freedom and becomes established as a community. It is no wonder that this heroic figure bursts forth into the biblical narrative in a memorable and dramatic birth story. Filled with suspense and intrigue, the opening ten verses of Exodus 2 depict simple human kindness as well as the presence of God lurking behind the providential coincidences that bring about a happy ending. These features have made the first ten verses of Exodus 2 a favorite and oft-told "Bible story." It begins with information about his natal family (2:1), and it ends by situating him in his Egyptian family (2:10). In between unfolds the account of the bravery of his mother and sister and the humanity of the Egyptian princess.

With great literary artistry, this episode presents the protagonist of the exodus, the individual who will fulfill the promise of Genesis and enable the creation of liberated Israel.[22]

A CLOSER LOOK: MIDWIVES AND WET-NURSES

This episode and the previous one provide a glimpse of childbirth and childcare practices in the biblical world. Midwifery is among the oldest and most specialized functions in human society.[23] Virtually always a woman's profession, it involves women helping other women in the intimate circumstances of a natural biological process. As the Genesis account (35:16–17) of Benjamin's birth indicates, midwives offered what might be termed holistic care, tending to the emotional needs of the new mother while also assisting in the birth process.[24] Very little information is available about Israel's health care system in general and the practice of midwifery in particular. However, data from the surrounding cultures as well as allusions in biblical texts indicate the existence of a developed midwifery profession in ancient Israel.

Practitioners of midwifery drew upon technical knowledge as well as clinical skills. Egyptian and Babylonian texts from the third or second millennium BCE contain rules and procedures for attending childbirth and suggest that bodies of knowledge about gynecological and obstetrical practice were collected and transmitted in writing and probably also orally. Mesopotamian documents, especially literary works describing goddesses as midwives, depict the series of activities that were performed in attending a woman in childbirth.[25] The practice of midwifery was situated in the magico-medical world. Prayers, incantations, and religious rituals were an integral part of the professional services provided by midwives (cf. Isa 26:16–18).[26] This feature of midwifery has persisted in traditional cultures of the Middle East that are rooted in biblical religion.[27] Because of the technical skills and religious functions of a woman dealing with the profound experience of bringing a new life into the world, a midwife was often called a "wise woman" in ancient Near Eastern cultures, including in early postbiblical

22 James A. Ackerman, "The Literary Context of the Moses Birth Story (Exodus 1–2)," *Literary Interpretations of Biblical Narratives,* ed. Kenneth R. R. Gros Louis (Nashville: Abingdon, 1974), 74–119.

23 Jean Towler and Joan Bramall, *Midwives in History and Society* (London: Croom Helm, 1986).

24 Carol Meyers, "Midwife (Gen 35:17; 38:28)," *WIS,* 182–3.

25 Marten Stol, *Birth in Babylonia and the Bible: Its Mediterranean Setting* (Cuneiform Monographs 14; Groningen: STYX Publications, 2000), 171–81.

26 Gary M. Beckman, *Hittite Birth Rituals* (Wiesbaden: O. Harrassowitz, 1983), 234.

27 Michele Klein, *A Time to Be Born: Customs and Folklore of Jewish Birth* (Philadelphia: JPS, 2000), 121–6; Lucy M. J. Garnett, *The Women of Turkey and Their Folk-lore* (London: David Nutt, 1890), 315.

Jewish texts (*m. Roš. Haš.* 2:5; *m. Šabb.* 18:3). Note that the French (*sage-femme*) and Dutch (*vroedvrouw*) terms for midwife both literally mean "wise woman" and that English "midwife" goes back to *wid-wife*, "knowing woman."[28] Because they were believed to have the power to transform childbirth from a life-threatening experience to a joyful one, midwives were valued members of most societies until the advent of modern, male-dominated medicine.

Among the specific practices mentioned in ancient texts, delivering a woman while she was positioned on two large bricks resonates most directly with biblical information. In Exod 1:16, the word rendered "birthstool" is literally "two stones" in Hebrew. The Israelites equated stones, common in Palestine, with the bricks used for various purposes in both Egypt and Mesopotamia, where stones were not nearly so plentiful (cf. Gen 11:3). The Exodus text thus designates a practice known from both Egyptian and Mesopotamian literature.[29] However, some difficulties with the Hebrew text make it possible that a different and more technical procedure, involving a prenatal examination, is involved, with the Hebrew reflecting an Egyptian term referring to that procedure.[30]

The services of midwives were probably sought for every delivery. In contrast, the use of wet-nurses was far less common, with most women suckling their own children. Only royal families seem to have resorted to such services, with other elite women perhaps doing the same to emulate the prestige and prerogatives of royalty.[31] Wet-nurses were paid for their services, often under contract; and such documents, along with many laws dealing with the problems that could arise when a woman suckles another woman's child, are found in Mesopotamian texts.[32] Although it is sometimes supposed that wet-nurses were employed to care for foundlings or for the children of women who died in childbirth, the fact that natural mothers were often involved in arranging for someone to nurse their offspring suggests that this was not so.[33] Moreover, most families probably lived at the subsistence level and could not afford to hire a wet-nurse. It is not clear how they might have dealt with the sustenance of an infant if the mother died or failed to lactate. Perhaps a relative or neighbor who herself was nursing an infant would feed an additional child; another possibility is that the infant would be adopted by another family.

[28] M. Stol, *Birth in Babylonia and the Bible* (2000), 171.
[29] Gay Robins, *Women in Ancient Egypt* (Cambridge, Mass.: Harvard University Press, 1993), 83; M. Stol, *Birth in Babylonia and the Bible* (2000), 171.
[30] Scott Morschauser, "Potters' Wheels and Pregnancies: A Note on Exodus 1:16," *JBL* 122 (2003): 731–3.
[31] G. Robins, *Women in Ancient Egypt* (1993), 89.
[32] M. Stol, *Birth in Babylonia and the Bible* (2000), 181–90.
[33] Mayer I. Gruber, "Breast-feeding Practices in Biblical Israel and in Old Babylonian Mesopotamia," *The Motherhood of God and Other Studies* (South Florida Studies in the History of Judaism 57; Atlanta: Scholars Press, 1992), 89–95.

The prestige attached to the ability to hire a wet-nurse, along with the notion that it was natural and beneficial for a woman to suckle her own offspring, come together in the story of Moses. As one of very few biblical characters said to have been suckled by a wet-nurse, his status as a prominent figure is anticipated. Yet, because his own mother is in fact the wet-nurse, his identity as one of the Hebrew people is likewise conveyed.

The parsimonious introductory verse tells us about the parents of Moses. Their names – Amram and Jochebed – are known from other biblical texts, including Exod 6:20. But they are omitted here in a break with the pattern, seen so often in Genesis as well as elsewhere in the Bible, for the parents of major figures to be mentioned. Lineages are important in societies such as ancient Israel that are organized by kinship and that conceive of themselves in family terms. The patronymic (father's name) would be expected but is omitted; and the name of the older brother Aaron, who will have a significant part to play in the story of exodus as well as in the establishment of the priesthood, does not appear at all. Yet the issue of lineage is not completely ignored. By mentioning that both parents are from the priestly tribe of Levi, the sacerdotal pedigree of Moses is provided. His role as the one who will establish the desert sanctuary and its personnel is anticipated and legitimized.

The other characters in this episode appear in subsequent verses. The infant's sister (not named until later in the narrative) succeeds in arranging for his biological mother to nurse him. The Egyptian princess has compassion on the apparently abandoned child, makes him her son, and names him. The handmaids of the princess give the narrative a flavor of the royal house to which the child will be taken. And the servant girl, unlikely to dissuade her mistress from defying the king's order, is alone with the princess when the baby is spotted. All these women are unnamed, to good rhetorical effect. The culmination of the birth story comes with the naming of Moses. As the only character with a name, his centrality in the tale is signaled.

Ironies abound in this episode. The Nile, for example, is meant to be the pharaoh's instrument for killing male children; and instead it becomes the vehicle for saving Moses. And a member of the powerful pharaonic household agrees to the suggestions of a lowly member of society, a foreigner whose people are in bondage to the royal administration.[34] Indeed, the ability of the powerless (including the midwives) to achieve their goals and disrupt political hierarchies through cleverness is a strong message of this segment of the exodus tale and

---

[34] For other examples of irony, see Terence E. Fretheim, *Exodus* (IBC; Louisville, Ky.: John Knox, 1991), 37.

adumbrates the ultimate ability of the Israelites to secure their freedom through the diplomacy of their leaders.

Links with the Book of Genesis, alluding to the creation account of Genesis 1 and the new creation of the flood story, also are part of the opening of Exodus 2.[35] The word "fine" used for the baby in verse 2 is part of a phrase in Hebrew that replicates the way God repeatedly exclaims "it was good" in the Genesis 1 creation account. The word for "basket" in Hebrew is *tēbâ*, a term that appears elsewhere in the Bible only in the story of Noah, where it denotes Noah's "ark." Both basket and ark are vehicles for the saving a significant figure from watery demise, thus signaling a new era.

The rescue of a doomed child is a motif known from other ancient literatures.[36] The miraculous recovery of a helpless infant communicated to the ancient audience that such a child is destined for greatness. Perhaps the closest parallel comes in the story of Sargon of Agade (near modern Baghdad in Iraq), who was the powerful ruler of an extensive empire in the early third millennium BCE. Yet the biblical version of this folk motif differs from the typical pattern, notably in that Moses is hardly raised in obscurity. He is a prince virtually from birth and is raised in the household of the very ruler who sought to have him killed. In that sense, Moses is like the sons of a Hittite queen, who are rescued and raised by gods; however, unlike Moses' mother, the queen wants to get rid of her offspring. If Exodus is using a familiar motif, it has adjusted it to its own purposes.

ANCIENT TEXT: THE BIRTH OF SARGON[37]

Call me Sargon. I am the child of a priest and an unknown pilgrim from the mountains. Today, I rule the empire from the city of Agade. Because my mother did not want anyone in the city of Asupiramu to know that she had given birth to a child, she left me on the bank of the Euphrates River in a basket woven from rushes and waterproofed with tar.[38] The river carried my basket down to a canal, where Akki, the royal gardener, lifted me out of the water and reared me as his own. He trained me to care for the garden of the great king. With the help of Ishtar, divine patron of love and war, I became king of the black-headed people and have ruled 55 years.

---

[35] Gary Rendsburg, "The Literary Approach to the Bible and Finding a Good Translation," in *Biblical Translation in Context*, ed. Frederich W. Knobloch (Bethesda, Md.: University Press of Maryland, 2002), 184–5.

[36] Donald B. Redford, "The Literary Motif of the Exposed Child," *Numen* 14 (1967): 202–28.

[37] Translation from Victor H. Matthews and Don C. Benjamin, *Old Testament Parallels: Laws and Stories from the Ancient Near East* (New York: Paulist Press, 1997), 85.

[38] The language is very similar to that of Exod 2:3.

ANCIENT TEXT: THE BIRTH OF THE SONS OF QUEEN KANESH[39]

The Queen of Kanesh in the course of a single year gave birth to thirty sons. She said, "What a multitude I have begotten!" She filled the interstices of the baskets with grease, put her sons into them, and carried them down to the river. The river carried them down to the sea, to the land of Zalpuwa. The gods recovered the children from the sea and raised them.

Moses' dual identity as a Hebrew child and an Egyptian prince is contained in the name he is given. There are grammatical problems with the name and its etymology. Yet most commentators agree that an Egyptian word *Mose* (meaning "child of"), an element found in the names of Egyptian rulers such as Thutmoses and Ahmoses, is provided with a Hebrew origin, that is, a word meaning "to draw out (of the water)." The double meaning symbolizes the youth's membership in two communities, and the Hebrew etymology may anticipate his eventual role in rescuing all the Israelites from the waters of the Reed Sea (NRSV "Red Sea"). Now that his name, which indicates his complex identity and hints at his ultimate destiny, has been explained, the narrative turns to Moses' life as an adult – with no intervening stories of his childhood or adolescence.

The first of two compelling vignettes, in verses 11–15, reveals how he comes to value his lowly Hebrew origins over his lofty Egyptian upbringing, with the result that he flees from the comforts of the royal palace into the unfamiliar and uninviting land of Midian. This remarkable change is the result of his killing an Egyptian who is beating a fellow Hebrew. In a somewhat similar incident, he then intervenes in a struggle between two Hebrews and learns that his violent act in the first incident is known to the pharaoh, who now seeks – once again – to take his life. Moses' deadly blows to the Egyptian are hardly just, for the Egyptian he kills has not fatally struck a Hebrew man; yet there is no hint of disapproval in the narrative. Moses' violent and reprehensible treatment of the Egyptian is best understood as symbolic of the similarly problematic violence soon to be perpetrated by God on the Egyptians. After all, the verb used when Moses kills this Egyptian (*nkh*, "to strike, kill") is used repeatedly for God's destruction of Israel's enemies, especially the Egyptians.[40] God has not yet appeared in the narrative, but his human counterpart Moses has begun to act in ways that anticipate divine actions against Israel's foes. At the same time, one of the Hebrews challenges his authority to intervene, thus adumbrating the difficulties Moses will face later in establishing himself as a credible leader.

The second vignette functions in a similar way, this time foreshadowing what God will do for Israel. At an oasis in the barren land, Moses comes to the aid of

---

[39] "The Queen of Kanesh and the Tale of Zalpa," translated by Harry A. Hoffner, Jr. (*COS* 1.71), 181.
[40] See Exod 3: 20 and 12:12.

the *seven* daughters of a Midianite priest who are being harassed by some local shepherds. The NRSV has the daughters report to their father that Moses has "helped" them, an unfortunate translation. The Hebrew is more powerful – it uses the verb *nṣl*, "to rescue, deliver," which is a key word referring to divine deliverance of the Israelites from oppression in the exodus narratives, beginning in 3:8, when God says, "I have come down to *deliver* them from the Egyptians." In rescuing the Midianite women, Moses prefigures Yahweh's saving deeds.

He also gains a wife, one of the daughters of the Midianite priest Reuel, whose name means "friend (or kinsman) of El (God)."[41] Not only does Moses come from a priestly tribe; but also, we now learn, his spouse comes from a family with a similar pedigree. And later in Exodus (chap. 18), we see Moses' Midianite father-in-law instructing him in administrative matters and providing a sacrificial meal. Just who were the Midianites? Does their appearance in narratives about Moses signify an important role in the account of Israel's national origins? In the Introduction, I described the compelling hypothesis that the origins of Israel's god came about through the interaction of the Moses group with the Midianites, a group of pastoralists moving about the desert regions southeast of the land of Canaan. Moses' marriage to Zipporah would be a cultural memory of the connection of Israelites with Midianites, as represented by the genealogy in Genesis (25:1–4) that sees the Midianites as descendants of Abraham through his wife Keturah.

The Moses and Zipporah union also provides a thematic connection with the ancestor narratives of Genesis. Like the account of Isaac's engagement to Rebekah, Exod 2:15–21 is a betrothal type-scene, albeit somewhat more compact and stylized than the Genesis example.[42] Both involve a foreign land and a well scene, with previously unknown parties coming together in marriage. The ancient audience for such a story, familiar with its general outlines and conventions and the way it highlights a critical juncture in the life of a hero, would have understood that they were being given a glimpse of a larger-than-life figure. The heroic quality of Moses again looms large via the literary artistry in the dramatic account of his encounter with the Midianite women at the well.

Literary artistry also appears in the immediate result of the marriage of the hero – namely, the birth of a son. The child's name, Gershom, is from a Hebrew verb that means "to drive out/off." The same word was used for the action of the shepherds in verse 17; and it will reappear in Exod 6:1, 11:1, and 12:39 in relating how the pharaoh will "drive" the Israelites from his land. At the same time, a folk etymology is provided for the name, treating it as if it were the combination of two short words (*gēr šām*), meaning "a stranger there." The word for stranger echoes God's promise to Abraham that his descendents would

---

[41] Moses' father-in-law is subsequently called Jethro as well as Hobab, perhaps reflecting a separate tradition; see W. H. C. Propp, *Exodus 1–18* (1998), 172–3, and n. 105.

[42] R. Alter, *Art of Biblical Narrative* (1980), 56–7.

be strangers (NRSV "aliens") in a land not theirs (Gen 15:13). The firstborn child of Moses thus provides a link with the ancestor stories, symbolizes the status of his people, indicates the way his parents met, and anticipates how the entire people will depart from Egypt – all in a name.

This section began with the marriage of Moses' parents and the birth and eventual naming of their son; and it ends with Moses' own marriage and the birth and naming of his son. These life cycle events form an *inclusio*.[43] Between them is contained the emergence of the hero in narrative segments that account for his Egyptian identity, his Hebrew origins, and his Midianite connection – all important elements in the story about to unfold.

An addendum to the Midianite episode follows (vv. 23–25). We learn that the Egyptian king – presumably the one from whom Moses had fled – dies, making it possible for Moses to return to Egypt. And we learn that the new regime does not provide any relief for the Israelites; if anything their oppression seems greater. The terms for "groaning" and "crying out" are repeated four times, signifying the agony of the Israelites. But, more important, this addendum finally brings God into the picture. Although the divine presence may have been hovering in the background of the fortuitous saving of the infant Moses, the narrator does not tell us anything about God's response to the suffering of the people until this passage. Each of the four words for Israel's cries and groans elicits a reaction from God. There is symmetry between the human predicament and the divine response. And there is drama and intensification in the fourfold repetition. Moreover, the word "God" is repeated as the subject of each verb, when one would expect it to be used only with the first verb (with pronouns accompanying the next three verbs). Such unusual repeating of the subject ("God heard ... God remembered ... God looked ... God took notice") brings God into the forefront and anticipates the remarkable burning-bush theophany that follows. In addition, the mention of the ancestral covenant in the addendum implies that the promise to the ancestors must be fulfilled by bringing the descendents of Jacob back to the land of Canaan. The stage is set for Moses' call and mission.

MOSES' CALL AND MISSION – EXODUS 3:1–7:7

NRSV 3 Moses was keeping the flock of his father-in-law Jethro, the priest of Midian; he led his flock beyond the wilderness, and came to Horeb, the mountain of God. ²There the angel of the LORD appeared to him in a flame of fire out of a bush; he looked, and the bush was blazing, yet it was not consumed. ³Then Moses

---

43 *Inclusio* is a Latin term designating a literary device in which the end of a passage or a section of text repeats or is similar to the beginning, thereby framing a literary unit.

said, "I must turn aside and look at this great sight, and see why the bush is not burned up." ⁴When the LORD saw that he had turned aside to see, God called to him out of the bush, "Moses, Moses!" And he said, "Here I am." ⁵Then he said, "Come no closer! Remove the sandals from your feet, for the place on which you are standing is holy ground." ⁶He said further, "I am the God of your father, the God of Abraham, the God of Isaac, and the God of Jacob." And Moses hid his face, for he was afraid to look at God.

7 Then the LORD said, "I have observed the misery of my people who are in Egypt; I have heard their cry on account of their taskmasters. Indeed, I know their sufferings, ⁸and I have come down to deliver them from the Egyptians, and to bring them up out of that land to a good and broad land, a land flowing with milk and honey, to the country of the Canaanites, the Hittites, the Amorites, the Perizzites, the Hivites, and the Jebusites. ⁹The cry of the Israelites has now come to me; I have also seen how the Egyptians oppress them. ¹⁰So come, I will send you to Pharaoh to bring my people, the Israelites, out of Egypt." ¹¹But Moses said to God, "Who am I that I should go to Pharaoh, and bring the Israelites out of Egypt?" ¹²He said, "I will be with you; and this shall be the sign for you that it is I who sent you: when you have brought the people out of Egypt, you shall worship God on this mountain."

13 But Moses said to God, "If I come to the Israelites and say to them, 'The God of your ancestors has sent me to you,' and they ask me, 'What is his name?' what shall I say to them?" ¹⁴God said to Moses, "I AM WHO I AM." He said further, "Thus you shall say to the Israelites, 'I AM has sent me to you.'" ¹⁵God also said to Moses, "Thus you shall say to the Israelites, 'The LORD, the God of your ancestors, the God of Abraham, the God of Isaac, and the God of Jacob, has sent me to you':

This is my name forever,
and this my title for all generations.

¹⁶Go and assemble the elders of Israel, and say to them, 'The LORD, the God of your ancestors, the God of Abraham, of Isaac, and of Jacob, has appeared to me, saying: I have given heed to you and to what has been done to you in Egypt. ¹⁷I declare that I will bring you up out of the misery of Egypt, to the land of the Canaanites, the Hittites, the Amorites, the Perizzites, the Hivites, and the Jebusites, a land flowing with milk and honey.' ¹⁸They will listen to your voice; and you and the elders of Israel shall go to the king of Egypt and say to him, 'The LORD, the God of the Hebrews, has met with us; let us now go a three days' journey into the wilderness, so that we may sacrifice to the LORD our God.' ¹⁹I know, however, that the king of Egypt will not let you go unless compelled by a mighty hand. ²⁰So I will stretch out my hand and strike Egypt with all my wonders that I will perform in it; after that he will let you go. ²¹I will bring this people into such favor with the Egyptians that, when you go, you will not go empty-handed; ²²each woman shall ask her neighbor and any woman living in the neighbor's house for jewelry of silver and of gold, and clothing, and you shall put them on your sons and on your daughters; and so you shall plunder the Egyptians."

NRSV 4 Then Moses answered, "But suppose they do not believe me or listen to me, but say, 'The LORD did not appear to you.'" [2] The LORD said to him, "What is that in your hand?" He said, "A staff." [3] And he said, "Throw it on the ground." So he threw the staff on the ground, and it became a snake; and Moses drew back from it. [4] Then the LORD said to Moses, "Reach out your hand, and seize it by the tail" – so he reached out his hand and grasped it, and it became a staff in his hand – [5] "so that they may believe that the LORD, the God of their ancestors, the God of Abraham, the God of Isaac, and the God of Jacob, has appeared to you."

6 Again, the LORD said to him, "Put your hand inside your cloak." He put his hand into his cloak; and when he took it out, his hand was leprous, as white as snow. [7] Then God said, "Put your hand back into your cloak" – so he put his hand back into his cloak, and when he took it out, it was restored like the rest of his body – [8] "If they will not believe you or heed the first sign, they may believe the second sign. [9] If they will not believe even these two signs or heed you, you shall take some water from the Nile and pour it on the dry ground; and the water that you shall take from the Nile will become blood on the dry ground."

10 But Moses said to the LORD, "O my Lord, I have never been eloquent, neither in the past nor even now that you have spoken to your servant; but I am slow of speech and slow of tongue." [11] Then the LORD said to him, "Who gives speech to mortals? Who makes them mute or deaf, seeing or blind? Is it not I, the LORD? [12] Now go, and I will be with your mouth and teach you what you are to speak." [13] But he said, "O my Lord, please send someone else." [14] Then the anger of the LORD was kindled against Moses and he said, "What of your brother Aaron the Levite? I know that he can speak fluently; even now he is coming out to meet you, and when he sees you his heart will be glad. [15] You shall speak to him and put the words in his mouth; and I will be with your mouth and with his mouth, and will teach you what you shall do. [16] He indeed shall speak for you to the people; he shall serve as a mouth for you, and you shall serve as God for him. [17] Take in your hand this staff, with which you shall perform the signs."

18 Moses went back to his father-in-law Jethro and said to him, "Please let me go back to my kindred in Egypt and see whether they are still living." And Jethro said to Moses, "Go in peace." [19] The LORD said to Moses in Midian, "Go back to Egypt; for all those who were seeking your life are dead." [20] So Moses took his wife and his sons, put them on a donkey, and went back to the land of Egypt; and Moses carried the staff of God in his hand.

21 And the LORD said to Moses, "When you go back to Egypt, see that you perform before Pharaoh all the wonders that I have put in your power; but I will harden his heart, so that he will not let the people go. [22] Then you shall say to Pharaoh, 'Thus says the LORD: Israel is my firstborn son. [23] I said to you, "Let my son go that he may worship me." But you refused to let him go; now I will kill your firstborn son.'"

24 On the way, at a place where they spent the night, the LORD met him and tried to kill him. [25] But Zipporah took a flint and cut off her son's foreskin, and touched

Moses' feet with it, and said, "Truly you are a bridegroom of blood to me!" [26]So he let him alone. It was then she said, "A bridegroom of blood by circumcision."

27 The Lord said to Aaron, "Go into the wilderness to meet Moses." So he went; and he met him at the mountain of God and kissed him. [28]Moses told Aaron all the words of the Lord with which he had sent him, and all the signs with which he had charged him. [29]Then Moses and Aaron went and assembled all the elders of the Israelites. [30]Aaron spoke all the words that the Lord had spoken to Moses, and performed the signs in the sight of the people. [31]The people believed; and when they heard that the Lord had given heed to the Israelites and that he had seen their misery, they bowed down and worshiped.

NRSV 5 Afterward Moses and Aaron went to Pharaoh and said, "Thus says the Lord, the God of Israel, 'Let my people go, so that they may celebrate a festival to me in the wilderness.'" [2]But Pharaoh said, "Who is the Lord, that I should heed him and let Israel go? I do not know the Lord, and I will not let Israel go." [3]Then they said, "The God of the Hebrews has revealed himself to us; let us go a three days' journey into the wilderness to sacrifice to the Lord our God, or he will fall upon us with pestilence or sword." [4]But the king of Egypt said to them, "Moses and Aaron, why are you taking the people away from their work? Get to your labors!" [5]Pharaoh continued, "Now they are more numerous than the people of the land and yet you want them to stop working!" [6]That same day Pharaoh commanded the taskmasters of the people, as well as their supervisors, [7]"You shall no longer give the people straw to make bricks, as before; let them go and gather straw for themselves. [8]But you shall require of them the same quantity of bricks as they have made previously; do not diminish it, for they are lazy; that is why they cry, 'Let us go and offer sacrifice to our God.' [9]Let heavier work be laid on them; then they will labor at it and pay no attention to deceptive words."

10 So the taskmasters and the supervisors of the people went out and said to the people, "Thus says Pharaoh, 'I will not give you straw. [11]Go and get straw yourselves, wherever you can find it; but your work will not be lessened in the least.'" [12]So the people scattered throughout the land of Egypt, to gather stubble for straw. [13]The taskmasters were urgent, saying, "Complete your work, the same daily assignment as when you were given straw." [14]And the supervisors of the Israelites, whom Pharaoh's taskmasters had set over them, were beaten, and were asked, "Why did you not finish the required quantity of bricks yesterday and today, as you did before?"

15 Then the Israelite supervisors came to Pharaoh and cried, "Why do you treat your servants like this? [16]No straw is given to your servants, yet they say to us, 'Make bricks!' Look how your servants are beaten! You are unjust to your own people." [17]He said, "You are lazy, lazy; that is why you say, 'Let us go and sacrifice to the Lord.' [18]Go now, and work; for no straw shall be given you, but you shall still deliver the same number of bricks." [19]The Israelite supervisors saw that they were in trouble when they were told, "You shall not lessen your daily number of bricks."

²⁰ As they left Pharaoh, they came upon Moses and Aaron who were waiting to meet them. ²¹ They said to them, "The LORD look upon you and judge! You have brought us into bad odor with Pharaoh and his officials, and have put a sword in their hand to kill us."

22 Then Moses turned again to the LORD and said, "O LORD, Why did you ever send me? ²³ Since I first came to Pharaoh to speak in your name, he has mistreated this people, and you have done nothing at all to deliver your people."

NRSV 6 Then the LORD said to Moses, "Now you shall see what I will do to Pharaoh: Indeed, by a mighty hand he will let them go; by a mighty hand he will drive them out of his land."

2 God also spoke to Moses and said to him: "I am the LORD. ³I appeared to Abraham, Isaac, and Jacob as God Almighty,ᵃ but by my name 'The LORD' I did not make myself known to them. ⁴I also established my covenant with them, to give them the land of Canaan, the land in which they resided as aliens. ⁵I have also heard the groaning of the Israelites whom the Egyptians are holding as slaves, and I have remembered my covenant. ⁶Say therefore to the Israelites, 'I am the LORD, and I will free you from the burdens of the Egyptians and deliver you from slavery to them. I will redeem you with an outstretched arm and with mighty acts of judgment. ⁷I will take you as my people, and I will be your God. You shall know that I am the LORD your God, who has freed you from the burdens of the Egyptians. ⁸I will bring you into the land that I swore to give to Abraham, Isaac, and Jacob; I will give it to you for a possession. I am the LORD.'" ⁹Moses told this to the Israelites; but they would not listen to Moses, because of their broken spirit and their cruel slavery.

10 Then the LORD spoke to Moses, ¹¹"Go and tell Pharaoh king of Egypt to let the Israelites go out of his land." ¹²But Moses spoke to the LORD, "The Israelites have notlistened to me; how then shall Pharaoh listen to me, poor speaker that I am?" ¹³Thus the LORD spoke to Moses and Aaron, and gave them orders regarding the Israelites and Pharaoh king of Egypt, charging them to free the Israelites from the land of Egypt.

14 The following are the heads of their ancestral houses: the sons of Reuben, the firstborn of Israel: Hanoch, Pallu, Hezron, and Carmi; these are the families of Reuben. ¹⁵The sons of Simeon: Jemuel, Jamin, Ohad, Jachin, Zohar, and Shaul, the son of a Canaanite woman; these are the families of Simeon. ¹⁶The following are the names of the sons of Levi according to their genealogies: Gershon, Kohath, and Merari, and the length of Levi's life was one hundred thirty-seven years. ¹⁷The sons of Gershon: Libni and Shimei, by their families. ¹⁸The sons of Kohath: Amram, Izhar, Hebron, and Uzziel, and the length of Kohath's life was one hundred thirty-three years. ¹⁹The sons of Merari: Mahli and Mushi. These are the families of the Levites according to their genealogies. ²⁰Amram married Jochebed his father's sister and she bore him Aaron and Moses, and the length of Amram's life was one

---

ᵃ Traditional rendering of Heb *El Shaddai*

hundred thirty-seven years. [21] The sons of Izhar: Korah, Nepheg, and Zichri. [22] The sons of Uzziel: Mishael, Elzaphan, and Sithri. [23] Aaron married Elisheba, daughter of Amminadab and sister of Nahshon, and she bore him Nadab, Abihu, Eleazar, and Ithamar. [24] The sons of Korah: Assir, Elkanah, and Abiasaph; these are the families of the Korahites. [25] Aaron's son Eleazar married one of the daughters of Putiel, and she bore him Phinehas. These are the heads of the ancestral houses of the Levites by their families.

26 It was this same Aaron and Moses to whom the LORD said, "Bring the Israelites out of the land of Egypt, company by company." [27] It was they who spoke to Pharaoh king of Egypt to bring the Israelites out of Egypt, the same Moses and Aaron.

28 On the day when the LORD spoke to Moses in the land of Egypt, [29] he said to him, "I am the LORD; tell Pharaoh king of Egypt all that I am speaking to you." [30] But Moses said in the LORD's presence, "Since I am a poor speaker, why would Pharaoh listen to me?"

NRSV 7 The LORD said to Moses, "See, I have made you like God to Pharaoh, and your brother Aaron shall be your prophet. [2] You shall speak all that I command you, and your brother Aaron shall tell Pharaoh to let the Israelites go out of his land. [3] But I will harden Pharaoh's heart, and I will multiply my signs and wonders in the land of Egypt. [4] When Pharaoh does not listen to you, I will lay my hand upon Egypt and bring my people the Israelites, company by company, out of the land of Egypt by great acts of judgment. [5] The Egyptians shall know that I am the LORD, when I stretch out my hand against Egypt and bring the Israelites out from among them." [6] Moses and Aaron did so; they did just as the LORD commanded them. [7] Moses was eighty years old and Aaron eighty-three when they spoke to Pharaoh.

THEOPHANY AT THE BUSH AND GOD'S DIALOGUE WITH MOSES (3:1–4:17)

God has noticed the suffering of the people. But how will God act to bring them relief? A leader is needed to span the chasm between divine will and the actions of humans in the arena of events. Moses, of course, has been introduced and his special role anticipated. But he does not yet know what that role will be, and he has not yet encountered God. All this is about to change in another dramatic episode that unfolds in three scenes: theophany (3:1–6); call (3:7–10); and dialogue (3:11–4:17).

The first verse in the first scene reveals that Moses has been serving as a shepherd for his father-in-law, here called Jethro, not Reuel. Jethro may be a name for Reuel in a different literary source for the present book of Exodus;[44] or it may be an honorary title, something like "your Excellency," used for a priestly

---

[44] Another tradition calls Moses' father-in-law Hobab (see Judg 1:16 and 4:11); and Num 10:29 calls Hobab the "son of Reuel the Midianite, Moses' father-in-law."

official.[45] Either way, the shepherd motif becomes part of the Moses narrative. What better role could there be for one about to become the shepherd of his people! Later in the Hebrew Bible, David will be called from tending his flock to be the "shepherd" for his people (1 Sam 17:15; 2 Sam 5: 2); and biblical poetry frequently uses shepherd imagery for God as ruler and protector of Israel (e.g., Psalm 23; Isa 40:10–11).

The locale is also set: the mountain of God, Horeb. Sinai is more often the designated mountain in the exodus traditions, and perhaps this – like the name of Moses' father-in-law – reflects a different literary source.[46] Another possibility is that this wilderness peak is not the same as the mountain of the covenant theophany (Exodus 19). The importance of a mountain for the revelation obtains, whatever the name. Mountains are nearly coterminous in ancient Semitic culture with the presence of a deity.[47] The initial revelation of Israel's deity must come at a mountain. The manifestation of God to Moses at Horeb anticipates the manifestation to Moses at Sinai, with all the people gathered there. But now Moses is alone, a fire miraculously burns in a bush, and a messenger appears.

The burning bush – a bush that is on fire but is not harmed – is perhaps the first of the sequence of miracles that accompany the story of the difficult transition from Egyptian servitude to freedom in the land promised to the ancestors. The word for bush, *sĕneh*, is a rare biblical term, likely chosen for use here (and in Deut 33:16) because of its assonance with Sinai. But the choice of a messenger (*mal'āk*, "angel") to precede God in appearing to Moses is less comprehensible. Such divine beings, whose role as emissaries from God is rooted in Near Eastern culture and the use of messengers to provide communication between two parties,[48] appear throughout the Hebrew Bible. Even prophets – think of the prophet Malachi, whose name means "my messenger" – are conceptualized as individuals sent by God with messages for the people. But why does an angel, with no apparent role in the unfolding interaction between God and Moses, appear here? And how does the presence of an intermediary fit with the tradition of Moses' uniquely intimate relationship with God? There are no easy answers to these questions. The angel in some sense is the same as God, because the angel is in the bush as is God (v. 4). Perhaps the biblical narrator is uncomfortable with the idea of a physical manifestation of God and so resorts to the introduction of a mediatory figure, at least at the outset of this encounter. Another, related possibility is that the presence in Israelite culture of angelic beings who can be seen and heard is an accommodation to

---

[45] Nahum M. Sarna, *Exodus* (The JPS Torah Commentary; Philadelphia: JPS, 1991), 12; in Gen 49:3, where *yeter* (a word related to Jethro) means "excelling."

[46] Source criticism assigns the name Horeb to the Elohist (E) and Deuteronomist (D) and the name Sinai to the Yahwist (J) and the Priestly writer (P).

[47] Richard Clifford, *The Cosmic Mountain in Canaan and the Old Testament* (HSM 4; Cambridge, Mass.: Harvard University Press, 1972).

[48] Samuel A. Meier, *The Messenger in the Ancient Semitic World* (HSM 45; Atlanta, Ga.: Scholars Press, 1988).

Israel's aniconic tradition, which deprives the people of a visible image of the deity.[49]

Moses' amazement at the visual impact of the intact fiery bush is intensified by the sound of God's voice calling his name. God is initiating a dialogue that will continue throughout the exodus account. God pronounces Moses' name twice, as is apparently the pattern when the deity calls out to a human (cf. God's call to Abraham in Gen 22:11, to Jacob in Gen 46:2, and to Samuel in 1 Sam 3:4). Similarly, Moses responds in the characteristic way by saying "Here I am" (v. 4).[50]

At this point, the notion of sacred space becomes an explicit part of the narrative for the first time in the Hebrew Bible. Certain locales, such those marked by trees (as in Gen 18:1 and perhaps the bush of this text), have already appeared as congenial to manifestations of the divine presence; and the importance of this site as "the mountain of God" (v. 1) has been noted. But two terms appear in verse 5 that signify directly the sanctity of a particular locale. The word for "place," *māqôm*, is often a technical term in biblical Hebrew for a sanctuary or holy place (cf. Gen 28:11, 19);[51] and "holy ground" likewise connotes sacred space. Together (as in Josh 5:15), they introduce a theophany. Here they provide mountain-and-fire imagery that will reappear in the narrative of the central theophany in ancient Israel's experience at Sinai (chap. 19). In ancient Near Eastern temple typologies, the *holy mountain* as the place where God resides is conceptualized as the center or axis of the universe, the place where heaven and earth meet. But this passage differs from such patterns in that it presents a unique event, one that neither arises from nor establishes ongoing sanctity at this location. This sanctity of place is expressed by the word "holy" (from the root *qdš*). Although the verbal form occurs in Gen 2:3, the noun "holiness" is used here, in the phrase "holy ground" (literally, "ground of holiness"), for the first time in the Bible and signifies what will be a dominant concept in Exodus – in the Sinai chapters and in the extended presentation of the tabernacle and its personnel.

Moses removes his shoes at this holy place as an indication of respect, according to ancient Near Eastern custom. We will see that the descriptions of priestly attire in the tabernacle passages do not mention priestly footwear; presumably priests went barefoot as they traversed the sacred precincts of Israel's god. A similar removal of shoes as a sign of respect in the domain of the deity is found in the custom of Muslims taking off their footwear as they enter a mosque; and to this very day, members of priestly families traditionally remove their shoes when they recite certain blessings in the synagogue.

---

49 W. H. C. Propp, *Exodus 1–18* (1998), 198–9. See also my discussion of the injunction concerning images in Exod 20:4–6.

50 Other prominent biblical figures utter this response to God or God's messenger: Abraham (Gen 22:1, 11), Jacob (Gen 46:2), Samuel (1 Sam 3:4, 6, 8), and Isaiah (Isa 6:8).

51 J. Gamberoni and Helmer Ringgren, "*māqôm*," *TDOT* 8:532–44. Deuteronomy often mentions the "place," presumably the Jerusalem temple, of divine presence.

With the sanctity of the site established and with Moses appropriately bare-foot, a voice – the voice of God – now discloses the divine identity. The authoritative "I am ... " (v. 6) seems formulaic, given the way it introduces proclamations in the ancient Near East[52] as well the fact that it occurs when God appears to the ancestors in Genesis. And indeed, the ancestors themselves are invoked as part of this self-identification of God to Moses. The mention of Abraham, Isaac, and Jacob is yet another link to the Genesis narratives as well as to the end of the preceding section of Exodus (2:24). Identifying the deity as the one to whom the ancestors were allied is also an implicit acknowledgment that there are other gods but that it is the ancestors' god who is to liberate Israel.

But God's self-identification as the ancestors' deity is not enough. God reiterates awareness of the Israelites' plight (vv. 7, 9) and intention to rescue them through Moses (vv. 8, 10).[53] They will not only leave Egypt; they will also have a place in which to relocate. The well-known description of Israelite territory as a "land flowing with milk and honey" (v. 8) appears here for the first time in the Bible. The products of animal husbandry (represented by "milk") and viticulture (represented by "honey," or grape syrup[54]) represent the productivity of a land that, in fact, has a difficult topography and chronic water shortages. This idealization is difficult to understand, and none of the theories that have been proposed is compelling.[55] But we must remember that in the covenant perspective that permeates the Hebrew Bible, an unproductive land is understood to be the result of human failures rather than of innate infertility.[56] Thus the land of divine promise is explicitly fertile.

The land of divine promise is also occupied; and verse 8 provides one of several biblical versions of a listing, which occurs twenty-seven times in the Hebrew Bible, of the occupants of the land. This list contains six peoples, fewer than the ten that comprise the most comprehensive one (Gen 15:19–21), and ends with the Jebusites, perhaps anticipating David's eventual success in routing the Jebusites from their stronghold in Jerusalem and thus culminating with the last of the foreign peoples, according to the Deuteronomic narrator, to be subjugated.[57] More problematic than the matter of which peoples are listed is the way God promises a land that is already inhabited. What will happen to those peoples? This passage leaves that question unanswered, but the deeply troubling response – that those peoples will be destroyed – comes in chapter 23 (vv. 23–24).

---

[52] E.g., the opening words of "The Inscription of King Mesha," translated by K. A. D. Smelik (*COS* 2.23), 137, and many other northwest Semitic monumental texts.

[53] The reiteration may derive from the blending of Yahwistic (J) and Elohist (E) sources; or it may simply be stylistic emphasis.

[54] The word for "honey" in the Hebrew Bible probably does not, except in Judg 14:8–9, mean bee honey; rather, it denotes a thick syrup usually made from grapes.

[55] The possibilities are summarized by André Caquot, "*dᵉbhash*," *TDOT* 3:130–1.

[56] E.g., Lev 26:18–20 and Deut 28:15–24.

[57] A detailed discussion of these lists appears in William H. C. Propp, *Exodus 19–40* (AB 2A; New York: Doubleday, forthcoming), Appendix B.

God's address to Moses in verses 7–10 culminates in the announcement of Moses' role in the divine plan to free the Israelites. It is also the prelude to the first of a series of eight exchanges between God and Moses, in which Moses protests his mission and God responds. The repetitions in the ongoing dialogue well may be the result of the merging of different traditions. Equally plausible is that this eight-part dialogue is the ultimate prophetic interaction with God; for in Semitic rhetorical style *seven*-plus-one enhances the symbolism of seven as a number meaning totality or completeness.[58]

The Moses–God Dialogue of 3:1–7:7[59]	
MOSES OBJECTS	GOD RESPONDS
first set	
Moses is unworthy (3:11)	God will be "with" him (3:12)
Moses does not know God's name (3:13)	God reveals the name (3:14–15)
the people will not heed Moses (4:1)	God provides signs (4:2–9)
Moses is unable to speak (4:10)	God will be with him and tell him what to say (4:12)
Moses asks God to send another (4:13)	God will help Moses and Aaron speak (4:14–17)
second set	
God has not done what was promised (5:22–23)	God repeats the promise (6:1–8)
the people and Egyptians will not heed (6:12)	God repeats the mission (6:13, 26–27)
Moses again says he is unable to speak (6:30)	God makes Aaron the speaker (7:1–7)

Moses is thus hardly a passive recipient of the divine mandate; rather he is a person responding to a daunting challenge with human doubt. At the same time, the reluctance that permeates Moses' dialogue with God signifies that God's initial appearance to Moses, although invoking the ancestors, is radically different from God's interaction with the ancestors, who are not similarly charged with a mission that they resist. Rather, this theophany follows a pattern that long has been identified as a prophetic *call narrative*, which typically contains a series of exchanges between the deity and a prophetic messenger.

The call marks the formative moment in which an individual's prophetic mission is initiated; and it appears for figures such as Isaiah, Jeremiah, and Ezekiel.

---

[58] E. Otto, "*šeḇaʿ; šāḇûʿôt*," 351; Amit, "Progression as a Rhetorical Device," *JSOT* 28 (2003).

[59] Cf. T. E. Fretheim, *Exodus* (1991), 52; for a more elaborate schema, see Gregory Y. Glazov, *Bridling of the Tongue and the Opening of the Mouth in Biblical Prophecy* (JSOTS 311; Sheffield: Sheffield Academic Press, 2001), 98–102.

Form critics, who analyze small units of biblical literature with attention to genre and life setting, have identified a distinctive literary pattern in the call narrative, which typically includes the appearance of God to the prophet (3:1–4a), an introductory statement by the deity (3:4b–9), a statement of commission (3:10), an objection (3:11), and reassurance along with an empowering sign (3:12).[60] The presence of this genre in the Moses account has the effect of identifying him as a prophetic figure, even though he is not explicitly identified as such until the end of the Pentateuch (Deut 34:10). As the Exodus story unfolds, Moses becomes such a multifaceted leader that attaching the "prophet" label would perhaps limit the range of his functions, which in the aggregate far transcend the roles of the other apostolic prophets of the Hebrew Bible. But situating the beginning of Moses' mission within a call narrative made it clear to the ancient audience that his leadership is rooted in the will of God.

The expected objection is followed by the requisite sign – but with a difference. God first responds with an assurance of being "with you," words that typically signify divine presence and the concomitant protection and power that the recipient of the call will need in order to carry out the mission.[61] Then God proclaims the sign, meant to corroborate a message from God, in language fraught with ambiguity. It is not clear what the sign is – it could be the miraculous burning bush, the very presence of God, the fact that God is sending him, or even the ultimate outcome of the mission, in which Moses effects the miraculous deliverance of his people from Egypt. Perhaps the language is intentionally ambiguous, allowing for all these possibilities, which encompass past, present, and future events, as one might expect in mnemohistory. In any case, the vague openness of the statement is far different from the specificity of the signs accompanying or preceding God's directives in other *sign* texts.[62] It is only fitting that the call narrative for Moses, an unparalleled figure in the Hebrew Bible, has unique features.

If the identity of the sign is purposefully vague, the identity of the one who gives the sign becomes strikingly specific in the episode that follows (vv. 13–15), in which the divine name is revealed. Identifying God as the one who appeared to the ancestors is apparently sufficient for Moses but not for the people. In a polytheistic world, gods are individuated by their names; and the god of Israel is no exception. Moses anticipates that the people will insist on knowing the name of this god who is sending Moses to free them. But such a request is not without its problems. For one thing, Gen 4:26 suggests that God's name (Yahweh) has been known since the third generation after creation. Yet the ancestral narratives

---

[60] Norman Habel, "The Form and Significance of the Call Narratives," *ZAW* 77 (1965): 297–323, and more recently G. Y. Glazov, *Bridling of the Tongue* (2001), 27–53.

[61] Baruch A. Levine, "On the Presence of God in Biblical Religion," in *Religions in Antiquity: Essays in Memory of Erwin Ramsdell Goodenough*, ed. Jacob Neusner (Leiden: Brill, 1968), 76.

[62] For the nature and function of signs, see Franz-Josef Helfmeyer, "'ôth," *TDOT* 1:167–88.

call God by various El names, such as El Shaddai (God Almighty, Gen 17:1) and El Elyon (God Most High, Gen 14:19–22), which are indicative of El traditions well entrenched among Israelites. Furthermore, the precise meaning of the name given in this passage is difficult to ascertain. The ambiguity about the name of God and when it was first used may be the result of the mingling of various sources with different traditions about when the name of God was first made known as well as different ways of referring to God.[63]

The name itself is first announced in this passage, uniquely in the Bible, as a first-person statement (*'ehyeh 'ăšer 'ehyeh*) translated "I AM WHO I AM" in the NRSV. It could also be rendered "I AM THAT I AM" or "I WILL BE WHO/WHAT I WILL BE;" and there are other similar renditions. Perhaps more important than the actual translation is the fact that the name (*'ehyeh*) seems to be some form of the verb "to be, become" (*hyh*) and thus asserts God's existence, God's identity as one who brings about existence, and perhaps even God's mystery as the one who is whatever the one is. The divine name as it is found throughout the Hebrew Bible finally appears in the third person form in v. 15, when God tells Moses to say that he has been dispatched to the Israelites by the "LORD [*yhwh*], the God of your ancestors, the God of Abraham, the God of Isaac, and the God of Jacob." Obscured in the English translation of this verse is the juxtaposition of God's name with memory: "This is my name forever, and this is how I am to be remembered [NRSV, and this is my title] for all generations."

A CLOSER LOOK: THE NAME OF GOD

Not only is a name intrinsically related to identity; but also in the biblical world deities, or people for that matter, do not exist without a name. An ancient text from the Nineteenth Dynasty in Egypt (ca. 1350–1200 BCE) illustrates the significance of a name. In this document, the goddess Isis says to the god Re, "Say to me your name, my divine father, for a man lives when one recites his name."[64] Not only existence but also power is inherent in the name of a deity, so that pronouncing it could be a source of blessing or disaster. Such a notion perhaps persists in the way people swear something today "in the name of God"; and it certainly is related to the stipulation in the Decalogue, "You shall not make wrongful use of the name of the LORD your God, for the LORD will not acquit anyone who misuses his name" (Exod 20:7). The personal name of God thus takes on extraordinary significance.

The name revealed to Moses is known as the Tetragrammaton ("four letters") because it is written with four letters in Hebrew. In transliteration, the name appears as YHWH and occurs some 6,823 times in the Hebrew Bible as

---

63 W. H. C. Propp, *Exodus 1–18* (1998). 204–5, 223–6.
64 "The Legend of Isis and the Name of Re," translated by Robert K. Ritner (*COS* 1.22), 34.

well as several times in inscriptions of the biblical period.[65] Ancient biblical manuscripts were basically consonantal, written without vowel signs. When vowels were added to the consonantal text in the early medieval period (seventh to ninth centuries CE) by the Masoretes, Jewish scholars who sought to preserve the traditional text of the Hebrew Bible, the four consonants of the divine name were left unvocalized. They refrained from adding vowels because, by that time, Jews considered the name of God so sacred that they did not pronounce it. Doing so might inadvertently cause them to violate the injunction not to "make wrongful use" of God's name. Thus, when they read aloud from the Bible, they substituted the word Adonai (*'ădōnāy*), which is a term of respectful address meaning "my Lord," or "my Lordship." This practice has continued among Jews to the present. In order to signify this substitution without removing the actual letters of God's name, the Masoretes added the vowels for Adonai to the existing consonants. The result was a hybrid form that made it appear, incorrectly, that God's name would have been Yehovah or Jehovah, which is how it has often been pronounced since the sixteenth century. The original pronunciation of the four-letter name of God, in fact, has been lost. However, current scholarship strongly suggests that the original pronunciation would have been "Yahweh."

Ancient translations of the Bible followed the reverential Jewish treatment of the divine name by rendering it "Lord." The Greek translation (Septuagint) reads YHWH as *Kyrios* and the Latin (Vulgate) has *Dominus*. Most English translations continue this practice by substituting LORD for the divine name. While this practice is respectful, it also is problematic. For one thing, as an epithet it obscures the fact that God has a proper name and reduces awareness of the polytheistic context of ancient Israel – the very situation that necessitated a name for God. Furthermore, as a masculine term, LORD may correctly reflect the third-person masculine nature of the verbal form of God's name but at the same time it perpetuates the masculine identity of a god for whom female imagery is also present.[66] Some translations, such as many of those in the Anchor Bible series, now simply insert the transliteration in capitals (YHWH) wherever the divine name appears in the Hebrew text. An interesting recent treatment is that of the liturgical text of the Bible used in Reform Judaism, where "the Eternal," indicating the everlasting existence of God, is used for the divine name.

The issues of how to render the divine name in English translations pale, however, in comparison with the difficulties in understanding its grammatical structure and its spelling. These are technical problems for which there is an extensive scholarly literature.[67]

---

[65] The Mesha stele of the tenth century, Kuntillet 'Ajrud inscriptions of the ninth–eighth centuries, and the Lachish and Arad ostraca of the seventh and sixth centuries BCE.

[66] Carol Meyers, "Female Images of God in the Hebrew Bible," *WIS*, 525–8. See also the supplementary section, A Closer Look: Gendered Images of God, pp. 122–3.

[67] See D. N. Freedman, M. P. O'Conner, and H. Ringgren, "*YHWH*," *TDOT* 5:500–21.

The origins of the name are also subject to much discussion and specula-tion. In the biblical world, personal names of individuals as well as toponyms often incorporated the names of deities – that is, they had what are known as theophoric elements. Tracing such elements of God's name in personal and place names in the Hebrew Bible and also in extrabiblical inscriptions shows that the worship of Yahweh by at least some elements in ancient Israel precedes the Davidic monarchy.[68] But can anything be said about earlier awareness of the god Yahweh that might inform the traditions associating Moses with the beginnings of Yahwism among Israelites?

The Introduction describes inscriptional data mentioning a land of the "Shasu of *ya-h-wa* [or *yhw*]." The intimate connections of Moses to the Midianites, probably one of the Shasu desert-dwellers, is likely the collective memory of an exodus group interacting with the Midianites and their deity. Another consid-eration is the name of Moses' mother. Jochebed is a theorphoric personal name with a shortened form of Yahweh (see Exod 6:20), making her arguably the first person in the Hebrew Bible to bear such a name and signifying the origin of Yahweh as the name of god with her son.

These old traditions linking the name of Israel's god with the Midianites and Moses aside, the etymology attached to the name ("I AM WHO I AM" or some variant thereof) remains a powerful expression of the nature of Israel's god. A name is related to identity; and the name of Israel's god indicates an open and fluid identity, not linked to any specific cosmological, natural, or functional phenomena, as was the case for other deities in the biblical world. Yahweh is presented as a god whose nature would become manifest in the exodus and thereafter in the ongoing story of that one god's relationship with one people, Israel. Moreover, Yahweh's role in this unfolding story was anticipated, so the narrator tells us, in the story of God's prior interaction with the ancestors. Thus Yahweh becomes inextricably part of the story of this people. All told, as the culmination of the passage in which God's name is revealed indicates, Yahweh's name and nature exist in time in all directions, "forever . . . for all generations" (3:15).

Having provided Moses with the divine name, God now reiterates in an extended speech (3:16–22) what lies ahead for him. Some of the language echoes that of verses 7–12, but this time it is presented as rhetoric that Moses is to use in bringing the case for departure from Egypt to the oppressed people, who are here identified as "Hebrews" (v. 18).[69] The anticipated redemption is to be presented as a declaration, or promise, from God. Even more striking is the sense that, from

[68] Z. Zevit, *Religions of Ancient Israel* (2003), 586–7, 604–9.
[69] Yahweh is here called "the God of the Hebrews," an epithet found only in this verse and several others in the exodus narrative (5:3; 7:16; 9:1, 13; 10:3).

God's perspective, the departure from Egypt will not be a simple matter but will necessitate adjustments and strategies. The agonizing series of negotiations with the Egyptian king, in which the Israelite leaders repeatedly request that their people be allowed to sacrifice to their god, is thus foreshadowed.[70] The "mighty hand" and outstretched hand of verses 19, 20 are similar to expressions of superior strength in Egyptian and Canaanite literature[71] and convey the notion that the power of Israel's god, manifest in "wonders" (v. 20), will prevail. Yahweh's power is repeatedly emphasized with the imagery of "an outstretched arm" or "a mighty hand" in Exodus (6:1; 13:3, 14; 15:6, 12, 16; 32:11). In all, the image of the hand of God appears twenty-seven times in Exodus and becomes part of stock biblical language referring to God's redemptive acts (e.g., Deut 26:8) as distinct from the deeds of humans.[72]

Another kind of foreshadowing occurs in the last two verses of this section (vv. 21–22). Moses is to instruct the women to solicit jewelry as well as clothing from their Egyptian neighbors, a request repeated in 11:2 where men, too, are so enjoined. This wealth would later become part of the precious metals and fabrics used in the construction of the tabernacle (Exod 35:22–24, 29; 36:2–7). In addition to anticipating the contributions to the wilderness shrine, the expected departure from Egypt with valuable goods links the exodus with the promise in Gen 15:13–14, where Abram is told that his descendents would leave the land of their oppression "with great possessions."[73] A troublesome ironic twist is contained in the final words of the instructions, for the Israelite victims of oppression will victimize ("plunder") their oppressors, a concept that is in tension with the notion that the valuables are given freely to the Israelites.

Moses is not convinced that the strategy set forth by God will succeed, and Exodus 4 begins with a third objection – that the people (not the "elders" to whom he was supposed to bring the message of deliverance) might not believe what he has to say. At this point we are introduced to the world of magic at God's

---

[70] The idea that the Israelites will sacrifice is somewhat anachronistic, for the sacrificial system is presented in the Pentateuch as part of divine revelation in the wilderness, after the exodus.

[71] Horus is called "strong in arm" in "Karnak, Campaign against the Libyans (Undated)," translated by Kenneth A. Kitchen (*COS* 2.4F), 30; and Ramesses II attributes his thirteenth century BCE victory over the Hittites to his "strong arm" in "The Battle of Qadesh – The Poem, or Literary Record," translated by Kenneth A. Kitchen (*COS* 2.5A), 36. The phrase "strong hand (arm) of the king" appears in three of the letters of the fourteenth-century BCE ruler of Jerusalem to his Egyptian overlord; see W. L. Moran, *Amarna Letters* (1992), 326–32 (letters 286, 287, 288).

[72] David R. Seely, "The Image of the Hand of God in the Book of Exodus," in *God's Word for Our World: Biblical Studies in Honor of Simon John De Vries* (vol. 1), eds. J. Harold Ellens, Deborah L. Ellens, Rolf P. Knierim, and Isaac Kalimi (JSOTS 388; London: T&T Clark, 2004), 38–54.

[73] Carol Meyers, "Women (and Men) with Jewelry and Clothing (Exod 3:22; 11:2; 32:2–3; 35:22–24, 29; 36:2–7)," *WIS*, 188.

initiative. Moses' staff is turned into a snake and back into a staff.[74] The skin of his hand becomes afflicted and then cured of some sort of dermatological ailment – probably not leprosy (Hansen's disease), which is not attested earlier than the third century BCE. A third sign is the turning of some Nile water to blood, an act that, much magnified, will become the first sign (7:15–25) in the signs-and-wonders sequence soon to come. The word "believe" recurs five times in 4:1–9, signifying the plight of a leader attempting to gain the trust of his people as well as the notion that disbelief can be dispelled by magical means.

A deity who engages in magic hardly fits our contemporary ways of thinking about God, even the god presented in the ancient, Iron Age biblical texts. Magic is too often, in modern theological considerations of religion, seen as occult, heretical, quasi-religious, idolatrous, even pagan. Yet for the ancients, magic was one of the few ways in which humans could attempt to manipulate and influence both the positive and negative forces that they believed existed in the world. Once we let go of the notion that magic is incompatible with biblical religion, we can see that a god who performs signs and wonders and also enables the god's emissaries to do so does not contradict other aspects of divine power that are manifest in the exodus narrative. Moreover, the fascinating details of God's acts of magic situate Israel's god in the wider Near Eastern world with its manifold expressions of ritual magic.[75]

In this ascending series of objections and responses, Moses' next (fourth) statement of reluctance is perhaps the best known; he expresses his sense of inadequacy with the terms "slow of speech and slow of tongue" (literally, "heavy of mouth and heavy of tongue;" cf. 6:12 and 30, where the repetition of this demurral uses the expression "poor speaker," literally, "uncircumcised of lips"). The appearance of parts of the mouth in this extended prophetic call narrative has parallels in the empowering "opening the mouth" rituals in ancient Near Eastern texts, especially Egyptian ones.[76] These parallels make it likely that this is metaphoric language and not the description of a speech impediment. They also bring into focus the genuine human predicament of prophetic reluctance to engage in a task that gives the prophet such an intimate knowledge of God and God's intentions. Although Moses' reluctance may be metaphoric, the language of God's beautifully aphoristic response plays upon the physical qualities that Moses has mentioned. God's rhetorical questions about who gives speech and sight to humanity bring God's role as creator into juxtaposition with the liberator

---

[74] The staff is an instrument of magic, often associated with serpents, in the ancient Near East; cf. Exod 7:9–12, etc., and "Ugaritic Incantation against Sorcery," translated by Daniel Fleming (*COS* 1.96), 301.

[75] See Geraldine Pinch, *Magic in Ancient Egypt* (Austin: University of Texas Press, 1994), and Karel van der Toorn, Bob Becking, and Pieter W. van der Horst, eds., *Dictionary of Deities and Demons in the Bible* (2nd ed.; Leiden: Brill; Grand Rapids, Mich: Eerdmans, 1999).

[76] Collected, with relevant biblical texts, in the Appendix to G. Y. Glazov, *Bridling of the Tongue* (2001), 361–83.

role that dominates the exodus narratives.[77] And God's persistence in assigning the prophetic role to Moses indicates that Moses has special attributes for what lies ahead.

Moses' continued reluctance now has no specific reason. His simple plea that someone else be sent (v. 13) occasions the introduction of Aaron as a prominent figure in the exodus account. We know that Moses has a sister, but this is the first we hear of a brother. Aaron's fate here becomes intermingled with that of his brother. Although it is not visible in English translations, the word for "mouth" appears *seven* times in this section (4:10–17), making the brothers fully intertwined leaders, together bringing God's will to the people. Aaron will eventually become the chief priestly figure of ancient Israel. His authoritative sacerdotal position, presented in Exodus as integral to Israel's national life, is made clear in this passage, where he receives the charge to function along with Moses as a spokesperson for God. It is no accident that his Levitical identity accompanies the first mention of him in the text (4:14). Yet the prophetic role of Moses is to dominate, for whatever Aaron will do is construed as being in the service of Moses. A memorable analogy is offered: being a "mouth" (i.e., spokesperson, or, more specifically, a prophet) for Moses is equated with Moses having the role of God vis à vis Aaron (v. 16; cf. 7:1). The time has come for Moses to return to Egypt and carry out his mission.

MOSES' POWER AND PROBLEMS (4:18–6:1)

Moses, staff of God in hand, sets out to return to Egypt along with Zipporah and their sons – two of them, according to 18:2–3. He is charged with performing wonders to win over the Pharaoh, and he is directed to call Israel God's "firstborn," a term that anticipates the ironic and tragic outcome of the signs-and-wonders sequence, with the death of Egyptian firstborns (12:29), and also the Israelite rite of the firstborn (13:1–2). In addition, firstborn invokes the parent–child image, one that appears often in the Hebrew Bible to portray the intimacy of the relationship between God and Israel. Furthermore, it implies that there are other children, that other peoples of the world are also God's children, just not in the privileged place of the firstborn.[78]

As Moses sets out, he has the permission of his father-in-law to leave Midian; he also has God's guarantee that those who sought to kill him are no longer alive – a strange assurance in light of what will soon confront him on his journey when none other than God apparently seeks to kill him. What is notable about God's directive is that the formulaic language with which prophets introduce authoritative statements appears for the first time: Moses is to say, "Thus says the

---

[77] B. S. Childs, *Book of Exodus* (1974), 78–9.

[78] In the ancient Near East, the firstborn son typically receives a larger share of his father's estate than does his brothers; see Deut 21:17.

Lord" in approaching Pharaoh (v. 22). God's directive also introduces (v. 21) the "harden the heart" motif that will recur many times in the signs-and-wonders (plagues) narrative. In addition, the ostensible reason for which the Israelites are to be released – that they may worship their god – appears here (v. 23) and will recur often as the drama unfolds. The word "sacrifice," first used in the introduction of this reason in 3:18, is here replaced by "worship," which provides irony to the whole exodus narrative for it is from the root *'bd* ("to work") and also signifies the forced service of the Israelites to the Egyptians (cf. Exodus 1) as well as the ultimate goal of the Israelites to serve (worship) their god.

The brief episode reported in 4:24–26 is among the most enigmatic and troubling passages in the Hebrew Bible. Is it Moses whom God tries to kill? Or is it one of his sons? The Hebrew is ambiguous here. And what is the reason for such an attempt? It may have been clear to ancient readers but remains mysterious to us. We can be sure of only three things in this cryptic account. The first is that the deity is the attacker – the God who so clearly wants to save lives here inexplicably wants to take a life; yet God only "tried" to do this.[79] We may not ever know God's motivation, despite the many hypotheses offered by commentators since antiquity. But a powerful god could easily have succeeded and this attempt therefore is something of a wake-up call, apparently involving the importance of circumcision – perhaps an object lesson for later generations who wavered at the use of circumcision as an ethnic marker.

A second fact is that the acute threat is averted through the action of a woman, Moses' wife Zipporah. Her decisive and quick response makes her a heroic figure.[80] She clearly knows exactly what to do and does it expertly. The procedure has a ritualistic flavor to it, not only because of what we know about circumcision as a rite in many cultures, but also because of what the passage tells us about her choice of instruments (a "flint"), her use of the foreskin she removes, and the ritual statement – enigmatic to us but having the quality of an incantation – that she recites as she completes her response to the perceived threat. Zipporah's Midianite identity, as part of a priestly family, may be the key to her ritual proficiency, for female priestly roles were part of many Near Eastern cultures. The passage also has unusual terminology. When Zipporah cuts off the foreskin, the root *krt* is used for "cut" instead of the root *mwl* found in all other biblical references to circumcision; and "bridegroom of blood" is a unique expression in the Hebrew Bible (see Bridging the Horizons: Circumcision, pp. 64–6). This odd language may indicate the presence of ancient Midianite terms

---

[79] "Was on the verge of" would be a better translation of the Hebrew than NRSV "tried" or NJPS "sought to"; so N. M. Sarna, *Exodus* (1991), 25

[80] See Ilana Pardes, "Zipporah and the Struggle for Deliverance," chapter 5 in *Countertraditions in the Bible: A Feminist Account* (Cambridge, Mass.: Harvard University Press, 1992), 79–97.

maintained in collective memory.[81] In any case, in this passage Zipporah functions as a savior, as do two other women (his sister and the Egyptian princess) in Moses' life. But professional expertise rather than sibling ties or human kindness characterizes her salvific deed. (See A Closer Look: Musicians and Midwives as Professionals, pp. 117–9).

The third fact – that circumcising the son and then touching Moses with the foreskin are actions that dispel mortal danger – likewise points to the ritualistic and magical nature of the procedure and to Zipporah's ritual expertise in knowing what to do.

BRIDGING THE HORIZONS: CIRCUMCISION

Circumcision of males, the surgical removal of all or part of the foreskin from the penis, arguably is the oldest and only surgical procedure performed on an otherwise healthy individual. It seems mysterious and archaic as we encounter it in the Hebrew Bible. Involving the genitalia, it arouses awareness of puzzling aspects of male sexuality. In contrast to the flesh-denying spirituality of Christianity, this intensely corporeal act of religio-ethnic identity (as in Exod 12:43–49) seems strange indeed. And it also is troubling to us in its gender exclusivity. As practiced by most Jews to this day as a sign of the covenant, does it mean that only males were true members of the covenant community?[82]

The Israelites were not the only people to practice circumcision. It became a rite practiced by Muslims and Coptic Christians as well as by Jews. Anthropologists have documented its widespread use among peoples in western Asia, Africa, and parts of the Pacific rim, including Australia. In the ancient biblical world, it was already practiced by Egyptians, although perhaps not by all of them, as well as some Semitic groups (cf. Jer 9:25–26) by the mid-third millennium BCE.[83] An eighth-century BCE text indicates that circumcision served as an exclusionary ethnic marker for the Egyptians.[84] What is striking about its appearance in global contexts is that, with the exception of biblical religions, it appears as a rite performed on males at adolescence or early adulthood, or at the time of marriage (although some Muslims delay it beyond the early weeks or years of life). A second-millennium BCE Egyptian text celebrates a group circumcision of adults in which all endured without flinching or injury: "When I was circumcised, together with one hundred and twenty men, there was none

---

81 N. M. Sarna (*Exodus* [1991], 25) calls them "fossilized" terms.

82 For a recent analysis of Israelite circumcision with particular attention to gender issues, see John Goldingay, "The Significance of Circumcision," *JSOT* 88 (2000): 3–18.

83 Jack M. Sasson, "Circumcision in the Ancient Near East," *JBL* 85 (1966): 473–6.

84 "The Victory Stela of King Phye (Piankhy)," translated by Miriam Lichtheim (*COS* 2.7), 50. The text reads, "They could not enter the palace because they were uncircumcised and were eaters of fish, which is an abomination to the palace"; cf. the exclusionary language for the Passover meal in Exod 12:48.

thereof who hit out, there was none thereof who hit, there was none thereof who was scratched."[85]

In considering Israelite circumcision two questions typically emerge: Why did it become such an important rite? And why it was uniquely performed on newborns rather than adolescents or young men?

Answering these questions means looking at the range of possibilities suggested by anthropological theorists.[86] None of the theories is particularly compelling, although the fact that circumcision in traditional societies is so often linked with rites of passage into manhood, at adolescence or marriage, seems to indicate that it has some relationship to male sexuality, more specifically, to the controlling of sexuality in ways suitable for mature, marriageable, full-fledged males. The relationship to sexuality for the Israelites might have been as a way to increase sexuality for a population with recurrent demographic problems – that is, like vegetation, male sexuality would be "pruned" in order to increase fertility.[87] But such theories do not do justice to the strange circumstances of the Zipporah incident nor to the fact that it is presented as a birth ritual.

In the phrase "bridegroom of blood," marriage and circumcision are linked.[88] The word for "bridegroom" is *ḥātān*, which is from the same stem as an Arabic and Akkadian word meaning "to protect"; in an extended form, that meaning fits extraordinarily well the powerfully apotropaic quality of this episode. What generally is overlooked in considering this passage and infant circumcision in general is the tenuous nature of new life in the biblical world. With as many as one in two infants failing to live until the age of five, and with early Israelites aware of the need for demographic increase to maintain farmsteads and rural communities, the powerfully protective nature of the act – appeasing the deity by producing life-blood at the dangerous transition from neonate to infant – perhaps warranted practicing it upon newborns rather than adolescents or bridegrooms. That it is depicted as a rite performed on the eighth day after birth (that is, right after the *seventh* day, which is when the infant fully exists) contributes to such an interpretation.[89]

---

85 "Circumcision in Egypt," translated by John A. Wilson (*ANET*, 326).

86 Summarized by Thomas O. Beidelman, "Circumcision," *Encyclopedia of Religion*, ed. Mircea Eliade (16 vols.; New York: Macmillan, 1987), 1:511–14.

87 Howard Eilberg-Schwartz, "The Fruitful Cut," chapter 6 in the *Savage in Judaism: An Anthropology of Israelite Religion and Ancient Judaism* (Bloomington, Ind.: Indiana University Press, 1990), 141–76.

88 Ernst Kutsch, "*ḥtn*," *TDOT* 5:270–7, summarizes the complex linguistic and kinship features of this connection.

89 In Exod 4:24–26, a woman performs the act. This is one example of the little-recognized but highly significant rituals carried out by women as part of the reproductive process; see Carol Meyers, "From Household to House of Yahweh: Women's Religious Culture in Ancient Israel," in *Congress Volume Basel 2001*, ed. André Lemaire (VTS 92; Leiden: Brill, 2002), 277–303.

Whatever the actual origin of the Israelite transfer of this rite to infancy in hoary Israelite beginnings, it clearly becomes associated with covenant in the Hebrew Bible. By the time of the exile, if not before, it becomes attributed to the ancestral period; the priestly narrator in Gen 17:9–27 has it instituted by God as a sign of the covenant and as an unmistakable physical marker of membership in the community. Its history in the early post-Hebrew Bible period was problematic for both Jews and early Christians. For many Jews in that era, it seemed to thwart the desire to participate in the wider Greco-Roman culture; and for Christians, it was part of the general controversy about adherence to Torah law.[90] Christianity, except for the Copts, ultimately rejected the physical practice although it retained its use as a metaphor for spiritual fitness. But for Jews it emerged as the *sine qua non* for their religio-ethnic identity, as is apparent in the fact that the Jewish circumcision ritual came to be known as *brit* (*bĕrît*), which means "covenant" and is an abbreviated form of *brit milah*, "covenant of circumcision."

Although not practiced as a religious ritual by Christians, in the modern period, especially in the United States, it was understood to have prophylactic qualities and was widely performed as a medical procedure. By the 1970s, approximately 90% of male infants in the United States were circumcised soon after birth. But since the closing decades of the twentieth century, that practice has been challenged by activists, within and outside the medical profession, who call it a dangerous, psychologically damaging, and even barbaric mutilation of the male body, as well as by a minority of Jewish feminists who resist the gender exclusivity of the rite. The medical data about the value of this surgery are not yet conclusive; and because there seems to be evidence that in some circumstances circumcision may be a sensible preventative measure, it is still performed on more than half of male babies born in the United States.[91] For most Jews, the powerful historic meaning of the rite seems to override their egalitarian impulses; they maintain the practice albeit with new interpretive understandings so that it transcends its inherently masculinist features.[92]

Whatever archaic and cryptic memories may be encoded in the circumcision passage, its function on a literary level is noteworthy. It foreshadows the way

---

[90] The issues for early Jews and Christians are summarized in Robert G. Hall, "Circumcision," *ABD* 1:1027–31.

[91] In 1999 the American Academy of Pediatrics recommended that circumcision not be performed routinely but that parents be given accurate and unbiased information to help decide whether to have their sons circumcised.

[92] E.g., Elyse Goldstein, "Blood and Men: A Feminist Looks at Brit Milah," in *Revisions: Seeing Torah Through a Feminist Lens* (Woodstock, Vt.: Jewish Lights, 1998), 114–22. See also Elizabeth Wyner Mark, ed., *The Covenant of Circumcision: New Perspectives on an Ancient Jewish Rite* (Hanover, N.H.: Brandeis University Press, 2003).

blood will save the firstborn Israelites from the final plague that God will visit upon the Egyptians (12:7, 13, 22–23), and it anticipates the role of circumcision in defining the legitimate participants in the Passover (12:43–49). It also allows Moses to continue on his way back to Egypt and to establish his liaison with his brother, whom God addresses directly for the first time in 4:27. Moses and Aaron meet at the "mountain of God" so that Aaron too can partake of the sanctity of the locale in which his brother's charge – and now his, too – was proclaimed. With Aaron speaking, together they bring God's message to the leaders of the people, who respond positively, clearing the way for Moses and Aaron to begin their diplomatic mission – negotiating with the pharaoh.

The cast of characters in the first interaction with the Egyptians (5:1–6:1) includes Moses and Aaron, the pharaoh, the Israelite taskmasters, their Egyptian supervisors, the people, and, of course, God, who is identified as Yahweh, the "God of Israel" (5:1) and the "God of the Hebrews" (5:3). All of these actors have their say, save for the people themselves – for they have Moses and Aaron as their spokespersons. The intricate set of exchanges, which fails to gain any release for the Israelites but rather brings about even harder labor and harsher treatment, is punctuated by the repetition of the words for service (NRSV "work," "servants") and forced labor (NRSV "working"), thus connecting this passage with the notion of service introduced in 1:11–14. The vivid language of dialogue, in keeping with the propensity of biblical narrators to use articulated language to portray the essence of an event or situation, represents the cruelty of oppression perhaps more than would any simple narrative.[93]

The exchange begins with the mention of a religious event – a festival involving pilgrimage to an unnamed site in the wilderness (5:1). Yet aspects of political maneuvering, and especially political subjugation, abound. God and the pharaoh are in a power struggle (5:2). The pharaoh carries out his harsh measures by co-opting the oppressed, that is, by engaging Hebrews to serve as taskmasters over their kin – a "divide-and-conquer" maneuver that has the effect of pitting Hebrews against each other. Through bureaucratic hierarchy, the pharaoh distances, and thereby protects, himself from the protests of the oppressed. And in a cruel twist, the oppressor depicts his measures as necessary treatment for an inherently lazy people (5:17) – a classic case of "blame the victim" as a justification for tyranny. In the end of this abortive attempt at negotiation, even Moses and God are at odds, with Moses indicting God for the increased suffering of the people (5:22–23), thereby initiating the second set of interactions between God and Moses. The result? God declares that divine power will overcome even the mighty pharaoh (6:1), apparently circumventing Moses' mission. The pharaoh has revealed his evil intent, and God's "mighty hand" (6:1) will have to intervene directly.

---

[93] R. Alter, *Art of Biblical Narrative* (1980), 63–87.

REAFFIRMATION AND RENEWAL (6:2–7:7)

Divine reaffirmation begins with divine identification: "I am the LORD" (6:2). This echoes God's self-revelation of 3:15, a repetition that helps convey the great difficulty Moses has in securing Israelite allegiance and Egyptian compliance. Another possibility is that, because it adds the priestly term "God Almighty" (El Shaddai), which is one of the epithets for Yahweh in the ancestor narratives (Gen 17:1 and 35:11), it may represent a separate ancient source (P) in which the god El is identified with Yahweh. In any case, it initiates a passage that has many of the same features of the call narrative of 3:1–12: a commission, objections, and further assurance follow God's introductory statement.

Despite the similarities to the first call narrative, this set of exchanges between Moses and God introduces several new features, which appear in God's affirmation of the promise in 6:2–8. The ancestral covenant is mentioned in verses 3–5, using language similar to that of 2:24. In both instances, God "remembers my covenant," with divine memory evoking human recollection. However, the language of covenant – "I will take you as my people, and I will be your God" (v. 7) – appears here for the first time, anticipating the Sinai covenant. This formulaic language, perhaps the most succinct expression of the bond between God and Israel (cf. Deut 26:16–19), may originate in the language of civil contracts. Note that the word for "covenant" (*bĕrît*) is also used in the Hebrew Bible for marriage bonds (e.g., Prov 2:17). Another word for covenant (*'ēdût*) appears eslewhere in Exodus (e.g., 16:24; see A Closer Look: Covenant, pp. 148–51).

God's insistence that the covenantal promise of freedom and return to the land is valid then comes in verses 6–8 in a staccato of dynamic verbs, with God in the first person as subject: "I will free ... deliver. ... redeem. ... take ... will be ... will bring ... will give." This eloquent *sevenfold* declaration of God's promise is a forceful indication of the totality of the divine commitment. In another way of counting the verbs, by including two ("swore," "freed") in dependent clauses, these verses have a series of *nine* verbs. This sequence of verbs denoting God's deeds anticipates the narrative of the *nine* signs-and-wonders (discussed in the next section) and also conveys the inalienable legal right of the Israelites to the land.[94] The series of verbs closes with the declaration "I am the LORD" (v. 8), repeating the opening assertion (v. 2); God's covenantal promises are thus framed in the most direct and forceful language for divine authority.[95]

Another new feature of this second set of exchanges between God and Moses is the insertion of a genealogical passage, 6:14–25. To our eyes, it seems to interrupt the passionate series of exchanges between the two main characters, God and Moses. But its rhetorical and literary purposes in its present position are clear. For one thing, the Levitical ancestry of Moses and Aaron is foregrounded

---

[94]   Isaac B. Gottlieb, "Law, Love, and Redemption: Legal Connotations in the Language of Exodus 6:6–8," *JANES* 26 (1998): 47–57.

[95]   Walther Zimmerli, *I Am Yahweh* (trans. Douglas W. Stott; Atlanta: John Knox, 1982), 1–28.

in the lineages. This information reasserts the qualifications of Israel's leaders, as members of the priestly family. In addition, because the genealogy lists Aaron's descendents but not those of Moses, the authority of the Aaronide priesthood, as it will emerge later in Exodus, is foreshadowed. Note too that Aaron's seniority over Moses, as firstborn son, appears within the genealogy, for he is mentioned first in verse 20. His name also precedes that of Moses at the beginning of the transitional summation, in verses 26–27, again anticipating his leadership in priestly matters (although Moses' preeminent role in the ensuing events is reasserted by his being named before Aaron in v. 27). Another way in which the genealogy draws attention to Aaron is by mentioning three women: his mother, wife, and daughter-in-law. Women do not usually figure in such lineages, and their presence contributes to an aristocratic claim for Aaron and his descendents.[96]

One of those women is Jochebed. In a context that highlights Aaron, the names of Moses' – and Aaron's – parents finally appear. We learn that Jochebed is married to Amram and that she is also her husband's aunt. Levitical stipulations forbid the marriage of a man to his father's sister (Lev 18:12), and this unusual instance of such a liaison perhaps is meant to highlight or intensify the Levitical pedigree of the Israelite leaders, with both parents descended from Levi. Jochebed's name is also significant – using a shortened form of *yhwh*, it means "Yahweh is glory." Moses' mother is the first biblical personage whose name contains the name of God. The Israelite cultural memory of Moses as the first to know God's name finds expression in the name of his mother.[97]

The genealogy itself is framed by Moses' reluctance, in verses 12 and 30, to carry out the mission. This section then concludes, in 7:1–7, with God's last response in the intricate and extended dialogue with Moses. With an astonishing analogy, God reiterates Moses' mission as God's messenger by saying that he will be "like God to Pharaoh," with Aaron as mouthpiece becoming Moses' prophet (7:1; cf. 4:10–16). Moses' sense of inadequacy is matched by the ultimate reassurance that, through God's action in calling him to this mission and sending him to the pharaoh, Moses will be god-like. Uniquely the recipient of orders from on high, Moses will represent the will of the Israelite god to one of the most powerful rulers of the ancient world. With this unparalleled prophetic role announced for Moses, God informs Moses that the road to freedom for the Israelites will not be quick and easy, for God will "harden Pharaoh's heart" (v. 3). However, the pharaoh eventually will acknowledge that the power manifest in "acts of judgment" (v. 4) originates in Moses' god; and then the people will depart Egypt. This section is a preview of the signs-and-wonders narrative that unfolds in the next section of Exodus; and it ends with the seemingly mundane information about the ages, 80 and 83 respectively, of Moses and Aaron. Their advanced years indicate their importance and wisdom, critical attributes as they are about to embark upon their negotiations with the pharaoh.

---

[96] Susan Tower Hollis, "Daughter of Putiel (Exod 6:25)," *WIS*, 189.
[97] Carol Meyers, "Jochebed," *WIS*, 103.

A CLOSER LOOK: HARDENING THE PHARAOH'S HEART

One of the most prominent and troublesome aspects of the series of signs-and-wonders that God performs through the agency of Moses and Aaron is the fact that the pharaoh's heart is "hardened," meaning that he is not convinced, despite the terrible effects of the wonders, that he should allow the Israelites to leave Egypt. Sometimes he agrees to let them depart and then reneges; at other times his refusal precedes the horrific unleashing of some aspect of nature. The pharaoh's obstinacy seems to present a case of a power struggle between the human ruler and the sovereignty of God. How can an all-powerful deity be pushed around by the whims of an Egyptian despot?

Such a reading of the pharaoh's obduracy, however, is complicated by the biblical terminology. The NRSV and most English translations of the Hebrew text use the verb "to harden." However, such translations mask the variety of Hebrew terms represented by the English verb. In five instances, the verb is *kbd*, "to be heavy." Using this verb creates a sustained set of puns: Moses claims to be "heavy" (NRSV "slow") of mouth and tongue in 4:10; the labor of the Israelites becomes "heavier" in 5:9; and four of the wonders are considered "heavy" (NRSV "great," for flies, 8:24; NRSV "deadly," for pestilence, 9:3; NRSV "heaviest/heavy," for hail, 9:18, 24; NRSV "dense," for locusts in 10:14).[98] The dominant Hebrew term, however, is *ḥzk*, "to be strong," which appears in those wonders attributed to the priestly source. That term should be translated literally as pharaoh's heart becoming "strong" in its resolve to refuse to release the Israelites, for it does not necessarily have the negative connotations of hardheartedness conveyed by the NRSV. One other term, *qšh*, "to harden," appears once (7:3), probably as an alternative term for P. The use of separate Hebrew terms suggests that the signs-and-wonders narrative is a composite literary work, with not all of the series of disastrous events found in each of its components; or, the varied terminology may simply be literary artistry. Either way, it indicates a narrative arrangement rather than a historiographic record.

A similar conclusion derives from noting that the subject of the English verb "to harden" varies in the course of the several chapters in which it is found. In the first five wonders, "Pharaoh" is the subject; in the subsequent ones, God is the subject and therefore the one who controls how the pharaoh responds. This shift keeps the overall sequence from seeming blatantly deterministic. Instead, we see a pattern indicating that what may begin as the pharaoh's resistance to doing something deemed against his or his nation's best interests ultimately becomes an act produced by God. Divine causality, although in tension with human will, is understood as part of the human as well as the natural realm, that is, as part of the decisions that humans make as well as of the workings of

---

[98] R. E. Friedman (*Bible with Sources Revealed* [2003], 130–1) points out these and other examples of "heavy" in the E tradition in Exodus.

nature. The fact that the "heart," which is consistently part of the idiom of the pharaoh's resistance, represents all aspects of a person – cognitive and rational as well as affective[99] – in the anthropology of the Hebrew Bible indicates that the pharaoh's recalcitrant behavior is considered conscious and deliberate, affecting the course of events.

The structured set of wonders leads to the conclusion provided by God's last response in the extended dialogue with Moses: that the Egyptians would "know" that Yahweh was responsible for the signs-and-wonders (7:5). As we shall see, the wonders are organized in sets of three. In the first of each triad, perhaps signifying what will take place in all the wonders in that set, the theme of Egyptians knowing Yahweh recurs, increasing its scope each time. In the first wonder, water turns to blood so that the pharaoh "shall know that I am the LORD" (7:17). In the fourth one, the flies ruin the land so that the pharaoh will "know that I the LORD am in this land" (8:22). Finally, in the seventh wonder, hail will strike down humans, animals, and plants so that the pharaoh will "know that there is no one like me [the LORD] in all the earth." The pharaoh's recognition of the *universal* sovereignty of Israel's god, and not merely his granting the Israelites permission to leave Egypt, is the ultimate goal of the structured set of wonders. Other features of this structure will become apparent as we examine the signs-and-wonders. In this literary context, what seems at first to be a power struggle between Yahweh and the pharaoh, in fact, is an artful and gripping display of how an ancient and prosperous culture, with understandable human difficulty – with hardness of heart – can acquiesce to the inevitable outcome ordained by God.

SIGNS-AND-WONDERS (NINE CALAMATIES) – EXODUS 7:8–10:29

NRSV 7:8 The LORD said to Moses and Aaron, [9]"When Pharaoh says to you, 'Perform a wonder,' then you shall say to Aaron, 'Take your staff and throw it down before Pharaoh, and it will become a snake.'" [10]So Moses and Aaron went to Pharaoh and did as the LORD had commanded; Aaron threw down his staff before Pharaoh and his officials, and it became a snake. [11]Then Pharaoh summoned the wise men and the sorcerers; and they also, the magicians of Egypt, did the same by their secret arts. [12]Each one threw down his staff, and they became snakes; but Aaron's staff swallowed up theirs. [13]Still Pharaoh's heart was hardened, and he would not listen to them, as the LORD had said.

14 Then the LORD said to Moses, "Pharaoh's heart is hardened; he refuses to let the people go. [15]Go to Pharaoh in the morning, as he is going out to the water; stand

---

[99] Heinz-Josef Fabry, "*lēḇ; lēḇaḇ*," *TDOT* 7:399–437.

by at the river bank to meet him, and take in your hand the staff that was turned into a snake. [16]Say to him, 'The LORD, the God of the Hebrews, sent me to you to say, "Let my people go, so that they may worship me in the wilderness." But until now you have not listened. [17]Thus says the LORD, "By this you shall know that I am the LORD." See, with the staff that is in my hand I will strike the water that is in the Nile, and it shall be turned to blood. [18]The fish in the river shall die, the river itself shall stink, and the Egyptians shall be unable to drink water from the Nile.'" [19]The LORD said to Moses, "Say to Aaron, 'Take your staff and stretch out your hand over the waters of Egypt – over its rivers, its canals, and its ponds, and all its pools of water – so that they may become blood; and there shall be blood throughout the whole land of Egypt, even in vessels of wood and in vessels of stone.'"

20 Moses and Aaron did just as the LORD commanded. In the sight of Pharaoh and of his officials he lifted up the staff and struck the water in the river, and all the water in the river was turned into blood, [21]and the fish in the river died. The river stank so that the Egyptians could not drink its water, and there was blood throughout the whole land of Egypt. [22]But the magicians of Egypt did the same by their secret arts; so Pharaoh's heart remained hardened, and he would not listen to them, as the LORD had said. [23]Pharaoh turned and went into his house, and he did not take even this to heart. [24]And all the Egyptians had to dig along the Nile for water to drink, for they could not drink the water of the river.

25 Seven days passed after the LORD had struck the Nile.

NRSV 8 Then the LORD said to Moses, "Go to Pharaoh and say to him, 'Thus says the LORD: Let my people go, so that they may worship me. [2]If you refuse to let them go, I will plague your whole country with frogs. [3]The river shall swarm with frogs; they shall come up into your palace, into your bedchamber and your bed, and into the houses of your officials and of your people, and into your ovens and your kneading bowls. [4]The frogs shall come up on you and on your people and on all your officials.'" [5]And the LORD said to Moses, "Say to Aaron, 'Stretch out your hand with your staff over the rivers, the canals, and the pools, and make frogs come up on the land of Egypt.'" [6]So Aaron stretched out his hand over the waters of Egypt; and the frogs came up and covered the land of Egypt. [7]But the magicians did the same by their secret arts, and brought frogs up on the land of Egypt.

8 Then Pharaoh called Moses and Aaron, and said, "Pray to the LORD to take away the frogs from me and my people, and I will let the people go to sacrifice to the LORD." [9]Moses said to Pharaoh, "Kindly tell me when I am to pray for you and for your officials and for your people, that the frogs may be removed from you and your houses and be left only in the Nile." [10]And he said, "Tomorrow." Moses said, "As you say! So that you may know that there is no one like the LORD our God, [11]the frogs shall leave you and your houses and your officials and your people; they shall be left only in the Nile." [12]Then Moses and Aaron went out from Pharaoh; and Moses cried out to the LORD concerning the frogs that he had brought upon Pharaoh. [13]And the LORD did as Moses requested: the frogs died in the houses, the

courtyards, and the fields. [14]And they gathered them together in heaps, and the land stank. [15]But when Pharaoh saw that there was a respite, he hardened his heart, and would not listen to them, just as the LORD had said.

16 Then the LORD said to Moses, "Say to Aaron, 'Stretch out your staff and strike the dust of the earth, so that it may become gnats throughout the whole land of Egypt.'" [17]And they did so; Aaron stretched out his hand with his staff and struck the dust of the earth, and gnats came on humans and animals alike; all the dust of the earth turned into gnats throughout the whole land of Egypt. [18]The magicians tried to produce gnats by their secret arts, but they could not. There were gnats on both humans and animals. [19]And the magicians said to Pharaoh, "This is the finger of God!" But Pharaoh's heart was hardened, and he would not listen to them, just as the LORD had said.

20 Then the LORD said to Moses, "Rise early in the morning and present yourself before Pharaoh, as he goes out to the water, and say to him, 'Thus says the LORD: Let my people go, so that they may worship me. [21]For if you will not let my people go, I will send swarms of flies on you, your officials, and your people, and into your houses; and the houses of the Egyptians shall be filled with swarms of flies; so also the land where they live. [22]But on that day I will set apart the land of Goshen, where my people live, so that no swarms of flies shall be there, that you may know that I the LORD am in this land. [23]Thus I will make a distinction between my people and your people. This sign shall appear tomorrow.'" [24]The LORD did so, and great swarms of flies came into the house of Pharaoh and into his officials' houses; in all of Egypt the land was ruined because of the flies.

25 Then Pharaoh summoned Moses and Aaron, and said, "Go, sacrifice to your God within the land." [26]But Moses said, "It would not be right to do so; for the sacrifices that we offer to the LORD our God are offensive to the Egyptians. If we offer in the sight of the Egyptians sacrifices that are offensive to them, will they not stone us? [27]We must go a three days' journey into the wilderness and sacrifice to the LORD our God as he commands us." [28]So Pharaoh said, "I will let you go to sacrifice to the LORD your God in the wilderness, provided you do not go very far away. Pray for me." [29]Then Moses said, "As soon as I leave you, I will pray to the LORD that the swarms of flies may depart tomorrow from Pharaoh, from his officials, and from his people; only do not let Pharaoh again deal falsely by not letting the people go to sacrifice to the LORD."

30 So Moses went out from Pharaoh and prayed to the LORD. [31]And the LORD did as Moses asked: he removed the swarms of flies from Pharaoh, from his officials, and from his people; not one remained. [32]But Pharaoh hardened his heart this time also, and would not let the people go.

NRSV 9 Then the LORD said to Moses, "Go to Pharaoh, and say to him, 'Thus says the LORD, the God of the Hebrews: Let my people go, so that they may worship me. [2]For if you refuse to let them go and still hold them, [3]the hand of the LORD will strike with a deadly pestilence your livestock in the field: the horses, the donkeys, the camels, the herds, and the flocks. ⁴But the Lord will make a distinction between the livestock of Israel and the livestock of Egypt, so that nothing shall die of all that belongs to the Israelites.'" ⁵The Lord set a time, saying, "Tomorrow the Lord will do this thing in the land." ⁶And on the next day the Lord did so; all the livestock of the Egyptians died, but of the livestock of the Israelites not one died. ⁷Pharaoh inquired and found that not one of the livestock of the Israelites was dead. But the heart of Pharaoh was hardened, and he would not let the people go.

8 Then the Lord said to Moses and Aaron, "Take handfuls of soot from the kiln, and let Moses throw it in the air in the sight of Pharaoh. ⁹It shall become fine dust all over the land of Egypt, and shall cause festering boils on humans and animals throughout the whole land of Egypt." ¹⁰So they took soot from the kiln, and stood before Pharaoh, and Moses threw it in the air, and it caused festering boils on humans and animals. ¹¹The magicians could not stand before Moses because of the boils, for the boils afflicted the magicians as well as all the Egyptians. ¹²But the Lord hardened the heart of Pharaoh, and he would not listen to them, just as the Lord had spoken to Moses.

13 Then the Lord said to Moses, "Rise up early in the morning and present yourself before Pharaoh, and say to him, 'Thus says the Lord, the God of the Hebrews: Let my people go, so that they may worship me. ¹⁴For this time I will send all my plagues upon you yourself, and upon your officials, and upon your people, so that you may know that there is no one like me in all the earth. ¹⁵For by now I could have stretched out my hand and struck you and your people with pestilence, and you would have been cut off from the earth. ¹⁶But this is why I have let you live: to show you my power, and to make my name resound through all the earth. ¹⁷You are still exalting yourself against my people, and will not let them go. ¹⁸Tomorrow at this time I will cause the heaviest hail to fall that has ever fallen in Egypt from the day it was founded until now. ¹⁹Send, therefore, and have your livestock and everything that you have in the open field brought to a secure place; every human or animal that is in the open field and is not brought under shelter will die when the hail comes down upon them.'" ²⁰Those officials of Pharaoh who feared the word of the Lord hurried their slaves and livestock off to a secure place. ²¹Those who did not regard the word of the Lord left their slaves and livestock in the open field.

22 The Lord said to Moses, "Stretch out your hand toward heaven so that hail may fall on the whole land of Egypt, on humans and animals and all the plants of the field in the land of Egypt." ²³Then Moses stretched out his staff toward heaven, and the Lord sent thunder and hail, and fire came down on the earth. And the Lord rained hail on the land of Egypt; ²⁴there was hail with fire flashing continually in the midst of it, such heavy hail as had never fallen in all the land of Egypt since it became a nation. ²⁵The hail struck down everything that was in the open field throughout all the land of Egypt, both human and animal; the hail also struck down all the plants of the field, and shattered every tree in the field. ²⁶Only in the land of Goshen, where the Israelites were, there was no hail.

27 Then Pharaoh summoned Moses and Aaron, and said to them, "This time I have sinned; the Lord is in the right, and I and my people are in the wrong. ²⁸Pray to the Lord! Enough of God's thunder and hail! I will let you go; you need stay no longer." ²⁹Moses said to him, "As soon as I have gone out of the city, I will stretch out my hands to the Lord; the thunder will cease, and there will be no more hail, so that you may know that the earth is the Lord's. ³⁰But as for you and your officials, I know that you do not yet fear the Lord God." ³¹(Now the flax and the barley were ruined, for the barley was in the ear and the flax was in bud. ³²But the wheat and the spelt were not ruined, for they are late in coming up.) ³³So Moses left Pharaoh, went out of the city, and stretched out his hands to the Lord; then the thunder and the hail ceased, and the rain no longer poured down on the earth. ³⁴But when Pharaoh saw that the rain and the hail and the thunder had ceased, he sinned once more and hardened his heart, he and his officials. ³⁵So the heart of Pharaoh was hardened, and he would not let the Israelites go, just as the Lord had spoken through Moses.

NRSV 10 Then the Lord said to Moses, "Go to Pharaoh; for I have hardened his heart and the heart of his officials, in order that I may show these signs of mine among them, ²and that you may tell your children and grandchildren how I have made fools of the Egyptians and what signs I have done among them – so that you may know that I am the Lord."

3 So Moses and Aaron went to Pharaoh, and said to him, "Thus says the Lord, the God of the Hebrews, 'How long will you refuse to humble yourself before me? Let my people go, so that they may worship me. ⁴For if you refuse to let my people go, tomorrow I will bring locusts into your country. ⁵They shall cover the surface of the land, so that no one will be able to see the land. They shall devour the last remnant left you after the hail, and they shall devour every tree of yours that grows in the field. ⁶They shall fill your houses, and the houses of all your officials and of all the Egyptians – something that neither your parents nor your grandparents have seen, from the day they came on earth to this day.'" Then he turned and went out from Pharaoh.

7 Pharaoh's officials said to him, "How long shall this fellow be a snare to us? Let the people go, so that they may worship the Lord their God; do you not yet understand that Egypt is ruined?" ⁸So Moses and Aaron were brought back to Pharaoh, and he said to them, "Go, worship the Lord your God! But which ones are to go?" ⁹Moses said, "We will go with our young and our old; we will go with our sons and daughters and with our flocks and herds, because we have the Lord's festival to celebrate." ¹⁰He said to them, "The Lord indeed will be with you, if ever I let your little ones go with you! Plainly, you have some evil purpose in mind. ¹¹No, never! Your men may go and worship the Lord, for that is what you are asking." And they were driven out from Pharaoh's presence.

12 Then the Lord said to Moses, "Stretch out your hand over the land of Egypt, so that the locusts may come upon it and eat every plant in the land, all that the hail

has left." [13]So Moses stretched out his staff over the land of Egypt, and the LORD brought an east wind upon the land all that day and all that night; when morning came, the east wind had brought the locusts. [14]The locusts came upon all the land of Egypt and settled on the whole country of Egypt, such a dense swarm of locusts as had never been before, nor ever shall be again. [15]They covered the surface of the whole land, so that the land was black; and they ate all the plants in the land and all the fruit of the trees that the hail had left; nothing green was left, no tree, no plant in the field, in all the land of Egypt. [16]Pharaoh hurriedly summoned Moses and Aaron and said, "I have sinned against the LORD your God, and against you. [17]Do forgive my sin just this once, and pray to the LORD your God that at the least he remove this deadly thing from me." [18]So he went out from Pharaoh and prayed to the LORD. [19]The LORD changed the wind into a very strong west wind, which lifted the locusts and drove them into the Red Sea[a]; not a single locust was left in all the country of Egypt. [20]But the LORD hardened Pharaoh's heart, and he would not let the Israelites go.

21 Then the LORD said to Moses, "Stretch out your hand toward heaven so that there may be darkness over the land of Egypt, a darkness that can be felt." [22]So Moses stretched out his hand toward heaven, and there was dense darkness in all the land of Egypt for three days. [23]People could not see one another, and for three days they could not move from where they were; but all the Israelites had light where they lived. [24]Then Pharaoh summoned Moses, and said, "Go, worship the LORD. Only your flocks and your herds shall remain behind. Even your children may go with you." [25]But Moses said, "You must also let us have sacrifices and burnt offerings to sacrifice to the LORD our God. [26]Our livestock also must go with us; not a hoof shall be left behind, for we must choose some of them for the worship of the LORD our God, and we will not know what to use to worship the LORD until we arrive there." [27]But the LORD hardened Pharaoh's heart, and he was unwilling to let them go. [28]Then Pharaoh said to him, "Get away from me! Take care that you do not see my face again, for on the day you see my face you shall die." [29]Moses said, "Just as you say! I will never see your face again."

*M*ost of us are familiar with the rubric *ten plagues* as a designation for this section of Exodus. That phrase, however, does not appear in the biblical account of the exodus nor in any other passage of the Hebrew Bible. Indeed, "plague" (from the root *ngp*, "to strike, smite"), denoting a sudden punitive blow meted out by God, is used in this section of Exodus only once in the nominal form (although it does appear in 8:2, somewhat inappropriately, in a verbal form in relation to the infestation of frogs). In 9:14, "plagues" denotes the disaster (hail) that will strike pharaoh, his courtiers, and the rest of his people – at least those who do not seek shelter. This is the only one among the nine

---

[a] Or *Sea of Reeds*

calamities that results in the loss of human life, and therefore the term plague is justified. However, in the next section (11:1–13:16), which presents the slaying of the firstborn, plague appears several times: In 12:13, God assures the Israelites that they will not suffer the "plague" – the slaying of the firstborn – that will soon afflict the Egyptians; and the verbal form (NRSV "strike") is used twice in 12:23 and once more in 12:27 in reference to this fatal blow to the Egyptians. A closely related term (*nega*, "affliction" [NRSV "plague"]), found in 11:1, also refers to the slaying of the firstborn, although it may retrospectively include the nine preceding events and thus anticipate postbiblical tradition, which links the nine calamities with the slaying of the firstborn and labels them "ten blows," which becomes the familiar English "ten plagues." It is to be noted in this respect that "blows" is the noun form of the verb "to strike," which is used for two of the calamities: bloody water in 7:17, 25 and gnats in 8:16–17.

That the "ten plagues" nomenclature is postbiblical is supported by the fact that biblical passages outside Exodus do not resort to plague terminology, let alone the number ten, in referring to the exodus account. Rather, "signs and wonders" or just "signs" or just "wonders" appears repeatedly in other biblical　— books in explicit reference to this series of episodes (e.g., Deut 4:34; Ps 78:43–51; 105:26–27; Jer 32:20–21). These texts reflect the language of the exodus account itself, which uses "signs" and/or "wonders" rather than "plagues" to refer collectively to the mighty acts of God that ultimately cause the pharaoh to release the oppressed Israelites. "Wonders" as an allusion to what God will do to the Egyptians first appears in 3:20, when God commissions Moses; it is next found in 4:21, when God is sending Moses back to Egypt to begin his mission; in 7:8 it is part of the introduction to the sequence of calamities; and it refers to all but the slaying of the firstborn in the recapitulation, before that last devastating blow, of 11:9 and 10. "Signs" alone appears in 4:17, when God tells Moses that he will use his staff to perform such portents; in 8:23 it denotes the flies episode; and in 10:1–2, "signs" seems to refer more generally to all that God does to the Egyptians. Finally, "signs" and "wonders" together appear in God's last response to the reluctant Moses, before he begins his negotiations with the pharaoh, in 7:3.

Because the exodus account itself as well as other biblical texts use "signs" and "wonders" for what postbiblical tradition calls plagues, the discussion here will avoid the latter term, which connotes horrific and extensive loss of life, a condition that does not obtain for all nine events. Moreover, because both "signs" and "wonders" more generally are God-focused terms, indicating divine intervention in human affairs, signs-and-wonders better represents the function of these episodes as manifestations of divine power on Israel's behalf.

In addition to terminology, the literary arrangement of the nine signs-and-wonders deserves attention. Diverse literary sources with different traditions of what the calamities were and how they were effected may underlie the canonical narrative. The two other biblical passages with the most detailed references to the signs-and-wonders, Psalms 78 and 105, diverge in the number, sequence, and content of these calamities. The presence of such varying traditions contributes to the notion that there were also different prose versions (perhaps P, J, and/or E), each with their own distinctive vocabulary and focus. Whether or not it originated as a composite of sources, its present canonical form is a sophisticated literary structure that has been recognized as such since early postbiblical times. It consists of three triads:

Structure of the Signs-and-Wonders			
bloody water (7:14–25)	warning	outside	morning
frogs (8:1–15)	warning	palace	–
gnats (8:16–19)	–	–	–
flies (8: 20–32)	warning	outside	morning
pestilence (9:1–7)	warning	palace	–
boils (9:8–13)	–	–	–
hail (9:13–35)	warning	outside (?)	morning
locusts (10:1–20)	warning	palace	–
darkness (10:21–29)	–	–	–

The first sign-and-wonder in each triad (bloody water, flies, hail) has the same format, with the pharaoh being warned of the impending calamity in the morning when he is on his way to the river. The second sign-and-wonder in each set (frogs, pestilence, locusts) mentions a warning, and the confrontation with the pharaoh appears to take place in the palace. The third sign-and-wonder in each set (gnats, boils, darkness) comes about abruptly, with no warning or indication of locale.

Another feature of the organization of these triads is that there seems to be some thematic focus to each. The first set (bloody water, frogs, gnats) contains calamities related to water and its denizens. The next three (flies, pestilence, boils) affect people, then livestock, and then people and animals. The third group (hail, locusts, darkness) consists of airborne menaces. The instrumentality of the calamities also seems to follow these triads: Aaron's hand or staff is responsible for the first three; Moses' hand brings about the last three; and the central set is varied, involving Moses praying, God striking, and Moses throwing soot into the air.

This artful structuring of the signs-and-wonders narrative is a message unto itself. That there is a pattern to what happens as the result of the pharaoh's sinful intransigency provides the message that God controls the natural world in order to effect divine purpose. The oppression of peoples cannot go unanswered. The signs-and-wonders are not random natural occurrences, although they are not unrelated to known ecological events. But it is the intensity and timing of these calamities that takes them out of the realm of the ordinary and casts them into the arena of deliberate divine activity for a specific purpose. They are over the top in terms of severity, as indicated by the frequent use of "all" to indicate how widespread they were and also the recurrence of phrases such as "had never been seen before" to denote how utterly extreme they were. Moreover, they are collectively comprehensive, affecting all of creation as depicted in Genesis 1: water and its inhabitants, vegetation and land animals, and the air. In reflecting the priestly account of creation, they suggest the presence of a priestly hand in arranging them. To see them simply as sequential natural occurrences is to ignore their presentation as deliberate, supernatural or hypernatural events and to deprive them of their theological significance.[100] As the discussion in A Closer Look: Hardening the Pharaoh's Heart suggests, the signs-and-wonders are meant to bring about universal knowledge of God and God's power (7:17; 8:10, 19, 22; 9:14). They also signify "mighty/great acts of judgment" (6:6; 7:4).

The striking literary arrangement of the signs-and-wonders does not, however, mean that the nine individual calamities fit an overall mold. On the contrary, there is considerable variation in the details of each calamity and the language with which it is presented. For example, in several instances the Egyptian magicians compete with Moses and Aaron, and in others they do not. Some of the calamities affect only the Egyptians and their possessions, and others involve Egyptians and non-Egyptians alike. The reason Moses gives for requesting permission for the Israelites to leave is stated somewhat differently whenever it appears. Sometimes the pharaoh is unmoved by the disaster, and other times he seems to relent or appears willing to negotiate. Pharaoh's voice is heard in some of the negotiations but not others. In several instances God reverses the calamity, although most seem to run their course. In short, the narrator skillfully varies the account of each sign-and-wonder, maintaining interest and suspense as the narrative moves inexorably to its climax, the slaying of the first-born Egyptians. Despite the increasingly intense episodes, the pharaoh does not relent and something more drastic must be implemented.

The evidence for a literary structure for the signs-and-wonders as a whole, albeit with significant variations among the individual components, does not mean that these disasters are the pure invention of a storyteller. Indeed, no consideration of this extraordinarily graphic part of the exodus narrative can ignore the issue of the natural phenomena that are represented by each of the calamities. Scholars long have attempted to place these occurrences against the backdrop of the *realia* of the ecology of the Nile basin and delta.[101] Examining the narratives in the light of geographical, microbiological, climatic, and medical data leaves little doubt that the biblical descriptions represent salient aspects of well-known occurrences of pestilence and disease in eastern North Africa.

---

[100]   T. E. Fretheim (*Exodus* [1991], 109) introduces the term "hypernatural" (nature in excess).
[101]   E.g., Greta Hort, "The Plagues of Egypt," *ZAW* 69 (1957): 84–104 and 70 (1958): 48–59, and the summary in K. A. Kitchen, *Reliability of the Old Testament* (2003), 250–1 and Table 18.

Documents of the late fourteenth century BCE, in particular, refer to epidemics so devastating that they remained in Egyptian memory for centuries; similar recollections are likely to have been reshaped in the Israelite collective memory as the signs-and-wonders narrative.[102]

In the idiom of ancient Semitic literature, the structured succession of signs-and-wonders and the accompanying hyperbole expresses divine intervention. Stripped of the exaggerated language that characterizes their presentation, the calamities are neither miraculous nor are they always unusual. Yet in their extent and intensity and as an aggregate, the natural becomes the hypernatural. The narrator draws upon the memory of known occurrences and skillfully weaves them, in their canonical form, into a gripping account of divine power in the service of liberation. Reality, folklore, and creative imagination come together in the composite biblical narrative. Attempts to correlate it with an interlocking sequence of disasters within a single specific year in Egyptian history miss the genius of the literary construction of the signs-and-wonders sequence and undervalue the profundity of its theological message.

Acknowledging the a historical character of the signs-and-wonders segment of the exodus story not only allows us to appreciate its literary and theological features; it also relieves our concern that innocent people would have suffered and that there was enormous damage to plants and animals, all at the hand of God. It does not, however, mitigate the problem, which recurs throughout the Hebrew Bible, of the Israelite conception of a god who might bring about freedom for some at the expense of the affliction of others.

INTRODUCTION (7:8–13)

The three major human figures, as well as the subsidiary ones, of the signs-and-wonders narrative are brought together in a prelude. Major themes and motifs – wondrous acts (v. 9), hardening of the pharaoh's heart (v. 13), competition with Egyptian magicians (vv. 11–12), and the power of staffs (vv. 9–10, 12; cf. 17:5–6) – appear in this brief vignette showing the initial appearance of Moses and Aaron in the pharaoh's court. The magicians appear for the first time, although their presence in the Egyptian court is established in the Joseph narrative at the end of Genesis (41:8, 24). Here, as in Genesis, they are linked with "wise men," a clue that the somewhat pejorative English term "magician" may be unjustified. Indeed, the Hebrew *ḥarṭôm* is derived from an Egyptian term designating an important priestly official.[103] Egypt was renowned in the ancient world for its sages and its workers of magic and wonders. The positive function of magic for Israelites as well as others in the biblical world has already been noted in the discussion of Moses' staff (4:2–5). Similarly, magic is not viewed negatively here.

---

[102] R. S. Hendel, "Exodus in Biblical Memory," *JBL* 120 (2001): 608–15.
[103] Thomas O. Lambdin, "Egyptian Loanwords in the Old Testament," *JAOS* 73 (1953): 15–51.

The techniques of Israel's leaders are not contrasted with those of the Egyptians. Rather, this scene shows Israel's god to be more powerful; for the magic rods of the Egyptian court, when turned into snakes, are consumed by Aaron's staff.

This fascinating vignette not only introduces the signs-and-wonders narrative; it also anticipates the climax of the story of departure, when the Egyptians perish in the divided Reed (Red) Sea. In the poetic celebration of the escape of the Israelites in chapter 15, God's outstretched hand, the equivalent of Aaron's staff, causes the earth to "swallow" the pharaoh's army (v. 12); the verb is the same as in 7:12. Moreover, the Hebrew term for snakes in this prelude (vv. 9, 10, 12) is not the usual biblical term, *nāḥāš*, which is used in 4:3 and 7:15. Instead, the word *tannîn* appears. That word denotes a larger, more terrifying beast or sea monster and is part of the mythic vocabulary of the Hebrew Bible; it represents the forces of chaos as antithetical to God's will. It serves to "dragonize" the pharoah, in keeping with the mythic imagery also present in Ezek 29:2–3.[104] Note that Ps 74:13 equates the splitting of the sea with breaking the heads of the *tannînîm* (NRSV "dragons") in the waters. Thus the swallowing of the Egyptians' rods/serpents anticipates the swallowing of the Egyptians in the sea and the termination of oppression/chaos.

#1, BLOODY WATER (7:14–25)

The image of the Nile turning to blood may originate in its appearance, full of sediment, in its spring flood stages. Yet its significance goes beyond such apparently harmless physical changes to the Nile and the other bodies of water in its flood plain, for bloodlike water in ancient Near Eastern literature is an omen, a portent of impending disasters.[105] As the first of the signs-and-wonders sequence, it is a harbinger of calamities to come. In addition, it is a water event par excellence. Note how many different terms (water, river, Nile, pools, canals, ponds) appear and how often many of them are repeated. This repetition foregrounds water and thereby foreshadows the ultimate water catastrophe, the splitting of the sea and the drowning of the pharaoh's forces.

There are other notable features of the bloody water episode. We are introduced to the resounding phrase "let my people go," which appears here for the first time as part of the request, recurring often, that the people be permitted to leave Egypt to worship in the wilderness (7:16). We see the confluence of human and divine power when Moses is instructed to tell the pharaoh that he will strike the Nile with his staff and Moses then tells Aaron to stretch his staff over the waters. They both seem to do as instructed, with their acts merged in the summary statement that God "had struck the Nile" (7:25); humans performing wonders are the agents of God. We also see the Egyptian magicians replicating

---

[104] Ph. Guillaume, "Metamorphosis of a Ferocious Pharaoh," *Bib* 85 (2004): 232–6.
[105] Examples are given in W. H. C. Propp, *Exodus 1–18* (1998), 348.

what Moses and Aaron do as instruments of Yahweh, although it is not clear whether they are acting simultaneously or sequentially with the Israelite leaders. And this is the only calamity for which a specific time period – the symbolically significant *seven* days – is given before Moses is sent back to the pharaoh.

#2, FROGS (8:1–15)

We have not seen the last of the Nile and its canals and pools. They appear in the second sign-and-wonder episode as the source of the frogs that penetrate every corner of the land. The verbal form of "plague" appears here (v. 2), uniquely, among the nine signs-and-wonders. Usually reserved for deadly afflictions, it is not quite appropriate for the infestation of frogs. Perhaps it is used here to give the frogs the status of a warning, anticipating the truly mortal affliction – the slaying of the firstborn, where, as already noted, "plague" appears several times. Otherwise, the vivid language reveals how intimately the frogs will affect everyone: they will be in the homes of all, even in their beds and food. The narrative indicates the totality of Egyptians involved by listing three elements of the population – pharaoh, the officials, and the people. This list, which reflects the hierarchical structure of Egyptian society, will recur frequently – *nine* times in all – in the narrative of *nine* signs-and-wonders.

As they do with the bloody waters, the Egyptian magicians replicate this feat. Yet the pharaoh, whose voice we finally hear, offers conditional release – if the scourge of frogs be lifted. The request goes not to his own magicians but to Moses and Aaron, who are asked to pray (Hebrew '*tr*, "plead") to Yahweh to remove the frogs. For the first time the pharaoh seems to acknowledge the existence of Yahweh. Could it be that he is becoming aware of the greater power of the Israelite god and that he is beginning to understand that there is "no one like the LORD our God" (8:10)? Or is his request a subterfuge, meant simply to rid Egypt of this affliction? These tantalizing possibilities emerge but are unanswered. In any case, the disappearance of the frogs, like their arrival, fails to bring the desired result.

#3, GNATS (8:16–19)

As the third calamity in the first triad, this one is presented with no warning and with little narrative detail. At the command of God, mediated through Moses, Aaron stretches out his staff and turns dust into clouds of some kind of biting insects, perhaps gnats. In hyperbolic fashion, they infest all of Egypt, for they come from "dust," which is often an image in the Hebrew Bible for what is countless (as in Gen 13:16). The magicians again try to duplicate the nasty deed, but this time they fail. It becomes apparent that what the Egyptians are experiencing is not simply magic. Rather, in a variant of the "mighty hand" and "outstretched arm" imagery, the "finger of God" (v. 19) is at work. Yet the pharaoh is unyielding.

#4, FLIES (8:20–32)

The next sign-and-wonder, which is the first of the second triad, is introduced by a warning in the morning. But new elements appear. For one thing, a one-day time delay is specified ("tomorrow," v. 23) before God sends the swarms of flies upon the hyperbolic everyone ("you, your officials, and your people ... also the land," v. 21). This heightens the suspense, suggests that a prophet of God can predict what will happen, and also provides ironic contrast with the way Moses ends a calamity "tomorrow" in 8:10. Another significant innovation is that God this time will distinguish between the Egyptians and the Israelites; the flies will not infest the land of Goshen, where God's people dwell (v. 22). This differentiation, which appears directly or indirectly in the rest of the calamities and of course in the slaying of the firstborn, adds a new dimension to the way the signs-and-wonders will bring knowledge of Israel's god to the Egyptians. It will surely be a "sign" (v. 23) that will convince the pharaoh of the legitimacy and power of Moses' god. We who read or listen to the story, from antiquity to the present, can conjure up the dramatic image of a wall of flies cutting off sharply at the border of Goshen, a place not mentioned in Egyptian texts nor locatable by historical geographers. Whether it is the designation of a real area in the eastern Nile Delta, as is often assumed on the basis of the exodus narrative, or a contribution of the storyteller cannot be established. It has become a place of the mnemohistorical imagination.

At first, the ruination of the land and the simultaneous sparing of the Israelites seem to have the desired effect. The pharaoh agrees that Moses and his people can offer sacrifices to their god. But there's a hitch – the sacrifices are to be done within Goshen and not in the wilderness as they had requested (7:16). Moses' response is somewhat enigmatic. He suggests that his people need to be distant – now he says three days distant (as in 4:18) – because their rituals will be offensive to the Egyptians, who would then stone them (8:26–27). What might be odious about Israelite rituals? Classical sources describe Egyptian fastidiousness as well as reluctance to sacrifice goats or sheep, animals that were part of the Israelite sacrificial cult.[106] How ancient such features of Egyptian culture were is uncertain, but the appearance of the concept of ethnic differentiation is notable. Unhappily, the sense of cultural difference involves the disapproval by one group of the customs of another. As for the possible result of such offensive behavior, the anticipated stoning may be more a reflection of Israelite punitive measures than the depiction of an authentic Egyptian response, given the paucity of stones available for use as projectiles in the alluvial Nile valley.[107] Amazingly, the pharaoh relents, but with two conditions: that the people will not go far; and that Moses will "pray" for the pharaoh – that is, entreat his god to remove the flies. Moses does so, accompanied by an unsuccessful proviso of

---

[106] Herodotus, Diodorus Siculus, Plutarch, and others; see ibid., 330.
[107] M. Greenberg, *Understanding Exodus* (1969), 202.

his own, namely, that the pharaoh not again revoke permission for the people to leave.

#5, PESTILENCE (9:1–7)

The outcome of the preceding calamity hinges on an allusion to animal sacrifice. This provides a link to the next sign-and-wonder, pestilence, which involves animals alone. Pestilence is one of the trilogy of afflictions (sword, famine, and pestilence) that appears frequently in prophetic and deuteronomic texts in connection with the destruction of Judah in the sixth century BCE. In those texts, it denotes disasters affecting humans as well as animals. Here it refers only to animals essential for transport and food: horses, donkeys, camels, herds, and flocks.[108] Yet, as in the tripartite list, pestilence signifies judgment, the consequence of the fact that the pharaoh is still holding the Israelites against God's will. The outbreak of pestilence is similar to the flies infestation in that it selectively destroys only Egyptian livestock, sparing Israelite animals. A time delay of one day is also involved (9:5), but now there is no hint of pharaonic interest in releasing the Israelites, who, this time, have asked more generally to "worship" (= serve) rather than to sacrifice (9:1).

#6, BOILS (9:8–12)

This sign-and-wonder is similar to the swarms of gnats in that it originates from dust, which is formed when Moses throws soot into the air. He does this without advance warning and with no prior request to worship or sacrifice, for this is the third item in the second group of three. The dust this time will cover all humans as well as animals, causing inflamed and painful skin eruptions (NRSV "boils"). For the first time, people – apparently only the Egyptians (9:11) – suffer directly, thus signaling an escalating severity in the sequence of calamities. Several other features of this calamity are noteworthy. The magicians, victims themselves of the outbreak of boils and unable to function, make their final appearance. And this is the last time in the signs-and-wonders narrative that Aaron has an active role. Even so, his actions are limited; he takes dust in his hands but only Moses throws it into the air so that it can turn to soot and cause boils. The cast of characters is now reduced to the major actors: Moses, the pharaoh, and Yahweh. Significantly, it is Yahweh who here, for the first time, directly hardens the pharaoh's heart (9:12). The indirect language of previous calamities, in which the pharaoh's heart is simply hardened or he is said to harden it himself, now gives way to unmediated divine causality.

---

[108] "Camels" is often thought to be anachronistic in this list, but the spread of the domesticated dromedary had apparently begun by the twelfth century BCE. See Paula Wapnish, "Camels," *OEANE* 1:408–9.

There may be a touch of poetic justice in the outbreak of boils. The soot that becomes the harmful dust is taken from furnaces (NRSV "kilns"). We learn nothing about these industrial installations. We do not know if they were used in the production of metal or bricks or ceramics. But if they are kilns for firing bricks, which figure prominently in the account of the harsh forced labor of the Israelites (5:7–19), they ironically become the source of the boils that now afflict the Egyptians. They also prefigure the smoldering appearance of Sinai – "like the smoke of a kiln" (19:18) – when God appears there to Moses.

#7, HAIL (9:13–35)

This is the first sign-and-wonder of the third triad, and Moses thus goes to the pharaoh in the morning with a warning. But this time, as the signs-and-wonders escalate, the warning is more protracted. The destructive element, hail, is uniquely called a plague (9:14) because, unlike the lethal pestilence that struck only livestock, this calamity will destroy humans as well as animals and vegetation. Perhaps that is why the noun "plague" is used in its plural form here. Also, it may anticipate the ultimate loss of human life in the slaying of the firstborn, for which "plague" is used several times. In any case, the Egyptian people have been spared to this point, although their crops and animals have been decimated. Now they too will be afflicted, that they may witness and acknowledge the power of the Israelite god (9:14–16).

The frequent repetition of the Hebrew word *'ereṣ*, variously translated "earth" and "land" in the NRSV, signals an important motif of this passage. The term refers to the land of Egypt several times (twice in 9:22 and once each in 9:23, 24, and 25) as well as to the land of Goshen (9:26), which is untouched by the devastating torrent of hail. Egyptian territory is also indicated in 9:23 and 33, which refer to the land affected by the hail. But more abstract meanings also appear. Being on the earth is equated with being alive in 9:15. In 9:14, the pharaoh will soon know the incomparability of Yahweh and Yahweh's power in all the world (NRSV "earth"). Indeed, Yahweh's name will be heard throughout all the world (NRSV "earth") in 9:16. And finally, the pharaoh's knowledge of God will mean an acknowledgment that all creation is God's: "the earth is the LORD's" (9:29).

The extensive warning is followed by another extensive sequence in which torrents of hail wreak havoc and cause the pharaoh to request an end to the deadly downpour. These expanded sections include vivid details, far more than are given for other signs-and-wonders. We find out that the hailstorm itself is accompanied by flashing fire (probably lightning), thunder, and rain (9:23, 24, 33, 34), anticipating in part the phenomena marking the theophany at Sinai in Exodus 19. We are told that the hailstorm is lethal to exposed beasts and people and that it also destroys all the crops of field and orchard, including flax and barley but excluding wheat and spelt, which were not yet in bud (9:21, 25, 31–32).

We feel the enormity of the devastation through the repeated hyperbolic use of *kōl*, variously translated "all, everything, the whole of" in the NRSV, even though we are also informed that not all the crops had been lost (9:32). We sense the narrator's awareness of the antiquity of Egypt in the statement that such hail has not fallen since Egypt was established (9:18, 24). We learn that some Egyptian officials heed the warning and bring into shelter the two categories of living beings, slaves and livestock, that are endangered because they are in open fields. And at the end, when the pharaoh implores Moses to end the hail and then reneges yet again on his willingness to release the Israelites, we see that ignoring God and hardening one's heart are now considered sinful behavior (9:27, 34).

#8, LOCUSTS (10:1–20)

The account of the second sign-and-wonder in the last triad begins in an unusual fashion. The notice of the pharaoh's obstinacy, caused by God, appears at the outset as a reason for Moses' mission and the use of signs, and again at the end (10:1 and 20). Another new feature is that the hearts of the officials are also hardened, yet eventually they for the first time challenge their ruler and urge him to heed Moses lest their nation be ruined (10:1 and 7). And a pedagogic tone is introduced. As we near the end of the signs-and-wonders sequence, the larger significance of these episodes is first articulated. That the exodus story will become a central and enduring way for the Israelites and then the Jews to know that God has the power to liberate the oppressed is anticipated in the directive of 10:2: "tell your children and grandchildren." The signs-and-wonders are not simply for the sake of demonstrating divine might to the Egyptians; they are part of the collective experience of the Israelites and, as such, will be extended to future generations. This future-looking aspect of the exodus narrative also appears in relation to several Israelite rituals and will be discussed in the next section (Plagues, Rituals, and Departure – Exodus 11:1–13:16).

Another unusual feature of the locust scourge is that it has elements found in the account of the climactic event of the exodus from Egypt, the splitting of the sea so that the Israelites can pass to safety. The locusts are brought into Egypt by "an east wind," emphatically mentioned twice in 10:13, and are removed by "a very strong west wind" (10:19). Similarly, God parts the sea with "a strong east wind" (14:21). And, amazingly, the locusts do not simply vanish, as seems to be the case for the flies when God removes them (8:31), but rather are thrust into the Reed Sea (NRSV "Sea of Reeds").[109] The body of water that will figure so prominently in the last stage of the Israelite escape from Egypt is mentioned here for the first time in Exodus. It hardly plays a pivotal role in how this

---

[109] The identification of this body of water is discussed in the supplementary section, A Closer Look: The Red/Reed Sea and the Exodus Route, pp. 112–13.

calamity unfolds, and its introduction surely serves to foreshadow the imminent culmination of the efforts to secure freedom.

The hardening of the pharaoh's heart at the beginning of this calamity displaces Moses' plea that his people be allowed to leave. After the initial threat, and with the urging of the anxious officials, Moses and Aaron are brought again to the pharaoh, who then agrees that the Israelites may go out to worship their god. But he imposes conditions. Moses specifies that all Israelites – young and old, men and women – must leave to celebrate the "LORD's festival" (10:9); this Israelite cultic event is gender and age inclusive. But the pharaoh will have none of this and imposes his own cultural values. He will allow only men to leave, thereby, in effect, holding women and children hostage. God's response to this intolerable situation is to send the locusts, a notoriously damaging natural disaster in the biblical world (see Joel 1–2:29). As such it is often a signal of divine judgment (e.g., Amos 4:9) as well as a metaphor for the size and destructiveness of enemy forces (e.g., Judg 7:12).

Whatever vegetation survived the ferocious hailstorm (10:5, 15) is now to be destroyed by swarms of locusts of unprecedented severity. In an ironic counterpart to the future storytelling proclaimed for the children and grandchildren of the Israelites, the parents and grandparents of the Egyptians are mentioned (10:6). But they are to look back in time, searching their collective memory in vain for a scourge of locusts of this magnitude. As was the case for the hailstorm, the pharaoh admits his sin (10:16–17) and has Moses entreat God to remove the locusts. God responds, the locusts disappear, yet God predictably again hardens the pharaoh's heart. The stage is set for the final sign-and-wonder.

#9, DARKNESS (10:21–29)

As the last episode in a triad, the onset of darkness is sudden and unannounced. But it is not completely unexpected. The locust experience, in which the swarming insects are so numerous as to make the land "dark" (NRSV "black") so that none can see (10:5, 15), is a harbinger of the darkness so palpable and thick that people "could not see one another" (10:23). And the darkness in turn anticipates the dreadful plague to come – the slaying of the firstborn in the darkness of the midnight hour (12:29) – and even the dramatic sea crossing in the dark of night (14:20). As the last calamity, darkness serves as a motif that links the nine signs-and-wonders with the subsequent firstborn plague and then the deliverance at the sea. It also arguably represents chaos, the pre-creation status of the cosmos (Gen 1:2) and an apt metaphor for the cruelty of the Egyptian pharaoh and his officials.[110] For the Egyptians, for whom the sun god and sunlight were the source of all life, darkness would signify death – the loss of life in many of the

---

[110] T. E. Fretheim, *Exodus* (1991), 129.

signs-and-wonders as well as the fatalities to come for the firstborns and for the pharaoh's army at the sea.

Other aspects of the darkness calamity are notable. It lasts three days, a duration that mirrors the three-day journey that the Israelites requested (5:3; 8:27). It spares the Israelites, as do some of the other signs-and-wonders. And it causes the pharaoh to relent and to allow all but the Israelites' livestock to depart. But Moses rejects this proviso with two demands. He insists that the pharaoh allow them to have "sacrifices and burnt offerings";[111] and they are adamant about taking their own livestock, some of which they will also use for sacral purposes (10:25–26). For the last time, the pharaoh reneges – but this time there is a postscript that marks this as the final direct interaction between Moses and the Egyptian ruler. The pharaoh dramatically banishes Moses from his court on pain of death, to which Moses readily accedes. The intricately constructed series of negotiations between the two major human protagonists has come to naught. Although Moses and Aaron will continue to be divine emissaries, God will now act more directly. Moses will give one more speech to the pharaoh, an announcement of what will happen rather than a warning, at the beginning of the next section, before angrily departing from the Egyptian court.

PLAGUE, RITUALS, AND DEPARTURE – EXODUS 11:1–13:16

NRSV 11 The LORD said to Moses, "I will bring one more plague upon Pharaoh and upon Egypt; afterwards he will let you go from here; indeed, when he lets you go, he will drive you away. [2] Tell the people that every man is to ask his neighbor and every woman is to ask her neighbor for objects of silver and gold." [3] The LORD gave the people favor in the sight of the Egyptians. Moreover, Moses himself was a man of great importance in the land of Egypt, in the sight of Pharaoh's officials and in the sight of the people.

4 Moses said, "Thus says the LORD: About midnight I will go out through Egypt. [5] Every firstborn in the land of Egypt shall die, from the firstborn of Pharaoh who sits on his throne to the firstborn of the female slave who is behind the handmill, and all the firstborn of the livestock. [6] Then there will be a loud cry throughout the whole land of Egypt, such as has never been or will ever be again. [7] But not a dog shall growl at any of the Israelites – not at people, not at animals – so that you may know that the LORD makes a distinction between Egypt and Israel. [8] Then all these officials of yours shall come down to me, and bow low to me, saying, 'Leave us, you and all the people who follow you.' After that I will leave." And in hot anger he left Pharaoh.

---

[111]   These two terms refer to burnt sacrifices, usually of cattle. Cattle, of course, would be absent from Egypt at this point, were the signs-and-wonders literal and sequential historical events.

9 The LORD said to Moses, "Pharaoh will not listen to you, in order that my wonders may be multiplied in the land of Egypt." [10]Moses and Aaron performed all these wonders before Pharaoh; but the LORD hardened Pharaoh's heart, and he did not let the people of Israel go out of his land.

NRSV 12 The LORD said to Moses and Aaron in the land of Egypt: [2]This month shall mark for you the beginning of months; it shall be the first month of the year for you. [3]Tell the whole congregation of Israel that on the tenth of this month they are to take a lamb for each family, a lamb for each household. [4]If a household is too small for a whole lamb, it shall join its closest neighbor in obtaining one; the lamb shall be divided in proportion to the number of people who eat of it. [5]Your lamb shall be without blemish, a year-old male; you may take it from the sheep or from the goats. [6]You shall keep it until the fourteenth day of this month; then the whole assembled congregation of Israel shall slaughter it at twilight. [7]They shall take some of the blood and put it on the two doorposts and the lintel of the houses in which they eat it. [8]They shall eat the lamb that same night; they shall eat it roasted over the fire with unleavened bread and bitter herbs. [9]Do not eat any of it raw or boiled in water, but roasted over the fire, with its head, legs, and inner organs. [10]You shall let none of it remain until the morning; anything that remains until the morning you shall burn. [11]This is how you shall eat it: your loins girded, your sandals on your feet, and your staff in your hand; and you shall eat it hurriedly. It is the passover of the LORD. [12]For I will pass through the land of Egypt that night, and I will strike down every firstborn in the land of Egypt, both human beings and animals; on all the gods of Egypt I will execute judgments: I am the LORD. [13]The blood shall be a sign for you on the houses where you live: when I see the blood, I will pass over you, and no plague shall destroy you when I strike the land of Egypt.

14 This day shall be a day of remembrance for you. You shall celebrate it as a festival to the LORD; throughout your generations you shall observe it as a perpetual ordinance. [15]Seven days you shall eat unleavened bread; on the first day you shall remove leaven from your houses, for whoever eats leavened bread from the first day until the seventh day shall be cut off from Israel. [16]On the first day you shall hold a solemn assembly, and on the seventh day a solemn assembly; no work shall be done on those days; only what everyone must eat, that alone may be prepared by you. [17]You shall observe the festival of unleavened bread, for on this very day I brought your companies out of the land of Egypt: you shall observe this day throughout your generations as a perpetual ordinance. [18]In the first month, from the evening of the fourteenth day until the evening of the twenty-first day, you shall eat unleavened bread. [19]For seven days no leaven shall be found in your houses; for whoever eats what is leavened shall be cut off from the congregation of Israel, whether an alien or a native of the land. [20]You shall eat nothing leavened; in all your settlements you shall eat unleavened bread.

21 Then Moses called all the elders of Israel and said to them, "Go, select lambs for your families, and slaughter the passover lamb. [22]Take a bunch of hyssop, dip

it in the blood that is in the basin, and touch the lintel and the two doorposts with the blood in the basin. None of you shall go outside the door of your house until morning. ²³For the LORD will pass through to strike down the Egyptians; when he sees the blood on the lintel and on the two doorposts, the LORD will pass over that door and will not allow the destroyer to enter your houses to strike you down. ²⁴You shall observe this rite as a perpetual ordinance for you and your children. ²⁵When you come to the land that the LORD will give you, as he has promised, you shall keep this observance. ²⁶And when your children ask you, 'What do you mean by this observance?' ²⁷you shall say, 'It is the passover sacrifice to the LORD, for he passed over the houses of the Israelites in Egypt, when he struck down the Egyptians but spared our houses.'" And the people bowed down and worshiped.

28 The Israelites went and did just as the LORD had commanded Moses and Aaron.

29 At midnight the LORD struck down all the firstborn in the land of Egypt, from the firstborn of Pharaoh who sat on his throne to the firstborn of the prisoner who was in the dungeon, and all the firstborn of the livestock. ³⁰Pharaoh arose in the night, he and all his officials and all the Egyptians; and there was a loud cry in Egypt, for there was not a house without someone dead. ³¹Then he summoned Moses and Aaron in the night, and said, "Rise up, go away from my people, both you and the Israelites! Go, worship the LORD, as you said. ³²Take your flocks and your herds, as you said, and be gone. And bring a blessing on me too!"

33 The Egyptians urged the people to hasten their departure from the land, for they said, "We shall all be dead." ³⁴So the people took their dough before it was leavened, with their kneading bowls wrapped up in their cloaks on their shoulders. ³⁵The Israelites had done as Moses told them; they had asked the Egyptians for jewelry of silver and gold, and for clothing, ³⁶and the LORD had given the people favor in the sight of the Egyptians, so that they let them have what they asked. And so they plundered the Egyptians.

37 The Israelites journeyed from Rameses to Succoth, about six hundred thousand men on foot, besides children. ³⁸A mixed crowd also went up with them, and livestock in great numbers, both flocks and herds. ³⁹They baked unleavened cakes of the dough that they had brought out of Egypt; it was not leavened, because they were driven out of Egypt and could not wait, nor had they prepared any provisions for themselves.

40 The time that the Israelites had lived in Egypt was four hundred thirty years. ⁴¹At the end of four hundred thirty years, on that very day, all the companies of the LORD went out from the land of Egypt. ⁴²That was for the LORD a night of vigil, to bring them out of the land of Egypt. That same night is a vigil to be kept for the LORD by all the Israelites throughout their generations.

43 The LORD said to Moses and Aaron: This is the ordinance for the passover: no foreigner shall eat of it, ⁴⁴but any slave who has been purchased may eat of it after he has been circumcised; ⁴⁵no bound or hired servant may eat of it. ⁴⁶It shall be eaten in one house; you shall not take any of the animal outside the house, and you

shall not break any of its bones. [47] The whole congregation of Israel shall celebrate it. [48] If an alien who resides with you wants to celebrate the passover to the LORD, all his males shall be circumcised; then he may draw near to celebrate it; he shall be regarded as a native of the land. But no uncircumcised person shall eat of it; [49] there shall be one law for the native and for the alien who resides among you.

50 All the Israelites did just as the LORD had commanded Moses and Aaron. [51] That very day the LORD brought the Israelites out of the land of Egypt, company by company.

NRSV 13 The LORD said to Moses: [2] Consecrate to me all the firstborn; whatever is the first to open the womb among the Israelites, of human beings and animals, is mine.

3 Moses said to the people, "Remember this day on which you came out of Egypt, out of the house of slavery, because the LORD brought you out from there by strength of hand; no leavened bread shall be eaten. [4] Today, in the month of Abib, you are going out. [5] When the LORD brings you into the land of the Canaanites, the Hittites, the Amorites, the Hivites, and the Jebusites, which he swore to your ancestors to give you, a land flowing with milk and honey, you shall keep this observance in this month. [6] Seven days you shall eat unleavened bread, and on the seventh day there shall be a festival to the LORD. [7] Unleavened bread shall be eaten for seven days; no leavened bread shall be seen in your possession, and no leaven shall be seen among you in all your territory. [8] You shall tell your child on that day, 'It is because of what the LORD did for me when I came out of Egypt.' [9] It shall serve for you as a sign on your hand and as a reminder on your forehead, so that the teaching of the LORD may be on your lips; for with a strong hand the LORD brought you out of Egypt. [10] You shall keep this ordinance at its proper time from year to year.

11 "When the LORD has brought you into the land of the Canaanites, as he swore to you and your ancestors, and has given it to you, [12] you shall set apart to the LORD all that first opens the womb. All the firstborn of your livestock that are males shall be the LORD's. [13] But every firstborn donkey you shall redeem with a sheep; if you do not redeem it, you must break its neck. Every firstborn male among your children you shall redeem. [14] When in the future your child asks you, 'What does this mean?' you shall answer, 'By strength of hand the LORD brought us out of Egypt, from the house of slavery. [15] When Pharaoh stubbornly refused to let us go, the LORD killed all the firstborn in the land of Egypt, from human firstborn to the firstborn of animals. Therefore I sacrifice to the LORD every male that first opens the womb, but every firstborn of my sons I redeem.' [16] It shall serve as a sign on your hand and as an emblem on your forehead that by strength of hand the LORD brought us out of Egypt."

The nine signs-and-wonders have failed to convince the pharaoh to release the Israelites. Consequently, the worst is yet to come: the slaying of the firstborn, a catastrophe that is truly a plague and that will bring a change of heart to the stubborn pharaoh. This climactic event is embedded in passages that set forth ritual practices – the paschal lamb, the unleavened bread, and the consecration of the firstborn – that make the exodus a foundational part of Israel's collective memory. Indeed, the ritual practices themselves likely affected the way the accompanying narratives were shaped. It becomes impossible to determine, in this complex set of materials, how much of the narrative draws upon authentic experience and how much of it developed over time in relation to existing customs. What seems certain – given the repetition, overlap, choppiness, expansiveness, mix of story and ritual, as well as the presence of details that seem to be drawn from different stages of the development of the Passover celebration – is that the present narrative combines multiple layers and genres of tradition. In its present form, the story line of the slaying of the firstborn, interrupted as it is with directions for ritual acts, is thereby drawn out in a way that heightens the dramatic interest in the unfolding narrative.[112] The canonical whole provides a compelling mnemohistorical basis for the Passover, a major component of Israelite cultural and religious identity. This festival "repeats" the past annually so that every future generation will know the redemptive nature of God (see 12:14, 24–26). It becomes a commemorative institution that provides identity, shared values, and thus group cohesiveness to those who celebrate it. See the discussion in Bridging the Horizons: The Passover Celebration, pp. 103–7.

ANNOUNCEMENT OF THE SLAYING OF THE FIRSTBORN (11:1–10)

What God will finally do to secure the release of the people is not specified at first; it is simply called one more affliction (NRSV "plague"; 11:1), thus linking the impending disaster to the nine signs-and-wonders. The pharaoh will not simply let the people go but rather will forcibly expel them. We thus sense that the plague will transcend all the signs-and-wonders in its devastation and impact. But first, the Israelites begin to prepare for their departure. In 11:2–3, we are reminded of what was anticipated when the Israelites were instructed (in 3:21–22) to request silver and gold from their Egyptian neighbors. Despite the pharaoh's policies, the Egyptian populace seems to be favorably disposed toward the foreigners in their midst, for they comply. Moreover, Moses enjoys prominence among all Egyptians, including the pharaoh's officials, save the pharaoh himself. The unnamed Egyptian ruler has become a parody of a powerful sovereign, isolated in his adherence to a misguided and doomed policy.

This retrospective and perhaps misplaced introduction to the account of the slaying of the firstborn is followed by a declaration from God (via Moses) announcing the tragic event about to take place (11:4–8). Moses and Aaron, with their arms and hands and staffs, are no longer the agents of God as they were for the signs-and-wonders. God will act directly (11:4; cf. 12:23). The focus of

---

[112]   T. E. Fretheim, *Exodus* (1991), 135–6.

the speech is the comprehensiveness of the plague. All firstborns will perish, regardless of class. The extremes of the Egyptian social hierarchy are clearly portrayed (11:5; cf. 12:29). The sedentary enthroned male at the top and the laboring female servant at the bottom, and thus everyone in between, will lose their first offspring. Moreover, animals as well as humans will be affected. The cry of the afflicted Egyptians (11:6) in hyperbolic fashion will be unprecedented and total. And the impending plague is presented as recompense for the suffering they have inflicted on others, for the Hebrew word for the loud "cry" of the Egyptians is the same as that used for the cries of the Israelites bemoaning their oppression (3:7, 9; cf. 2:23, where a slightly different term is used). The Israelites, however – as for so many of the signs-and-wonders – again will be spared. The striking image, in which Israelites are not disturbed by so much as a growling dog (11:7), epitomizes how God distinguishes between Israel and Egypt.

With the parameters of the slaying of the firstborn now specified, Moses has convinced the courtiers, but still not their ruler. Moses makes his final irate exit from the royal court. A summation follows (11:9–10), reiterating the futility of the signs-and-wonders and therefore, in effect, justifying the widespread loss of human and animal life about to take place.

The intentional destruction of innocent life in God's slaying of the firstborn has long troubled readers of this narrative. What kind of deity was it, whose deeds could benefit one group at the expense of others? Already in the early postbiblical period, rabbinic commentators sought ways to rationalize such a horrific act.[113] Such attempts take the plague account at its face value. But we now can recognize the literary rather than literal nature of these stylized narratives. Understanding them to be ahistorical materials may ameliorate somewhat the otherwise stark injustice of divine acts. And this troubling characterization of God also can be understood as a function of the portrayal of divine actions as the source of knowledge of divine might; that is, God causes political events, which inevitably benefit one group at the expense of others. Yet such modern scholarly interpretations should not obscure the fact that people in the biblical world would attribute horrific acts of violence to divine power. Still, the view that humans cannot presume to comprehend acts of God that seem unjust also cannot be put aside. Either way, we twenty-first-century readers must struggle with the narrative presentation of the tragic slaughter of Egyptian firstborns. At the same time, understanding the significance of a firstborn in biblical antiquity can help us evaluate the meaning of this episode in the larger exodus story.

As we shall see in the ritual commemoration proclaimed in 13:11–16, the firstborn holds a symbolic place in the psychology of the biblical world. The first of any series represents all to come, and the death of all Egyptian firstborns serves as a death knell to the society as a whole. This harsh view of the Egyptians makes them the enemy par excellence, a position they hold throughout the

---

[113] Cited in N. M. Sarna, *Exodus* (1991), 52 and 244, n. 5.

Pentateuch. They become the quintessential other.[114] In their behavior toward the Israelites, in the differential way they suffer whereas Israelites are spared in many of the signs-and-wonders, and finally in their complete vulnerability to the slaying of their firstborns in contrast to the total invulnerability of the Israelites, the Egyptians are the evil other against which the distinctiveness of the Israelites is portrayed. The oppositional positions of Egyptians and Israelites in the exodus narrative reflect Israel's struggle to find and maintain her distinctive identity in the fluid cultural waters of the ancient Near East. This was certainly the case in the mid-first millennium BCE, and it may have been equally so in the late second millennium BCE as Israelites differentiated from others in their land.[115] Such difficult struggles perhaps are the only way to understand how the God of justice and mercy, the liberator of the oppressed, can also be characterized as the direct perpetrator of a mass slaughter of many innocent people.

SLAYING OF THE FIRSTBORN, PASCHAL LAMB, AND UNLEAVENED
BREAD (12:1–51)

That the slaying of the firstborn will loom large in the collective memory of the exodus becomes apparent in chapter 13. But first, chapter 12 sets forth, in a long and complex interweaving of present actions with their future meaning, the details of the escape from Egypt. Looking at this section millennia later, we see this chapter not only as a vivid tale of departure but also as an etiology for the most enduring of Israelite festivals, the Passover. Situated within the narrative of the exodus, the major elements of the festival – the roasted lamb and the unleavened bread – become forever intertwined with the notion of freedom from bondage.

The character of the narrative changes radically. Gone is the preoccupation with the Egyptians. The shift is signified by God's announcement about the reckoning of time. The month of exodus and concomitant freedom will be the first month of the year for the Israelites (12:2). This is a springtime New Year, unlike the autumnal one also in evidence in the Hebrew Bible. Whatever its origins as a celebration of spring, in this text it initiates the marking of time in relation to the memory of the past rather than to the seasonal changes of nature.[116] The months are to be designated by ordinal numbers with the month of the exodus as "the first month of the year" (12:2). The exodus thus becomes the implied referential point for all mentions of dates (cf. 16:2; 19:1). For the Israelites, the understanding of time is to be inextricably linked with the beginning of national freedom.

---

[114] See F. Volker Greifenhagen, *Egypt on the Pentateuch's Ideological Map: Constructing Biblical Israel's Identity* (JSOTS 361; London: Sheffield Academic Press, 2003).

[115] E. Bloch-Smith, "Israelite Ethnicity in Iron I," *JBL* 122 (2003): 401–25.

[116] W. H. C. Propp, *Exodus 1–18* (1998), 383–8, provides a detailed discussion of the reckoning of time in ancient Israel.

The inclusiveness, across all social classes, with which the Egyptians will suffer from the slaying of the firstborn is now mirrored by the totality with which the Israelites will participate in what is mandated for them. We learn at the beginning (12:3) that the "whole congregation" will hear the instructions, and at the end (v. 47) we see that phrase repeated for all who will participate in the celebration. Using the same language at the beginning and the end of a section forms an *inclusio*. The use of this literary device unifies the section and indicates that the whole congregation, past, present, and future ("throughout your generations . . . as a perpetual ordinance"; vv. 14, 17) is involved throughout. A festival including an entire group has the effect of unifying a population and giving people a corporate identity, connecting everyone with the shared past it commemorates. This seems to be the case in general, across cultures, with ritual heightening and preserving a sense of "communitas."[117]

Just how inclusive is the term "congregation"? The Hebrew word is ʿēdâ, which ordinarily refers to an assembly of adult males; but sometimes, as here, it functions as an age- and gender-inclusive term.[118] Also, although deuteronomic regulations for the Passover as a pilgrimage festival seem to require its celebration only for males (Deut 16:1–8, 16), the stipulations in the exodus narrative apparently include women. They are part of the total community said to experience the departure and then commemorate it in ritual acts. The involvement of households (vv. 3–4) and families (v. 21) indicates this, as does the use of the term *nepeš* ("person"), a generic term for people of both genders in priestly texts such as this one.[119] This inclusiveness, however, does not apply to non-Israelites. Again, we see explicit boundary-forming stipulations in the way such persons – foreigners, slaves, indentured (NRSV "bound") servants, hired laborers, and alien residents[120] – are treated. Foreigners and bound or hired laborers, who are also considered non-natives, are excluded from the community of Passover observers. The others, who are permanent or semipermanent members of the community, may be included after first becoming Israelites in the flesh, that is, undergoing circumcision (vv. 43–45, 48–49). The converse is also true: those who fail to observe the festival, whether they are natives or alien residents, forfeit their place in the community (v. 19).

The components of the commemorative festival are set forth, beginning with a detailed presentation of the meal to be eaten before the departure from Egypt. Because the time is spring, the major component of the meal is to be a ruminant

---

[117] E. Turner, "Rites of Communitas," in *Encyclopedia of Religious Rites* (2004), 98.

[118] D. Levy, Jacob Milgrom, Helmer Ringgren, Heinz-Josef Fabry, "ʿēdâ," *TDOT* 10:470–5.

[119] Mayer I. Gruber, "Women in the Cult According to the Priestly Code," *The Motherhood of God and Other Studies* (Atlanta, Ga.: Scholars Press, 1992), 63–6.

[120] "Aliens" (gērîm) are free people living voluntarily among the Israelites for an extended period of time and participating in their culture, even though they are not related by kinship, whereas "foreigners" are either non-Israelite slaves or more likely someone living temporarily among the Israelites as a merchant, traveler, diplomat, or the like. See D. Kellerman, "gûr, gēr, gērûth, měgûrim," *TDOT* 2:443–9.

(12:3–5). The feast described in this passage likely contains vestiges of the annual celebrations, common among people who keep herd animals, at the time of year when such animals leave their winter shelters. These festivals mark the beginning of a season and the hopes for fertile animals that will provide plentiful milk.[121] The animal of the Passover tradition is often understood to be lamb. The NRSV translates "lamb" for the designation of the animal in verses 3 and 4, but the Hebrew term *śeh* can also mean baby goat, or kid, as verse 5 indicates. The Passover regulations in Deuteronomy (16:2) mention "flocks and herds," allowing for the possibility that even a cow might be used. What is noteworthy, from an economic and ecological perspective, is that the animal, whatever it may be, is to be a year-old male. Slaughtering a male yearling is optimal because up to that point, around the time of weaning, no major investment has been made in the animal. Also, its mother is in full milk production, which of course is maintained for human use once the young animal is killed.[122] Choosing the male animal preserves the females and their potential as producers of more animals as well as milk. The frequency of one-year-old animals in biblical texts mandating sacrifice as well as among the bones recovered by archaeologists from the remains of cultic structures reflects these economic considerations. In any case, the slaughter of an animal for meat is not an everyday occurrence in premodern cultures, and its ceremonial function is not surprising. This was so in the ancient Near East in general.

The ritual slaughter of ruminants, often young ones, is characteristic of the larger biblical world. Similarly, some of the particulars of the sacrifice in this passage are comparable to practices known from other ancient Near Eastern groups. Performing sacrifices in the evening in the middle of the first month, for example, is recorded at Emar (cf. v. 6).[123] This twilight time may also explain why the biblical rite is to take place on the fourteenth day of the month and not the beginning – the full moon in mid-month would provide maximum light for an evening ritual. Eating a sacrifice until it is gone is mentioned in Ugaritic documents (cf. v. 10).[124] Sacrifices in the ancient Near East are typically of unblemished animals (cf. v. 5); meat offerings were considered food for the gods and would have to come from perfect specimens. Also, special treatment of the "head, legs, and inner organs" (cf. v. 9) was apparently part of Egyptian sacrificial practices.[125]

---

[121] Oded Borowski, *Every Living Thing: Daily Use of Animals in Ancient Israel* (Walnut Creek, Calif.: AltaMira Press, 1998), 216.

[122] See Simon J. M. Davis, *The Archaeology of Animals* (New Haven: Yale University Press, 1987), 157.

[123] "Rituals from Emar," translated by Daniel Fleming (*COS* 1.122), 428, 442, 433. Emar is a Syrian city at which a Late Bronze Age (fourteenth to twelfth centuries BCE) archive, including cultic documents, has been discovered.

[124] "Ritual Extispicy (RS 24.312)," translated by Dennis Pardee (*COS* 1.92), 292.

[125] According to Herodotus; cited in W. H. C. Propp, *Exodus 1–18* (1998), 396.

But it would be a mistake to look at this animal sacrifice only in terms of its ecological and cultural context. It also has commemorative functions, especially to the story of the slaying of the firstborn. An etiology is provided for the Passover sacrifice, in the account of the "first" such one, when the blood of the animals is smeared on the doorposts and lintel of Israelite dwellings in Egypt before the animals are roasted and consumed. The blood marks the homes that God will "pass over" (v. 13) when the plague destroying the firstborns is brought upon the Egyptians. All this is to be done hurriedly; the people should be dressed, with shoes on and staff in hand, ready for a hasty departure. Because preparing and roasting a whole animal are hardly speedy procedures, the instructions here may derive from different levels of tradition. Or they may simply be a reflection of how episodes are constructed to suit the larger purposes of the narrative, for this dramatic sequence of escape from death, when the firstborns are killed, as prelude to escape from Egypt becomes the narrative understanding of the paschal sacrifice.

Although the English translation ("pass over") of this passage provides the etymology and source of the English designation Passover, the Hebrew term *pesaḥ*, as a verb, probably means "to protect."[126] Note that in verse 13, God will "protect" (NRSV "pass over"), in contrast to what God will do in the second part of the verse: "destroy." The powerful apotropaic function of blood to protect against evil demons is incorporated into the symbolic power of the narrative to demonstrate God's guardianship of Israel. As for the noun (or adjective) "passover," it sometimes is a designation for the sacrificed animals, as in 12:21, 27, and 43; in those contexts it would be more appropriate for English translations to use "paschal," or "paschal sacrifice" ("paschal" is derived from the root *psḥ*) rather than "passover lamb" or "passover sacrifice." The extended meaning of the noun, to designate the festival originating in this act of protection, is properly translated Passover.

The paschal sacrifice is not the whole of the festival meal. Verse 8 introduces two other elements – bitter herbs and unleavened bread. The former probably signifies a kind of green plant that serves as a condiment. In postbiblical lore, the bitterness of the herbs has a commemorative function (see Bridging the Horizons: The Passover Celebration, pp. 103–7). But the latter, the unleavened bread, receives its commemorative role within the biblical narrative. It is the second major component of the festival and is presented in greater detail in verses 14–20, 33–34, and 39 (and also in 13:3–10). The term *maṣṣâ*, usually spelled matzah (or matzo) in English, denotes a bread of barley or wheat. All grain offerings to God under the sacrificial system were unleavened (e.g., Exod 29:2; Lev 2:4–5, 11). Thus it is not surprising to find such bread as part of the Passover meal, which

---

[126] The term was usually thought to be from a root meaning "to limp," but now its origin in a root for "protect" seems more likely; see Eckart Otto, "*pāsaḥ pesaḥ*," *TDOT* 12: 1–24.

is conceptualized here as a sacrificial meal carried out in the home rather than at a sanctuary.

The transition into a discussion of the matzah in verse 14 explicitly mentions the commemorative function of "this day," a phrase probably referring to both the Passover and unleavened bread components, as a "day of remembrance." The considerable detail about removing leaven and about the length of the festival authenticates features of what undoubtedly was an important festival by the time of the late monarchy, when it involves a pilgrimage to the Jerusalem temple as well as a family celebration. Like the paschal animal, which was to be eaten in haste, the matzah is linked with a hurried departure from Egypt. The collective memory of departure and freedom is ritualized. In addition, in stipulating a seven-day period for eating unleavened bread, Passover as the spring New Year festival acquires the symbolic aura of *seven*. Festivals constructed with seven-day units may in fact be typical of the Syro–Palestinian world – the spring New Year festival in Late Bronze Age Syria lasts seven days.[127]

The commemorative aspect of the spring festival, anticipated already in 10:2 and proclaimed in 12:14, recurs in 12:24–26 with respect to the paschal sacrifice. The tone is akin to deuteronomic language. The insertion of a question that children will ask as a rhetorical device is strikingly similar to that of Deut 6:20. In both cases the answers, which have an etiological flavor, serve to make the past an ongoing and vital part of the community's present. A similar didactic ploy, with an explanation of the custom of eating unleavened bread provided for children, appears in 13:7–8.

Aside from the aspects of the story that pertain to festival regulations, chapter 12 continues the story line of the slaying of the firstborn as announced in chapter 11. The narrative includes several notable features. One is that the firstborn plague not only affects people and livestock but also is tantamount to the punitive "judgment" of the Egyptian gods (12:12). This image invokes the notion of Yahweh as the presiding judge in a heavenly court, doling out punishment to lesser deities as well as errant humans. Such imagery is prominent in Canaanite mythology and is found widely in the Hebrew Bible.[128] The divine justice meted out to Egyptian gods in this passage, like the language of 15:11 and 18:11, is part of a range of biblical texts that preclude the attribution of absolute monotheism to the Israelites, at least not before the exilic period. The singularity of Israel's god, however, should not be seen as standing in tension with the representation of a divine sphere populated by numerous lesser, albeit active, supernatural entities.[129]

---

[127] "Rituals from Emar," translated by Daniel Fleming (*COS* 1.222), 434.

[128] See especially Isa 24:21–23 and also 1 Kgs 22:19–23; Pss 82; 89:6–9; Job 1–2; Isaiah 6.

[129] Barbara N. Porter, "One God or Many? A Brief Introduction to a Complex Problem," *One God or Many? Concepts of Divinity in the Ancient World*, ed. Barbara Newling Porter (Transactions of the Casco Bay Assyriological Institute, Volume 1; Chebeague Island, Maine: Casco Bay Assyriological Institute, 2000), 1–2.

The existence of such lesser numinous beings is part of another notable feature of this episode: the ambiguity surrounding God as the direct instrument of destruction. That God will "strike down" every firstborn in Egypt appears several times (12:12, 23, 27, 29); but in verse 23 a mysterious "destroyer" will keep away from the blood-marked dwellings of the Israelites. This may be a hint of beliefs about night demons, which were part of the folklore of all ancient Near Eastern cultures. At the same time, it reflects a larger angelology associated with Israel's god, in which lesser divine beings were dispatched as messengers or, especially relevant here, as instruments of destruction. The widespread destruction of humans, as is the case in the slaying of the Egyptian firstborns, is attributed in the Hebrew Bible to such destructive angels (e.g., 2 Sam 24:16–17; 2 Kgs 19:35; cf. Exod 33:2).

As the story continues, we are taken back one last time to the Egyptians. The repeated use of "midnight" and "night" in 12:29–31 reminds us that the slaying of the firstborn is a nighttime event, which is linked ritually to the slaughter and consumption of the paschal offering (12:6–10). We find a reference to stratified Egyptian society in verse 29, which echoes 11:5 in portraying the totality of the populace affected by the midnight plague; this time prisoners represent the bottom of the social hierarchy. And we learn that the pharaoh finally gets it – that death is everywhere. His people fear that the killing will soon go beyond the firstborn and that all will die (v. 33). Somewhat unexpectedly, for the days of diplomatic haggling with the Israelite leaders are long gone, he sends for Moses and Aaron and commands them, with all their people and herds, to leave Egypt on their own terms ("as you said," v. 31). He concludes with a surprising request to be blessed. Can this reflect the notion that the freeing of slaves brings a blessing to the master (cf. Deut 15:18)? Does it also echo the ancestor Jacob's parting words to the pharaoh when he leaves Egypt (cf. Gen 47:7, 10)?[130] We are not told whether such a blessing is forthcoming, but we are reminded once more in verses 35–36 (cf. 3:21–22 and 11:2–3) of the largesse of many Egyptians in giving economic resources to the departing people.

Finally the departure itself is recorded. The numerous and often vexing geographical references in the Hebrew Bible relating to the route of the exodus begin in verse 37, with the mention of Rameses and Succoth. The former (cf. 1:11) is the unidentified eastern Delta site associated with the enforced labor of the Israelites; the latter, likewise lacking clear identification, seems to lie, appropriately, about a day's journey from Rameses.[131] This notice of departure is the first of what will become twelve stages of a wilderness journey, each marked in the narrative by formulaic language: the people journey or set out from *place name*

---

[130] David Daube (*The Exodus Pattern in the Bible* [London: Faber & Faber, 1963], 52–3) suggests the first possibility, U. Cassuto (*Commentary* [1983], 145–6) the second.

[131] According to a letter of Seti II (1204–1196); see Jeffrey H. Tigay, "Exodus," *The Jewish Study Bible*, eds. Adele Berlin and Marc Zvi Brettler (New York: Oxford University Press, 2003), 129.

a and come to or encamp at *place name b*. This arrangement, which continues into the book of Numbers, presents the transition from Egypt to the Promised Land as a purposeful journey rather than a period of wandering and is usually attributed to the final priestly redaction of the Pentateuch.[132] The wilderness journey formula thus links Exodus to the ongoing story line that takes the Israelites from Sinai to the land of Canaan. Like the connections to Genesis in Exodus, especially in the opening sections, the journey passages situate Exodus in its pentateuchal context.

Verse 37 also contains the startling demographic information that the departing people numbered 600,000 adult males, a tradition somewhat different from the 603,550 men of 38:26. Adding an estimation of the number of women and children accompanying the men, to say nothing of the additional "mixed crowd" of verse 38, would yield a figure of more than 2.5 million people. This astronomical and impossible number is likely hyperbole, as such large round figures often are in the literary mode of the Hebrew Bible. It functions here to echo the assertion of 1:7 that the Israelites became so numerous that they filled the land. It also serves to include all later populations of Israelites, who themselves would experience the exodus in the rituals grounded in this chapter. The number itself, a multiple of six, may have originated in the fact that 600 was a military unit in ancient Israel (see, e.g., Exod 14:7 and Judg 18:11). That these men are "on foot," a phrase used for infantry, supports this possibility and also foreshadows the military aspect of the departure yet to come, with the Egyptian chariotry in pursuit. Similarly, military terminology in verse 41 denotes the departing "companies," that is, all Israel; and in the summation at the very end of this chapter (12:50–51), "troop by troop" (NRSV "company by company") designates the Israelites. Perhaps more important than the number itself is the presence of the "mixed crowd," a term designating non-Israelites among those departing Egypt.[133] The inclusion of other peoples here, from the very beginning, may reflect the diversity of groups that constituted early Israel; it also makes the story of liberation one that can transcend the national or ethnic identity of the Israelites.

Another numerical datum, this one concerning chronology, appears in verses 40–41: the duration of the sojourn in Egypt is given as 430 years, a figure somewhat larger than the 400 years predicted in Gen 15:13 (cf. Gen 15:16). Another amplification of 400 appears in 1 Kgs 6:1, which states that construction of the Jerusalem temple began 480 years after the exodus. As mentioned in the Introduction, the 1 Kings passage is often used in attempts to date the exodus. Indeed, since the early postbiblical period, all these numbers have evoked considerable attention – concerning their accuracy, how they were obtained, and

---

[132]   Frank Moore Cross, *Canaanite Myth and Hebrew Epic: Essays in the History of the Religion of Israel* (Cambridge, Mass.: Harvard University Press, 1973), 308–17.

[133]   H.-J. Fabry and H. Lamberty-Zielinsky, "II/III 'rb II/III," *TDOT* 11:332.

their relationship to biblical notions of a "generation" – but little consensus.[134] Perhaps it is best to recognize that 430 is a large number used rhetorically to indicate how extensive the Egyptian experience was. Another important aspect of this figure is that it is part of an overall attempt in the Hebrew Bible to give chronological "information" that provides both continuity and symmetry to the story of ancient Israel, beginning with the ancestral narratives. These dates may be dubious indicators of absolute chronology, but they are powerful markers of two major features of the biblical story: the exodus and the temple. Those two pivotal elements are linked in the book of Exodus, which begins with the extended narrative of the departure from Egypt and concludes with a detailed account of the construction of the institutional, theological, and architectural antecedent of the temple – namely, the tabernacle.

Chapter 12 ends rather briefly in verses 50–51 with the report that the Israelites obeyed God's instructions and were brought out of Egypt. This rather simple statement contrasts with the report of departure in verses 41–42 (before the intervening instructions about who might participate in the paschal celebration). There an apt *double entente* – the Hebrew word translated "vigil" means both "to watch" and "to keep" – marks God's vigilant protection of the Israelites, who in turn would vigilantly keep their experience on the night of escape alive for all generations. As is so often the case in this chapter, language describing the past accommodates and affirms the present customs of the storyteller. Verses 50–51 lack that dimension and probably serve simply as an introduction or transition to the next section, where the ongoing commemoration of the past becomes prominent again.

UNLEAVENED BREAD AND CONSECRATION OF THE FIRSTBORN (13:1–16)

Just as instructions for the paschal offering appear multiple times (12:3–13, 21–27, 43–49) in this section of Exodus (11:1–13:16), so too do those for unleavened bread. The directions for the matzah festival of 12:14–20 recur here in chapter 13:3–10, where they are sandwiched between instructions for the consecration of the firstborn. All of this is to take place, as does the exodus from Egypt, in the month of Abib, literally "the month of new grain." Cereal crops are the basic foodstuffs in the land of the Bible; they are central to life. Thus the new life of grain in the spring, celebrated as a renewal of life, is an appropriate vehicle for celebrating, in the matzah festival, the Israelites' new life in freedom.

Like the first unleavened-bread section in chapter 12, the one in chapter 13 is strongly oriented toward its commemorative function. The injunction to remember the exodus in verse 3 means more than simple recollection. Rather, recollection of the past is intimately tied to activity – ritualization – which, in

---

[134] These attempts are summarized in W. H. C. Propp, *Exodus 1–18* (1998), 365, 415–16.

turn, creates and maintains identity.[135] To remember is to engage in a series of behaviors: eating unleavened bread but not leavened bread for seven days; a festival on the seventh day; removal of leaven from the entire land (cf. 3:8, 17); teaching the meaning of the past to future generations by formally instructing children; and even wearing "it" as a "reminder" (v. 9; cf. v. 16). The ambiguous "it" (memory of the exodus?) is to be "as a sign on your hand and as a reminder on your forehead." This is likely a somewhat elliptical metaphoric expression, meant to accentuate the way the memory of the exodus functions as do jewelry or amulets worn on the wrist or as a circlet on the head; that is, the exodus and its meaning are to be ever precious and always present.[136] This text (along with Deut 6:8 and 11:18), literally interpreted in postexilic times, is related to the Jewish custom that began in that period of wearing phylacteries (*tĕpillîn*) – small boxes containing scriptural verses and strapped to the arm and forehead – during study or prayer. Whether the text precedes or postdates the beginnings of that custom is debatable. Either way, this passage is also notable for the first appearance in the Bible of the phrase "the torah [NRSV, teaching] of the LORD." *Torah* is a term that comes to mean the entire Pentateuch, or even God's teaching more generally. Its use here may simply indicate a conviction that certain divine precepts were authoritative and should be known and communicated – "be on your lips" – by members of the community.

The final ritual associated with the exodus, though not with the Passover, is the consecration of firstborn males, both animals and humans. The first to open the womb bears special significance, perhaps as a harbinger of future fertility, in many premodern cultures. Thus they are "returned" to the deity as sacrifice in gratitude to the provider of fertility. Males in particular are singled out for special treatment in patrilineal societies such as ancient Israel. The firstlings of livestock (like first fruits; cf. 23:16, 19 and 34:19) "belong" to God and become sacrificial animals, except for the donkey, which was not considered an animal suitable for sacrifice and was either destroyed or replaced with a sheep. Firstborn sons likewise belong to God but are not sacrificed; rather, they are redeemed. The procedure for this is not explained and must have been familiar to the ancient audience. Elsewhere in the Pentateuch, in Num 18:36, an exchange of five silver shekels made to the priest, for a month-old male child, is specified.[137]

Again, connecting a ritual to the past is central, as is the explicitly didactic mode in which the link is made. In response to a child's question (13:14), the slaying of the firstborn Egyptian humans and animals is proclaimed as the reason

[135] Marc Brettler, "Memory in Ancient Israel," *Memory and History in Christianity and Judaism*, ed. Michael A. Singer (Notre Dame, Ind.: University of Notre Dame Press, 2001), 5.

[136] W. H. C. Propp, *Exodus 1–18* (1998), 423–4.

[137] Traditional Jews maintain this practice by ceremonially presenting five silver coins to a member of the congregation who is a descendent of the priestly tribe when their first son is a month old.

for this custom. However, there is some dissonance. The firstborn plague is not gender specific, whereas this consecration of the firstborn pertains only to males. Because the consecration does not quite fit the event it commemorates, it is likely that the association enters Israel's collective identity as a rationale for an existing ancient practice. It is another example of the accretion of hoary customs into the cultural memory of the exodus story.

Two other aspects of the consecration passage deserve mention. In reviewing the episode of the exodus story that is commemorated in the consecration of the firstborn (v. 15), the text attributes the loss of innocent life to flawed Egyptian leadership. Casting blame on the pharaoh is perhaps an indication that the narrator was already struggling with this profoundly troublesome aspect of the exodus story. Another way of evaluating the consecration passage is in terms of the overall exodus narrative. The consecration of firstborn sons perhaps functions as an ironic and intensified reversal of the pharaoh's directive (1:22) to slay newborn Hebrew males. It thus forms a fitting conclusion to the sojourn narrative, and the account of journey to the sea and deliverance there (13: 17–15:21) can begin.

BRIDGING THE HORIZONS: THE PASSOVER CELEBRATION

No festival of the Hebrew Bible better epitomizes the ritualization of the past in order to shape and preserve group identity than does the Passover in relation to the memory of exodus. The narrative of exodus is not history, as explained in the Introduction, but rather represents the characteristic way in which traditional societies remember their past.[138] Authentic experience and the folklore and customs of a farming people receive narrative elaboration of epic proportions in Exodus. The paschal lamb and unleavened bread were probably elements of agricultural festivals that were well entrenched in the festival calendar of the inhabitants of ancient Palestine. Earlier generations of scholars tended to look at the two components of the Passover, animals and grain, as originating in two discrete socioeconomic groups: settled agriculturalists and nomadic pastoralists. However, it is now recognized that throughout the biblical period the ancient Israelites practiced a mixed economy in which peasant farmers raised crops and also kept animals. Springtime celebrations conceivably involved both aspects of their agrarian regime.

Linking agricultural festivals with commemoration of the past taps into their affective quality. Festivals associated with the productivity of lands and live-stock are imbued with strong emotion, for the fertility of fields and animals is integrally related to the very survival of subsistence farmers. Seasonal fertility

---

[138] Paul Connerton, *How Societies Remember* (Cambridge: Cambridge University Press, 1985), 70.

celebrations therefore have a life–death dimension, which makes them deeply meaningful. The Passover in turn makes these intense emotional properties part of the community's remembrance of its past. The ability of the Passover to represent and sustain the identity of the Israelites is enormously enhanced. Carrying out the Passover rituals has the effect of making all those who observe the Passover know for themselves the powerful central value of the exodus: liberation by a salvific deity. The practices associated with the Passover thus are not simply commemorative, although they are that. They are also experiential. As a festival engaged with the past, the Passover becomes a prototypical event. It takes an episode that "happened" in the past and makes it, and the values it represents, part of the experience of all subsequent generations. The exodus story is transformed from a past event to a living reality for the community that observes the Passover. Shared values and experiences are incorporated into the celebration and its narrative; together they give Israel its identity.[139] The Passover reproduces the rupture that gave rise to the community in the first place. Ritual institutions not only commemorate the story accounting for the origins of some; they also bind the larger group to that story and the values it represents, just as all Americans share the Mayflower experience and the journey to freedom.

In its agricultural roots, the Passover was a household celebration with its commemorative dimension arguably originating at the instigation of a group that had experienced an exodus and who joined up with Iron Age settlers in the highlands of Canaan. The festival apparently survived as a household celebration despite the seventh-century BCE nationalism, reflected in the deuteronomic regulations for the Passover (Deut 16:1–7), which mandate that the paschal offering be made at the "place the LORD your God will choose" (i.e., the Jerusalem temple). That it was observed as a family festival in early Second Temple times is attested by extra-biblical sources. Two fifth-century BCE documents from the diaspora community at Elephantine (in Egypt) refer to the observation of Passover in the household.[140] Its vital connection to the concept of freedom, as expressed in the exodus story, along with its household setting have made it a central and enduring part of Jewish religious and cultural tradition.

The development of a sequential order of customs and accompanying readings or prayers to celebrate the Passover probably began when the Second Temple was destroyed in 70 CE, thus precluding the offering of the paschal sacrifice.[141] Liturgical substitutions were instituted, and family rather than temple rituals

---

[139]　P. Spikard and W. J. Burroughs, "We Are a People," in *We Are a People* (2000), 10.

[140]　"The Passover Letter," translated by Bezalel Porten (*COS* 3.46), 117, and "Instructions Regarding Children and Inquiry Regarding Passover" (*TAD* D7.6), translated by Bezalel Porten (*COS* 3.87A), 208–9.

[141]　Baruch Bokser, *The Origins of the Seder* (Berkeley: University of California Press, 1964).

were developed (or renewed). The result of these practices is a separate book or guide, called the Haggadah ("telling" or "narration"), which sets forth the rituals and readings that comprise the household Passover service, known as the Seder ("order"), which is held on the first evening of the Passover. The rituals involve six foodstuffs that connect those celebrating the festival with a shared past. In the order in which they come in the Seder, they are

1. *Karpas,* a green vegetable such as parsley or lettuce that represents the new growth of springtime. However, it is dipped in heavily salted water before it is eaten, so that the tears of the suffering Hebrews in Egypt can be tasted.
2. *Zeroah,* a roasted shank-bone of a lamb, which represents the paschal sacrifice. This is not actually consumed, but it is mentioned in the Seder service in reference to the slain animal whose blood marks the doors of Israelite homes at the time of the slaying of the Egyptian firstborn.
3. *Matzah,* the unleavened bread, which is eaten at the Seder and all during the eight-day festival of Passover. It is called the "bread of affliction."
4. *Maror,* bitter herbs, usually raw horseradish. Eating the *maror* brings tears to the eyes and recaptures the agony of the period of oppression in Egypt (cf. 12:8).
5. *Charoset,* a mixture of chopped fruits, nuts, and wine meant to resemble the mortar used by the Hebrews in making bricks in Egypt.
6. *Beitzah,* a roasted egg, symbolizes life and is also reminiscent of sacrificial foods.

The Seder meal typically begins with everyone present eating a boiled egg. In addition to these ceremonial foods, the Seder service includes the drinking of four cups of wine, with appropriate blessings. Wine represents joy and celebration and is part of all Sabbath and festival meals in Jewish tradition.

Many customs have been added to the celebration of the Seder over the centuries. For example, in the medieval period, Jews began leaving their doors open during the Seder as a way of welcoming into their homes any who were hungry; to this day, the door is opened, if only for a brief moment, during the Seder. Another example comes from the last few decades – a Cup of Miriam is placed on the Seder table in many homes to remind those present of the role of Miriam and of other women in the exodus story. These women are not mentioned in the traditional Haggadah itself.

It is important to recognize that the Haggadah is not a straightforward reading of the biblical chapters recounting the exodus. Rather, it is a mixture of blessings, prayers, stories, rabbinic comments, and songs, as well as directions for using the symbolic foodstuffs. Many of its components have been carefully designed to engage children in the celebration and to help them understand the value of freedom as well as the power and compassion of God. The commemorative intent and didactic consciousness of the narratives in Exodus dealing with the Passover have been taken seriously. Although based on the narrative of sojourn and departure in Exodus, the Haggadah quotes relatively few biblical verses. The result is a document that never mentions Moses; instead God becomes the sole focus of the story of redemption.

The Haggadah itself, which probably originated in the Roman period, does not have the authority of a canonical text and is not immutable. Consequently, it has been an expression of Jewish creativity for nearly two millennia and arguably is the most popular form of Jewish religious literature. The earliest surviving versions, from the Middle Ages, differ from one another in their texts and illustrations, thus demonstrating the freedom with which Jews through the centuries and all over the world have changed or augmented the traditional Haggadah to suit the needs and values of their communities. Since the 1940s, for example, the Haggadahs used by many liberal Jews have omitted the traditional reciting of the so-called Ten Plagues as part of the Seder. This change comes from an unwillingness to commemorate any experience that involves the suffering of innocent people, and it allows Jews to cope with the difficult moral problems of some aspects of the biblical account of exodus. Also, prayers are often added that express the idea of freedom for all who are subjugated or exploited and that invoke God's blessing on all peoples. Such changes continue the process of engaging the past so that it speaks to the present; they recognize that oppression was not a one-time occurrence but rather persists in every generation and must always be challenged.

Christian responses to the Passover also have had a long and complex history. The paschal theme of sacrifice and redemption are surely part of the Passion narratives of the New Testament. The firstborn son Jesus, in a sense, becomes a substitute offering (John 19:36; cf. 1:29, 36), his death and resurrection a transposition of the Passover rituals and a vehicle for salvation (1 Cor 5:7; Rev 5:6–14). The synoptic gospels set Jesus' Last Supper at the beginning of Passover (e.g., Mark 14:12–18), although the Gospel of John suggests that it preceded the Passover. The Last Supper may not actually have been a Seder, but it does have some elements that are parallel to the Seder. Its close ties with the symbolism and message of the Seder and paschal sacrifice are prominent aspects of the New Testament.[142]

This fundamental connection between Passover and Jesus as Savior plays out in Christian tradition in many ways. Early Christian communities, for example, believed they should celebrate Passover; and subsequent groups felt that Easter should coincide with Passover. Theological discussions of the relationship between the Eucharist and elements of the Passover celebration

---

[142] Joseph Klawans, "Was Jesus' Last Supper a Seder?" *BR* 17 (2001): 24–33, 47.

abound.[143] Since antiquity, churches have struggled to decide whether and in what form to incorporate aspects of the exodus motif or the Seder meal into their understanding of scripture and their ritual experience of Christ's redemptive death and resurrection.

THE DELIVERANCE – EXODUS 13:17–15:21

NRSV 13:17 When Pharaoh let the people go, God did not lead them by way of the land of the Philistines, although that was nearer; for God thought, "If the people face war, they may change their minds and return to Egypt." [18]So God led the people by the roundabout way of the wilderness toward the Red Sea.[a] The Israelites went up out of the land of Egypt prepared for battle. [19]And Moses took with him the bones of Joseph who had required a solemn oath of the Israelites, saying, "God will surely take notice of you, and then you must carry my bones with you from here." [20]They set out from Succoth, and camped at Etham, on the edge of the wilderness. [21]The LORD went in front of them in a pillar of cloud by day, to lead them along the way, and in a pillar of fire by night, to give them light, so that they might travel by day and by night. [22]Neither the pillar of cloud by day nor the pillar of fire by night left its place in front of the people.

NRSV 14 Then the LORD said to Moses: [2]Tell the Israelites to turn back and camp in front of Pi-hahiroth, between Migdol and the sea, in front of Baal-zephon; you shall camp opposite it, by the sea. [3]Pharaoh will say of the Israelites, "They are wandering aimlessly in the land; the wilderness has closed in on them." [4]I will harden Pharaoh's heart, and he will pursue them, so that I will gain glory for myself over Pharaoh and all his army; and the Egyptians shall know that I am the LORD. And they did so.

5 When the king of Egypt was told that the people had fled, the minds of Pharaoh and his officials were changed toward the people, and they said, "What have we done, letting Israel leave our service?" [6]So he had his chariot made ready, and took his army with him; [7]he took six hundred picked chariots and all the other chariots of Egypt with officers over all of them. [8]The LORD hardened the heart of Pharaoh king of Egypt and he pursued the Israelites, who were going out boldly. [9]The Egyptians pursued them, all Pharaoh's horses and chariots, his chariot drivers and his army; they overtook them camped by the sea, by Pi-hahiroth, in front of Baal-zephon.

---

[143] E.g., Enrico Mazza, *The Celebration of the Eucharist: The Origin of the Rite and the Development of Its Interpretation* (Collegeville, Minn.: Liturgical Press, 1999).
[a] Or *Sea of Reeds*

10 As Pharaoh drew near, the Israelites looked back, and there were the Egyptians advancing on them. In great fear the Israelites cried out to the LORD. ¹¹They said to Moses, "Was it because there were no graves in Egypt that you have taken us away to die in the wilderness? What have you done to us, bringing us out of Egypt? ¹²Is this not the very thing we told you in Egypt, 'Let us alone and let us serve the Egyptians'? For it would have been better for us to serve the Egyptians than to die in the wilderness." ¹³But Moses said to the people, "Do not be afraid, stand firm, and see the deliverance that the LORD will accomplish for you today; for the Egyptians whom you see today you shall never see again. ¹⁴The LORD will fight for you, and you have only to keep still."

15 Then the LORD said to Moses, "Why do you cry out to me? Tell the Israelites to go forward. ¹⁶But you lift up your staff, and stretch out your hand over the sea and divide it, that the Israelites may go into the sea on dry ground. ¹⁷Then I will harden the hearts of the Egyptians so that they will go in after them; and so I will gain glory for myself over Pharaoh and all his army, his chariots, and his chariot drivers. ¹⁸And the Egyptians shall know that I am the LORD, when I have gained glory for myself over Pharaoh, his chariots, and his chariot drivers."

19 The angel of God who was going before the Israelite army moved and went behind them; and the pillar of cloud moved from in front of them and took its place behind them. ²⁰It came between the army of Egypt and the army of Israel. And so the cloud was there with the darkness, and it lit up the night; one did not come near the other all night.

21 Then Moses stretched out his hand over the sea. The LORD drove the sea back by a strong east wind all night, and turned the sea into dry land; and the waters were divided. ²²The Israelites went into the sea on dry ground, the waters forming a wall for them on their right and on their left. ²³The Egyptians pursued, and went into the sea after them, all of Pharaoh's horses, chariots, and chariot drivers. ²⁴At the morning watch the LORD in the pillar of fire and cloud looked down upon the Egyptian army, and threw the Egyptian army into panic. ²⁵He clogged their chariot wheels so that they turned with difficulty. The Egyptians said, "Let us flee from the Israelites, for the LORD is fighting for them against Egypt."

26 Then the LORD said to Moses, "Stretch out your hand over the sea, so that the water may come back upon the Egyptians, upon their chariots and chariot drivers." ²⁷So Moses stretched out his hand over the sea, and at dawn the sea returned to its normal depth. As the Egyptians fled before it, the LORD tossed the Egyptians into the sea. ²⁸The waters returned and covered the chariots and the chariot drivers, the entire army of Pharaoh that had followed them into the sea; not one of them remained. ²⁹But the Israelites walked on dry ground through the sea, the waters forming a wall for them on their right and on their left.

30 Thus the LORD saved Israel that day from the Egyptians; and Israel saw the Egyptians dead on the seashore. ³¹Israel saw the great work that the LORD did against the Egyptians. So the people feared the LORD and believed in the LORD and in his servant Moses.

NRSV 15 Then Moses and the Israelites sang this song to the LORD:

"I will sing to the LORD, for he has triumphed gloriously;
    horse and rider he has thrown into the sea.
²The LORD is my strength and my might,
    and he has become my salvation;
  this is my God, and I will praise him,
    my father's God, and I will exalt him.
³The LORD is a warrior;
    the LORD is his name.
⁴"Pharaoh's chariots and his army he cast into the sea;
    his picked officers were sunk in the Red Sea.ᵃ
⁵The floods covered them;
    they went down into the depths like a stone.
⁶Your right hand, O LORD, glorious in power –
    your right hand, O LORD, shattered the enemy.
⁷In the greatness of your majesty you overthrew your adversaries;
    you sent out your fury, it consumed them like stubble.
⁸At the blast of your nostrils the waters piled up,
    the floods stood up in a heap;
    the deeps congealed in the heart of the sea.
⁹The enemy said, 'I will pursue, I will overtake,
    I will divide the spoil, my desire shall have its fill of them.
    I will draw my sword, my hand shall destroy them.'
¹⁰You blew with your wind, the sea covered them;
    they sank like lead in the mighty waters.
¹¹"Who is like you, O LORD, among the gods?
    Who is like you, majestic in holiness,
    awesome in splendor, doing wonders?
¹²You stretched out your right hand,
    the earth swallowed them.
¹³"In your steadfast love you led the people whom you redeemed;
    you guided them by your strength to your holy abode.
¹⁴The peoples heard, they trembled;
    pangs seized the inhabitants of Philistia.
¹⁵Then the chiefs of Edom were dismayed;
    trembling seized the leaders of Moab;
    all the inhabitants of Canaan melted away.
¹⁶Terror and dread fell upon them;
    by the might of your arm, they became still as a stone
  until your people, O LORD, passed by,
    until the people whom you acquired passed by.

ᵃ Or *Sea of Reeds*

¹⁷You brought them in and planted them on the mountain of your own
   possession,
   the place, O LORD, that you made your abode,
   the sanctuary, O LORD, that your hands have established.
¹⁸The LORD will reign forever and ever."

19 When the horses of Pharaoh with his chariots and his chariot drivers went
into the sea, the LORD brought back the waters of the sea upon them; but the
Israelites walked through the sea on dry ground.

20 Then the prophet Miriam, Aaron's sister, took a tambourine in her hand;
and all the women went out after her with tambourines and with dancing. ²¹And
Miriam sang to them:

"Sing to the LORD, for he has triumphed gloriously;
horse and rider he has thrown into the sea."

*T*he complex and dramatic story of the crossing of the sea is the culmination
of the exodus narrative. From the beginning of the book of Exodus, when
it becomes clear that the days of the sojourn in Egypt must come to an end,
through the recounting of the oppressive Egyptian measures to keep the Israelites
on foreign soil, the ultimate goal of leaving Egypt is always part of the narrative
thread. Sometimes it appears explicitly, as when Moses and Aaron repeatedly
request permission for their people to depart, and sometimes it hovers in the
background. At the same time, the narrative makes it clear that Israelite success
in overcoming Egyptian dominance will be related to the power of their god.
All the signs-and-wonders and then the horrific slaying of the firstborn seem
to make the pharaoh relent, but the overarching tension between pharaoh (and
his gods) and the Israelite god will have to play out in one final event. Egyptian
power must be overcome categorically. And how can that be done? Power is
embodied in military capability, and so the armies and chariots of the mighty
Egyptian empire must be destroyed. This is a daunting task for an unarmed
group of refugees. The difference for them will be the might of a power greater
than that of the Egyptians. That power, we shall see, lies incontrovertibly in the
god of the Israelites; and it is displayed in spectacular form by the episode of the
sea.

The account of this climactic event has been preserved in the Hebrew Bible
in a prose account and also in a poetic version. The latter (15:1–21) is a victory
hymn, befitting a military triumph, and arguably is the oldest literary unit in
the Hebrew Bible. As such, it is likely the basis for the prose account, which
precedes it in Exodus. The earliest version (J) of the prose account, to which
other elements (E and P) were added later, may date to the tenth century BCE.
The hymn, or Song of the Sea, thus would be earlier. Analysis of the Song's
archaic grammatical features and some of its thematic elements, both similar

to characteristics of Ugaritic literature of the Late Bronze Age, indicate that it is considerably older – perhaps as old as the late thirteenth or early twelfth century BCE – than the prose narratives for which it is a source, although some dispute the early date.[144] Information internal to the Song, however, seems to fit the political and social scene in the Levant at the end of the Late Bronze Age or early Iron Age – that is, before Edom and Moab had become small states. Because such information probably would not have been available half a millennium later, a date for the Song not long after the exodus experience but as late as the early monarchy seems likely.[145]

As a victory hymn, the Song does not set out to provide a record of the sea event but rather to celebrate it and to proclaim the sovereignty of Israel's god. It is lyric poetry and has its own conventions, which are different from what we might expect in a prose account or even in epic poetry. This means that some aspects of the sea event are alluded to but not specified and also that a logical chronological sequence is not maintained. The departure from Egypt is never mentioned. Indeed, the Song would be difficult to understand were it not for the accompanying narrative version. Perhaps this is why the prose account precedes the song in the canonical ordering of the materials concerning the final and climactic episode of the deliverance of the Israelites from oppression in Egypt. The audience first needs to be familiar with the subject of the Song in order to understand and appreciate it and to be caught up in its emotional imagery.

TO AND THROUGH THE SEA (13:17–14:31)

The prose account of the crossing of the sea begins with the departure from Egypt. In this telling, it is the pharaoh who lets the people go (13:17) rather than God who brings them out (as in the preceding verse, 13:16). Shifting credit for the release to the Egyptian ruler appears to conclude the theme of his heart being hardened; his obstinacy seems to have ended, for he accedes to the request for freedom for the Israelites (but see 14:4, 8, 17). Yet God is immediately involved in choosing their escape route. Put in military terms ("if the people face war," v. 17; "prepared for battle," v. 18), the outset of the journey foreshadows the military confrontation that lies ahead. Rather than take the direct coastal route ("by way of the land of the Philistines"), the Israelites are directed to follow a circuitous path as they make their way to the Reed Sea (NRSV "Red Sea"). They are to be led by pillars of clouds and fire, perhaps similar to the signals that caravans

---

[144] Most American scholars support the argument for an early date, as set forth by F. M. Cross, *Canaanite Myth* (1973), 112–44. Many European scholars hold that the archaic features are intentionally inserted into a much later (sixth or fifth century BCE) composition; see Martin L. Brenner, *The Song of the Sea: Ex 15:1–21* (BZAW 195; Berlin: de Gruyter, 1991).

[145] See Mark S. Smith, *The Pilgrimage Pattern in Exodus* (JSOTS 239; Sheffield: Sheffield Academic Press, 1997), 222–3.

use, except that in the Hebrew Bible smoke or clouds and fire are fraught with divine imagery (cf. 19:18; 24:16–17).

Clouds and fire, one linked with day and the other with night, also can be understood as a figure of speech; they form a merism (two opposites that together denote a totality), providing an inclusive view of time and indicating that God will always be present as the Israelites' guide. The momentous journey out of Egypt is also a funeral procession of sorts, for Joseph's embalmed skeletal remains are transported for burial in the land of promise. This connection with the ancestral past is marked by language that echoes the end of Genesis (Gen 50:24–26; cf. Josh 24:32).

A CLOSER LOOK: THE RED/REED SEA AND THE EXODUS ROUTE

Looking at the exodus narrative from the cinematic perspective of the twenty-first century, one is struck by the special-effects character of the signs-and-wonders. Perhaps most dramatic of all, however, is what happens when God splits the sea, providing dry land on which the Israelites can cross, and then restores the sea, in which the pursuing army drowns. But where is this body of water and how does it fit into the overall route of the Israelites in their departure from Egypt and journey to the Promised Land? Such questions have engaged students and scholars for millennia.[146]

The Hebrew text reads *yam sûp*, which occurs more than twenty times in the Hebrew Bible and is best translated "Sea of Reeds," or sometimes "reed sea" when it seems to be a descriptive term for a body of water with an abundance of reeds or rushes rather than the name of a specific lake or sea. The earliest Bible translations (Septuagint and Vulgate) used "Red Sea"; and most English translations maintain this translation tradition, despite the fact that reeds do not grow in the Red Sea and that crossing the Red Sea – which is the body of water along the west side of the Arabian peninsula and has two northward arms, the Gulfs of Suez and Aqaba/Eilat[147] – does not fit very well the apparent departure point of the Israelites from the eastern Delta. Moreover, attempts to find a body of water compatible with all the references to the Sea of Reeds in the exodus account as well as elsewhere in the Hebrew Bible have not succeeded. Because at least eight different options have been suggested for its identity, the term *yam sûp* remains ambiguous. At best, we should recognize that the term does not always refer to the same body of water or marshy area. One possibility is that the poetic sea-crossing tradition of Exodus 15 involves a kind of mythic reference to the Gulf of Aqaba/Eilat. That tradition then is superimposed on the prose narratives

---

[146] The chapter on the Re(e)d Sea in J. K. Hoffmeier, *Israel in Egypt* (1999), 199–222, provides a summary.

[147] In antiquity, "Red Sea" likely designated only the Gulf of Aqaba/Eilat as in Exod 23:31 and 1 Kgs 9:26.

of Exodus 13 and 14 with respect to a more northerly location, without concern for the resulting geographical ineptness.[148] In any case, attempts to identify the term with an existing lake, sea, or marsh, especially if the storyteller may not have intended an exact locale, are futile and detract from focusing on the significance of the miraculous rescue of the escaping Israelites.

Similar problems arise in attempts to identify and locate the various place names mentioned in the stages of the wilderness journey, as well as Sinai itself, and to reconstruct the itinerary using the information in Exod 12:37, 13:17–20, 14:2, and Numbers 33.[149] Some of the toponyms can be related to known sites in the Sinai Peninsula, whereas others remain unknown or represent sites unoccupied until much later. Even more disconcerting is the fact that using the existing data does not allow for a reconstruction of a feasible route. Several possibilities – a northern, a central, and a southern route – remain viable because of the ambiguity of the biblical information. Some would argue that the southern route is least problematic and most likely.[150] Unfortunately, such assertions depend on reading many of the narratives in which the toponyms are embedded as if they are exact records, a procedure that does not sufficiently acknowledge either their literary artistry or their composite nature. One other feature of the itinerary traditions contributes further to the difficulty in finding an "original" itinerary. Chronological information also is given in the notices of the Israelites' journey (e.g., 16:1) as part of the wider Pentateuchal timetable of events. The details in Exodus and Numbers are at variance with those in Deuteronomy, suggesting that the route may have been constructed to a certain extent with a timetable in mind.[151] In the aggregate, the information in the itinerary about time and place is part of a structure that organizes salient aspects of the Pentateuch and is hardly a record of an actual journey.

These complications indicate that it may be best, as for the references to the Reed Sea, not to take the information in the wanderings passages at face value. The depiction of a route through Sinai, in Numbers and Deuteronomy as well as in Exodus, may not be based on records of any single journey but instead is more of an impressionistic collage of geographic materials gathered from various sources over an extended period of time and used to recreate the journey of the exodus generation. Geographic veracity was not a concern in that process, as it might be for us today.

The sea-crossing event itself is presented in chapter 14, which is divided into three sections: Egyptian pursuit (vv. 1–14), the splitting of the sea (vv. 15–25),

---

[148] Hedwig Lamberty-Zielinski and Magnus Ottosson, "*sûp; yam sûp,*" *TDOT* 10:190–6.
[149] Summarized by J. K. Hoffmeier, *Israel in Egypt* (1999), 176–98.
[150] K. A. Kitchen, *Reliability of the Old Testament* (2003), 265–74.
[151] William D. Johnstone, "Exodus," in *Eerdmans Commentary to the Bible*, eds. James D. G. Dunn and John W. Rogerson (Grand Rapids, Mich.: Eerdmans, 2003), 86.

and the rejoining of the separated waters (vv. 26–30). Each section is introduced by "Then the Lord said to Moses" (vv. 1, 15, 26). Divine instrumentality thus underlies the three main actions of this account.

When the Israelites reach Etham, their next destination after Succoth, they are told to turn back and go a different way, causing the Egyptians to think they are lost. The stage is set for one last recurrence of the theme of the pharaoh's heart becoming hardened (14:4, 8, 17). God causes the Egyptians to attempt to reclaim the Israelites as a labor force, and God's purpose is clear. The Egyptians will fail in a spectacular way. By overcoming the Egyptian ruler, his officers, and his military forces, the greater power of the Israelite god Yahweh will once and for all be established. In language similar to that of some of the signs-and-wonders episodes, the narrative proclaims that the outcome will be Egyptian knowledge of the Israelite god (v. 18).

Ruing the decision to let the Israelites leave, the pharaoh musters his forces and sends them in pursuit. To the Israelites, Egyptian power seems overwhelming, as they look back and see the amassed chariotry – six hundred elite chariots among many others – and accompanying army that soon overtakes them. Their agony has come full circle: they cry out to God, as they had when their oppression began (2:23). The intensity of their fears is expressed in a series of urgent and panicky rhetorical questions to Moses (14:11–12). In effect, they are challenging Moses' leadership, his very wisdom in persuading them to respond to God and allow him to seek their release. They now perceive their journey as a path to immediate and certain death. This is the first instance of the periodic and perhaps predictable complaints – the murmurings – of the Israelites as they travel in the wilderness. Such defiance is inevitable. It is the normal response of people who are embarking on a journey away from the familiar, however abhorrent it may be, into the unknown. Indeed, the psychological verity of their outcry makes it less an indication of their lack of faith in God and in Moses' abilities as God's spokesperson than a sign of the natural human anguish involved in accepting an immediate future that is uncertain and seems fraught with danger. Moses may be painted as superhuman; the people are not.

Moses must reply, and he does, in an aptly comforting, rather than critical, tone. The three rhetorical and challenging questions of his people are answered with three successive and reassuring imperatives: "Do not be afraid, stand firm, and experience [NRSV, see] the deliverance" that God will perform (14:13). The first of these commands is one commonly used in military contexts, to steady the troops before battle; and it is also a directive from God in theophanies (as in Gen 26:24), assuring a person that the power of God's presence will be for good and not for ill. Those meanings converge here: there is a military threat, for the Israelites face an incredibly powerful army; and they are about to see God's presence manifest in an act of astonishing redemptive power. The second command may also be a technical military term for assuming battle readiness (as when Goliath takes his stand in 1 Sam 17:16).

The third command is especially noteworthy in its use of the term "salvation" (NRSV "deliverance") as part of the phrase *yĕšûʿat YHWH ʾăšer-yaʿaśeh*, "salvation [NRSV, deliverance] that the LORD will work." This word for salvation is used often and prominently in the Hebrew Bible in very specific theological contexts – namely, in association with the military victories of various Israelite leaders, in particular those attributed to divine intervention. It also regularly appears in deuteronomic passages to highlight the redemptive power of Israel's god.[152] The model for these and other related theological usages is the victory over pharaoh's forces at the Reed Sea and is introduced in this passage and 15:2. The term never is used for the departure from Egypt itself but, rather, apparently is reserved to denote miraculous divine help. What more dramatic instance of such salvation could there be than the rescue of a motley and dispirited group of powerless refugees from the well-equipped army of a mighty imperial state? The people need only "stay calm" (NRSV "keep still") – God will do the fighting (v. 14). The image of God as a warrior–savior, prominent in the Song of the Sea, is incorporated into the prose account.

God may seem impatient at the Israelite cry but immediately engages Moses in the task at hand. As for many of the signs-and-wonders, Moses is to stretch out his staff (14:16; cf. "hand" in vv. 21 and 26 and also in v. 16), an act that will divide the sea. The resulting dry land becomes the escape route for the Israelites. They cross between the walls of water to the other side of the sea, accompanied by God's angel, the beneficent counterpart to the destroyer who took the lives of the firstborns (12:23). And they are protected by the visible manifestation of God, the pillars of fire and cloud, which now are behind the Israelites. After a night of pursuit, the Egyptians waver in their resolve, but it is too late. The dramatic chase scene comes to a stunning end: the walls of water crash in on them, as Moses raises his hand over the seas. The Israelites have been "saved" (v. 30); they now have reason to "trust" (NRSV, "believe in") God. The NRSV translation is somewhat misleading, for the Hebrew word means commitment and loyalty, not belief in any creedal sense.

The splitting of the sea takes the exodus story to a new level. As phenomenal as were all the signs-and-wonders, those calamities reflect known patterns of natural devastation, writ large by their sequential timing and intensity. Even the plague of the firstborn, when viewed in terms of its role as a counterpart to the Egyptian decree of infanticide and as the vehicle for giving Israelite festivals and rituals a commemorative grounding, is not of the same ilk as the division of the sea. It should not surprise us, then, to see that the descriptive language in chapter 14 takes us into the realm of cosmic battle. The defeat of the Egyptian forces is nothing less than the defeat of chaos, of the universal forces antithetical to life and represented in mythic terms by raging waters. The "dragons" and "leviathan" that are crushed when God divides the primordial seas – doing so

---

152 See John F. Sawyer and Heinz-Josef Fabry, "*yšʿ*," *TDOT* 6:445–6.

brings about "salvation" in the world in Ps 74:12–17 – here are the pharaoh's armies. Crushing them brings redemption to the Israelites. The prose narrative echoes these mythic ideas, and the following Song gives resounding emotional expression to them.

THE SONG OF THE SEA (15:1–21)

Because the prose introduction to chapter 15 mentions Moses and because Moses is the chief human actor in the exodus story, most of the poetic section of Exodus 15 usually has been called the Song of Moses. That designation for verses 1–18, for example, still appears as a section heading in many English translations. The snippet of a song in verse 21, attributed in the text to Miriam, then is called the Song of Miriam. Her song is introduced by the mention of Miriam performing along with a cohort of female musicians. The traditional ascription of the authorship of verses 1–18 to Moses initially was challenged in the mid–twentieth century, and many other studies have since appeared.[153] One recent example concerns a Dead Sea Scroll fragment containing eight lines of poetic text that have survived as Miriam's Song and represent at least one manuscript tradition preserving an extended poem associated with Miriam.[154] The accumulated weight of literary, textual, historical, sociological, musicological, and feminist research on Exodus 15 indicates that Miriam is the more likely author. Indeed, the fact that the Song is a victory hymn, a genre associated with female rather than male musicians, in itself is a compelling enough reason to assign composition to Miriam rather than to her more famous brother. That being said, it may be better to designate the poetic lines of chapter 15 as the Song of the Sea, acknowledging its content rather than its authorship. The focus of the Song is on God's cosmic power, and anything that would distract us from the Song's message and role should be avoided.

The prose introduction to verse 21 informs us that Miriam sang this victory song with a cohort of women and that their performance involved song, dance, and drums. The use of drums, along with dance and celebratory song, is exemplified in the victory song genre, of which there are several examples in the Hebrew Bible (1 Sam 18:6; Jer 31:4; cf. Judg 11:34 and 5:1). What these texts have in common, in addition to directly or indirectly mentioning dance and drums, is that a song is involved – a particular kind of song. The context for all of these passages is unexpected military victory, which is why the term "victory song" describes this performance genre. But that designation does not do justice to the kind of victory involved in each case. The victories – of unarmed, outnumbered,

---

[153] The scholarship on the Song's authorship is summarized in Carol Meyers, "Miriam, Music, and Miracles," *Mariam, the Magdalen, and the Mother*, ed. Deirdre Good (Bloomington, Ind.: Indiana University Press, forthcoming).

[154] George J. Brooke, "The Long-Lost Song of Miriam," *BAR* 20 (1994): 62–5.

underequipped, or otherwise disadvantaged Israelites – are attributed to ahistorical, wondrous circumstances, namely, the intervention of God in human affairs. It is no accident that celebrating such miraculous saving acts takes poetic form. Miracles involve what humans understand to be a causal connection between heaven and earth, and only poetry or song can convey the affective meaning of the escape from defeat and death.[155] The miracle of divine salvation is captured in the Hebrew Bible by the medium of song.

A CLOSER LOOK: MUSICIANS AND MIDWIVES AS PROFESSIONALS

God's redemptive deeds at the sea may be central to a consideration of the Song, but the fact of Miriam's authorship has its own importance. It provides information about the role of women in ancient Israel as composers and performers of music within the well-developed and sophisticated musical culture of the Israelites.[156] Performance in ancient Israel was hardly an amateur matter but rather was in the hands, depending on the genre and setting, of trained musicians. Ensembles of instrumentalists, singers, and/or dancers contributed to religious as well as secular events. The Hebrew Bible has a rich vocabulary of musical terms, and it mentions dozens of different musical instruments. In most cases, the gender of the performers is not specified, but the Song tradition reveals a performance genre associated exclusively with women.

The instrument mentioned in Exod 15:20 is probably a hand-drum, a small hand-held frame drum anachronistically translated "tambourine" in many English versions. It happens to be the only percussion instrument mentioned in the Hebrew Bible; and in every case in which the gender of the musicians is stipulated, women are the drummers. This raises the possibility that when ensembles including hand-drums are mentioned (e.g., Ps 150:3–5), at least some of the instrumentalists are female. Support for that likelihood comes from archaeology. Small terra-cotta figurines from the Iron Age, probably used for votive purposes, often represent musicians; and only women are depicted as drummers.[157] Women in the biblical world apparently were expert percussionists. Because ancient Semitic music was more rhythmic than tonal or melodic, their hand-drum skills would have made women essential for most musical performances. The victory song genre itself was exclusively female because of the performance context – that is, in the wake of a military victory. In a world with

155 David Noel Freedman, "Pottery, Poetry, and Prophecy: An Essay in Biblical Poetry," *JBL* 96 (1977): 20.
156 That culture is documented in Joachim Braun, *Music in Ancient Israel/Palestine: Archaeological, Written, and Comparative Sources* (Grand Rapids, Mich.: Eerdmans, 2002).
157 Carol Meyers, "Mother to Muse: An Archaeomusicological Study of Women's Performance in Ancient Israel," in *Recycling Biblical Figures,* eds. Athalya Brenner and Jan Willem van Henten (Leiden: Deo Publishing, 1999), 66–73.

men as the primary combatants, the women who remain behind typically are the ones to greet triumphant soldiers returning from battle. It is no wonder that the composition and performance of celebratory hymns became a women's genre in ancient Israel.

Playing musical instruments, learning dances, and composing and singing hymns and songs so they can be performed before an audience are activities that involve both knowledge and practice. Women who participated in such expressive events can be termed professionals. Midwives – with their knowledge of esoteric rituals, clinical procedures, and medicinal substances (see A Closer Look: Midwives and Wet-Nurses, pp. 40–2) – would share with musicians the dynamics of learning, practicing, and transmitting their skills. And musicians and midwives were not the only professional women in ancient Israel. Exodus refers to female cultic functionaries (4:24–26; 22:18; 38:8) and textile artisans (35:25–26; 36:6); other biblical books mention several more (e.g., mourning women, wise women, perfumers, and prophets).

What can the existence of these and other female professional roles tell us about the lives of women in ancient Israel? Ethnographic data from premodern societies provide valuable insights into the social dynamics.[158] Professional knowledge in traditional societies is transmitted from experts to apprentices, usually several such novices meeting with or working with one or more experts. Group preparation takes place when the professional activity, as for musicians, involves public performance. Training and practice sessions mean that the women involved have frequent contact with their female peers. Such connections, which transcend household boundaries, afford women the opportunity to achieve status and recognition that is not dependent on the parameters set by male-oriented kinship patterns. Senior women who are experts in a professional activity exercise control over themselves and their cohort that affords them prestige and enables them to experience a sense of power rather than powerlessness, at least with respect to the dynamics of their female-gendered group. In their mentoring roles they exercise leadership. Moreover, professional women providing services that are both expected and needed by their community act autonomously and authoritatively.

It thus seems certain that professional women in ancient Israel had opportunities for contribution to the community and for self-expression and fulfillment apart from their daily activities in household life. They functioned in ways that would have crosscut the male-dominated hierarchies of their communities. Recognizing the existence of female professionals therefore means contesting

---

[158] See Carol Meyers, "Guilds and Gatherings: Women's Groups in Ancient Israel," in *Realia Dei: Essays in Archaeology and Biblical Interpretation in Honor of Edward F. Campbell, Jr. at His Retirement*, eds. Prescott H. Williams, Jr. and Theodore Hiebert (Atlanta: Scholars Press, 1999), 161–70.

the appropriateness of the designation "patriarchal" for all aspects of Israelite society.[159]

It is also important to note that the work of midwives and many musicians (and other female professionals) was hardly secular. For midwives, the recitation of prayers and incantations was an essential facet of their professional expertise. Similarly, the performers of victory songs composed and performed hymns that were imbued with religious meaning, the celebration of God's redeeming acts. The Song of the Sea, as one of the earliest theological statements in the Hebrew Bible, therefore is arguably a contribution of female creativity.

As a celebration of miraculous rescue, the Song is highly exuberant, full of evocative imagery and superlatives. Its opening line in 15:1 (and 15:21) is likely the title of the Song as well as its first verse, according to the practice in Semitic antiquity of titling poems or other literary works by their first words or lines. It addresses the Song to God, making it a heaven-centered hymn of praise for what God has done on earth. Moses disappears, and the hand or staff with which he divides and closes the waters is here the hand of God (vv. 6, 12). The waters are not split, with dry land in between; rather they become cosmically turbulent. Scholars do not agree about whether and how the poem is organized. One possibility is to treat verse 1 as the title and verse 18 as a coda and then divide the rest into four poetic sections or strophes of uneven length, according to content. Equally compelling is a three-strophe structure based on considerations of form. A two-part division has considerable merit, at least in terms of its relation to the overall structure of Exodus.[160] However it is structured, its emotional and poetic qualities are clear, even in English translation.

Many aspects of the Song are decidedly mythological in both form and content. It resembles and likely draws from the epic poetry of ancient Canaan, which recounts the conquest of the god Baal over the sea-monster and his subsequent sovereignty. As in other mythologies of the ancient Near East and also ancient Greece, the forces of chaos, represented by turbulent waters, are quelled so that order can exist in the created realm. The threat of the Egyptians to the Israelites is assimilated into the wider notion of primordial dangers, and the victory of order and the vanquishing of the enemy are epitomized by God's rescue of the Israelites at the sea. The vocabulary of conquest is inevitably military, and the language of the poem is accordingly replete with divine warrior imagery.[161] Elements of nature – wind and water – are God's weapons. The metaphor of

---

159 Carol Meyers, "Hierarchy or Heterarchy? Archaeology and the Theorizing of Israelite Society," in *Confronting the Past: Essays in Honor of William G. Dever*, eds. Seymour Gitin, J. P. Dessel, J. Edward Wright (Winona Lake, Ind.: Eisenbrauns, forthcoming).

160 M. S. Smith, *Pilgrimage Pattern* (1997), 207–18.

161 Patrick D. Miller, Jr., *The Divine Warrior in Early Israel* (Cambridge, Mass.: Harvard University Press, 1973).

God as "warrior" (v. 3), signifying cosmic power, is the ultimate expression of this historicization of a mythic theme.

An important consequence of the cosmic language of the Song is that God's deeds transcend the particular in their impact. The Israelites and Egyptians are directly and intimately affected by the sea episode, but all peoples are aware of what happened. That awareness is not simple cognition, however. The response of other peoples is visceral; they are shaken to the core by the display of Yahweh's power. This gives a universal dimension to the reality of Israel's god. In addition, the specific peoples that are mentioned (Philistines, Edomites, Moabites, and Canaanites) figure among the early enemies of Israel. The idyllic poetry of verses 14–15, in which all those nations cringe in fear, often is used in attempts to date the poem; for some it idealizes and for others it anticipates or reflects Israel's embattled experience in the land.

One of the most striking and controversial features of the Song is its proclamation of the incomparability of Israel's god, "Who is like you, O LORD, among the gods?" (v. 11). This claim flows from the unique divine power exemplified by the saving deeds at the sea. Yahweh is mightier than any other deity, as the Egyptians themselves acknowledge in the preceding narrative account. Because the existence of other deities is not explicitly denied, this passage presumably would predate the exclusive monotheism that probably does not emerge until the sixth century BCE. Other possibilities are that the phrase "among the gods" refers to lesser heavenly beings in the host of heaven or that it may be vestigial poetic language. The issue cannot be easily resolved, and making this verse an issue in understanding Israelite concepts of God is probably unjustified; to do so retrojects postbiblical theological concerns onto an ancient text with a different worldview. What should remain in the foreground is that, regardless of whether or not it acknowledges the existence of other divine beings, the resounding rhetorical question captures Israel's exclusive devotion to Yahweh and Yahweh's might. So central was this concept that verse 11 became an integral part of daily Jewish liturgy by the early postbiblical period.[162]

Another controversial feature of the Song is its supposed reference to the Jerusalem sanctuary, which would mean that the poem would not predate the monarchic era and the construction of the temple in the capital. God's "holy abode" appears in verse 13, and the mountain of God's "inheritance" (NRSV "possession") and God's "sanctuary" are mentioned in verse 17. The terminology, especially the term "inheritance," is frequently used to designate Israel's homeland in Canaan. However, such usage itself may derive from this passage rather than the other way around; scholars are divided on this issue. Looking at Ugaritic poetry is informative in support of an early date for the Song. The mythic language of Exodus 15, with its reference to the divine habitation in

---

[162] The whole Song had already become part of the Sabbath liturgy in the Second Temple period; see N. M. Sarna, *Exodus* (1991), 76.

heaven as God's possession, or inheritance, resonates with the description – "holy place, the mountain that is my personal possession"[163] – of the shrine built for the victorious Canaanite deity Baal.

Moreover, a close examination of the language for God's shrine (v. 17) does not support identifying it with the Jerusalem shrine or another cultic site of early Israel. For one thing, the term "holy place" (NRSV "sanctuary") is never used to designate the temple in the Kings account; and it appears in other texts more generally to designate holy areas or objects possessing sanctity. But it certainly does designate the abode for God in the celestial sphere; such divine abodes throughout the ancient Near East were considered models for the gods' earthly dwellings – i.e., temples. "Sanctuary" in Exod 25:8 has such a meaning, and we will consider the function of the shrine as God's dwelling in our discussion of the tabernacle (see A Closer Look: Temples and Temple Service, pp. 220–2). In this passage, God's hands-on role – the shrine is established with "your hands" (v. 17) – indicates that God (and not Solomon or Bezalel) is the builder of the sanctuary. In addition, the term translated "place" of abode is more accurately translated "dais" of God's throne or seat, language reflecting the furnishings of God's heavenly, not earthly, abode (cf. Ps 33:13–14, which refers to God seated on a heavenly "dais"; NRSV "where he sits enthroned"). The verbs in verse 17 are thus accurately translated in the past tense by the NRSV ("You brought them in and planted them . . . [at the] place, O LORD, that you made your abode").[164] But the sanctuary that has been built is not the one in Jerusalem.

These verses probably are not later additions to an early twelfth- or eleventh-century poem, nor do they necessarily mean that the Song as a whole must come after the tenth-century construction of a national shrine in Jerusalem. Rather, they are the culmination of the second part of the poem. The first twelve verses are a poetic expression of the victory at the sea; the second part of the poem takes the Israelites from the sea to the sacred mountain. That unnamed mountain is perhaps the same as the mountain of God's initial theophany to Moses, or it may reflect traditions of a premonarchic sacred site in the land. It is only its context within Exodus that makes it the place where God would soon appear to all the people. Countless efforts, by those who assume Sinai to be the mountain of the poem, have been made to identify Sinai with a specific geographical locale.[165] More likely, the lack of specificity in the poem is appropriate, given the way Exodus blends different traditions and also echoes mythological notions. All mountainous shrines can therefore be God's holy mountain.

---

[163] "The Ba'lu Myth," translated by Dennis Pardee (*COS* 1.86), 251.

[164] The verbs of the Song and especially verse 17 are among the most notoriously difficult to understand, with respect to tense, in the Hebrew Bible; see David Noel Freedman, "Moses and Miriam: The Song of the Sea (Exodus 15:1–18, 21)," in *Realia Dei: Essays in Archaeology and Biblical Interpretation in Honor of Edward F. Campbell, Jr. at His Retirement*, eds. Prescott H. Williams, Jr. and Theodore Hiebert (Atlanta: Scholars Press, 1999), 73–83.

[165] Summarized in W. H. C. Propp, *Exodus 1–18* (1998), 562–71. I discuss the problem of locating Sinai in the section on Theophany at the Mountain – Exodus 19.

The Song of the Sea thus functions as the centerpiece (but not the center point) of the book of Exodus in terms of Israel's existence in freedom versus bondage.[166] All the movement of the narrative until this point is moving toward a destination, the mountain of the LORD; and the rest of the narrative concerns the revelation at the mountain. Indeed, the Song is as much a song of God's holy mountain as it is a song of a sea. But the people are not yet at the mountain at the Song's end. The prose narrative of their journey to the mountain (15:22– 18:27) immediately follows the Song, balancing the prose narrative of the sea that immediately precedes the poetic account.

A CLOSER LOOK: GENDERED IMAGES OF GOD

The poetic imagery of God as "warrior" in verse 3 of the Song of the Sea gives the impression that the Israelite deity is male. Other anthropomorphic images of God – such as king and even father – are also derived from stereotypical male roles and similarly contribute to that notion. Indeed, the variety of such masculine images and the frequency with which they occur produce an over-whelming sense of a male deity. For example, although "father" as an epithet for God actually is quite rare in the Hebrew Bible, God is called "king" some forty-seven times, almost all in poetic passages.[167] The nature of Hebrew as a gendered language further leads to such a conception of God. All nouns in Hebrew are either masculine or feminine, and the word for God ('ēl or 'ĕlōhîm) as well as the name of God (Yahweh) both are masculine. Thus all pronouns referring to God are also masculine.

The presence of male images and the accompanying nouns and pronouns obscure the presence of imagery that is derived from female roles in Israelite society. Gynomorphic images for God can, in fact, be identified throughout the Hebrew Bible.[168] The most common of those are maternal ones. God is depicted as giving birth to Israel and then providing nurturance – food, water, clothing, and healing, as well as maternal instruction (e.g., Num 11:12; Hos 11:3–4). Most of these images are quite direct, with metaphors and similes used to convey God's maternal creativity and care giving. But indirect images are also present. God sometimes performs for Israel what were almost exclusively women's tasks in ancient Israel, thus giving a female aura to certain divine acts. The preparation of bread, for example, is virtually always a woman's role in the biblical world; and so God's sending bread in the wilderness (Exod 16:4, 15) evokes female imagery. God's male military might in redeeming the Israelites gives way to female nurturance in sustaining them on their journey. The notion of God as

[166] M. S. Smith, *Pilgrimage Pattern* (1997), 214–18; W. H. C. Propp, *Exodus 1–18* (1998), 37–8.
[167] Marc Zvi Brettler, *God Is King: Understanding an Israelite Metaphor* (JSOTS 76; Sheffield: Sheffield Academic Press, 1989), 31.
[168] Carol Meyers, "Female Images of God in the Hebrew Bible," *WIS*, 525–8.

the source of sustenance and safety is also present in texts depicting God as a maternal eagle, providing food and protection in the wilderness (Exod 19:4; cf. Deut 32:10–14).

In addition, the use of the epithet "merciful" for God as the source of divine compassion is probably related to such maternal images. The adjective "compassionate" (or "merciful") and the noun "compassion" (or "mercy"), as well as the verb "to be compassionate, merciful," all are related to the Hebrew word for "womb" (*reḥem*); and they all are used in relation to God more often than to humans in the Bible. Especially noteworthy in this regard is the oft-repeated creedal statement of Exod 34:6–7 (cf. 33:19), which proclaims the abundant, unending, and steadfast nature of divine love. Such divine compassion evokes *uteral* imagery – God has powerful maternal love for Israel.[169]

What does the presence of such imagery indicate about the Israelite conception of God with respect to gender? The Hebrew Bible does not provide a systematic or dogmatic exposition of the nature of God. Rather, ideas about God are conveyed by what God does, so that the actions attributed to God – such as God's redemption of Israel from oppression at the exodus – reveal something of the divine character. Similarly, both female and male imagery for God, especially in poetry, depict the nature of God. Whether the gendered images had a literal meaning for some or all of the ancient Israelites probably never can be determined. What does seem certain is that they would not have understood our current interest in the sex or gender of God. The dominant male metaphors for God may seem sexist and problematic in today's world, when wrenched from their Iron Age context. But it is worth considering that the many male images and the fewer female ones together were powerful vehicles for expressing the fundamentally nonhuman character of God.

---

[169] Phyllis Trible, *God and the Rhetoric of Sexuality* (Overtures to Biblical Theology; Philadelphia: Fortress, 1978), 31–59.

IV. Commentary Part II. Sinai and Covenant – Exodus 15:22–24:18

WILDERNESS JOURNEY – EXODUS 15:22–18:27

NRSV **15:22** Then Moses ordered Israel to set out from the Red Sea,[a] and they went into the wilderness of Shur. They went three days in the wilderness and found no water. [23]When they came to Marah, they could not drink the water of Marah because it was bitter. That is why it was called Marah.[b] [24]And the people complained against Moses, saying, "What shall we drink?" [25]He cried out to the LORD; and the LORD showed him a piece of wood; he threw it into the water, and the water became sweet.

There the LORD made for them a statute and an ordinance and there he put them to the test. [26]He said, "If you will listen carefully to the voice of the LORD your God, and do what is right in his sight, and give heed to his commandments and keep all his statutes, I will not bring upon you any of the diseases that I brought upon the Egyptians; for I am the LORD who heals you."

27 Then they came to Elim, where there were twelve springs of water and seventy palm trees; and they camped there by the water.

NRSV **16** The whole congregation of the Israelites set out from Elim; and Israel came to the wilderness of Sin, which is between Elim and Sinai, on the fifteenth day of the second month after they had departed from the land of Egypt. [2]The whole congregation of the Israelites complained against Moses and Aaron in the wilderness. [3]The Israelites said to them, "If only we had died by the hand of the LORD in the land of Egypt, when we sat by the fleshpots and ate our fill of bread; for you have brought us out into this wilderness to kill this whole assembly with hunger."

4 Then the LORD said to Moses, "I am going to rain bread from heaven for you, and each day the people shall go out and gather enough for that day. In that way I

---

[a] Or *Sea of Reeds*
[b] That is *Bitterness*

will test them, whether they will follow my instruction or not. ⁵On the sixth day, when they prepare what they bring in, it will be twice as much as they gather on other days." ⁶So Moses and Aaron said to all the Israelites, "In the evening you shall know that it was the LORD who brought you out of the land of Egypt, ⁷and in the morning you shall see the glory of the LORD, because he has heard your complaining against the LORD. For what are we, that you complain against us?" ⁸And Moses said, "When the LORD gives you meat to eat in the evening and your fill of bread in the morning, because the LORD has heard the complaining that you utter against him – what are we? Your complaining is not against us but against the LORD."

9 Then Moses said to Aaron, "Say to the whole congregation of the Israelites, 'Draw near to the LORD, for he has heard your complaining.'" ¹⁰And as Aaron spoke to the whole congregation of the Israelites, they looked toward the wilderness, and the glory of the LORD appeared in the cloud. ¹¹The LORD spoke to Moses and said, ¹²"I have heard the complaining of the Israelites; say to them, 'At twilight you shall eat meat, and in the morning you shall have your fill of bread; then you shall know that I am the LORD your God.'"

13 In the evening quails came up and covered the camp; and in the morning there was a layer of dew around the camp. ¹⁴When the layer of dew lifted, there on the surface of the wilderness was a fine flaky substance, as fine as frost on the ground. ¹⁵When the Israelites saw it, they said to one another, "What is it?" For they did not know what it was. Moses said to them, "It is the bread that the LORD has given you to eat. ¹⁶This is what the LORD has commanded: 'Gather as much of it as each of you needs, an omer to a person according to the number of persons, all providing for those in their own tents.'" ¹⁷The Israelites did so, some gathering more, some less. ¹⁸But when they measured it with an omer, those who gathered much had nothing over, and those who gathered little had no shortage; they gathered as much as each of them needed. ¹⁹And Moses said to them, "Let no one leave any of it over until morning." ²⁰But they did not listen to Moses; some left part of it until morning, and it bred worms and became foul. And Moses was angry with them. ²¹Morning by morning they gathered it, as much as each needed; but when the sun grew hot, it melted.

22 On the sixth day they gathered twice as much food, two omers apiece. When all the leaders of the congregation came and told Moses, ²³he said to them, "This is what the LORD has commanded: 'Tomorrow is a day of solemn rest, a holy sabbath to the LORD; bake what you want to bake and boil what you want to boil, and all that is left over put aside to be kept until morning.'" ²⁴So they put it aside until morning, as Moses commanded them; and it did not become foul, and there were no worms in it. ²⁵Moses said, "Eat it today, for today is a sabbath to the LORD; today you will not find it in the field. ²⁶Six days you shall gather it; but on the seventh day, which is a sabbath, there will be none."

27 On the seventh day some of the people went out to gather, and they found none. ²⁸The Lord said to Moses, "How long will you refuse to keep my

commandments and instructions? ²⁹See! The LORD has given you the sabbath, therefore on the sixth day he gives you food for two days; each of you stay where you are; do not leave your place on the seventh day." ³⁰So the people rested on the seventh day.

31 The house of Israel called it manna; it was like coriander seed, white, and the taste of it was like wafers made with honey. ³²Moses said, "This is what the LORD has commanded: 'Let an omer of it be kept throughout your generations, in order that they may see the food with which I fed you in the wilderness, when I brought you out of the land of Egypt.'" ³³And Moses said to Aaron, "Take a jar, and put an omer of manna in it, and place it before the LORD, to be kept throughout your generations." ³⁴As the LORD commanded Moses, so Aaron placed it before the covenant, for safekeeping. ³⁵The Israelites ate manna forty years, until they came to a habitable land; they ate manna, until they came to the border of the land of Canaan. ³⁶An omer is a tenth of an ephah.

NRSV 17 From the wilderness of Sin the whole congregation of the Israelites journeyed by stages, as the LORD commanded. They camped at Rephidim, but there was no water for the people to drink. ²The people quarreled with Moses, and said, "Give us water to drink." Moses said to them, "Why do you quarrel with me? Why do you test the LORD?" ³But the people thirsted there for water; and the people complained against Moses and said, "Why did you bring us out of Egypt, to kill us and our children and livestock with thirst?" ⁴So Moses cried out to the LORD, "What shall I do with this people? They are almost ready to stone me." ⁵The LORD said to Moses, "Go on ahead of the people, and take some of the elders of Israel with you; take in your hand the staff with which you struck the Nile, and go. ⁶I will be standing there in front of you on the rock at Horeb. Strike the rock, and water will come out of it, so that the people may drink." Moses did so, in the sight of the elders of Israel. ⁷He called the place Massah[a] and Meribah,[b] because the Israelites quarreled and tested the LORD, saying, "Is the LORD among us or not?"

8 Then Amalek came and fought with Israel at Rephidim. ⁹Moses said to Joshua, "Choose some men for us and go out, fight with Amalek. Tomorrow I will stand on the top of the hill with the staff of God in my hand." ¹⁰So Joshua did as Moses told him, and fought with Amalek, while Moses, Aaron, and Hur went up to the top of the hill. ¹¹Whenever Moses held up his hand, Israel prevailed; and whenever he lowered his hand, Amalek prevailed. ¹²But Moses' hands grew weary; so they took a stone and put it under him, and he sat on it. Aaron and Hur held up his hands, one on one side, and the other on the other side; so his hands were steady until the sun set. ¹³And Joshua defeated Amalek and his people with the sword.

14 Then the LORD said to Moses, "Write this as a reminder in a book and recite it in the hearing of Joshua: I will utterly blot out the remembrance of Amalek from

[a] That is *Quarrel*
[b] That is *Test*

under heaven." ¹⁵And Moses built an altar and called it, The LORD is my banner. ¹⁶He said, "A hand upon the banner of the LORD! The LORD will have war with Amalek from generation to generation."

NRSV 18 Jethro, the priest of Midian, Moses' father-in-law, heard of all that God had done for Moses and for his people Israel, how the LORD had brought Israel out of Egypt. ²After Moses had sent away his wife Zipporah, his father-in-law Jethro took her back, ³along with her two sons. The name of the one was Gershom (for he said, "I have been an alien[a] in a foreign land"), ⁴and the name of the other, Eliezer[b] (for he said, "The God of my father was my help, and delivered me from the sword of Pharaoh"). ⁵Jethro, Moses' father-in-law, came into the wilderness where Moses was encamped at the mountain of God, bringing Moses' sons and wife to him. ⁶He sent word to Moses, "I, your father-in-law Jethro, am coming to you, with your wife and her two sons." ⁷Moses went out to meet his father-in-law; he bowed down and kissed him; each asked after the other's welfare, and they went into the tent. ⁸Then Moses told his father-in-law all that the LORD had done to Pharaoh and to the Egyptians for Israel's sake, all the hardship that had beset them on the way, and how the LORD had delivered them. ⁹Jethro rejoiced for all the good that the LORD had done to Israel, in delivering them from the Egyptians.

10 Jethro said, "Blessed be the LORD, who has delivered you from the Egyptians and from Pharaoh. ¹¹Now I know that the LORD is greater than all gods, because he delivered the people from the Egyptians, when they dealt arrogantly with them." ¹²And Jethro, Moses' father-in-law, brought a burnt offering and sacrifices to God; and Aaron came with all the elders of Israel to eat bread with Moses' father-in-law in the presence of God.

13 The next day Moses sat as judge for the people, while the people stood around him from morning until evening. ¹⁴When Moses' father-in-law saw all that he was doing for the people, he said, "What is this that you are doing for the people? Why do you sit alone, while all the people stand around you from morning until evening?" ¹⁵Moses said to his father-in-law, "Because the people come to me to inquire of God. ¹⁶When they have a dispute, they come to me and I decide between one person and another, and I make known to them the statutes and instructions of God." ¹⁷Moses' father-in-law said to him, "What you are doing is not good. ¹⁸You will surely wear yourself out, both you and these people with you. For the task is too heavy for you; you cannot do it alone. ¹⁹Now listen to me. I will give you counsel, and God be with you! You should represent the people before God, and you should bring their cases before God; ²⁰teach them the statutes and instructions and make known to them the way they are to go and the things they are to do. ²¹You should also look for able men among all the people, men who fear God, are trustworthy, and hate dishonest gain; set such men over them as officers over thousands, hundreds, fifties, and tens.

---

[a] Hebrew *ger*
[b] Hebrew *Eli*, my God; *ezer*, help

^{22}Let them sit as judges for the people at all times; let them bring every important case to you, but decide every minor case themselves. So it will be easier for you, and they will bear the burden with you. ^{23}If you do this, and God so commands you, then you will be able to endure, and all these people will go to their home in peace."

24 So Moses listened to his father-in-law and did all that he had said. ^{25}Moses chose able men from all Israel and appointed them as heads over the people, as officers over thousands, hundreds, fifties, and tens. ^{26}And they judged the people at all times; hard cases they brought to Moses, but any minor case they decided themselves. ^{27}Then Moses let his father-in-law depart, and he went off to his own country.

The escape from oppression in Egypt is not the same, the people soon realize, as a secure existence as an autonomous community. No sooner do they depart from the sea than they are faced with two enormous problems. The first concerns their very survival. How can the Israelites secure the food and water that are necessary for the long and arduous trek through the virtually barren wilderness? The second concerns another kind of survival. How are they to function as a people? How can they survive without mechanisms to deal with internal dynamics and external threats, and how can they establish a cultural identity? Both problems reflect the ongoing struggles of the Israelites to secure sustenance and to maintain national social, political, and religious integrity in the land of promise; they are problems of any people at any time. This section of Exodus (15:22–18:27) sets forth the crises and resolutions, with respect to both physical and cultural survival, that the liberated Israelites face in their journey from the sea to Sinai. It also adds to the impressive list of roles Moses plays in the exodus account.

WATER CRISIS (15:22–27)

Moses resumes his leadership as the people set out on the next stage of their journey into the wilderness of Shur. This place is unknown and differs from the area mentioned in the wilderness account in Numbers (33:8). Its literal meaning in Hebrew – "wall" – may be an allusion to a barrier fortification that the Egyptians apparently constructed at times to protect their eastern border from incursions of marauders from the Sinai Peninsula (cf. Gen 25:18). The indeterminacy of place also characterizes the next geographical locale mentioned, Marah. The site is unknown and its reliability as an authentic toponym is doubtful. Rather, it is the meaning of the name ("bitterness") that is critical to the episode that unfolds there. It also is a link with the bitterness of the work imposed on the Israelites in Egypt (1:14) and commemorated in the bitter herbs of the Passover ritual (12:8). The name is repeated three times, providing some convergence with the three days required to reach the site. A three-day period is a standard segment or stage of a long journey in ancient Near Eastern literature, including the Hebrew Bible (e.g., Gen 22:4).[1] It also recalls the three-day trek that Moses mentions so often in his negotiations with the pharaoh. These features of the arrival at Marah indicate that details of chronology and geography have symbolic and literary significance and are unlikely to preserve information about any single or specific journey.

The crisis of Marah concerns the fundamental human need for survival, namely, water. After three days without water, the Israelites come to a place that does have water – but it is bitter. Understandably, the people confront their leader. The motif of complaint is introduced to the narrative and will recur multiple times as the Israelites continue their journey across desolate and dangerous terrain. Moses, in turn, cries out to God, who provides the solution. Reminiscent of the wonders in Egypt, when he and his brother used their staffs to turn the Nile bloody and undrinkable, Moses now uses wood to achieve the opposite, that is, to make water potable. This magical act becomes the occasion for a message from God to the people. In language very similar to that of the deuteronomist, God gives them "a statute and an ordinance," also called God's "commandments" and "statutes" (vv. 25–26). The significance of these terms designating regulations for community life will be considered in the section on the covenant and its contents. At this point, it is important simply to recognize that they are introduced at the same time as water is provided, far in advance of the revelation of the covenantal precepts at Sinai according to the sequence of the book of Exodus. Perhaps the message is that both water and regulations are essential for survival. The connection between this introduction of community regulations and the complaints at Marah otherwise is rather tenuous.

Regulations by their nature require obedience, and that aspect of community order also is introduced. In return for their compliance with these unspecified precepts, God will offer protection from the maladies that were endemic in Egypt. God is thus identified in 15:26 as "healer" (NRSV "who heals you"), with ultimate sovereignty over health and disease, life and death. Also introduced in this first post-sea episode is the idea of testing the Israelites. Their ability to obey God's words will hereafter be scrutinized closely. Time and again, the Israelites will come up short but God nonetheless will sustain them. What happens at Marah, the very first stop after the sea, epitomizes their entire journey. Raw human needs and the struggle to obey God's statutes will characterize their wilderness sojourn; and these issues, in the view of deuteronomists and priestly leaders alike, reach a crisis point at the period of destruction and exile in the sixth century BCE.

---

[1] U. Cassuto, *Commentary* (1983), 183, gives examples.

FOOD CRISIS (16:1–36)

The next stage – Elim – brings the people to *twelve* springs of water and *seventy* date palms (15:27). These numbers are symbolic – a spring and water to drink for each tribe, and a perfect and full complement of trees with sweet fruit to eat. God is indeed sustaining them.

But no sooner do they embark on the next stage of their journey than they face deprivation. This time they are without food, and they complain to Moses again and to Aaron too. The intensity of their outcry is expressed by the frequent – *sevenfold* – repetition of the word "complain" in 16:1–12. The need for sustenance is real, but their outcry is ominous as they accuse their leaders of trying to starve them to death. But God understands this distress to be directed toward God, not to God's emissaries, and so responds with the miraculous provision of bread and meat from heaven.[2] The wondrous appearance of ample food in the wilderness is no less amazing than the way adequate quantities are assured. An *omer* (a measure of grain, the equivalent of one tenth of an *ephah*, which would be about two quarts; cf. v. 36) per person per day is the amount needed for survival; and that amount is exactly what each person obtains, whether they gather much or little (v. 17–18).

As at Marah, a test is involved; this time the test becomes the vehicle for the introduction of a community observance, the Sabbath. Situated in the narrative before the Sinai event and the giving of the Decalogue with its stipulation of a weekly day of rest, the seventh day is proclaimed as a "day of solemn rest, a holy sabbath to the LORD" (v. 23; cf. v. 25) and thus a day of rest for the people (v. 30). The people are to collect an omer of food daily for five days and a double amount on the sixth day so that they will have enough for both the sixth and the seventh days. This process becomes the test, in that the people are to gather no more than what they need on a given day; they are to have faith that God would provide what they need each day. But this proves to be too difficult. The people gather extra and, except for the double portion picked up on the sixth day, the surplus rots. Moreover, some people even try to collect food on the seventh day itself. Clearly, obedience to God does not come easily to this people, despite the wonders and miracles they have experienced. But God does not abandon them, and apparently they eventually learn how to deal with the food from heaven, for they continue to receive it for the "forty years" (v. 35) of their journey. The testing in the wilderness of Sin is a microcosm of the Israelite experience: God continues to care for them despite their disobedience.

Also noteworthy in this episode is the use of four terms. The first is the word "instruction" (*tôrâ*; v. 28), which is not a specifically legal term but rather more broadly signifies teaching, a concept that underlies the body of instructions,

---

[2] The quails are a one-time occurrence, quelling the outcry of the people but, unlike the manna, not recurring during the wilderness journey.

both stories and rules, that comes to be known as the Torah. Although it is sometimes translated "law," its conceptual origin in the idea of divine direction should be kept in mind. This term already has appeared in the narrative with respect to the instructions regarding Passover (12:49, NRSV "law") and amulets (13:9, NRSV "teaching"), and it may be a term that best fits the exhortations or norms that are part of the body of regulations collected in 20:17–23:33.

The second term, "glory," also has appeared before, in verbal form ("to gain glory, honor"; 14:4, 17, 18). But in 16:7 and 10, the phrase "glory of the Lord" (*kĕbôd YHWH*) is found for the first time in the Hebrew Bible. This phrase is prominent, especially in priestly sections, as a designation for the actual presence of God. Drawing upon conventions in Near Eastern literature, in which the majesty of gods and kings is expressed by the image of blazing or fiery radiance surrounding them, "glory of the Lord" becomes the language of theophany.[3] God indeed appears to humans; but a cloud covers God's physical manifestation, which only Moses among humans can see (24:16–18; cf. 40:34–35).

The third is the designation, "manna," for the food that God provides. This word comes only at the end of the episode in an appendix (vv. 31–36) that provides additional details about the name, appearance, and enduring significance of this food from heaven. Its name seems to have an etymological relationship to the question the Israelites ask when they first see it (v. 15): "what (*mān*) is it?" The description of what it looked like and how it tasted cannot be matched with any substance known from the Sinai region. There is no naturalistic explanation. Rather, the manna tradition of food for a multitude in the barren wilderness is a miraculous aspect of the arduous journey. The powerful God who can perform the miracle of the sea is also a nurturing deity who can provide sweet water and now delectable food where neither exists.

The fourth term is "covenant," which the NRSV uses in verse 34 for a Hebrew word, '*ēdût*, which means "pact" or "contract" (cf. "testimony" in some older translations) and is a synonym for *bĕrît*, also translated "covenant" in the NRSV Although "covenant" (*bĕrît*) has appeared twice (2:24 and 6:4) in relation to the ancestral pact with God presented in Genesis, this usage anticipates the Sinai covenant. It may, in fact, be an elliptical reference to the "ark of the covenant," in which the tablets of the covenant ('*ēdût*) are to be kept.[4]

The description of the manna is situated in a commemorative ritual (vv. 33–34) – one that, unlike the Passover, does not seem to have survived the biblical period. Aaron is to place some of the manna in a jar to be kept "before the Lord," a phrase alluding to a shrine, for future generations to see.[5]

---

[3] Moshe Weinfeld, "*kābōd*," *TDOT* 7:29–33.

[4] The ark is discussed in Commentary Part III, in relation to Exod 25:10–22.

[5] Just as the Sabbath appears before it is proclaimed at Sinai, so the existence of a shrine with a priestly role for Aaron is assumed before tabernacle and priesthood are established. These are example of the composite and mnemohistorical nature of Exodus.

A CLOSER LOOK: THE SABBATH

The experience in the wilderness of Sin relates the observance of the Sabbath to the earliest experience of the Israelites as a free people, even before the rules of the Sabbath have been proclaimed at Sinai. This is the first occurrence of the noun "Sabbath" (*šabbāt*) in the Hebrew Bible, but the narrative offers no reason for the existence of a special seventh day; nor does a reason appear in the Sabbath ordinance of 34:21, which may be its simplest and earliest form. When it appears in Exodus in the community precepts known as the Decalogue, the paradigm for the Sabbath is a priestly one, linked to the creation of the cosmos; it is a ritual of remembrance (20:8) marking God's cessation from work on the *seventh* day after six days of creation (20:11; cf. Gen 2:2–3). A similar rationale appears in the priestly tabernacle texts, in 31:12–17. Quite different is the rationale in Deuteronomy, where the Sabbath precept is explicitly commemorative of Israel's past. It uses language recalling the redemption of the people from Egypt: "Remember that you were a slave in the land of Egypt, and the LORD your God brought you out from there with a mighty hand and an outstretched arm; therefore the LORD your God commanded you to keep the sabbath day" (Deut 5:15). As a hallowed day that becomes a premier social and religious institution of the Israelites and, whether observed on Saturday or Sunday, a hallmark of the religious week of both Jews and Christians since postbiblical times, it is linked in the Bible to both the order of the cosmos and the origins of Israel.

The rationales may differ in Exodus and Deuteronomy, but the implications of the Sabbath for the people are the same. Both sources stipulate that the sanctity of the seventh day is meant to provide a respite for all. Unlike the Passover regulations, there is no distinction between Israelites and uncircumcised servants or foreigners. Noncitizens and servants and even animals are to observe the Sabbath. The regulations also are gender and age inclusive. The somewhat puzzling omission of the wife can probably be understood as a function of the conjugal pair being understood as a unit, with the masculine singular "you" (20:9) being used inclusively, as it is in the verbs that proclaim the negative imperatives (such as "You shall not murder...."). It should be noted, in addition, that 20:10 lists *seven* categories of household members: the male (and female?) head of house, son, daughter, male slave, female slave, livestock, and alien resident. That symbolic number may be intended to emphasize the totality of household members required to observe the Sabbath.

A humanitarian impetus for such an institution seems likely, and it would have been especially meaningful in an agrarian society such as ancient Israel, in which most people were engaged in arduous subsistence labor. The information in Exodus about the Sabbath, a word that literally means "cessation" (probably from the root *šbt*, meaning "to cease, rest") provides few details about what is to be done on the Sabbath other than to cease from work even during labor-intensive periods (34:21), and to refrain from kindling fires (35:3). But other biblical texts, especially in the prophetic books, provide evidence that the Sabbath was apparently an entrenched Israelite institution, sometimes observed and sometimes not, during the monarchy. Such texts also indicate other parameters for its observance. In addition to cessation from labor, cultic practices – special sacrifices and setting out loaves for God – connected with the Sabbath apparently were part of temple practice (Num 28:9–10; Lev 24:8). The somewhat shocking attachment of the death penalty to Sabbath disobedience (31:14–15; 35:2) may be a function of the fact it was not always observed and thus required a strong penal deterrent as well as religious and historical rationales. At the same time, one wonders whether imposing cessation from work on everyone might itself have been a hardship for some, curtailing productivity.

However difficult it may be to reconstruct the nature and scope of Sabbath observance, attempting to understand the origins of the Sabbath are even more problematic. Various astrological, sociological, cultic, and etymological hypotheses have been suggested.[6] Prominent among them is the notion that the Hebrew term *šabbāt* and the Akkadian word *šab/pattu(m)*, which designates a day of evil omen, were the same and that the Hebrew Sabbath was simultaneously appropriating and negating such an ominous day. However, like all the others, this theory has serious philological and etymological problems and cannot be sustained. What remains then is the strong possibility that the Sabbath actually originated among the Israelites, perhaps for the humanitarian reasons that the biblical texts suggest.[7] The Israelites presumably added a special day to the existing six-day week of the biblical world, thereby creating the unit of time, the seven-day week, that culminates in a day with enduring social and religious significance. It was a day that became particularly important in late First Temple times as a benchmark of covenant obedience. And in the exilic and postexilic periods, it took on added significance as an institution that was not dependent on temple cult and that would help the people, including many now living in diaspora communities, maintain their identity and faith.

WATER AND MILITARY CRISES (17:1–16)

Two episodes mark the next stage of the journey. The water issue recurs (vv. 1–7) and a military problem emerges (vv. 8–16) – the problems of drought and enmity again are shown to have had antecedents in Israel's past. The Israelites resume their trek and come to Rephidim, the last stop before the encampment at Sinai and another place that cannot be identified. The name Rephidim, which is from a root meaning "to support," may be linked etiologically to the way Moses' arms are supported in the military episode. The narrative introduces a new

---

[6] Summarized in Gerhard F. Hasel, "Sabbath," *ABD* 5:849–51.
[7] Mayer I. Gruber, "The Source of the Biblical Sabbath," *JANES* 1 (1969): 20–1.

and stronger term to indicate the distress of the people. Now the thirsty people
"quarrel" with Moses and "test" God (v. 2) as well as "complain" about their lot
(v. 3). Fearing that they and their livestock will perish, their unhappiness has
escalated to the point that Moses fears for his life. God immediately intervenes
by directing Moses to go with some of the elders some distance from the people
and to use the very staff with which he had struck the Nile to hit a rock, where
God would be standing.[8] This act brings a flow of water and results in a new
designation for the locale, Massah ("test") and Meribah ("quarrel"); the motif
of testing again appears in the form of the place-name, only this time it is
God who is being tested. The place also seems to be called Horeb (v. 6), the
mountain of God and the place where God first appears to Moses, and perhaps
another designation for Sinai. The geography here is unclear. But the result of
the testing is certain: God has responded positively by providing water. The
dramatic appearance of water from a rock at Horeb not only relieves the thirst
of the people but also imbues the place with cosmic significance, anticipating
the theophany soon to come at the mountain. In the mythologies of the ancient
Near East, the holy or cosmic mountain is the source of all waters.

This episode ends with the penetrating question of the people in their quarrel
with Moses and test of God – "Is the LORD among us or not?" (v. 7). This query
reveals a fundamental concern about divine presence.[9] On the one hand, the
Hebrew Bible contains the notion that God is everywhere, or at least wherever
humans call out to God (e.g., Ps 145:18). On the other hand, the idea of divine
omnipresence is not entirely convincing; like their neighbors, the Israelites felt
that God was somehow nearby and more accessible in specific places and especially in the succession of earthly homes they constructed for the divine presence
(e.g., Ps 63:1–2; 84:1–4). The need to have God nearby reflects attitudes about
God's two-fold role as protector and provider. Because deities are generally understood to be the source of sustenance and also of power to ward off enemies,
believing that God is present is tantamount to trusting that God will provide
material needs and protection. The agonizing question about whether God is
"among us" thus reflects a belief that the presence of God would surely mean
the availability of water.

In the next episode (17:8–16), the protective aspect of God's potent presence
becomes immediately apparent. While still at Rephidim, the Israelites are sud-
denly confronted with their first military challenge, an attack by the Amalekites.
The Israelites are able to overcome the enemy as long as Moses holds high his
hand, which presumably holds his staff, which is now called the "staff of God"
(v. 9), a designation that has not been used since its first appearance in 4:20.

---

[8] In the longer version of this episode in Numbers (20:2–13), God commands Moses to
     speak to the rock. But Moses strikes it, and this ostensible disobedience becomes the
     rationale for his being forbidden to enter the land of Canaan.
[9] B. A. Levine, "On the Presence of God," in *Religions in Antiquity* (1968), 71–87.

Moses does this while atop a "mountain," perhaps Horeb itself, the mountain of God. (The NRSV translation "hill" does not adequately render the poetic word for mountain in v. 9.) The staff held aloft miraculously empowers Joshua and his troops to prevail. This first appearance of Joshua provides no details about his role as Moses' assistant (cf. 24:13; 33:11); his position as heir apparent becomes explicit only in Numbers and Deuteronomy, and of course in the book of Joshua itself. Yet, as the warrior par excellence in the generations before David, his military leadership is prefigured in Israel's first battle.

This prototypical military victory over the Amalekites, the traditional enemy of Israel (see, e.g., 1 Samuel 15) then is commemorated in two ways. In the first mention of writing among the Israelites, God's promise to remove the Amalekites as a threat is recorded in a document, which will serve as a "reminder" that the "remembrance" of Amalek will disappear forever (v. 14). "Reminder" and "remembrance" are both from the root *zkr*, "to remember," and signify the commemorative processes of the biblical narrative. The second act involves the construction of an altar that Moses names "the LORD is my banner" (v. 15), in commemoration of God's part in the victory. Armies in the ancient Near East commonly used banners or standards with insignias, and the name of the altar apparently signifies God's presence in the battle. The accompanying statement, "a hand upon the banner of the LORD," may be an ancient oath, for oaths were often sworn by placing the hand in a significant place. This would be like saying "I swear on God's banner" – that is, in God's name. The concluding statement of this episode portends what will be a reality for the Israelites, especially in the early centuries: an ongoing struggle with the Amalekites, a people who are linked in biblical genealogies (Gen 36:12; 1 Chr 1:35–36) with the Edomite descendents of Esau.[10] This kinship connection makes their traditional enmity with the Israelites all the more troublesome. And the way they are marked for perpetual enmity, if not annihilation, is especially problematic to readers today. Like the slaughter of the firstborn Egyptians and the total destruction of many Canaanite cities as recounted in the book of Joshua, the story of ancient Israel contains dark moments of hatred and violence as well as uplifting messages of love and peace.

ORGANIZATIONAL CRISIS (18:1–27)

To this point, the narrative of the pre-Sinai wilderness trek has presented and solved the problems that continually threaten the Israelites: inadequate food and water, and the external threat of enemy attack. The message for all generations is that God will provide and protect the people. The narrative of journey also has

---

[10]　Cf. Num 14:42, where the Amalekites defeat the Israelites because God "is not with you"; God's absence means the lack of divine protection and thus military defeat. See Gerald L. Mattingly, "Amalek," *ABD* 1:169–71.

indicated the existence of community regulations and perhaps even a shrine. Moses remains the leader, assisted by Aaron and with Joshua waiting in the wings. All that is lacking is the mechanism for dealing with internal discord in order to maintain stability. The stage is set for the final episode before reaching the mountain of revelation. Chapter 18 introduces the problem of community organization and adjudication. At the same time, it is a transitional chapter; as an epilogue to chapters 1–17 and a prologue to chapters 19–40, it is a bridge between the exodus story and the Sinai event.[11] The first part of the chapter (vv. 1–12) brings Moses' father-in-law Jethro back into the narrative and provides an ending to the exodus narrative; and the second part (vv. 13–27), which explains how social order is established with Jethro's guidance, anticipates the guidelines for social order to be revealed in the theophany at the mountain of God.

Jethro appears here for the third and last time in the exodus account. He is first mentioned when Moses flees from Egypt and marries his daughter Zipporah (3:1) and then a second time when Moses leaves him to begin his mission in Egypt (4:18). Now, having heard of the exodus, Jethro reappears. In an aside, we learn that Zipporah has remained with her father during this period. The NRSV gives the impression that she was "sent away" (v. 2) by Moses, but it is more likely that the Hebrew term is referring to the dowry Jethro provides for Zipporah when she finally leaves her family.[12] The names of her two sons (Gershom and Eliezer), with their apt etymologies, are supplied parenthetically (vv. 3–4). Jethro's name appears *seven* times in verses 1–12, making him the focus of the narrative.

Sending word ahead that he is coming with Zipporah and her two sons, Jethro journeys to the mountain of God, where Moses comes out to meet him. They greet each other warmly and appropriately, with Moses bowing before his father-in-law. Once inside Jethro's tent, Moses recounts all that has happened – how God has rescued Moses and the people and sustained them in the wilderness. Learning of God's saving power causes Jethro to acknowledge the sovereignty of Yahweh over all other deities. As in the Song of the Sea (15:11), the manifestation of divine power leads to an acknowledgment of Yahweh's uniqueness, which is not quite the same as acclaiming Yahweh as the only divine being (cf. 12:12).

Jethro's theological statement is accompanied by a ceremonial act; he brings two sacrifices – a "burnt offering" and "sacrifices" to God (v. 12). The Hebrew term (*'ōlâ*) for the former, derived from a verb meaning "to go up, ascend," designates an offering that is completely burned by fire on an altar, with the rising smoke ascending to God in the heavens. The latter term (*zĕbāḥîm*) denotes

[11]   E. Carpenter, "Exodus 18," in *Biblical Itinerary* (1997), 91–108.
[12]   Raymond Westbrook, *Property and the Family in Biblical Law* (JSOTS 113; Sheffield: JSOT Press, 1991), 150–1. See also my discussion of the dowry in the supplementary section, A Closer Look: Marriage in Ancient Israel, pp. 195–9.

sacrifices that are only partially burnt, with the remaining part becoming part of a festive repast to be shared by God and humans. Jethro's sacrifice becomes the occasion for a ceremonial meal with the leaders of the Israelites.[13] Aaron, in anticipation of his eventual priestly role, takes precedence over Moses when they come together "to eat food [NRSV, bread]."[14] Yet Jethro is the one to bless God and make the offerings; Aaron and the others simply join in the subsequent meal. Given the incessant claim that the Israelites desired to leave Egypt to sacrifice to their god, it is astonishing that this Midianite priest is the first actually to do so after the departure from Egypt. His primacy in what is to become a well-ordered set of sacrificial practices, along with the glimpse of his daughter's ritual competency (in the circumcision episode of 4:24–26), lends credence to the possibility of a Midianite role in the origins of Israelite religion (see the discussion of Moses, God, and Midian in the Introduction). Where this sacrifice and meal take place is not specified; but altars for sacrifice, as soon becomes clear at the Sinai theophany, can be constructed of local materials virtually anywhere (20:24–25).

Jethro notices more than the supremacy of Israel's god; he also notices that Israel's leader is overburdened. The second part of chapter 18 (vv. 13–27) presents Jethro's solution to the problem of Moses having sole responsibility for maintaining social order by settling disputes among the people. This is a rather extraordinary episode. It unproblematically depicts a non-Israelite priest, from a people who were enemies of the Israelites for much of the biblical period, as the one who established something as fundamental for community life as an efficient way to achieve social stability. And it also reveals the mixed sacral and civic components of adjudication, so foreign to us in the modern world, that characterized the Israelites and other ancient peoples.

Jethro emphatically proclaims, via the threefold declaration "you will surely wear yourself out … the task is too heavy … you cannot do it alone" (v. 18), that Moses' caseload is too large. He recommends appointing officials who can adjudicate and then provides guidelines for selecting honorable and honest men and for organizing them over units of the population. Moses already knows the "statutes and instructions" (v. 16) – terms that together represent the community regulations (20:17–23:33; see the discussion of terms on p. 179) to be presented at Sinai – and he will teach them to these officials (v. 20). In this scheme, Moses will deal with only the most difficult cases. The result will be "well-being" (NRSV "peace") for all in addition to a more tolerable life for Moses (v. 23). Not surprisingly, Moses accedes to the wise counsel of his father-in-law, who, as a Midianite priestly authority, has expertise in these matters. Jethro then departs.

---

[13] The sacrifical system is explained in A Closer Look: Sacrifice, pp. 248–9.
[14] The word (*lehem*), commonly translated "bread," can also have the more generic meaning "food" as in 18:12.

This touching narrative of an overworked leader accepting sage advice from his father-in-law reveals Israelite notions of how order can be established among members of a community. In the present canonical sequence, this episode precedes the revelation at Sinai; yet the existence of community regulations is assumed (v. 20). But that is not enough. Community leadership – Moses being the prototypical leader – must take care of two concomitant needs. The people first must learn their community's code of behavior. They must know how to follow their life's "way" (*derek*); the Hebrew word literally means "path" or "road" but also is used figuratively, as it is here (v. 20), for the ethically responsible actions of people's lives as they follow the life course. No institutionalized mechanism for instruction is stipulated; it seems to remain in Moses' hands, probably in his priestly capacity but perhaps also in anticipation of his role in communicating God's covenantal law at Sinai. The second necessity – how to handle disputes that inevitably arise – sometimes involves priestly procedures and suggests that teaching the torah regulations for community order was to some extent a priestly responsibility. The role of the priesthood in the late biblical period (cf. Zech 3:6–7), and perhaps throughout, is made part of Israel's past.

The description of mechanisms for handling disputes involves the delegation of some of Moses' leadership responsibilities to others. It is a mistake to think of judiciary functions in the ancient world as if they constituted a discrete branch of community organization, as they do in secular states in the modern world. Rather, rendering justice was an administrative and sometimes a religious function. The word for judge is from a root (*špṭ*) that can refer to a variety of administrative roles, including ruling and delivering or saving in a military sense as well as rendering judgments. Sometimes elders are the community leaders who exercise judicial functions. English translations of the noun form almost always render it "judge," thus masking the administrative context.[15] This Exodus passage, it should be noted, does not use the nominal form. Rather, the verb appears in the four places in chapter 18 (vv. 13, 16, 22, 26) mentioning the rendering of justice; the NRSV's use of the noun "judge(s)" in two of those verses mistakenly implies a discrete judicial role for these officials.

That the noun "judge" does not appear in this passage is probably related to the fact that this term was not a title for forensic officials in ancient Israel, at least in the monarchic period. Not one of the 280 officials mentioned in the Hebrew Bible for the period of the monarchy is so designated; nor is the title found on any of the hundreds of bullae or seals of Israelite officials that date to the period of the Hebrew Bible.[16] Also, a synonymous Hebrew root for judging

---

[15] Hence the misleading designation of "judge" for the charismatic military leaders in the book of Judges.

[16] Nili Sacher Fox, *In the Service of the King: Officialdom in Ancient Israel and Judah* (Cincinnati: Hebrew Union College Press, 2000), Tables A.1 and A.2, 281–305.

(*dyn*) rarely is used as a noun; it appears only twice, both instances in reference to God as the supreme arbiter.[17]

This Exodus description of judicial functions gives the title "officer" (*śar*), not "judge," to the honest men who will adjudicate. That term has military connotations as well as administrative ones, and it is not clear how or if it is related to the judicial organization within lineages that probably existed for much of the biblical period.[18] But it does recall the use in 2:14 of "ruler and judge," meaning a ruler who judges, in reference to Moses. The list in verse 21 of qualifications for these officials – that they should be capable, God-fearing, honest men who detest illicit activity – reveals the ideal that implementation of justice rests on the shoulders of those with impeccable moral and spiritual credentials. Judging means being an arbiter of disputes and restorer of community peace more than conducting trials as such.

Even such well-qualified officials may not be able to handle every problem brought to them. The major or difficult cases are to be brought to Moses. A clue as to what such major cases might entail lies in the phrase "seek (inquire of) God" (v. 15), which is part of the sacral–juridical terminology of the Hebrew Bible. It is elliptical for "seek a word (or pronouncement) from God" and, as such, refers to the manner in which priests, who had divinatory methods for securing divine rulings, handled difficult cases.[19] The nature of such cases is not indicated, but the extended narrative in Num 5:11–31 concerning the woman suspected of marital infidelity may provide some insight into how an impossible situation, with lack of witnesses or admissible evidence, is resolved by sacral procedures.[20] An elliptical reference to divine decision is also found in Exod 22:7–9 (cf. 22:10–11), in which coming before God is meant to assess the veracity of the defendant for which there are no witnesses. Trials by ordeal, in which "the gods decide," have similar dynamics and are common in premodern societies;[21] they deal with the kinds of judicial impasses that lead to hung juries in today's courts. Thus Moses is functioning in a priestly capacity in bringing the disputes between people "before God" (v. 19). Indeed, the tent-of-meeting traditions also include an oracular function (33:7–9) in a sacral context (33:7–9); and the priestly garments of the tabernacle texts include an item involved in "judgment" (28:15–30). This priestly aspect of Moses' adjudication is related to

---

[17] In 1 Sam 24:15 and Ps 68:5; cf. the similar Aramaic term for some postexilic officials in Ezra 4:9 and 7:25.

[18] Paula McNutt, *Reconstructing the Society of Ancient Israel* (Library of Ancient Israel; Louisville, Ky.: Westminster John Knox, 1999), 100–1, 174–6.

[19] The same verb (*drš*, "to seek, inquire of") is used for seeking a prophetic oracle from God; see S. Wagner, "*dārash,*" *TDOT* 3:302–3.

[20] See Rhonda Burnette-Bletsch, "Woman Accused of Unfaithfulness (Num 5:11–31)," *WIS*, 216–17. A Mesopotamian law dealing with a case like the one in Numbers 5 likewise indicates divine resolution; see "The Laws of Hammurabi," translated by Martha Roth (*COS* 2.131), 344 (law §132).

[21] E.g., law §2 in "Hammurabi" (*COS* 2.131), 337.

his priestly role in providing instruction – both were responsibilities of Levitical priests (Lev 10:11; Deut 24:8; 33:8–10) that are often overlooked because of the biblical emphasis on the extensive sacrificial rituals performed and supervised by priests.[22]

The attention to the administration of justice in chapter 18 depicts one other aspect of judicial proceedings. The image of Moses sitting to judge with other people, presumably the disputants and perhaps also witnesses and counsel, standing around him (vv. 13–14, 22) reflects the way judicial matters were handled in the ancient Near East. Monarchic rule in ancient Israel, with the king as chief human adjudicator, involves a room, called "Hall of Justice," with a throne on which the king sits to hear cases (1 Kg 7:7). God as ultimate adjudicator likewise "sits in judgment" (Isa 28:6). The modern concept of a "seated judge" is undoubtedly rooted in this ancient imagery.

Several literary features of the Jethro episode also bear mention. In a variety of ways – such as the *sevenfold* use of a name or phrase, the *seventh* day or *seven* days for sacral events, *seven* parts or items of something – the number seven or its multiple seventy has been used symbolically in the exodus narrative. In this chapter, we find similar roles for the number ten.[23] The people are divided into administrative units by multiples of *ten*. These divisions are hardly literal but rather represent a nested set, perhaps corresponding to the family households, clans or lineages, tribes, and people/nation that formed the segmented sociopolitical structure of ancient Israel during the monarchic as well as premonarchic periods.[24] Two other sets of ten appear in the *tenfold* use of the verbs "to do" and "to come," emphasizing the important actions of this episode. A multiple of ten is also present in the references to Jethro; not only does his name appear *seven* times but his kinship designation "father-in-law" appears thirteen times, making a total of *twenty* references to the Midianite priest. Finally, perhaps the most significant symbolic use of numbers is the *tenfold* use of the Hebrew word *dābār*, which means "thing, word, matter, case." Unfortunately, the repetition of the term is not visible in English translations. But it punctuates the Hebrew text; and, even more than the other uses of ten, it prominently anticipates the *ten* "words," which come to be known as the Ten Commandments or Decalogue, that God soon will reveal to the people.

The chapter comes to a close with Moses' acceptance and implementation of his father-in-law's advice. He has provided for the administration of justice, as an adjunct of community organization. The stage is now set for the theophany that will establish community norms in a covenant context.

---

[22] According to the Chronicler (1 Chr 23:4; 26:29), David appoints "officers and judges," that is, officers who adjudicate, who are from a priestly family and whose judicial work takes them outside the temple precincts.

[23] U. Cassuto, *Commentary* (1983), 222.

[24] P. McNutt, *Reconstructing the Society* (1999), 75–94, 164–8.

THEOPHANY AT THE MOUNTAIN – EXODUS 19

NRSV 19 On the third new moon after the Israelites had gone out of the land of Egypt, on that very day, they came into the wilderness of Sinai. [2]They had journeyed from Rephidim, entered the wilderness of Sinai, and camped in the wilderness; Israel camped there in front of the mountain. [3]Then Moses went up to God; the Lord called to him from the mountain, saying, "Thus you shall say to the house of Jacob, and tell the Israelites: [4]You have seen what I did to the Egyptians, and how I bore you on eagles' wings and brought you to myself. [5]Now therefore, if you obey my voice and keep my covenant, you shall be my treasured possession out of all the peoples. Indeed, the whole earth is mine, [6]but you shall be for me a priestly kingdom and a holy nation. These are the words that you shall speak to the Israelites."

7 So Moses came, summoned the elders of the people, and set before them all these words that the Lord had commanded him. [8]The people all answered as one: "Everything that the Lord has spoken we will do." Moses reported the words of the people to the Lord. [9]Then the Lord said to Moses, "I am going to come to you in a dense cloud, in order that the people may hear when I speak with you and so trust you ever after."

When Moses had told the words of the people to the Lord, [10]the Lord said to Moses: "Go to the people and consecrate them today and tomorrow. Have them wash their clothes [11]and prepare for the third day, because on the third day the Lord will come down upon Mount Sinai in the sight of all the people. [12]You shall set limits for the people all around, saying, 'Be careful not to go up the mountain or to touch the edge of it. Any who touch the mountain shall be put to death. [13]No hand shall touch them, but they shall be stoned or shot with arrows; whether animal or human being, they shall not live.' When the trumpet sounds a long blast, they may go up on the mountain." [14]So Moses went down from the mountain to the people. He consecrated the people, and they washed their clothes. [15]And he said to the people, "Prepare for the third day; do not go near a woman."

16 On the morning of the third day there was thunder and lightning, as well as a thick cloud on the mountain, and a blast of a trumpet so loud that all the people who were in the camp trembled. [17]Moses brought the people out of the camp to meet God. They took their stand at the foot of the mountain. [18]Now Mount Sinai was wrapped in smoke, because the Lord had descended upon it in fire; the smoke went up like the smoke of a kiln, while the whole mountain shook violently. [19]As the blast of the trumpet grew louder and louder, Moses would speak and God would answer him in thunder. [20]When the Lord descended upon Mount Sinai, to the top of the mountain, the Lord summoned Moses to the top of the mountain, and Moses went up. [21]Then the Lord said to Moses, "Go down and warn the people not to break through to the Lord to look; otherwise many of them will perish. [22]Even the priests who approach the Lord must consecrate themselves or the Lord will break out against them." [23]Moses said to the Lord, "The people are not permitted

to come up to Mount Sinai; for you yourself warned us, saying, 'Set limits around the mountain and keep it holy.'" [24]The LORD said to him, "Go down, and come up bringing Aaron with you; but do not let either the priests or the people break through to come up to the LORD; otherwise he will break out against them." [25]So Moses went down to the people and told them.

The Sinai experience itself begins in chapter 19, which initiates a section of the Pentateuch – the encampment at the mountain of God – that extends from 19:1 through the rest of Exodus, the entire book of Leviticus, and well into Numbers. The Song of the Sea in chapter 15 may be the center point of Exodus, marking the end of servitude and the beginning of freedom. But the long Sinai episode is situated in the center of the Pentateuch. There are 68 chapters in the Pentateuch before Exodus 19 and 60 more after the Israelites depart Sinai in Numbers 10. The 58 chapters of Sinai materials thus form the socioreligious core of the Torah literature.

In centering Sinai in the Pentateuch, the shapers of the Torah reinterpret diverse traditions about the past to form a national identity. Features that constitute foundational Israelite beliefs and practices at a later period are integrated into the collective memories of the wilderness experience.[25] The Sinai block of the Torah presents not only the revelation itself but also the covenant, community policies, legal rulings and norms, and the institutionalized expression – a religious edifice with priesthood and offerings – of God's relationship to the Israelites. Recognition of Yahweh as the major, if not only, god of the Israelites, a development that comes at the end of the monarchic period, becomes associated with Sinai, making it seem as if Yahwism was a basic Israelite belief throughout the biblical period.

Given the complexities of the Sinai materials, it is no wonder that its first chapter, perhaps more than any section of the book of Exodus, is marked by profound redactional and source complexity, which generations of scholars have tried in vain to unravel.[26] It also contains a dizzying array of literary genres and motifs: cosmic mountain, covenant making, priestly instructions, and oracular statements – all embedded in the cataclysmic language of God's appearance to humans. Whether the final arrangement of materials has literary coherence or is the result of the attempts of the ancients to accommodate diverse yet equally authoritative traditions cannot be determined. Yet the existing text is a powerful narrative of great significance, presenting as it does the inauguration of an exclusive covenantal relationship between a single god, Yahweh, and a single people, Israel.

[25] M. S. Smith, *Memoirs* (2004), 233–55.
[26] See Marc Brettler, "The Many Faces of God in Exodus 19," *Jews, Christians, and the Theology of the Hebrew Scriptures*, eds. Alice Ogden Bellis and Joel S. Kaminsky (SBL Symposium Series 8; Atlanta: Society of Biblical Literature, 2000), 353–67.

Perhaps the difficult nature of the narrative flow of this chapter, such that one must read it slowly and repeatedly, is a fitting accompaniment to the theological magnitude of what it contains. Its most disorienting aspect is the chronological one; that is, it does not follow a chronological sequence with logical movement between actions that are adjacent in the text. Such temporal disorientation, in fact, permeates the larger Sinai narrative that chapter 19 introduces. It is possible that this characteristic is the result of a literary strategy that favors setting and characterization (of God, Moses, and the people) over story line or plot.[27] Whether or not such spatial rather than temporal orientation is intentional, the narrative impresses the reader more strongly with the scenario and the actors and the ultimate outcome than with the steps along the way. This is indeed a suitable mood for an episode that enters into the mysterious realm of divine revelation, in which the normal sequential processes of historic time are suspended. The experience at Sinai thus is presented not as a past event that happened in time but rather as an ongoing experience of the people whose covenanted relationship with God is understood to have been initiated there.

Chronological order may be suspended in this chapter; but it still is part of the overall journey narrative. As such, it is introduced by the formulaic language containing time information that is used repeatedly to mark the stages of Israel's passage from Egypt to the land of Canaan – on the third new moon after departing Egypt the people leave Rephidim and encamp in the wilderness of Sinai at the mountain of God. Yet there is an important change in the way this information is provided. Typically, the chronological details follow the geographic ones (as in 16:1). Here the order is reversed, thereby foregrounding the time of the arrival at Sinai. What might be the reason for such a shift? The time period is the key. If the departure from Egypt was on the fourteenth day of the first month (later called Nisan), the people would have been traveling for two weeks in that month and then four weeks in the following month. The third new moon thus marked the culmination of six weeks of travel, and the holy Sinai experience would be in the *seventh* week.[28] The sanctity of the number seven, used here for the designation of time, appropriately permeates the formative theophany of the Israelites. The actual moment of revelation, however, never is specified – as if pinning this divine revelation to a precise moment in time would mitigate its timeless qualities. The *seventh* week after departure from Egypt therefore is the beginning of an extended stay at the mountain; according to Num 10:11, which has the Israelites departing from the wilderness of Sinai in the second month of the second year, they remain there for just under a year.

---

[27] Thomas B. Dozeman, "Spatial Form in Exodus 19:1–8a and in the Larger Sinai Narrative," *Semeia* 46 (1989): 87–101.

[28] This coincides with the agricultural festival of Weeks (Pentecost; see 34:22), which became connected with the giving of the Torah at Sinai by the early postbiblical period.

Just as the moment of God's appearance to Moses and the people is vague, perhaps deliberately so, its location likewise is uncertain. Pilgrims and scholars alike have long tried to identify the mountain of God. As early as the Byzantine period, the peak known as Jebel Musa (Mountain of Moses) was believed to be the holy spot; and a monastery was built there by Justinian to commemorate the events of the Exodus narrative. But even earlier traditions place it in southern Sinai. And in more recent times, archaeological surveys in the Sinai Peninsula have produced many more proposals.[29] The fact is that the different names for the mountain (Horeb, Sinai, Mountain of the LORD), as well as divergent and imprecise biblical information, preclude definitive identification of the site. One can only speculate as to whether this indeterminacy is the result of the confluence of different traditions or is a deliberate strategy. Either way, the effect in practical terms is to preclude focus on an extraterritorial site for God's original "home" that might compete with the central and politically important earthly residence situated in the temple in Jerusalem. In theological terms, it reinforces the notion of divine omnipresence by diminishing the possibility that the mountain of God is a single known locale. Searching for Sinai is arguably a futile enterprise that violates the biblical depiction of revelation as a phenomenon that transcends space as well as time. Whether by accident or design, Sinai becomes a concept rather than a place. To put it another way, the cosmic symbolism of the "mountain of the LORD" situates the divine presence, wherever and whenever it transpires, in the center of the cosmos.

The chronological morass of chapter 19 has Moses climbing the mountain three times, with at least one other ascent apparently recounted in 24:1–3. The first of those ascents comes immediately, in verses 3–8. This semipoetic passage contains a concise summary, in a speech from God, of the covenant relationship between God and the people, who immediately affirm the agreement. The speech is addressed (v. 3) to the "house of Jacob," used in parallel to the "children of Israel" (NRSV "Israelites"). The former designation is used only here in the entire book of Exodus. Invoking the name of Jacob has the effect of linking the people who are present at Sinai with the descendents of Jacob mentioned at the outset of the exodus story, in 1:1 and 5, which is the only place in Exodus, in addition to this verse, where Jacob appears independently of the Abraham–Isaac–Jacob set. At the same time, of course, the name of Jacob is part of that set and thus a reminder of the ancestral covenant (as in 2:24; 6:2–4). Covenants have figured in the Genesis narratives that precede the exodus account, but this Sinai covenant declaration introduces new and key elements that go beyond what has been promised to the ancestors. The ancestral covenant is invoked even as it is transformed into a different sort of relationship.

---

[29] Graham I. Davies, "The Wilderness Itineraries and Recent Archaeological Research," in *Studies in the Pentateuch*, ed. John A. Emerton (VTS 22; Leiden: Brill, 1990), 161–75.

There is considerable scholarly debate about whether the special relationship of the Israelites with Yahweh as their god begins at Sinai. Because a strong connection between exodus and Sinai is absent in Exodus 15 and other preexilic biblical texts mentioning Egypt and exodus (e.g., Deut 26:5–10; 1 Sam 12:8; Psalms 105; 114) but appears in postexilic passages (such as Nehemiah 9), the antiquity of a Sinai covenant tradition seems doubtful. The question of a Sinai covenant may never be resolved in historical terms, but the collective memory that links exodus with a covenant at a holy mountain is quite clear in Exodus.

This covenant tradition in Exodus also situates it within the larger Penta-teuchal tradition of an ancestral covenant. The several references to the an-cestors (such as Jacob here at the beginning of the Sinai account) and their covenant imply that God already is uniquely connected with this people. More-over, the term "my people," which is part of technical covenant terminology, occurs repeatedly in the exodus narrative and virtually nowhere else in the Pentateuch (see 6:5–7). Indeed this so-called "election" of the Israelites, and the concomitant response of God to their plight, is assumed throughout Exodus.[30] However, the covenant bond made at Sinai is different in significant ways from the ancestral one.

The first new feature is that the Sinai covenant is inextricably related to the deliverance from oppression in Egypt. God has heard the cries of the peo-ple and has rescued them from the hardships of their forced labor in Egypt. The covenant becomes predicated upon Israelite awareness of divine salva-tion. Like other covenants known from the ancient world (see A Closer Look: Covenant, pp. 148–51), this one is predicated on beneficent actions that the sovereign ruler has performed on behalf of those with whom the covenantal agreement is being established. Indeed, the introduction (v. 2) to the formal "words" of chapter 20 contains a statement about what God has done for the people. Thus Israel's experience of redemption, rather than any specific belief, is presented as the premise on which the covenant rests. A second new element is that of reciprocity, again in keeping with what is known about covenants in the world of the Bible. The ancestral covenant requires nothing of Abraham and Sarah and their descendents.[31] This one includes conditions to which the people must adhere – God expects them to "listen diligently to my voice" (NRSV "obey my voice") and "keep [the stipulations of] my covenant" (v. 5). A third new aspect is the communal nature of the agreement: the revelation and ensuing bond are between God and a people, not an individual. A fourth new factor is the response of the people. Circumcision, sacrifice, and name change mark the response to the ancestral covenant; the people here respond with a simple and clear affirmative statement, repeated nearly verbatim at the covenant ratification

---

[30] T. E. Fretheim, *Exodus* (1991), 208–9.
[31] However, in the overall narrative of the Pentateuch, Abraham is linked with adherence to God's stipulations (Gen 17:1; 18:19; 22:18; and 26:5).

ceremony that concludes the covenant pericope, that they will do all that God says (v. 8; cf. 24:3, 7). Amazingly, there is unanimity in their acquiescence to the terms of the covenant. These refugees from Egypt, who have often grumbled in discord en route to Sinai, now speak through their representative elders "as one."

This initial account of Moses ascending the mountain includes several dramatic and theologically charged images. The first concerns the gender of God (discussed in A Closer Look: Gendered Images of God, pp. 122–3). In the poetic account of the sea crossing in Exodus 15, the warrior metaphor is dominant. But here the soaring image of Israel borne from Egypt on "eagles' wings" likely taps into the notion of the maternal behavior of these swift birds. Although biblical poetry frequently uses the speed of eagles to denote rapidity, one archaic poetic text (Deut 32:10–14) draws upon the way eagles protect their young to depict God's care for the Israelites (called "Jacob" in Deut 32:9 and 15) on their journey.[32] That female birds were understood to exhibit such behavior is clear from the development of this metaphor in the Deuteronomy passage – the eagle that bears Jacob on its wings in the wilderness also feeds and "suckled" (NRSV "nursed") its young with the choicest food and drink. The maternal care of a bird, providing sustenance (as at Marah and Massah/Meribah) as well as protection, can be paired with the powerful intervention of a warrior as complementary gendered images for Israel's god.

The next image is similarly dramatic but also troublesome. Israel, in affirming the covenant relationship, will become God's "treasured possession out of all the peoples" (v. 5). The words "treasured possession" translate a single Hebrew term, *sĕgullâ*. Used only eight times in the Hebrew Bible, its nuances can be determined from its frequent use in documents from Mesopotamia and Ugarit.[33] Unlike a possession that is inherited, a *sĕgullâ* is acquired and thus especially valued. It sometimes represents the personal fortune as opposed to the public wealth of kings. In the figurative sense in which it is used here, the sovereign God views Israel as such a possession, in this way emphasizing God's initiative and personal involvement in acquiring Israel and also denoting how cherished the Israelites are as a people belonging to God.

Yet this seemingly positive imagery of Israel as God's selected treasure is problematic because of the associated language: Israel seems to be unique among "all the peoples" in its relationship with Yahweh, who is depicted as owning the entire world. Exodus 19 intensifies and foregrounds the exclusivity of the relationship between God and this one people. Is this a particularistic vision of a people that God cares for more than any other? Why has God chosen to

---

[32] The use of "Jacob" in the eagle metaphor in both Exodus 19 and Deuteronomy 32 may indicate that one draws upon the other or that they each draw from a common poetic tradition.

[33] Edouard Lipiński, "*sĕgullā*," *TDOT* 10:148.

rescue this one group among all the downtrodden peoples of biblical antiquity? Is there any inclusive and universalistic dimension to Israel's treasured position in the divine scheme? Such troubling questions underlie some of the negative responses to Sinai found in Christian tradition.[34]

Those questions, of course, make sense largely in monotheistic cultures with universalistic notions of the deity. In the polytheistic world of ancient Israel, with national as well as local gods serving and being served by the inhabitants of sociopolitical entities, a god's connection to a single people would have been expected. Still, the moral tension inherent in the notion of the exclusivity of Israel's relationship with God perhaps is resolved to some extent by what follows the "treasured possession" statement. God is not neglecting the rest of the world. It is not only Israel that belongs to God; rather "the whole earth is mine" (v. 5). And Israel has a role in the larger scheme of things, a role that ultimately will include all other peoples. The next verse provides a significant concept in this regard: Israel is to function as if it were a "priestly kingdom and a holy nation" (v. 6).

What can such a designation for a people mean? Priests in the Hebrew Bible are a group set aside, with special responsibilities to carry out the many tasks associated with maintaining God's earthly dwelling, carrying out the sacrificial rituals associated with the sacred precinct, adjudicating certain disputes, and also instructing people in community regulations and traditions. We shall look more closely at both priests and sanctity in due course, but suffice it for now to recognize that the priests were a group apart who participated to a certain extent in divine sanctity yet also mediated God's word and holiness to the community. The notion of holiness can include, as it seems to here, the notion of separateness – of persons set aside from the rest of the populace by their service in God's earthly abode and by their adherence to God's word (see A Closer Look: Holiness, pp. 152–4). It therefore would seem to be an impossibility for an entire people to be conceived of as "priestly" and "holy." It is only in the context of the whole world belonging to God that Israel's sacerdotal role makes sense. We are looking at an elliptical analogy. God has not forgotten about the world and is not ignoring the rest of humanity. Israel with respect to other nations is as priests are to their community – they exemplify sanctity and transmit God's will.[35] All nations will thus ultimately be as is Israel, namely, treasured peoples of God. The concept of a holy nation also implies that holiness can be a corporate attribute.[36]

---

[34] See Brooks Schramm, "Exodus 19 and Its Christian Appropriation," in *Jews, Christians and the Theology of the Hebrew Scriptures*, eds. Alice Ogden Bellis and Joel S. Kaminsky (SBL Symposium Series, 8; Atlanta: Society of Biblical Literature, 2000), 327–52.

[35] This analogy bears some resemblance to the concept of Israel as a witness and "light to the nations" in Second Isaiah.

[36] Baruch A. Levine, "Biblical Concept of Holiness," in *Leviticus* (JPS Torah Commentary; Philadelphia: JPS, 1989), 256.

A CLOSER LOOK: COVENANT

The covenant concept is the dominant metaphor in the Hebrew Bible for the relationship between God and the Israelites. So central is it that it appears in Christian tradition in the designations for two parts of the Christian Bible – Old Testament (= Old Covenant) and New Testament. Drawn from the sphere of politics, a covenant is a legal document binding two parties in which they agree under oath to certain obligations vis-à-vis each other. Yet as a term for such agreements, it is virtually obsolete in English (except perhaps for its somewhat vestigial use in relation to the institution of marriage), making it difficult for contemporary readers to grasp the social and political meaning of covenants in the ancient world.

There are several words for covenant in Hebrew. Perhaps most prominent is *bĕrît*. Its etymology is uncertain, but it most likely is derived from a Semitic word for "clasp" or "bond." Its original meaning has more to do with the concept of an "obligation" between two parties than simply an agreement.[37] The term designates a variety of different agreements mentioned in the Hebrew Bible in addition to the Sinai covenant, but clearly the latter is the chief biblical exemplar of this ancient concept. Another term is *'ēdût*, which refers to a formal contractual agreement, or treaty – perhaps the written form of the covenant. The NRSV translates *'ēdût* as "covenant, although it might better be rendered "treaty," when it is paired with "ark" in the phrase "ark of the covenant" (see Exod 35:22). The national covenant associated with Sinai has been understood, since the middle of the last century, in terms of treaty documents known from other cultures of the ancient Near East. An extensive scholarly literature compares the biblical covenants to those of Israel's neighbors, tries to determine whether the Sinai covenant was an enacted reality for the Israelites or a symbolic construct representing its belief system (or both), and seeks to locate the emergence of the covenant concept within particular periods of Israelite history.[38] Examination of Hittite treaties from the second millennium BCE and Assyrian ones of the first millennium reveals several kinds of treaties. Some were what is known as "parity" treaties, in which equal parties enter into an oath-bound agreement. More relevant are the treaties known as "suzerainty treaties," in which a weaker ruler subordinates himself and his kingdom, in a kind of vassal relationship, to a stronger ruler. The covenant depicted for the ancestors in Genesis, with its

---

[37] Moshe Weinfeld, "*bĕrîth*," *TDOT* 2:255.

[38] George E. Mendenhall and Gary A. Herion ("Covenant" *ABD* 1:1170–1202) review the study of covenant and favor the theory that it was an early part of Israel's political existence.

lack of mutual obligations, would be similar to the covenant associated with Moses and Sinai but would have its prototype in the royal grants that an overlord might make to a lesser monarch.[39]

Suzerain treaties, and to a large extent grants, exhibit a series of formal elements that can be associated with some features of the Sinai covenant as it appears in Exodus and even more of those in Deuteronomy. It is important to remember that this list of elements is somewhat composite and that not all of them are necessarily part of every treaty document that has been recovered from the ancient world. The structure of covenants includes the following parts according to second millennium sources (with first millennium examples being somewhat simpler):

1. *Preamble.* The overlord is identified with the formula "The words of [proper name] ... " This would be equivalent to Exod 20:1–2a.

2. *Historical prologue.* The past beneficent deeds of the overlord toward the vassal are described. The second part of Exod 20:2 (v. 2b) would represent this element.

3. *Stipulations.* This means, first of all, that the vassal owes allegiance to the overlord, just as the Israelites vow to have no other overlord but Yahweh (Exod 20:3); and second, it requires the subordinate ruler to meet the specific demands that are listed. The entire contents of the Sinai covenant – the commandments and rulings, laws and judgments – might be considered the stipulations of the Sinai covenant.

4. *Deposition and reading of the document.* The treaty is deposited in a sacred place, usually the sanctuary of the deity. The tabernacle ark is depicted as a repository for the covenant (e.g., Exod 25:21). The treaty is also to be read periodically in public, which means it is binding on the people that the vassal rules. Biblical parallels to this are harder to ascertain, but the notion of citizens appearing several times a year "before the LORD God" (Exod 23:17) is arguably related to periodic public readings at festivals. Note also that Moses reads the covenant to the people in 24:7.

5. *Witnesses.* The witnesses are exclusively deities, hardly to be expected in the biblical covenant in which Israel's god happens to be the overlord and also greater than all other gods. But perhaps the pillars Moses erects in 24:4 are the equivalent (cf. Josh 24:26–27, where a stone placed in a shrine serves as witness to the covenant).

---

[39] Richard Elliott Friedman, "Torah and Covenant," in *Oxford Study Bible*, eds. M. Jack Suggs, Katherine Doob Sakenfeld, and James R. Mueller (New York: Oxford University Press, 1992), 156–60.

6. *Blessings and curses.* The consequences of obedience and disobedience are
    set forth as rewards and punishments respectively. Exodus seems to lack
    this element, but Leviticus (chap. 26) and Deuteronomy (chap. 28) both
    have extensive and graphic sets of blessings and curses.

Once these structural elements were in place, the document would be ratified
and formally accepted in rituals that included animal sacrifice. The assent of
the Israelites in 19:8 and 24:3 and 7 may represent such ratification, and the
accompanying sacrificial ritual is described in 24:4–6.

In sum, the items in this list have striking analogues to aspects of the Sinai
covenant. Moreover, the biblical language enjoining the people to "keep my
covenant," found in 19:5 and in many other biblical texts, echoes the instructions given in ancient Near Eastern documents by a sovereign to his officials,
commanding them to adhere to the stipulations imposed by a covenant.[40] Although there is disagreement about when the covenant metaphor became part
of biblical tradition and whether an actual covenant document ever served as
a charter for communal life during any period of Israelite history, the origin
of covenant language in these political arrangements of the ancient world is
not disputed. As important as the affinities are, however, it is also important
to acknowledge significant differences. The Near Eastern treaties are between
individuals: a strong ruler and one or more weaker ones who enter into a de-
pendency relationship with the suzerain. There may be a public dimension to
the vassal's role, in that the people he rules are implicated in the document to
which he agrees. But those people are not themselves party to the agreement. In
contrast, the Israelites are the corporate party to the agreement in the biblical
covenant. This unique feature of the Sinai covenant emerges as an important
and complicated aspect of the relationship between Israel and God. The adherence to the covenant involves the behavior of the entire populace, so that
the obedience of a portion of the people, no matter how large that portion is,
can be compromised or threatened by the disobedience of others, even if they
are few.

Only as an ideal could an entire people maintain the detailed stipulations
of the Sinai covenant. Would this mean the ultimate demise of the inevitably
disobedient people? One other unique feature of the covenant paradigm in
ancient Israel provides at least a partial solution to that dilemma. Israel as a
community may be one party to the covenant, but the other party is their god.

---

[40] Moshe Weinfeld, "The Common Heritage of Covenantal Traditions in the Ancient
World," in *I Trattati nel Mondo Antic: Forma, Ideologia, Funzione*, eds. Luciano Can-
forna, Mario Liverani, and Carlo Zaccagnini (Rome: "L'Erma" di Breitschneider, 1990),
175–91.

No treaty document known from the ancient Near East has the deity as the overlord. It is not impossible that other ancient peoples conceptualized their relationship with a deity in covenant terms, for we know that some peoples considered themselves the people of a certain god. Yet there is no documentary evidence establishing such relationships in treaty form. Moreover, those peoples had more than one deity, a fact that might have compromised the effectiveness of a treaty. The biblical covenant is exclusively with Yahweh. The deity is thereby placed above all political systems, and the ethic of the covenant is grounded in the transcendent.[41]

In thinking of the punitive aspect of the covenant, should its stipulations be disobeyed, it is important to note that Israel's relationship with God is characterized by other metaphors that ameliorate the implications of the covenant metaphor. For example, the parent metaphor, with God as parent and Israel as child, invokes gracious love and forgiveness as well as punishment for misdeeds. Consider, too, that the redemptive acts of God, on which the covenant is predicated, also serve as the model for subsequent graciousness – toward the people bonded to God in the covenant, and ultimately to all peoples.

The second account in Exodus 19 of Moses' ascent of the mountain to receive a direct revelation from God is found in verses 9–15. Yet the information in these verses is hardly consistent. There seem to be repeated versions of Moses' report to God. We do not quite see Moses going up to the mountain, yet at the end of the instructions that God gives to him, we learn that he comes down from the mountain (v. 14). It is not clear whether the people themselves can ascend the mountain, as verse 13 suggests, or must refrain from doing so according to verse 12. And it is not clear whether the people will see God or simply hear God's voice. However we are to understand the nature of the theophany, it is clear that the concept of revelation in these verses is embedded in ideas of holiness and ambiguity about how it may be approached. The extraordinary power of the concentrated holiness of divine revelation cannot be met with simple language and behavior, and the various responses are intermingled in these verses in overlapping and at times contradictory ways. The first mention of divine appearance in verse 9 proclaims that God will be in a "dense cloud," an image reminiscent of the pillars of fire and cloud of 13:21–22. But here a new dimension is given to the cloud as marker of divine presence – it apparently is intended to hide God's physical manifestation, for the people are meant to hear but not see the deity, who is the epicenter of holiness.

---

[41] George E. Mendenhall, "The Suzerainty Treaty Structure: Thirty Years Later," in *Religion and Law: Biblical-Judaic and Islamic Perspectives*, eds. Edwin B. Firmage, Bernard G. Weiss, and John W. Welch (Winona Lake, Ind.: Eisenbrauns, 1990), 97–8.

Holiness is a major concept in Exodus, reflecting at least in part the interests of priestly writers or editors. The term "holy" is used dozens of times, mainly in relation to the personnel, utensils, sacrifices, garments, and space associated with the Tabernacle in chapters 25–40. But the concept of sanctity in the sphere of human life already has appeared: first, with respect to place, in 3:5 in the burning bush episode, where the "holy ground" marking God's appearance to Moses at Horeb may be the same as the holy mountain, Sinai, of this chapter (19:23); second, with respect to time, in 16:23 in the establishment of the Sabbath; and third, with respect to people, in the designation of Israel as a holy nation in this chapter (19:6).

A CLOSER LOOK: HOLINESS

The concern for holiness in the Hebrew Bible exhibits certain characteristics that may seem strange to us in the modern world, where holiness is largely an abstract concept. Holiness in ancient Israel is difficult to define or understand, for it is linked with the nature of God and therefore is not fully knowable. A quality of mystery surrounds many uses of terms for holiness. The root (*qdš*) for "holy" and "holiness" appears hundreds of times in the Hebrew Bible and also has cognates in other Semitic languages, yet its etymology is still debated.[42] Moreover, not a single synonym for "holy" can be found in the Hebrew Bible, although "purity" in a technical, priestly sense (indicating ritual completeness or perfection) often overlaps with "holy."[43]

Holiness in biblical antiquity is a highly positive quality that sets places, people, animals, things, and time apart from the mundane, ordinary, or profane. It may be an inherent attribute, or it may be acquired through a ritual act. For people as well as objects and animals, it may involve the concept of consecration to the deity through the removal of impurity and evil. Whether inherent or acquired, all the manifestations of sanctity in the human realm are related to God as their source and major embodiment. The archaic Song of the Sea in Exodus 15 proclaims divine sanctity in announcing that God is "majestic in holiness" (v. 11).

Humans characteristically wish to feel the nearness of the holy God, as the source of protection and sustenance. Yet they cannot come too close to the cosmic center of holiness, God, because of God's enormous power and because all humans lack the kind of moral and physical perfection that characterizes divine sanctity. Thus in many biblical contexts, especially with respect to cultic matters in the book of Leviticus, approaching God to bring an offering or

[42] Helmer Ringgren and Walter Kornfeld, "*qdš*," *TDOT* 12:522–7.
[43] For the complex relationship between "holy/profane" and "pure/impure" in the divine and human spheres, see Philip Peter Jenson, *Graded Holiness: A Key to the Priestly Conception of the World* (JSOTS 106; Sheffield: Sheffield Academic Press, 1992), 40–54.

sacrifice means trying first to rid oneself of imperfections or contaminations by washing and other means.

Although holiness is a positive concept, in the ancient world it is also imbued in some of its manifestations with danger. Approaching God, the center of holiness, also means taking absolute care not to come too close, for divine power can be lethal as well as the source of life. In ancient Israel, as throughout the ancient Near East, the earthly residences of deities – temples – were enclosed domains, inaccessible to nonpriests (explained in the supplementary section, A Closer Look: Temples and Temple Service, pp. 220–2). Such precincts were permeated with the holiness of their divine resident, and all the appurtenances and personnel were deemed holy. A striking feature of the sanctity of a temple was that even within it there were gradations of holiness, with the inner sanctum, usually the place were a representation of the deity was placed, being most holy and the outer courts having a lesser degree of holiness. An important quality of this cultic holiness was contagion; that is, holiness and its ritual opposite, defilement, were virtually physical properties that could spread by contact. For this reason, a nonpriest (and thus someone not completely holy) could not touch any part of the holy domain lest it become defiled; this policy in effect created a protective barrier between the mysterious presence of God and the ordinary world.[44] Nor could the holiness of the sacred precinct be allowed to go outside it. Improper transgression of the boundary between the sacred and nonsacred realms could have dire consequences.

The reasons for such extreme separation between the holy and the ordinary, along with regulations to maintain it, are not clear. Perhaps the representation of divine power as hierarchically organized, from the most holy center to its less holy periphery, originated in support of a hierarchy of priestly control of sacral institutions as well as in a belief in the awesome destructive as well as beneficent power of deities. Anthropological analysis suggests that the radical separation between the holy and the profane, and the extraordinary measures taken to preserve that separation, may also be related to the way premodern peoples sought to order their world.[45] Another consideration is that the safety of the expensive cultic appurtenances and other resources kept within sacred precincts was involved in the development of these notions of sacred space. The idea of "dangerous sanctity" might deter elements seeking to steal some of the wealth of a sacral institution.

Holiness may be an essentially cultic concept, as many of the references to it in Exodus indicate. However, it also becomes extended in biblical usage to support human efforts to emulate the moral perfection of God. A long section

---

[44] Menahem Haran, *Temples and Temple Service in Ancient Israel* (New York: Oxford University Press, 1978), 175–81.

[45] P. P. Jenson, *Graded Holiness* (1992), 56–88.

(chaps. 17–26) of Leviticus is often called the "Holiness Code" because the rationale it provides for adhering to God's teachings is that God is holy (e.g., Lev 19:2). Surely the notion of a priestly and "holy nation" in Exodus 19 is rooted in the hope that everyone will be harmonized with divine sanctity and essential goodness so that evil and discord will disappear from the world. In this view, the opposition between sacred and profane, which seems to be part of cultures everywhere, will essentially vanish once Israel – and everyone else – embraces the way of life outlined in the covenant.

In the Sinai episode, the mountain serves as the equivalent of an earthly shrine of God, the equivalent of the tabernacle or temple. The gradations of holiness that characterize constructed shrines and temples in the biblical world have their equivalent in Sinai's zones.[46] The holiest spot is the summit, approachable only by Moses (19:20). The lower part of the mountain is a second zone of holiness; it seems to be accessible to Aaron and a select few priests (19:22; cf. 24). The area at the base of the mountain is the third zone, where the sanctified people can gather (19:12, 17, 23). Yet there are anomalies to this scheme. A somewhat different and perhaps more democratic tradition is preserved in the second half of verse 13,[47] which implies that when the trumpet sounds, everyone can ascend the mountain. Similarly, in verse 24, Aaron seems to share with Moses accessibility to the top of the mountain, with priests and people alike relegated to the bottom. This may reflect a tradition in which Aaron and the priesthood have an especially prominent role.

Whatever their access to the mountain, the people first must be consecrated by Moses (vv. 10–11, 14–15). This involves the washing of clothes (19:10) – utter cleanliness is a condition of holiness, not so much as a removal of dirt as a restoring of garments to their pristine state. The people also are to refrain from having sex (19:15), for the emission of bodily fluids (i.e., semen) renders one temporarily less than whole and imperfect. Because the directive to refrain from sexual relations is directed toward men, forbidding them to "go near a woman," the Israelites who are to experience the Sinai revelation appear to be males only. Yet the whole community seems to be present at Sinai, for the text repeatedly refers collectively to the "people" and to the "Israelites," which usually are gender inclusive terms. The phrasing of verse 15 may simply be conventional male language referring to sexual intercourse, typical of the androcentric orientation of the Hebrew Bible but not intended to exclude women from the experience of the theophany or from being party to the contents of the revelation. Note the inclusive language of Deuteronomy (29:10–11; 31:12) in a similar covenant context.

---

[46] The zones of holiness are explained in the disussion of the tabernacle and are represented in the table Tabernacle Texts; see pp. 224–5.

[47] See M. Brettler, "Many Faces of God," in *Jews, Christians, and the Theology* (2000), 362–3.

The belief that improper crossing of the boundaries between the holy and profane realms can have dire consequences (19:21, 24) underlies the instructions of 19:12–13, which specifies that any unqualified people (or even animals) must not touch the holy mountain lest they be put to death. Moreover, they are to be put to death by methods – stoning or shooting (with arrows) – that can be done from a distance. The reason for this is that those who are not qualified to touch the mountain, should they do so, will have contracted dangerous holiness, which is contagious; those who execute them must not have physical contact with them lest they too contract that dangerous quality.

Having prepared the people for being in the presence of God, Moses is ready for the third ascent of the mountain (vv. 16–20). The ensuing theophany – the most direct appearance of God to an entire people in the Hebrew Bible – is couched in the language of powerful phenomena of nature. In addition to the thick cloud of verse 9 (cf. 20:21; 24:15–18), thunder and lightning, enveloping smoke, and violent shaking (vv. 16–18; cf. 20:18) are present. This language has motivated attempts to locate a volcano in the Sinai Peninsula and attribute the Exodus 19 imagery to a Late Bronze Age eruption. However, there are no active volcanoes in Sinai. Also, the imagery of verses 9 and 16–19 (and 20:18) includes features that are not part of seismic activity. But most important is the fact that the intense noise and movement, along with visual extremes of lightning and dark clouds and smoke, are stereotypical features of theophany in ancient Semitic poetry, especially Ugaritic texts depicting storms or the convulsing of nature as a signal of divine presence.[48] Such combinations of seismic and meteorological language appear in other biblical passages, especially poetic ones, depicting the extraordinary power of God (e.g., Judg 5:4–5 and Hab 3:3–6). Ear-splitting trumpet blasts (vv. 16, 19; cf. 20:18) also accompany the images of violent natural phenomena, adding to the aural aspects of the theophany and perhaps also reflecting the use of trumpets at oath-making ceremonies (cf. 2 Chr 15:15).

The language of natural cataclysm is typical of attempts to describe what people believe to have been extraordinary events. One example from more recent times is instructive. The radical political rupture that marked the end of British dominance of the American colonies was described in seismic terms by observers who wrote close to the events of the 1770s. A late eighteenth-century commentator on the Boston Tea Party claims that Massachusetts Bay was "the *Volcano* from whence issued all the Smoak, Flame, & Lava which hath since enveloped the whole British american continent for the Length of above 1700 Miles."[49] And an early nineteenth-century historian describes the American Revolution in these terms: "Public commotions in human affairs, like the shocks of

---

[48] Mark S. Smith, *The Early History of God: Yahweh and the Other Deities of Ancient Israel* (San Francisco: Harper and Row, 1990), 49–55.

[49] Peter Oliver, *Origins and Progress of the American Rebellion*, eds. Douglass Adair and John A. Schutz (San Marino, Calif.: Huntington Library, 1961; odp, 1781), 9.

nature, convulse the lofty mountains, which have arisen for ages above the clouds, beneath the skies."[50] Metaphors drawn from nature, in these two instances, describe the cataclysmic end of British rule; in fire and brimstone, the old order must expire before the new order can begin.

One can imagine that the shapers of the Sinai tradition similarly believed that the theophany of God at Sinai marked a new order in human affairs, one that involved not simply the self-manifestation of God but also the inextricable connection of God's presence to the content of that prototypical event: the covenant as a charter for Israelite communal existence. The theophany is understood to be earthshaking in the principles it sets forth for the community. The explosive language of revelation initiates the "words" that God communicates to the people and that constitute most of the rest of Exodus.

The vehicle for conveying the charter for Israelite life to the people is none other than Moses, whose role in chapter 19 is truly remarkable, perhaps even more so than in the narrative up to this point. His name appears throughout this chapter, *fourteen* times in all; fourteen is twice the symbolic number seven and signifies his centrality in this episode. Moses' unique status also is manifest in the fact that he apparently is the only one allowed to approach the top of the mountain, the area closest to the presence of God. Indeed, with the exception of the "words" (i.e., Decalogue) of chapter 20, which God speaks directly to the people, all the other texts – the community regulations and the tabernacle instructions – presented as the content of the covenant are mediated through Moses. Moses looms large, his presence enveloping and lending authority to the diverse traditions gathered into the narrative of the Sinai theophany.

COVENANT – EXODUS 20:1–24:18

NRSV 20 Then God spoke all these words: [2]I am the LORD your God, who brought you out of the land of Egypt, out of the house of slavery; [3]you shall have no other gods before[a] me.

4 You shall not make for yourself an idol, whether in the form of anything that is in heaven above, or that is on the earth beneath, or that is in the water under the earth. [5]You shall not bow down to them or worship them; for I the LORD your God am a jealous God, punishing children for the iniquity of parents, to the third and the fourth generation of those who reject me, [6]but showing steadfast love to the thousandth generation of those who love me and keep my commandments.

---

[50] Mercy Otis Warren, *History of the Rise, Progress, and Termination of the American Revolution, Interspersed with Biographical, Political, and Moral Observations* (3 vols.; Boston: E. Larkin, 1805), 1: 216.

[a] Or *besides*

7 You shall not make wrongful use of the name of the LORD your God, for the LORD will not acquit anyone who misuses his name.

8 Remember the sabbath day, and keep it holy. ⁹Six days you shall labor and do all your work. ¹⁰But the seventh day is a sabbath to the LORD your God; you shall not do any work – you, your son or your daughter, your male or female slave, your livestock, or the alien resident in your towns. ¹¹For in six days the LORD made heaven and earth, the sea, and all that is in them, but rested the seventh day; therefore the LORD blessed the sabbath day and consecrated it.

12 Honor your father and your mother, so that your days may be long in the land that the LORD your God is giving you.

13 You shall not murder.ᵃ

14 You shall not commit adultery.

15 You shall not steal.

16 You shall not bear false witness against your neighbor.

17 You shall not covet your neighbor's house; you shall not covet your neighbor's wife, or male or female slave, or ox, or donkey, or anything that belongs to your neighbor.

18 When all the people witnessed the thunder and lightning, the sound of the trumpet, and the mountain smoking, they were afraid and trembled and stood at a distance, ¹⁹and said to Moses, "You speak to us, and we will listen; but do not let God speak to us, or we will die." ²⁰Moses said to the people, "Do not be afraid; for God has come only to test you and to put the fear of him upon you so that you do not sin." ²¹Then the people stood at a distance, while Moses drew near to the thick darkness where God was.

22 The LORD said to Moses: Thus you shall say to the Israelites: "You have seen for yourselves that I spoke with you from heaven. ²³You shall not make gods of silver alongside me, nor shall you make for yourselves gods of gold. ²⁴You need make for me only an altar of earth and sacrifice on it your burnt offerings and your offerings of well-being, your sheep and your oxen; in every place where I cause my name to be remembered I will come to you and bless you. ²⁵But if you make for me an altar of stone, do not build it of hewn stones; for if you use a chisel upon it you profane it. ²⁶You shall not go up by steps to my altar, so that your nakedness may not be exposed on it."

NRSV 21 These are the ordinances that you shall set before them:

2 When you buy a male Hebrew slave, he shall serve six years, but in the seventh he shall go out a free person, without debt. ³If he comes in single, he shall go out single; if he comes in married, then his wife shall go out with him. ⁴If his master gives him a wife and she bears him sons or daughters, the wife and her children shall be her master's and he shall go out alone. ⁵But if the slave declares, "I love my master, my wife, and my children; I will not go out a free person," ⁶then his master

---

ᵃ Or *kill*

shall bring him before God. He shall be brought to the door or the doorpost; and his master shall pierce his ear with an awl; and he shall serve him for life.

7 When a man sells his daughter as a slave, she shall not go out as the male slaves do. [8]If she does not please her master, who designated her for himself, then he shall let her be redeemed; he shall have no right to sell her to a foreign people, since he has dealt unfairly with her. [9]If he designates her for his son, he shall deal with her as with a daughter. [10]If he takes another wife to himself, he shall not diminish the food, clothing, or marital rights of the first wife. [11]And if he does not do these three things for her, she shall go out without debt, without payment of money.

12 Whoever strikes a person mortally shall be put to death. [13]If it was not premeditated, but came about by an act of God, then I will appoint for you a place to which the killer may flee. [14]But if someone willfully attacks and kills another by treachery, you shall take the killer from my altar for execution.

15 Whoever strikes father or mother shall be put to death.

16 Whoever kidnaps a person, whether that person has been sold or is still held in possession, shall be put to death.

17 Whoever curses father or mother shall be put to death.

18 When individuals quarrel and one strikes the other with a stone or fist so that the injured party, though not dead, is confined to bed, [19]but recovers and walks around outside with the help of a staff, then the assailant shall be free of liability, except to pay for the loss of time, and to arrange for full recovery.

20 When a slaveowner strikes a male or female slave with a rod and the slave dies immediately, the owner shall be punished. [21]But if the slave survives a day or two, there is no punishment; for the slave is the owner's property.

22 When people who are fighting injure a pregnant woman so that there is a miscarriage, and yet no further harm follows, the one responsible shall be fined what the woman's husband demands, paying as much as the judges determine. [23]If any harm follows, then you shall give life for life, [24]eye for eye, tooth for tooth, hand for hand, foot for foot, [25]burn for burn, wound for wound, stripe for stripe.

26 When a slaveowner strikes the eye of a male or female slave, destroying it, the owner shall let the slave go, a free person, to compensate for the eye. [27]If the owner knocks out a tooth of a male or female slave, the slave shall be let go, a free person, to compensate for the tooth.

28 When an ox gores a man or a woman to death, the ox shall be stoned, and its flesh shall not be eaten; but the owner of the ox shall not be liable. [29]If the ox has been accustomed to gore in the past, and its owner has been warned but has not restrained it, and it kills a man or a woman, the ox shall be stoned, and its owner also shall be put to death. [30]If a ransom is imposed on the owner, then the owner shall pay whatever is imposed for the redemption of the victim's life. [31]If it gores a boy or a girl, the owner shall be dealt with according to this same rule. [32]If the ox gores a male or female slave, the owner shall pay to the slaveowner thirty shekels of silver, and the ox shall be stoned.

33 If someone leaves a pit open, or digs a pit and does not cover it, and an ox or a donkey falls into it, ³⁴the owner of the pit shall make restitution, giving money to its owner, but keeping the dead animal.

35 If someone's ox hurts the ox of another, so that it dies, then they shall sell the live ox and divide the price of it; and the dead animal they shall also divide. ³⁶But if it was known that the ox was accustomed to gore in the past, and its owner has not restrained it, the owner shall restore ox for ox, but keep the dead animal.

NRSV 22 When someone steals an ox or a sheep, and slaughters it or sells it, the thief shall pay five oxen for an ox, and four sheep for a sheep.^a The thief shall make restitution, but if unable to do so, shall be sold for the theft. ⁴When the animal, whether ox or donkey or sheep, is found alive in the thief's possession, the thief shall pay double.

2 If a thief is found breaking in, and is beaten to death, no bloodguilt is incurred; ³but if it happens after sunrise, bloodguilt is incurred.

5 When someone causes a field or vineyard to be grazed over, or lets livestock loose to graze in someone else's field, restitution shall be made from the best in the owner's field or vineyard.

6 When fire breaks out and catches in thorns so that the stacked grain or the standing grain or the field is consumed, the one who started the fire shall make full restitution.

7 When someone delivers to a neighbor money or goods for safekeeping, and they are stolen from the neighbor's house, then the thief, if caught, shall pay double. ⁸If the thief is not caught, the owner of the house shall be brought before God, to determine whether or not the owner had laid hands on the neighbor's goods.

9 In any case of disputed ownership involving ox, donkey, sheep, clothing, or any other loss, of which one party says, "This is mine," the case of both parties shall come before God; the one whom God condemns shall pay double to the other.

10 When someone delivers to another a donkey, ox, sheep, or any other animal for safekeeping, and it dies or is injured or is carried off, without anyone seeing it, ¹¹an oath before the LORD shall decide between the two of them that the one has not laid hands on the property of the other; the owner shall accept the oath, and no restitution shall be made. ¹²But if it was stolen, restitution shall be made to its owner. ¹³If it was mangled by beasts, let it be brought as evidence; restitution shall not be made for the mangled remains.

14 When someone borrows an animal from another and it is injured or dies, the owner not being present, full restitution shall be made. ¹⁵If the owner was present, there shall be no restitution; if it was hired, only the hiring fee is due.

16 When a man seduces a virgin who is not engaged to be married, and lies with her, he shall give the bride-price for her and make her his wife. ¹⁷But if her

---

^a Verses 2, 3, and 4 rearranged thus: 3b, 4, 2, 3a

father refuses to give her to him, he shall pay an amount equal to the bride-price for virgins.

18 You shall not permit a female sorcerer to live.

19 Whoever lies with an animal shall be put to death.

20 Whoever sacrifices to any god, other than the LORD alone, shall be devoted to destruction.

21 You shall not wrong or oppress a resident alien, for you were aliens in the land of Egypt. [22]You shall not abuse any widow or orphan. [23]If you do abuse them, when they cry out to me, I will surely heed their cry; [24]my wrath will burn, and I will kill you with the sword, and your wives shall become widows and your children orphans.

25 If you lend money to my people, to the poor among you, you shall not deal with them as a creditor; you shall not exact interest from them. [26]If you take your neighbor's cloak in pawn, you shall restore it before the sun goes down; [27]for it may be your neighbor's only clothing to use as cover; in what else shall that person sleep? And if your neighbor cries out to me, I will listen, for I am compassionate.

28 You shall not revile God, or curse a leader of your people.

29 You shall not delay to make offerings from the fullness of your harvest and from the outflow of your presses.

The firstborn of your sons you shall give to me. [30]You shall do the same with your oxen and with your sheep: seven days it shall remain with its mother; on the eighth day you shall give it to me.

31 You shall be people consecrated to me; therefore you shall not eat any meat that is mangled by beasts in the field; you shall throw it to the dogs.

NRSV 23 You shall not spread a false report. You shall not join hands with the wicked to act as a malicious witness. [2]You shall not follow a majority in wrongdoing; when you bear witness in a lawsuit, you shall not side with the majority so as to pervert justice; [3]nor shall you be partial to the poor in a lawsuit.

4 When you come upon your enemy's ox or donkey going astray, you shall bring it back.

5 When you see the donkey of one who hates you lying under its burden and you would hold back from setting it free, you must help to set it free.

6 You shall not pervert the justice due to your poor in their lawsuits. [7]Keep far from a false charge, and do not kill the innocent and those in the right, for I will not acquit the guilty. [8]You shall take no bribe, for a bribe blinds the officials, and subverts the cause of those who are in the right.

9 You shall not oppress a resident alien; you know the heart of an alien, for you were aliens in the land of Egypt.

10 For six years you shall sow your land and gather in its yield; [11]but the seventh year you shall let it rest and lie fallow, so that the poor of your people may eat; and what they leave the wild animals may eat. You shall do the same with your vineyard, and with your olive orchard.

12 Six days you shall do your work, but on the seventh day you shall rest, so that your ox and your donkey may have relief, and your homeborn slave and the resident alien may be refreshed. ¹³Be attentive to all that I have said to you. Do not invoke the names of other gods; do not let them be heard on your lips.

14 Three times in the year you shall hold a festival for me. ¹⁵You shall observe the festival of unleavened bread; as I commanded you, you shall eat unleavened bread for seven days at the appointed time in the month of Abib, for in it you came out of Egypt.

No one shall appear before me empty-handed.

16 You shall observe the festival of harvest, of the first fruits of your labor, of what you sow in the field. You shall observe the festival of ingathering at the end of the year, when you gather in from the field the fruit of your labor. ¹⁷Three times in the year all your males shall appear before the Lord GOD.

18 You shall not offer the blood of my sacrifice with anything leavened, or let the fat of my festival remain until the morning.

19 The choicest of the first fruits of your ground you shall bring into the house of the LORD your God.

You shall not boil a kid in its mother's milk.

20 I am going to send an angel in front of you, to guard you on the way and to bring you to the place that I have prepared. ²¹Be attentive to him and listen to his voice; do not rebel against him, for he will not pardon your transgression; for my name is in him.

22 But if you listen attentively to his voice and do all that I say, then I will be an enemy to your enemies and a foe to your foes.

23 When my angel goes in front of you, and brings you to the Amorites, the Hittites, the Perizzites, the Canaanites, the Hivites, and the Jebusites, and I blot them out, ²⁴you shall not bow down to their gods, or worship them, or follow their practices, but you shall utterly demolish them and break their pillars in pieces. ²⁵You shall worship the LORD your God, and I will bless your bread and your water; and I will take sickness away from among you. ²⁶No one shall miscarry or be barren in your land; I will fulfill the number of your days. ²⁷I will send my terror in front of you, and will throw into confusion all the people against whom you shall come, and I will make all your enemies turn their backs to you. ²⁸And I will send the pestilence[a] in front of you, which shall drive out the Hivites, the Canaanites, and the Hittites from before you. ²⁹I will not drive them out from before you in one year, or the land would become desolate and the wild animals would multiply against you. ³⁰Little by little I will drive them out from before you, until you have increased and possess the land. ³¹I will set your borders from the Red Sea[b] to the sea of the Philistines, and from the wilderness to the Euphrates; for I will hand over to you the inhabitants of the land, and you shall drive them out before you. ³²You shall make

---

[a]   Or *hornets:* Meaning of Heb uncertain
[b]   Or *Sea of Reeds*

no covenant with them and their gods. [33] They shall not live in your land, or they will make you sin against me; for if you worship their gods, it will surely be a snare to you.

NRSV 24 Then he said to Moses, "Come up to the LORD, you and Aaron, Nadab, and Abihu, and seventy of the elders of Israel, and worship at a distance. [2] Moses alone shall come near the LORD; but the others shall not come near, and the people shall not come up with him."

3 Moses came and told the people all the words of the LORD and all the ordinances; and all the people answered with one voice, and said, "All the words that the LORD has spoken we will do." [4] And Moses wrote down all the words of the LORD. He rose early in the morning, and built an altar at the foot of the mountain, and set up twelve pillars, corresponding to the twelve tribes of Israel. [5] He sent young men of the people of Israel, who offered burnt offerings and sacrificed oxen as offerings of well-being to the LORD. [6] Moses took half of the blood and put it in basins, and half of the blood he dashed against the altar. [7] Then he took the book of the covenant, and read it in the hearing of the people; and they said, "All that the LORD has spoken we will do, and we will be obedient." [8] Moses took the blood and dashed it on the people, and said, "See the blood of the covenant that the LORD has made with you in accordance with all these words."

9 Then Moses and Aaron, Nadab, and Abihu, and seventy of the elders of Israel went up, [10] and they saw the God of Israel. Under his feet there was something like a pavement of sapphire stone, like the very heaven for clearness. [11] God did not lay his hand on the chief men of the people of Israel; also they beheld God, and they ate and drank.

12 The LORD said to Moses, "Come up to me on the mountain, and wait there; and I will give you the tablets of stone, with the law and the commandment, which I have written for their instruction." [13] So Moses set out with his assistant Joshua, and Moses went up into the mountain of God. [14] To the elders he had said, "Wait here for us, until we come to you again; for Aaron and Hur are with you; whoever has a dispute may go to them."

15 Then Moses went up on the mountain, and the cloud covered the mountain. [16] The glory of the LORD settled on Mount Sinai, and the cloud covered it for six days; on the seventh day he called to Moses out of the cloud. [17] Now the appearance of the glory of the LORD was like a devouring fire on the top of the mountain in the sight of the people of Israel. [18] Moses entered the cloud, and went up on the mountain. Moses was on the mountain for forty days and forty nights.

COMMUNITY POLICY – THE DECALOGUE (20:1–17)

The statements that appear in this section of Exodus are arguably the most famous and familiar set of precepts ever promulgated. Notwithstanding the pivotal position of the Song of the Sea, chapter 20 is the centerpiece of the entire book. The narrative has been leading inexorably up to this point; and what follows may be considered a continuation of the divine revelation that begins in chapter 20. The significance of these precepts in Exodus, in the Hebrew Bible, and in postbiblical tradition evokes questions about their origin and structure as well as their function in ancient Israel. But first, what should we call them?

The beginning of chapter 20 gives no title or designation; it simply states that God spoke certain "words" (v. 1). Three other passages (Exod 34:28; Deut 4:13; 10:4), however, contain the phrase "ten words" (NRSV "ten commandments") in reference to a covenant document Moses inscribes on tablets of stone. Because the Hebrew term for "word," *dābār*, also means "statement," it would be more appropriate to consider the content of chapter 20 as "ten statements." Yet the imperative verbs introducing nine of the statements, or all ten depending on how they are counted, afford some legitimacy to the interpretive label "Ten Commandments," especially because "commandment" implies official and formal authority. A more apt designation is "Decalogue," which comes from the Greek (*deka logoi*) for "ten words" or "ten statements." The word *logos* can also mean "law," and thus Decalogue implies to some that the ten statements are ten laws. But these statements are never referred to in the Hebrew Bible as *ḥuqqîm*, the term for statutes or laws; and to think of them as laws would be to misinterpret and distort their function.

The tradition that these "words" are ten in number is also problematic. How is one to count the sentences that comprise verses 2–17? How is the number ten attained? There are no uniform answers to these questions, perhaps because the present text is the result of a long stage of development or the combination of several sources. In some reckonings, for example, verse 17 contains two commandments because "you shall not covet" appears twice. Others count the introductory statement (v. 2) as the first commandment, and still others begin with the first imperative in verse 3. And there are additional possibilities.[51] These variations indicate that more than ten commandments are contained in chapter 20; in an earlier stage of their formation, there may have been as many as twelve or thirteen.[52] Yet the notion that there are *ten*, and no more, discrete imperatives seems integral to their incorporation into the present narrative of Exodus. The *tenfold* use of the Hebrew term for "word" in Exodus 18 is hardly coincidental in its anticipation of statements that would be ten in number. Given the central role that the "ten words" came to play in Israelite and Jewish society, the importance of ten may lie in its mnemonic value – ten fingers in order to count and remember ten brief and pithy stipulations.

[51] Ronald Youngblood, "Counting the Ten Commandments," *BR* 8 (1994): 30–5, 50, 52.
[52] Bernhard Lang, "Twelve Commandments – Three Stages: A New Theory for the Formation of the Decalogue," in *Reading from Left to Right: Essays on the Hebrew Bible in Honour of David J. A. Clines*, eds. J. Cheryl Exum and H. G. M. Williamson (JSOTS 373; London: Sheffield Academic Press, 2003), 290–300.

The fact that the Ten Commandments have a meaningful internal division into two groups of five, with respect to language and content, similarly argues for the importance of ten in conceptualizing them in their canonical aggregate. The first five (if one begins with v. 2) all contain the phrase "the LORD your God," whereas the other five do not mention God. Each of the first five includes explanatory statements, which are not present in any of the second group. Also, the first set contains obligations to God, with the second group containing admonitions directed toward behavior among humans. The link between these two realms is the fifth commandment, about honoring one's parents, who are perhaps the authorities from whom children learn about the ultimate authority of God. That the two groups are inextricably related means that religious and social behavior are intertwined aspects of the covenant. Transgressions in the social realm as well as the religious realm are thus sins against God as well as violations of group norms.

However they came into being in their present form, the importance of the Ten Commandments is also evident in the fact that they appear multiple times in the Hebrew Bible. In addition to Exodus 20, they are found in Deut 5:6–21, which differs slightly from the Exodus version (as in the rationale for the Sabbath observance, as mentioned on p. 132) and may be the earliest canonical iteration. Leviticus 19 contains a somewhat fragmented version, which is generally believed to contain multiple allusions to the Exodus version.[53] Also contributing to their importance is the fact, already noted, that God speaks these words directly to the people and not through the mediation of Moses (but cf. vv. 7, 9, and 12, where God does not seem to be the speaker), even though hearing God speak may be profoundly unsettling to them (v. 19). Similarly, in 31:18 (cf. 34:1) it is God's own finger that provides a written record, whereas that function is delegated to Moses for the so-called Covenant Code (24:4; see the discussion on p. 189). As the direct words of God, the Ten Commandments as situated in Exodus stand as absolute and unequivocal, immutable in ways that the other revealed precepts are not.

What makes these imperatives such a central part of biblical literature? Most are not innovative; regulations dealing with similar issues, especially in the second set of five, appear frequently in earlier Near Eastern documents. Also, except for the last of the commandments, all the other stipulations are found or assumed somewhere else in the Pentateuch. Moreover, by placing the Genesis narratives before the Sinai covenant, the biblical editors themselves presuppose that murder, adultery, and theft have always been unacceptable among humans and that prohibiting them does not originate at Sinai. Such factors make it unlikely that the importance of the Decalogue lies simply in its contents. Examining the form of the precepts may be more useful in this regard.

---

[53] Jacob Milgrom, *Leviticus 17–22* (AB 3A; New York: Doubleday, 2000), 1596–1602.

Those who are familiar with other ancient legal materials, including those in the Hebrew Bible, will notice that the precepts of Exodus 20 (and Deuteronomy 5) are strikingly different. Ancient laws typically present a legal situation and then specify a response; this arrangement is labeled "casuistic" because it presents a "case." In contrast, the statements of the Decalogue are normative. Consequently, many scholars call them "apodictic," a term designating absolute and unconditional statements about norms of behavior.[54] Such categorical imperatives are not common in the law codes recovered from the ancient Near East. Indeed, their absolute and imperative form calls into question whether it is even appropriate to consider them laws. Similarly, the fact that they are devoid of punishments, which are part and parcel of collections of law from biblical antiquity, gives them a conceptual status different from that of laws. And the final imperative, about coveting, can neither be enforced nor punished; it is completely outside the realm of human justice. The statement about honoring parents likewise cannot be dealt with in courts.

Also notable is that the imperatives are all in the second person masculine singular, whereas there is usually variation from singular to plural in the legal materials in the Pentateuch. The purpose of the singular is perhaps to relate each of the commandments to the members of the community as individuals; all the precepts apply directly to everyone. As for the masculine formulation, it can hardly be understood as exempting women from responsibility for obeying the commands. Rather it is likely a consequence of the androcentric nature of the Hebrew Bible and the way in which a marital pair is considered a single unit. This is especially clear in the Sabbath commandment, where wives are not included in the list of household members (and animals) who must cease their labors on the seventh day (see A Closer Look: The Sabbath, p. 132).

The negative formulation is also striking. Except for the Sabbath commandment and the one concerning parents, they begin with "You shall not ... " (or, in v. 3, "you shall have no ... "). In other words, they are prohibitions. They are not a catalogue of what members of the community must do but rather of what they must avoid doing. This negative formulation allows for considerable freedom – people can live their lives as long as they remember to desist from certain behaviors that violate the stability of the community. Or, to put it another way, this is a minimal list of the behaviors that would rupture community life. The stipulations themselves, for the most part, are rather tersely stated; the longer ones are possibly amplifications of an earlier, simpler form. Such factors, along with the five-plus-five pattern, also suggest that these are precepts meant to be easily learned and memorized.

Because so many of the features of the Ten Commandments set them apart from typical legal materials and because they are formulated to provide a brief and balanced set of values, it is more appropriate to think of them as community

---

[54] Rifat Sonsino, "Law: Forms of Biblical Law," *ABD* 4:252–3.

policy rather than a set of laws operating within the realm of jurisprudence.[55] They contain foundational precepts that are not laws themselves but provide the basis for the community's statutory and common (case) regulations. In concise and straightforward creedal form, they set forth the basic religious and social precepts that constitute the identity of all individuals in the community Israel.

BRIDGING THE HORIZONS: THE DECALOGUE

Recognizing that the Decalogue is a set of precepts that could be easily remembered raises questions about their function in ancient Israel and in postbiblical Judaism and Christianity. There seems to be sufficient evidence in the admonitions of some Psalms (e.g., 50; 81) and in several of the prophets (e.g., Hos 4:1–2; Jer 7:2) to claim that, as the essence of the covenant document, they would have been recited or repeated whenever Israelites gathered to express their allegiance to Yahweh and their acceptance of a covenant relationship with their deity. In other words, the "ten words" had a role in Israel's community existence.

Yet what that role was for most of the biblical period can only be conjectured. The antiquity of covenant forms and practices makes it plausible that these precepts were part of Israel's earliest identity. The function of the ark (25:10–22; 37:1–9) as a repository for the deposit of sacred documents also lends credibility to the antiquity of the Decalogue as a community charter. Still, its persistence in community, liturgical, and bureaucratic life throughout the monarchy is debatable. A document said to have been discovered in the temple in the seventh century BCE during the reign of Josiah is called the "scroll of the torah" (NRSV "book of the law") in 2 Kgs 22:8 and may have been some part of what is now the book of Deuteronomy. If so, it would have contained a version of the Decalogue. But, considering the response of the king, who institutes what the scroll proclaims, its contents were unknown and thus not in effect at that time. Such an account casts doubt on the prominence of the Decalogue during much of the monarchy.

Whether or not it was important during the period of the monarchy (tenth to sixth centuries BCE), there is evidence that the recital of the Decalogue was part of the daily temple ritual in the postexilic period.[56] The Nash Papyrus, a second-century document discovered in Egypt, contains a liturgical text that includes the Decalogue. A document from the Qumran community includes it in the text that was placed in phylacteries. The first-century CE Jewish historian

---

[55] Moshe Weinfeld, "The Decalogue: Its Significance, Uniqueness, and Place in Israel's Tradition," in *Religion and Law: Biblical-Judaic and Islamic Perspectives*, eds. Edwin B. Firmage, Bernard G. Weiss, John W. Welch (Winona Lake, Ind.: Eisenbrauns, 1990), 10–17.

[56] Ephraim E. Urbach, "The Role of the Ten Commandments in Jewish Worship," in *The Ten Commandments in History and Tradition*, eds. Ben-Zion Segal and Gershon Levi (Jerusalem: Hebrew University, Magnes Press, 1990), 161–89.

Josephus refers to it in a way that indicates its liturgical use. Early rabbinic sources also indicate such use; but, interestingly, they report that its place in the temple liturgy was discontinued so as not to detract from the importance of the rest of Sinaitic revelation.

Later Jewish thinkers likewise express ambivalence about privileging the Decalogue over the many other precepts in the Torah. Consequently, it was not incorporated into the enduring daily synagogue liturgy, although the custom of reciting it was revived from time to time over the centuries. To this day, even though the Ten Commandments are esteemed as important principles of Judaism, they are usually read in the synagogue only in their context within the portions that constitute the annual cycle of reading, week by week, the entire Pentateuch. Thus they would be read only twice in a year – once each for the versions in Exodus and Deuteronomy.

Because the Decalogue does not have a consistently prominent role in post-biblical Judaism apart from the Sinai revelation as a whole, it is not surprising that it is not depicted in Jewish art until the Middle Ages (ca. 1300). Traditional Jewish representations, which show two tablets, sometimes joined and in other instances separate, almost certainly are a product of Christian art, where they appear in sculpture, paintings, and manuscripts as early as the Byzantine period.[57] These depictions are based on biblical texts that refer to two tablets but do not indicate that they were joined (Exod 31:18; 32:15–16).

The appearance of the Decalogue in Christian art accompanies a complex history in Christian practice and thought. In the New Testament, concerns about its authority are part of the larger question of the continuing validity of Jewish scripture.[58] Different positions can be found in the New Testament, with some texts supporting the continued use of at least part of the Decalogue (Matt 19:16–19) and others suggesting the "end of the law" (e.g., Rom 10:4). Yet the Decalogue's sociomoral commandments are perhaps reformulated by Paul in the idea of loving one's neighbor as a fulfillment of the Torah (Rom 13: 8–10).

Positive regard for the Ten Commandments in early Christianity is reflected in their use in the early church.[59] Several second-century CE documents – the catechetical *De Doctrina Apostolorum*, the *Didache*, and the *Shepherd of Hermes* – include some of the commandments as part of a tendency toward establishing specific guidelines for morality. Other documents, perhaps as anti-Jewish

---

[57] Gad B. Sarfatti, "The Tablets of the Law as a Symbol of Judaism," in *The Ten Commandments in History and Tradition*, eds. Ben-Zion Segal and Gershon Levi (Jerusalem: Hebrew University, Magnes Press, 1990), 363–418.

[58] David Flusser, "The Ten Commandments and the New Testament," in *The Ten Commandments in History and Tradition*, eds. Ben-Zion Segal and Gershon Levi (Jerusalem: Hebrew University, Magnes Press, 1990), 219–46.

[59] Summarized in B. S. Childs, *Book of Exodus* (1974), 428–37.

polemic, tend to be more opposed to any legal formulations. Profound and sustained discussions of the Decalogue are found in the writings of many Christian thinkers of the pre-Reformation period, from Augustine to Aquinas. With the Reformation, it receives serious attention from Luther, Calvin, and others as principles for shaping Christian life. And it has since become an important part of systematic theology, although the rise of critical biblical scholarship in the nineteenth century, which called into question the antiquity and authority of the Pentateuch, has diminished its significance for some. Whether and how it might be relevant to the religious and liturgical lives of Christians today are part of the continuing consideration of the function of covenant and community within the church.[60]

Whatever its contemporary role in the religious lives of Jews and Christians, the Decalogue has been propelled into public prominence and discussion by the rise of conservative political forces in the United States. Claiming that the United States rests on biblical foundations, which, of course, may be partly true, some officials have encouraged the posting of replicas of the Ten Commandments in prominent public places, including courthouses and schools. Perhaps the best-known example of this policy is the placement, in 2000, of a large sculpture of the Decalogue in the courthouse in Birmingham, Alabama, by the Chief Justice of the Alabama Supreme Court. In the opinion of many, the explicitly religious quality of the first four (or five) commandments, with their mention of a single god, Yahweh, associated with Judaism and Christianity and not with many of the other religious traditions followed by Americans, makes that incident a violation of the pluralistic vision of American democracy. The removal of the sculpture several years later has not ended the debate. Whether legitimately used in public settings or not, it is clear that the Decalogue still figures prominently in the way many people think about their biblical heritage.[61]

Looking at each of the canonical ten statements means, of course, selecting a numbering system. Given its formulaic similarity to covenant documents, 20:2 ("I am the LORD your God . . .") can be understood as a preamble. It is a formula of self-identification that gives authority to what follows. Therefore, contrary to most but not all of the Jewish traditions of numbering the statements, verse 2 should not be considered the first commandment. Rather, the reference to

---

[60] Jay W. Marshall, "Decalogue," *DOTP*, 181.

[61] For an eloquent statement by a legal expert who opposes the public use of the Decalogue, see Marci Hamilton's "The Ten Commandments and American Law: Why Some Christians' Claims to Legal Hegemony are not Consistent with the Historical Record" (Sept. 2003). An example of the opposing viewpoint, by the president of the Southern Baptist Theological Seminary, is Albert Mohler's "The Secular Hatred of the Ten Commandments" (Sept. 2003). Both can be found at http://www.bibleinterp.com/Archives/news_BiblicalInterpretation.htm

what God did for the Israelites in the past becomes the motive for God's claim
on Israel to obey the imperatives that follow. Christian tradition is divided:
Orthodox and Reformed churches begin with 20:3; Roman Catholic, Lutheran,
and Anglican churches consider verses 4–6 as the first one and split verse 17 into
two. Because the former provides the possibility of greatest synchronicity with
the latter as well as with Jewish tradition, it shall be followed here; but the choice
is not meant to privilege one tradition over another.

    #1, no other gods (20:3). The footnote to the text here indicates that some
would translate this as "you shall have no other gods *besides* me" instead of
" . . . *before* me." The last two words in both renderings – and there are many
other possible ones (such as "*except for* me" and "*in spite of* me") – imply a
spatial relationship: that other gods not be next to or in front of Yahweh. There
is considerable scholarly debate about this phrase, and it is difficult to comprehend what it meant as a text that originated before the absolute monotheism of
the sixth century BCE. One thing is certain – it does not categorically deny the
existence of other gods. Such denial originates in exilic prophecy (e.g., Isa 45:5,
14, 18, 21–22); this formulation therefore would be preexilic.

    The Hebrew, which literally means "upon my face," perhaps is best translated
"in my presence" and indicates that other deities (or their cult statues) were not to
be in Yahweh's presence.[62] This is probably language originating in the concept
of Yahweh enthroned in heaven and exercising dominion over a heavenly court
as well as over the earth itself. Derived from Canaanite mythological notions of
a divine council, with the chief god El presiding over other deities, the biblical
version admits of secondary divine beings (e.g., "heavenly beings" [literally,
"sons of gods"] in Ps. 29:1 and 89:6; "the host of heaven" in 1 Kgs 22:19) as
well as angelic emissaries.[63] But it does not countenance other full deities in
Yahweh's court. This commandment thus serves as an interdiction against the
legitimacy of other primary deities for Israelites. It asserts the primacy of Yahweh
for Israel. Reading it together with the prologue, which proclaims that Yahweh is
Israel's god and implies that Yahweh is mightier than any Egyptian deities, and
also with the next verse, which prohibits images, it is a statement of monolatry –
the exclusive worship of one god without the denial of others. Yahweh's claim
to be Israel's god is based on having greater power than other gods and not on
singularity. Even if other gods exist, they are incomparable (cf. Exod 15:11) and
do not belong in Yahweh's presence.

    Coming as it does as the first in the series of ten, this assertion perhaps is
the most fundamental feature of what it means to belong to the covenanted
community of Israel. The claim for allegiance to Yahweh alone establishes the
major feature of Israel's collective identity. Its prominence in the Decalogue may

---

[62] Moshe Weinfeld, *Deuteronomy 1–11* (AB 5; New York: Doubleday, 1991), 266–7.
[63] E. Theodore Mullen, *The Divine Council in Canaanite and Early Hebrew Literature* (Chico,
    Calif.: Scholars Press, 1980).

indicate a cultural climate in which such exclusivity was difficult to establish. Scholars have used this fact to suggest when in the preexilic period the Decalogue, or at least this statement, may have originated; but no consensus has emerged. Many epochs in Israel's past, including the premonarchic period, would qualify as periods in which various other deities were a part of the religious lives of many people, even the royal court, and would have been opposed by the formulators of the Decalogue.[64]

#2, no images of God (20:4–6). Unlike the simple and pithy wording of the first and many of the other statements, this one includes details as well as an extended motive clause. Its basic intent is aniconic; that is, it forbids the construction and worship of images meant to represent a deity. There is some ambiguity in the wording: it may be forbidding people to make sculptured images, probably meaning metal ones, of any aspect of creation; or it may be forbidding the making of such images to represent a god. Given the fact that representations of flora and fauna are part of the specifications for the tabernacle and temple, the latter reading of the text seems more likely. Another question is whether the prohibition (here and in v. 23) forbids the construction of images of Yahweh as well as of other gods, or only images of other gods. The layers of tradition are so complex here that it is difficult to determine whether this prohibition assumes or prescribes aniconism for Yahweh as it does for other gods.[65]

What we know from the study of other ancient religious traditions is relevant. Statues of one or more gods were routinely placed within the inner sanctums of temples and shrines in the biblical world. The temple/tabernacle structures of the Israelites and the accompanying religious practices – animal, grain, and liquid sacrifices – were in so many ways similar to those of other peoples of the ancient Near East that it is striking to see this express prohibition of material renderings of any divine presence. Scholars have long sought to explain what motivated the Israelites to have their cultic practices diverge in this way from those of other ancient cultures. One important possibility is that the Israelites, like their Canaanite predecessors, established open-air worship sites (*bāmôt*) that used nonanthropomorphic symbols – such as standing stones (*maṣṣēbôt*) and sacred trees (*'ăšērîm*) – for the divine presence. This de facto aniconic tradition eventually became programmatic, as expressed in the Decalogue, even when those open-air shrines themselves were banned.[66]

Yet ancient Israel also had elaborate dwellings for God, not only open-air shrines. Such structures incorporated Near Eastern traditions that were much

[64] Z. Zevit, *Religions of Ancient Israel* (2001), *passim*.

[65] Tryggve D. N. Mettinger, "Israelite Aniconism: Developments and Origins," in *The Image and the Book: Iconic Cults, Aniconism, and the Rise of Book Religion in Israel and the Ancient Near East*, ed. Karel van der Toorn (Leuven: Uitgeverij Peeters, 1997), 175–7; see also B. S. Childs, *Book of Exodus* (1974), 406–8.

[66] Tryggve D. N. Mettinger, *No Graven Image? Israelite Aniconism in Its Ancient Near Eastern Context* (Coniectanea Biblica Old Testament Series 42; Stockholm: Almqvist & Wiksell International, 1995).

more apt to include anthropomorphic cult statues, which provided legitimiza-tion for monarchic rule. Given this function of iconic representation of deities, it also is possible that there was a sociopolitical as well as religious motivation for prohibiting images. Because earliest Israel was a segmentary society and arguably antimonarchic, an early and pervasive practice, incorporated into its cultic structures, may have been to find ways to represent God's presence with-out actually constructing images of God, which connoted monarchic rule as well as divine rule.[67] The tabernacle, as we shall see, like the Jerusalem temple, uses alternative means, without actual statuary, to represent God's presence. Moreover, by the time that the prohibition of images was expanded to include an explanation, it receives an explicitly theological and priestly rationale in the mention (in v. 4) of the realms of the created world: heavens above, waters below, and earth in between. The Israelites eventually believed that what God created is entirely separate from God, and depicting the deity in any material form would violate that understanding of a transcendent deity.

So widespread was the use of images to represent divine presence in shrines in the ancient world that this prohibition must have been especially difficult to promulgate. It is no wonder, then, that it is accompanied by an expanded proscription, which forbids bowing down to images or worshipping them as well as making them, and also a strongly worded statement explaining the gravity of the ban. It suggests that there will be dire consequences across generations should it be disobeyed – disobedience would be tantamount to rejecting God – but God's lasting love (and blessings) would come to those who adhere to it. The language of this statement includes many important concepts. One is the notion of an "impassioned" God. The NRSV "jealous" probably reflects an understanding of the term derived from the marriage metaphor for the covenant bond, which involves exclusivity and would mean jealousness were it to be broken. But "jealous" may not do justice to the Hebrew term, which denotes intense emotion more generally and which is used only of God in the Hebrew Bible. Despite the limitations of human language for depicting the nonhuman God, this term may indicate a degree of emotional intensity greater than that experienced by humans.

The result of this intense response by God, should the prohibition of images be sinfully violated, is strongly punitive. Its notion of punishments extended across four generations is also a powerful component of the creedal statement of 34:6–7 (see p. 264). This cross-generational accountability likely reflects the strong role of family lineages in premonarchic (twelfth–eleventh centuries BCE) and early monarchic Israel (tenth–eighth centuries BCE). Since antiquity, the idea of punishment to the fourth generation has been troubling to commenta-tors, who frequently suggest somewhat apologetically that the misdeeds of one

---

[67] Ronald S. Hendel, "Aniconism and Anthropomorphism in Ancient Israel," in *The Image and the Book: Iconic Cults, Aniconism, and the Rise of Book Religion in Israel and the Ancient Near East*, ed. Karel van der Toorn (Leuven: Uitgeverij Peeters, 1997), 224–8.

generation often affect succeeding ones. Both Jeremiah (31:29–30) and Ezekiel (18:2–4) contest cross-generational punitive measures; their emphasis on individual accountability is part of the societal changes of the late monarchic period. Deuteronomic law (24:16) also indicates that juridical process did not involve generational responsibility in the late monarchic period. We can only wonder if this is the language of hyperbole, meant to emphasize the importance of obeying this stricture, rather than an expression of belief that the innocent descendents of someone who disobeyed would have to pay the consequences. Support for such an understanding of the harsh language may lie in the even more exaggerated language describing what the results will be for contrasting behavior. Blessings will come to the "thousandth generation" (20:6) of those whose love for God means that they obey all God's teachings. Such blessings will last, in a sense, forever. Note that in Ps 105:8–10 the ancestral covenant will endure to the thousandth generation – it will be a "covenant forever" and an "everlasting covenant."

How effective was such strong language, along with the repetition of the prohibition in various forms in other parts of the Pentateuch? Usually, repeated strictures indicate opposition to existing practices. But it is also possible that in this case they are underscoring and attempting to maintain a central and ancient feature of Israelite cultural identity. In this respect, it is relevant that archaeological data support the effectiveness of the prohibition, or at least of the aniconic tradition, whether de facto or promulgated as policy. Significant numbers of metal figurines and statuettes from Canaanite sites of the Late Bronze Age have been identified as anthropomorphic representations of deities.[68] If one excludes ceramic pillar figurines depicting women holding their breasts, most of which are arguably votive objects and not representations of a goddess,[69] Iron Age sites that presumably are Israelite have yielded relatively few such artifacts. Although this is an argument from silence, it does suggest an important discontinuity in the material culture with respect to sculpted cult images and implies that many Israelites apparently accepted the aniconic aspect of their cultural identity.

#3, misuse of God's name (20:7). In ancient Semitic thought, the essence of a person or object was believed to be contained in its very name. Thus the sanctity and power inherent in God's name – God's very identity – could not be taken lightly. As explained in the supplementary section on A Closer Look: The Name of God, pp. 57–9, the traditional reluctance to pronounce the name of God is grounded in this notion. The NRSV translation ("You shall not make wrongful use...") masks a strong juridical component. The Hebrew says, literally, not to "lift the name of God," which is an idiom for oathtaking. Also, it uses the

---

[68] E.g., Ora Negbi, *Canaanite Gods in Metal* (Tel Aviv: Institute of Archaeology, 1976).
[69] C. Meyers, "From Household to House of Yahweh," in *Congress Volume Basel* (2002), 285–9.

term *laššāw*, which can mean "falsely" as well as "in vain, for nothing." Oath-taking by invoking God's name and thus divine power in judicial contexts was a serious matter, and this prohibition guards against egregious dishonesty in such situations as well as against more general blasphemy. The judicial aspect of the term is further underscored by the clause that expands the prohibition. The form of the Hebrew verb translated "acquit" is used almost exclusively with God as the subject in situations where God exempts someone from punitive judgment. In this prohibition, misusing God's name could not be so excused. However, despite the grounding of this prohibition in legal language, it is possible that it was meant to have wider application.[70]

#4, observing the Sabbath (20:8–11). The exodus narrative already has introduced the Sabbath. Securing food for their wilderness journey means that on the sixth day the Israelites are to gather quantities of manna to last for two days – the sixth and the seventh. This process is connected to the Sabbath and its prohibition of productive labor (16:22–30). (The origins and nature of the Sabbath are described in A Closer Look: The Sabbath, pp. 132–3). Its role in Israel's identity formation is marked by the imperative "remember."

This is one of the two commandments expressed in positive terms. But, like the prohibition of images, it has an extensive addition to what must have been an original brief adjuration to observe this day; and the added material includes a negative imperative ("you shall not do any work," v. 10). The expanded text also has an additional positive directive – the people are enjoined to work on six days as well as to refrain from doing so on the seventh. The priestly idea of holiness frames the additional materials: in another positive statement added to the original brief formulation, the Israelites are told to keep the day "holy" (v. 8), the reason being that God has "made it holy" (NRSV "consecrated it," v. 11). The separateness implied by the term "holy" is to be applied to a temporal unit, so that the seventh day is differentiated from the other six days because of the cessation of labor. Elsewhere in the Hebrew Bible the sanctity of the Sabbath is marked by special sacrifices; and in late biblical and postbiblical times, community worship and special liturgy are the hallmark of Sabbath observance. Yet the stipulations about the Sabbath in the Decalogue have no religious or cultic content but, rather, focus on the interests of the community.

#5, honoring parents (20:12). There is no word in biblical Hebrew for "parent," and the fifth statement expresses the behavior due to both parents by mentioning them individually. Like the previous statement, this one is expressed positively. As such, it resonates with many references to respecting one's parents in biblical wisdom traditions. When we examine the community regulations of chapters 21–23 that are closest to this, namely 21:15 and 17, the social context making the relationship to parents so important as to be included as one of the Decalogue's precepts will be explained.

---

[70] B. S. Childs, *Book of Exodus* (1974), 410–12.

At this point, however, it is important to note that, in the context of the Decalogue, this precept is part of community policy addressed to adults (as the adultery statement, and others, indicate). Although it is often cited today to encourage dependent children to be mindful of their parents, it is more likely that in biblical times it was an admonition to offspring, even after they themselves were adults, to maintain their respect for their mothers and fathers.[71] Like several others, this precept has an appended clause that provides an appropriate reward for adhering to it – (adult) children who honor those who bore them will themselves have long lives. It is no wonder then that the imperative verb used here is "honor" and not "obey." The former certainly is broader and is used in the Hebrew Bible to indicate human response to God as well as to other humans. "Honor" entails more than just obedience; it also means to show respect, to esteem, and even to exalt, just as it does when used for one's relationship to God.[72]

#6, murder (20:13). This statement, like the next three, is brief and is not augmented with an explanation or motive. Like the next two, it consists of only two words in Hebrew: the verb plus the negative adverb. As such, it may represent an "original" formulation of these community precepts. Understanding the nuances of the Hebrew verb translated "murder" is extremely important. Some translations (such as KJV, RSV, and NAB), in rendering the verb "kill," make it seem as if this prohibition was against the taking of human life under any circumstance. Yet that notion is clearly contradicted by the many military narratives in the Hebrew Bible as well as by the military metaphors for God; the intentional taking of human life in warfare is not presented as a violation of the covenant. Moreover, capital punishment is clearly specified in some of the legal materials in the Pentateuch.

At least three different Hebrew verbs can be used for killing. The one in this instance is *rṣḥ*, and its usage patterns elsewhere in the Hebrew Bible are instructive.[73] Appearing some forty-six times, it is never used for killing in battle or in self-defense nor for the slaughter of animals. The subjects of the verb are Israelites, members of the covenant community. Although it is clear that God sometimes strikes down or kills humans, this verb never has God as the subject. Moreover, in the several biblical narratives that use it to depict killing, the objects of the verb are Israelites. In the Decalogue, of course, as well as several times in the Prophets (e.g., Jer 7:9, echoing the Decalogue), the term is used absolutely, with no object specified. In light of this information, it is warranted to translate the term "murder" and to understand it as the illicit taking of the life of another human by force. How the community is

[71] Jon L. Berquist, *Controlling Corporeality: The Body and the Household in Ancient Israel* (New Brunswick, N.J.: Rutgers University Press, 2002), 122.

[72] P. Stenmans, "*kābēd* I," *TDOT* 6:19–20.

[73] Frank-Lothar Hossfeld, "*rāṣaḥ*," *TDOT* 13:630–40.

to deal with such a crime and how to handle the possibility that causing the death of another was an accident are both part of the legal materials of the Pentateuch.[74]

#7, adultery (20:14). This succinct precept proscribes sex outside of marriage. But for whom? The prohibition of adultery does not specify, and it is only by looking at other biblical texts that the range of adulterous behaviors can be ascertained. Male Israelites, their marital status unspecified, are forbidden on penalty of death to have sex with married or engaged Israelite women, who would also be put to death (Deut 22:23–24; Lev 20:10; strangely, no legal formulations in Exodus deal with adultery per se). Responses to adultery in wisdom and prophetic texts indicate that more lenient measures also existed.[75] Either way, it was apparently not considered adultery for Israelite men – their marital status again unspecified – to have sex with unmarried and unbetrothed women (see Exod 22:16–17); or, at least, the legal consequences did not involve the death penalty. Similarly, a man (not identified as being married) who has sexual relations with a betrothed female servant in his household is deemed to have committed sinful behavior for which he can atone and is not subject to the death penalty specified for adultery (Lev 19:20–22).

It thus seems reasonable to conclude that this precept forbids Israelite men from having sex with betrothed or married Israelite women. Another possibility, given the second person masculine form of the verb, is that it is addressed to Israelite men but subsumes into the imperative the wives or fiancées of those who are married, for they are partners of a marital unity and that makes them similarly subject to the ban on sex outside of marriage (just as the wife is likely considered part of the marital pair in the discussion of who must keep the Sabbath, 20:10). That is, a married or betrothed woman cannot have sex with anyone but her fiancé or husband. In any case, if the other biblical materials are taken into account, this prohibition cannot be taken as an absolute condemnation of all sexual relations outside of marriage.

Because adultery does appear in this foundational set of precepts, it is often alluded to when prophets charge Israel with violating the covenant. It was undoubtedly of great importance to prohibit a man from having sex with a woman betrothed or married to another man, but the rationale for the gravity of the offense is never made explicit. The reasons must have been so obvious to people in the world of the Hebrew Bible that it was not necessary to stipulate what they were. Because the prohibition is not against all extramarital sex, it is best

---

[74] See Exod 21:12–13. The verb does not actually appear in this passage, which is the starting point for other asylum laws (Deut 4:41–43; 19:1–13).

[75] See Carol Meyers, "Rape or Remedy? Sex and Violence in Prophetic Marriage Metaphors," in *Prophetie in Israel: Beiträge des Symposiums "Das Alte Testament und die Kultur der Moderne" anlässlich das 100 Gerburtstags Gerhard von Rads (1901–1971), Heidelberg, 18–21 Oktober 2001*, eds. Irmtraud Fischer, Konrad Schmid, and Hugh G. M. Williamson (Altes Testament und Moderne Bd. 11; Münster: Lit-Verlag, 2003), 185–98.

understood as originating in the social and economic spheres as much as in the religious and moral aspects of society.

Virtually all societies have some sort of interdictions against female adultery, in which a married or engaged woman has sex with another man. Social scientists who examine such extramarital liaisons do not agree about what is at the root of the apparently universal opposition to them, but many suggest that the abhorrence of female adultery lies in the fact that it can produce uncertainty about paternity and concomitant concern for the biological identity of any offspring that may result from an illicit union.[76] In agrarian societies in which unmovable property (land) is critical to family survival, the specter of transmitting property to another man's child, should a woman's extramarital sex lead to pregnancy, is especially problematic. With no means to determine paternity, the worst would be assumed. Thus a simple act of passion and pleasure, while not causing immediate harm as does murder and theft, could cause severe rupture in family trust and structure as well as in patterns of inheritance.

It is no wonder that the Decalogue, as a distillation of ancient Israel's essential beliefs and practices, should include a prohibition of adultery as a way of strengthening and emphasizing what is difficult to enforce by ordinary deterrents and which can so easily go undetected. Controlling the illicit expression of passion is a challenging proposition for any society. What may have originated in social and economic concerns becomes integral, for ancient Israel, to the notion of living in a covenantal relationship with God. The importance of the marriage bond is thereby given a sacral dimension. Although the adultery prohibition of the Decalogue is thus often cited as an example of Israelite concern for the institution of marriage, it likely originated in broader concerns than simply the sacral bond between a wife and a husband. Moreover, because it does not prohibit all male extramarital sex, we cannot assume that the Israelite conception of the marital relationship is comparable to contemporary ideas about mutual faithfulness.

 # 8, theft (20:15). The third in a series of brief, two-word (in Hebrew) statements, the prohibition of theft is categorical. Elsewhere in the Hebrew Bible the verb "to steal" (*gnb*) is typically followed by a direct object that indicates the stolen item or abducted person. The community regulations in Exodus dealing with theft exemplify such usage (e.g., 21:16; 22:1). But here no object of theft is given; it is categorically forbidden to steal.

The forbidden acts, murder and adultery, in the two preceding imperatives are so egregious that they are subject to capital punishment according to other pentateuchal texts. Because such is not the case for the theft of objects, some scholars have argued that verse 15 originally had "person" as a direct object

---

[76] Karen Erickson Paige and Jeffrey M. Paige, *The Politics of Reproductive Ritual* (Berkeley: University of California Press, 1981), 177.

and was meant to forbid kidnapping, an offense that *is* punishable by death.[77] However, such a reading does not take seriously enough the life–death problems caused by the theft of certain kinds of property – agricultural tools or even jars of food – in a society in which most people lived at the subsistence level. Thus it is more likely that generic theft, which could rupture the fabric of family and community life just as could murder and adultery, is the intent. The impact of the forbidden offense would have been more relevant in formulating this prohibition than its legal remedies, which, as we shall see, were apparently more lenient than in other ancient Near Eastern societies.

#9, false witness (20:16). The stability of any community depends on the ability of its leaders to adjudicate disputes and redress wrongs. Judicial procedures for doing so are often dependent on the testimony of victims, perpetrators, and/or witnesses. Unless such testimony is given honestly, justice cannot be served. This prohibition seeks to prevent false testimony in legal proceedings by asserting that one must not, literally, "answer [a question in court] with a lie." Like the prohibition against swearing falsely (20:7), its terminology is related to legal expressions found elsewhere in the Hebrew Bible. Because of the way it is formulated, it is unlikely to be a categorical support of truth-telling in all aspects of life, despite the critique of falsehood and deception more generally in prophecy.[78]

The strong concern in ancient Israel for the potential abuse of adjudicatory processes through false testimony is evident in the appearance in the pentateuchal laws of a policy forbidding the death penalty on the strength of a single witness (Num 35:30; Deut 19:15). The assumption is that it is not always possible to know if a witness has lied. Even in courts today, with the availability of lie detector tests and other means for assessing the truth of testimony, it is not always possible to detect sworn falsehoods. The problem would have been even more intractable in antiquity, as perhaps indicated by the distress voiced in a number of psalms about witnesses who deceive (e.g., Ps 24:4). Making lying in court one of the prohibitions of the Decalogue gives it, in the breach, the status of a sin against God as well as against another human. In that way settling disputes with integrity and preventing the conviction of someone who is innocent might more readily be achieved.

The prohibition of false testimony specifies that this is not to be done against one's "neighbor" and thereby evokes the question of what is meant by that word. Clearly contemporary parlance, in which neighbor refers simply to someone living nearby, is inadequate. The Hebrew term may indeed begin with the idea of residential proximity, but it entails a broader social connectedness. People

---

[77] Following Albrecht Alt, "Das Verbot des Diebstahls im Dekalog," in *Kleine Schriften zur Geschichte des Volkes Israel* (3 vols.; Munich: C.H. Beck'sche Verlagsbuchhandlung, 1953), 1:337–40.

[78] Cf. Walter Brueggemann, "Exodus," *NIB* 1:851–2.

in the villages of biblical Israel were embedded in a web of relations, based on kinship or proximity or both, that provided mutual help and security in a setting that lacked the social services to which we are accustomed in the modern world. Neighbors could be the source of life-giving economic or "medical" assistance. Biblical texts using the term "neighbor" are thus specifying people with close, interdependent community relationships. Trust among such people is crucial. Thus, just as this prohibition of false witness is not a categorical prohibition of lying, it also does not address a person's veracity with respect to all others.

#10, coveting (20:17). Neighbors appear again in the final statement, which is another precept concerned with social stability. This coveting imperative is an astonishing prohibition of an emotional state, not a deed; but it is an emotional state that can be the beginning of a wrongful deed. The term for "covet" (*ḥmd*) does not refer to the simple and natural human desire that can be aroused by viewing an attractive object or person. Rather it denotes the intense desire that is generated by passion and thus is not easily controlled.[79] Thus, to "covet" what is another's can have grave consequences for a community as well as an individual. This final precept is a perceptive psychological statement. If heeded, it can prevent the situations – adultery, theft, and even murder and false testimony – that many of the other imperatives forbid.

The admonition against coveting raises the important question of whether the emotional state implied by "covet" was understood as being separate from a consequent action. That is, is the Decalogue trying to rule against covetous feelings as such? Or is it interested specifically in forbidding emotions so strong that they cannot be contained and inevitably result in harmful deeds? It may be true that covetous individuals themselves suffer even if they do not act on their impulses. However, extensive study of the term "covet" in biblical and extrabiblical contexts indicates that coveting and the deeds it causes form a semantic unit.[80] The exhortation not to covet in the Decalogue thus attempts to prevent the kind of emotions that lead to the disruptive actions that are themselves prohibited.

Unlike the other precepts of the Decalogue, this one repeats its admonition. "You shall not covet . . . " appears twice in succession, each time with a different object. The first object is the general category "household" (*bayit*). The NRSV translation "house," which implies a building, does not do justice to the concept of the Hebrew term. The word often denotes not only a family's domicile but also the family members themselves, their livestock, their land, and also all the tools, installations, and materials associated with their daily lives. The object of the repeated admonition then enumerates what the "household" represents: spouse, servants, animals, and anything else. Strangely, children are not included in the list of human members of the household, perhaps because forestalling

---

[79] G. Wallis, "*chāmadh*," *TDOT* 4:454–7.
[80] Ibid.

adultery is the intent. Another factor may have been the desire to list a total of *seven* things not to be coveted (household, wife, male slave, female slave, ox, donkey, and anything else); in the aggregate, these seven symbolize the totality of a household.

COMMUNITY REGULATIONS: RULINGS, RULES, AND NORMS (20:18–23:33)

The first verse of chapter 21 is often considered a title for all the community regulations that follow. It uses the word *mišpāṭîm*, translated "ordinances" in the NRSV. This term usually denotes *rulings* that are casuistic and arose in juridical settings. Drawing on custom or precedent, they adjudicate a variety of civil and criminal matters; and they have a "secular" tone, with no reference to God. However, some of the cases in this part of Exodus mandate actions for handling certain situations that threaten community stability and are presented in more authoritative language and with more severe penalties; these strong *rules* may fit the designation *ḥuqqîm*, or "statutes," linked with "ordinances" in 15:25 and with "instructions" (*tôrôt*) in 18:16, 20. The latter term perhaps represents another kind of material, presented as direct address to all individuals; these *exhortations* seem to be covenant language that promulgates normative principles. Clearly "ordinances" is not an adequate designation for the range of community regulations in 20:18–23:33.

This collection is also often referred to as the "book of the covenant" because that designation appears in the complex chapter between these ordinances and the tabernacle texts that follow (24:7). However, that title more likely comes from a redactor or editor who is combining covenant stipulations or exhortations with various ordinances and statutes so as to situate all of them within the covenant context and give them an authoritative etiology. Although it is not certain that "book of the covenant" was meant to designate all the materials in 21–23, it nonetheless provides a convenient label for the canonical collection of discrete and diverse components. The designation Covenant Code is also used, although that phrase is somewhat misleading for it may give the impression that these regulations have the structure and comprehensiveness implied by the word "code." Not only do the regulations lack a clear or systematic organization, but also they fail to mention or deal only briefly with major aspects of life that communities typically regulate. Inheritance and divorce laws are absent, for example.

Giving a single title to this collection would mask its diversity. It is a blend of different forms: case rulings and rules, apodictic or normative statements, and mixed types. Also, a wide range of issues is treated – property, sexuality, liability, bodily injury, homicide, slaves, witchcraft, philanthropy, family relations, food-ways, animal "rights," court proceedings, and festivals. Its regulations include both social and religious behavior; that is, it deals with behavior with respect to God as well as human interactions.

Despite the diversity of content and form, an overall structure to these chapters can be discerned (see table below). Some introductory materials – a narrative resuming the account of the Sinai theophany and then a special religious ruling serve as an introduction (20:18–26) – and a concluding section of divine promises and admonitions (23:20–33) frame the legal materials, which themselves can be divided into two sections. The first is the set of stipulations or rulings in 21:1–22:20, which are largely case laws with attached punishments as appropriate; some are *rulings* and others are the more stringent *rules*. The second section, 22:21–23:19, consists mainly of ethical and religious *norms* or exhortations with attached motivational statements but no juridical actions. The overall organization can perhaps be understood as the merging of ancient customary rulings and rules (the first section) with the covenant orientation of the exhortations (second section).[81] Within the two main sections, materials on the same general subject are not necessarily grouped together. Thus internal ordering in each cannot easily be established despite many attempts to do so. No doubt the development of this collection of diverse materials took place over a long period of time, and this may account in part for its complexity.

Community Regulations: Rulings, Rules, and Norms	
introduction. 20:18–26	narrative resumption and instructions (norms)
section 1. 21:1–11	ordinances (rulings)
21:12-17	statutes (rules)
21:18–22:17	ordinances (rulings)
22:18–20	statutes (rules)
section 2. 22:21–23:19	exhortations or instructions (norms)
conclusion. 23:20–33	narrative of divine promises and admonitions

Whether the stipulations of this corpus, or at least its core ordinances and statutes, were actually in place as community law for all or part of Israelite communal existence has long been debated. If "law" consists of "the principles, regulations, and policies of a society that are recognized and enforced by judicial decision, thus constituting a form of social control,"[82] then classifying materials in Exodus 21–23 as law is problematic. The reason for this is that we know so little about the administration of justice in ancient Israel (as indicated in the discussion of Exodus 18). The written materials in Exodus 21–23 may be based on oral traditions that were used for nonformal dispute resolution and were only later formulated and formalized in regulations that were implemented

---

[81] W. Johnstone, *Exodus* (1990), 53–8.
[82] Barry L. Eichler, "Israelite Law: An Overview," in *Encyclopedia of Religion*, ed. Mircea Eliade (16 vols.; New York: Macmillan, 1987), 7:466.

through the involvement of third parties (judicial figures or bodies), often with the support of political authorities.[83]

An approximate time period for at least some items of the so-called "book of the covenant" can be suggested. Because certain features can be related to evolving sociopolitical conditions, this particular collection, especially in comparison with the legal materials in Deuteronomy and in Leviticus, may contain some of the earliest community rulings, rules, and norms in the Hebrew Bible.[84] The social context, especially of the first section, seems to reflect the village court practices and proclamations of an agrarian people, with the highest political officer being a chieftain. There is no mention of an army or a king, although this does not preclude a date during the monarchy for the compilation of the core of this collection.

Yet even a hypothetical date is not the same as evidence that all the people at the time, or later, would have known and accepted these materials as authoritative, despite the intent of the narrator to represent them as having been accepted by all Israel since its beginnings as a community. Evidence from biblical books outside the Pentateuch indicates that the cases and admonitions did not always have the force of law or at least that other legal traditions, not preserved in the Pentateuch, were in effect for some parts of the community in some periods of its existence. Legal traditions no doubt were evolving over time; and the differences among the several pentateuchal corpora surely attest that the items in the Exodus corpus, despite being presented as God's word, were not immutable. One intriguing suggestion is that the case rulings of the first section are among the oldest materials and that Deuteronomists, with their strong covenant orientation, combined them with the covenant-oriented exhortations of the second section. This process ultimately led to the further reformulations that constitute the largely covenant-oriented corpus in Deuteronomy 12–26.[85]

How and when these ordinances, statutes, and instructions were incorporated into community life remains uncertain; but the general authenticity of the regulations, especially the case rulings, is clear when one compares them with other legal materials from the ancient world.[86] The discovery in the last century and a half of extensive law collections from other societies in the biblical world has revolutionized our understanding of the stipulations in the Pentateuch. At least ten different documents, going back to the mid–third millennium BCE, preserve collections of laws. In addition, there are thousands of documents that record court cases and transactions from the practice of law. Human societies everywhere, no matter how simple, cannot exist without the stability of accepted

[83] Bernard S. Jackson, *Studies in the Semiotics of Biblical Law* (JSOTS 314; Sheffield: Sheffield Academic Press, 2002), 82–7.

[84] Jay W. Marshall, *Israel and the Book of the Covenant: An Anthropological Approach to Biblical Law* (SBLDS 140; Atlanta: Scholars Press, 1993).

[85] W. Johnstone, *Exodus* (1990), 58.

[86] Samuel Greengus, "Law: Biblical and ANE Law," *ABD* 4:242–52.

norms and without procedures for dealing with those who disrupt them. We now can understand that ancient Israel was in many ways similar to other ancient peoples, or to all peoples for that matter, in the kinds of regulations that appear to have governed its community life. At the same time, certain features of the biblical ordinances emerge as being quite different from those of other ancient cultures.

A CLOSER LOOK: ANCIENT NEAR EASTERN LAW

The law collections of the ancient Near East appear mainly as inscriptions on stone monuments erected by a prominent ruler, usually as a way of supporting if not aggrandizing his rule. Some also appear on sets of clay tablets. The oldest surviving legal corpora were written in Sumerian, a non-Semitic language spoken by peoples who lived in southern Mesopotamia in the third and early second millennia BCE. These inscriptions claim that the ruler has established justice and peace. The prologue to a set of laws promulgated by Ur-nammu (reigned 2112–2095 BCE), the renowned founder of a strong dynasty of kings based in Ur, asserts that he has standardized weights and measures, protected the poor, widows, and orphans, "eliminated enmity, violence, and cries for justice," and "established justice in the land."[87] The thirty-seven surviving casuistic (case) laws in this document cover a range of issues, including false accusations, assault, homicide, and miscarriage, that also appear in the ordinances of Exodus. In another group of Sumerian laws, from several centuries later, the king similarly claims to have established justice by, among other acts, liberating oppressed populations and ensuring that (adult) children support their parents.[88]

Perhaps the most famous of the surviving law texts is the so-called Code of Hammurabi, named for its promulgator, a powerful king who ruled the Babylonians from 1792 to 1750 BCE. Inscribed on a large stela depicting the sun god Shamash presumably investing authority in the king, the 282 laws are framed by a prologue and an epilogue. Many of the laws are clearly part of the legal tradition discernable in the earlier Sumerian laws. Moreover, copies of all or parts of them have survived on documents from as much as 1500 years later than the stela. Clearly we are looking at a legal tradition that spanned several millennia, exhibiting remarkable continuity. Most of the laws in the Hammurabi Code are casuistic and, as we might expect, deal with a variety of situations, many of them similar to those reflected in the ordinances of Exodus. (Laws in the Hammurabi Code that are directly relevant to Exodus rulings are quoted in Ancient Texts: Laws of Hammurabi, pp. 187–8). As befits a developed urban society with extensive commercial enterprises, an exceptionally large number

---

[87] "The Laws of Ur-Namma (Ur-Nammu)," translated by Martha Roth (COS 2.153), 409.
[88] "The Laws of Lipit-Ishtar," translated by Martha Roth (COS 2.154), 411. Lipit-Ishtar reigned from 1934 to 1924 BCE.

of laws are intended to protect private as well as state property. In most of them, the problem is first described, and then the solution is mandated. Often a rather simple case is followed by more complicated ones involving the same issue.

Several other Babylonian collections have been recovered, as have laws promulgated by the Assyrians and the Hittites. These range in date from the early second millennium to the mid-first millennium BCE. Some are more comprehensive than others, and the penalties show a clear variation, with some appearing quite harsh and others more lenient. Whatever their differences, they also have many points of contact with each other as well as with the Sumerian collections and the Hammurabi Code.

Examining these law collections individually and in comparison with each other reveals several important features.[89] One is that, like the several sets of regulations in the Pentateuch, none of them is truly comprehensive or exhaustive. There seems to have been no attempt to set forth a complete legal system that would cover all aspects of social, economic, and political existence. Although there are indirect allusions to certain areas of community life that almost certainly would have had to be regulated, direct statements or relevant cases are not always recorded. Despite the noticeable gaps in each individual collection, in the aggregate they have cases pertaining to most areas. Scholars understand the incomplete nature of the collections to be the result of the fact that many standard, widely accepted, and uncomplicated legal materials were probably transmitted in oral form, with only difficult or complicated cases that might be contested requiring the additional authority and perhaps wider promulgation that inscriptions provided. That is, there were likely traditional bodies of common law, with not all of their constituent regulations receiving formulation in written form.

Another important feature of the written collections is that their rulings do not seem to have been the basis for more than a handful of the thousands of court cases and legal transactions appearing in other documents from Mesopotamia and Anatolia. Thus the function of the laws appearing in compilations such as those of Ur-nammu and Hammurabi cannot be determined without taking into account the wide variety of other legal materials that have been recovered. It may never be possible to establish the relationship between the law "codes" and the records of cases, but it is certainly possible to recognize the strong concern for justice and order that permeates all the legal materials.

The concern for justice involves inequities, however. The law collections reveal differential treatment of persons, according to social class and in some cases gender. Specifically, three main categories of persons appear: free persons,

[89] Martha T. Roth, *Law Collections from Mesopotamia and Asia Minor* (2nd edition; SBL Writings from the Ancient World Series; Atlanta: Scholars Press, 1997), 2–7.

including men, women, and children; a secondary class of persons, the commoners of both genders; and male and female slaves in the households of either
commoners or free persons. In addition, a variety of other groups of persons,
specialists such as merchants and artisans, appear and were usually considered
free persons. Still other groups were apparently subsumed into the palace and
temple bureaucracies. Although justice for all is important, penalties can vary
according to the social status of the parties involved.

In form and content, the casuistic rulings in Exodus clearly are part of the
wider legal traditions found throughout the ancient Near East. Careful examination of the cases cited in chapters 21–23 reveals dozens of instances of close
correspondence with cases cited in one or more of the cuneiform law collections.[90] The Exodus cases frequently deal with similar legal problems and reflect
shared customs and attitudes. Sometimes the wording and even the prescribed
penalty are virtually identical. An oft-cited example is Hammurabi §120:

If a man stores his grain in another man's house, and a loss occurs in the storage bin or
the householder opens the granary and takes the grain or he completely denies receiving
the grain that was stored in his house – the owner of the grain shall establish his case
before the god, and the householder shall give to the owner of the grain twofold of the
grain that he took (in storage).[91]

This can be compared to the case in Exodus 22:7–8:

When someone delivers to a neighbor money[92] or goods for safekeeping, and they are
stolen from the neighbor's house, then the thief, if caught, shall pay double. If the thief
is not caught, the owner of the house shall be brought before God to determine whether
or not the owner had laid hands on the neighbor's goods.

Although they are organized somewhat differently, the similarities are striking.
In both texts, goods given to a neighbor for safekeeping are stolen; the person
with whom they have been entrusted may be guilty of having taken them; in the
absence of witnesses, guilt can be established only by the deity; and the amount
of restitution, should the neighbor be found accountable, is double the worth of
the goods given for safekeeping. Such correspondences suggest a direct textual
dependence of the Exodus rulings on the Code of Hammurabi.[93]

---

[90] B. S. Childs, *Book of Exodus* (1974), 462–3, lists those correspondences but does not
include the Neo-Babylonian laws of the mid-first millennium BCE and several other small
collections.

[91] "Hammurabi" (*COS* 2.131), 343.

[92] NRSV "money" is anachronistic and misleading here (and also in 21:11, 34; 22:25; 30:16);
money as we know it did not yet exist. The Hebrew word is *kesep* ("silver") and refers to
silver metal weighed out as payment.

[93] David P. Wright, "The Laws of Hammurabi as a Source for the Covenant Collection
(Exodus 20:23–23:19)," *Maarav* 10 (2003): 11–88.

Despite such correspondences, there are important differences. The ways in which the rulings and exhortations of Exodus 21–23 seem to depart from the legal traditions of the ancient Near East are instructive because they provide a way to identify specifically Israelite values. The context of the biblical materials is itself a notable difference. Their canonical position situates them within Israel's covenant with God (24:7). Instead of appearing on a monumental inscription set up by a powerful human ruler or on a set of royal administrative tablets, the rulings, rules, and norms are combined as a corpus promulgated by God, albeit through Moses' prophetic mediation (24:4). By virtue of the covenant context, adherence to them becomes a matter of loyalty and obedience to God, not to a human ruler. Ethical behavior is thus embedded in a moral framework in which God is invested in the behavior of humans. This merger of standards of behavior with the belief that those standards neither originate in nor serve political authority, but rather stem from the divine will, may be one of the most significant legacies of the covenant context.[94]

Another difference has to do with form. The appearance of so many non-juridical and unconditional exhortations in addition to the case rulings and rules is not typical of Near Eastern corpora. In strong, absolute terms, these normative statements deal with issues that affect the stability of society, show a concern for human life and justice, provide instructions for sacral activities, and mandate certain aspects of religious life. Moreover, an abundance of motive clauses appears in the exhortations. A motive clause is one that is added to a prohibition in order to provide a rationale.[95] A prominent example is the way an admonition is connected with a remembrance of the past, as in the stipulation that the people refrain from oppressing non-Israelites because they themselves once had such status: "for you were aliens in the land of Egypt" (22:21; 23:9). Other motive clauses provide an etiology (23:15; cf. 20:11) or are simply explanatory (e.g., 22:27; 23:7, 12; cf. 20:5–6).[96] Such clauses are not completely absent from other ancient legal materials, although they are estimated to appear in no more than five to six percent of the stipulations of some collections (and never provide reasons that recall the past). But they are much more common in the Bible, appearing in as many as half of the legal materials.[97] What could be the reason for this prominence of motive clauses? Their presence, like the exhortations themselves, may indicate a strong interest in conveying important

---

[94] D. N. Freedman, "Formation of the Canon," in *Religion and Law* (1990), 326–9.

[95] Rifat Sonsino, *Motive Clauses in Hebrew Law and Near Eastern Parallels* (SBLDS 45; Chico, Calif.: Scholars Press, 1980).

[96] Motive clauses also appear in the Decalogue: a promissory clause explains the positive results for proper treatment of parents (20:12), and a promise of negative consequences accompanies the command not to misuse the divine name (20:7).

[97] John W. Welch, "Reflections on Postulates: Power and Ancient Laws," in *Religion and Law: Biblical-Judaic and Islamic Perspectives*, eds. Edwin B. Firmage, Bernard G. Weiss, John W. Welch (Winona Lake, Ind.: Eisenbrauns, 1990), 118. Welch's statistics include all biblical laws, not only the ones in Exodus.

standards of behavior to a wide public and not simply providing authoritative statements for adjudicatory purposes.[98] After all, they are in the Torah (teaching) literature of ancient Israel. The motive clauses thus embody the didactic role of the canonical form of community regulations.

With respect to specific content, the legal issues are not significantly dissimilar to those of other ancient peoples. However, differences in the number of cases dealing with some matters or in the punitive measures taken can be discerned. The death penalty, for example, seems to be mandated less often in Exodus than in other law collections. The rulings in Exodus do not require capital punishment for stealing (except the abduction of persons; 21:16). In contrast, many Mesopotamian and Anatolian theft laws, perhaps reflecting societies with more developed mercantile economies and more wealth accumulated by elites, are apt to inflict death upon those convicted of theft, especially if they do not have the means to make restitution (e.g., Hammurabi §8). Such harsh penalties, protecting the estates of the royal and temple bureaucracies, make property seem more valuable than human life.

A related distinction concerns policies regarding restitution, fines, and corporal punishment. Near Eastern laws often vary the amounts in relation to the social status of the victim. For example, the liability of a person whose ox fatally gores a person is greater if the dead person is a free person than if a slave. Moreover, if someone is guilty of assaulting a person of his or her own class, the injury done to the victim is inflicted upon the assailant; but if the victim is a commoner or slave, a fine is levied. Comparable biblical materials have no class differentiation. Aside from the death penalty, corporal punishments such as flogging or mutilation do not appear at all in the rulings of Exodus (but cf. Deut 25:1–3, 11–12), unless the unmentioned punishment of 21:20 involves the body of the guilty person. The *lex talionis* or talion law (punishment commensurate with injuries suffered; Exod 21:22–25) may involve corporal punishment, although many feel that it is a legal principle mandating fairness but not literally imposed (see Exod 21:26–27). There is no mention of imprisonment.

These community regulations seem to discourage the accumulation of assets and attempt to provide resources for the needy.[99] By forbidding the collection of interest, for example, wealth is less likely to accumulate (Exod 22:25). Letting the land lie fallow in the seventh year restricts income while benefiting the poor (Exod 23:10–11). Such policies seem especially idealistic; and many scholars are skeptical about whether such stipulations were ever carried out. Be that as it may, an overall concern for those who lack independent means to support and protect themselves in an agricultural society – widows and orphans (22:22), the poor (22:25, 26–27; 23:6, 10–11), debt servants and slaves (21:2–11; 23:12), and

---

[98]   Moshe Greenberg, "Biblical Law: Establishing a Moral Order," *BR* 7 (1991): 43.
[99]   Ibid.

non-Israelite sojourners (22:21; 23:9, 12) – permeates Exodus 21–23 as well as other legal and also prophetic materials in the Hebrew Bible. This interest in social welfare, which is manifest in rulings meant to protect vulnerable people from abusive or unjust treatment and in exhortations that discourage abusive or exploitative behavior toward them, is not characteristic of other ancient Near Eastern cultures or even of classical Greece and Rome.[100] The social policies of the legal texts, together with the social concerns of the prophets, form the distinctive values of the Hebrew Bible. Some of those values can be appreciated only in the context of the Iron Age world of ancient Israel, and of course many others transcend the millennia.

ANCIENT TEXTS: LAWS OF HAMMURABI

Of the 282 laws in the Hammurabi Code, at least 18 of them are relevant to rulings in Exodus[101] :

§1. If one citizen charges another with murder, but has no evidence, then the sentence is death. (See Exod 23:1–3.)

§2. If one citizen charges another with witchcraft, but has no evidence, then the defendant is tried by ordeal in a river. If the defendant drowns, the plaintiff inherits the defendant's household. If the defendant survives, then the sentence is death for the plaintiff, and the defendant confiscates the plaintiff's household. (See Exod 22:18; cf. 22:8, 9.)

§5. If a judge accepts a bribe to render and seal a decision, then the judge is fined twelve times the settlement ordered in the decision, is expelled from the bench, and cannot serve as judge again. (See Exod 23:5–6.)

§8. If a citizen steals an ox or a sheep from a state or a temple official, then the citizen is fined thirty times the value of the stolen livestock. Likewise, if one citizen steals an ox or a sheep from another, then the fine is ten times the value of the stolen livestock. If a citizen fails to pay a fine for stealing livestock, then the sentence is death. (See Exod 22:1; cf. 20:15.)

§14. If a citizen kidnaps and sells a member of another citizen's household into slavery, then the sentence is death. (See Exod 21:16.)

§21. If one citizen tunnels through the wall of another's house and robs it, then the citizen is sentenced to death. The execution shall take place outside the tunnel, and the body is used to fill the tunnel. (See Exod 22:2–3.)

§57. If a herder does not have a covenant with the owner of a field to graze his sheep on it, but has grazed his sheep on the field without consent of the owner,

---

[100] Richard H. Hiers, "Biblical Social Welfare Legislation: Protected Classes and Provisions for Persons in Need," *JLR* 17 (2002): 50.

[101] Except for §250, which is taken from "Hammurabi" (*COS* 2.131), 350, the translations are the less literal and more reader-oriented renderings of V. H. Matthews and D. C. Benjamin, *Old Testament Parallels* (1991), 101–9.

when the owner of the field harvests it, then the fine is 140 bushels of grain for every sixteen acres of land. (See Exod 22:5.)

§117. If a citizen sells his wife, his son, his daughter, or himself into slavery to pay a debt, then the creditor cannot keep them as slaves for more than three years and must free them at the beginning of the fourth year. (See Exod 21:2–11.)

§120. (Quoted on p. 184.)

§125. If one citizen stores property in the warehouse of another, and if the property is stolen by a thief who tunnels through the wall or climbs over it, then the owner of the warehouse whose carelessness allowed the robbery to take place, must make every effort to find the thief and recover the stolen property. In any case, the warehouse owner must make full restitution of the whole of the stolen property to the owner. (See Exod 22:7–8.)

§195. If a citizen strikes his father, then his hand shall be cut off. (See Exod 21:15.)

§199. If one citizen blinds the eye or breaks the bone of another citizen's slave, the fine is one-half the price of the slave. (See Exod 21:26–27.)

§206–7. If a citizen accidentally hits another citizen and causes injury, then that citizen must swear, "I did not strike this citizen deliberately," and must pay for the cost of the physician. If the victim dies from the blow, then the citizen must swear the same oath, but if the citizen is a member of a royal household, then the fine paid to the household of the victim is nine ounces of silver. (See Exod 21:18–19.)

§209. If one citizen beats the daughter of another and causes her to miscarry, then the fine is six ounces of silver. (See Exod 21:22–23.)

§244. If a citizen rents an ox or an ass, and if a lion kills it while it is out in the open, then there is no fine. (See Exod 22:14–15.)

§249. If a citizen rents an ox and a member of the divine assembly strikes it with lightning and it dies, then the citizen who had rented the ox must swear in the name of a member of the divine assembly that the death of the ox was an act of god, and then there is no fine. (Exod 22:14–15.)

§250. If an ox gores to death a man while it is passing through the streets, that case has no basis for a claim. (See Exod 21:28–36.)

§251. If the ox of a citizen, who has neither tethered, nor blunted the horns of the animal, even after the city assembly has put the owner on notice that it was dangerous, gores a state official, then the fine is eighteen ounces of silver. (See Exod 21:28–36.)

Introduction: narrative resumption and altar instructions (20:18–26). Following the Decalogue, with its list of essential community principles (20:1–17), the narrative of the Sinai theophany resumes briefly, in 20:18–21. These verses represent both a response to the experience of God's revelation at the holy mountain and also an introduction to the continued revelation to follow. The language of natural cataclysm and trumpet blasts in verse 18 echoes the atmosphere, as portrayed in chapter 19, surrounding the mystery of God's appearance to humans. How do people respond to such an experience? The intense and dramatic effect on the Israelites literally moves them; that is, they are depicted as falling back from the pyrotechnics of revelation. Next they implore Moses to resume his role as mediator. If the Decalogue has come to them directly from God, the rest of what God has to say should come via Moses, whose prophetic authority to transmit God's word to the people is here accentuated.

This response of the Israelites to the presence of God provides a glimpse of how God's extraordinary holiness is a positive quality but also is fraught with danger (as already explained in the supplementary section, A Closer Look: Holiness). Humans cannot survive direct auditory or visual contact with God because of God's intense power. In this case, Moses assures the people that no harm will come, that God only intends to elicit their reverence by giving them the experience of being in the divine presence.[102] The result will be that they will not "go astray" (NRSV "sin"), verse 20; that is, they will adhere to what God reveals through Moses. Moses then approaches the dense darkness that envelops God's presence in order to receive the extensive set of community regulations that constitute chapters 21:1–23:19.

Set off, however, from those regulations is the so-called "altar law" of 20:22–26, a series of instructional statements regarding the kind of altars for sacrifice that Israelites are to build. It is prefaced with a prohibition of metal statues of gods, which is related to the prohibition of idolatry in verses 4–6. God's presence will not be in images but rather in the altars to be made "for me," probably an elliptical phrase indicating altars made for sacrificing to God, an act that brings people into God's presence.

Two aspects of these altars are striking. One is their simplicity; they are to be made of heaped-up earth (v. 24) or at most unhewn stones (v. 25) and are to be low, or at least have no steps (v. 26). No shape is prescribed, but the assumption is that altars must rise above the surrounding terrain. The other is their potential ubiquity; they can be constructed at virtually any site considered sacred, that is, wherever God is invoked ("remembered") and then responds by blessing the people (v. 24). These features are suitable for the kinds of offerings to be made on these altars: burnt offerings and offerings of well-being, which are the most common of the sacrifices mentioned in the Pentateuch. Yet they contrast with other information in the Hebrew Bible. The altar for sacrifice described in the instructions for tabernacle and temple is quite ornate; and Deuteronomy forbids sacrifice anywhere except at the temple altar. Moreover, there is no mention of priestly officiants – these low-tech altars imply easy access of all to the direct acts of animal sacrifice. Scholars have long struggled to determine

---

[102] Rather than NRSV "test them"; see J. Tigay, "Exodus," in *The Jewish Study Bible* (2004), 151.

how the instructions in 20:24–26 relate to other biblical texts. Resolution of this problem is uncertain; but the passage does seem to indicate a tradition of multiple, simple, and readily available altars for much of the biblical period.[103] Note that two figures in the book of Judges, Gideon and Manoah, use local altars without priests (Judg 6:20–27 and 13:16–19), as do the ancestors in Genesis.

Case rulings and rules, many with attached punishments (21:1–22:20). This first of the two sections of legal materials in Exodus contains rulings dealing with servitude (slavery), violence (homicide and assault), property (liability and restitution), and several social and religious situations. All of them can be considered remedial. They present cases, which consist of wrongful deeds and also their remedies – either compensation or punishment. However, there are two distinct types of formulation. Most of them (21:1–11, 18–36; 22:1–17) are of the "when/if . . . then . . ." variety, and usually are expressed in the third person; the second person ("when you . . . ") of 21:2–6 is unusual. They tend to be somewhat discursive in that they introduce specific conditions. But a small number (21:12–17; 22:19–20) are of the somewhat more terse "whoever . . . " type and are mainly in the third person; these strong rules (along with 22:18) deal with the most extreme cases and involve capital punishment. There are *seven* references to God in the third person in the case laws (21:6, 13; 22:8, 9, 11, 20) and one in the first person (22:13). Some of those present direct involvement of God in judicial proceedings; and the seven-plus-one pattern may be a way of emphasizing that God *fully* participates in maintaining a just community.

Discussion of every individual case is not possible, but some observations can be made about each set of cases as well as about certain specific ones that are especially difficult or informative.

Servitude (slavery; 21:2–11). As explained with respect to Hebrew servitude in Egypt (see A Closer Look: Bondage, Servitude, and Slavery, pp. 35–6), slavery among the Israelites included the debt servitude of people within their community. The NRSV's use of the term "slave" in 21:2–11 is somewhat misleading because this passage is concerned with debt servitude. "Slave" also has a negative connotation that may not be justified. Within the context of ancient agrarian villages, without banks or state welfare, debt servitude, in fact, serves a necessary social and economic function. It provides a way for struggling households to borrow essential resources by working off the debts thereby incurred. Usually older, unmarried children, rather than the adults of a household, would be "sold" to work off an obligation, which is why the manumission procedures reflect the likelihood that the indentured person will become a spouse during the period of indenture. A convicted indigent thief could also work off a fine through such service. The rights of servants and also the equitable

---

[103] Ziony Zevit, "The Earthen Altar of the Laws of Exodus 20:24–26 and Related Sacrificial Restrictions in Their Cultural Context," in *Texts, Temples, and Traditions: A Tribute to Menahem Haran*, eds. Michael V. Fox, Victor Avigdor Hurowitz, Avi Hurvitz, Michael L. Klein, Baruch Schwartz, and Nili Shupak (Winona Lake, Ind.: Eisenbrauns, 1996), 53–62.

treatment of a servant's spouse and offspring are apparent in these manumission rulings.[104] Servitude was not normally permanent; but indentured males who, for some reason could not or would not be able to achieve solvency on their own, could elect to remain a permanent part of the household to which they were indentured, in which case a symbolic ear-piercing ceremony rendered the servitude permanent. This may seem bizarre or even cruel from our contemporary perspective, but in its own context it rendered official a legitimate and humane way to provide security for destitute people.

For the most part, biblical rulings dealing with slavery treat female and male Hebrew servants with parity, as is the case in these manumission texts as well as in the Sabbath precept (20:10; cf. 23:12) and in protection from assault (21:26–27).[105] However, the sexuality of an unmarried bondswoman, which may mean she becomes a secondary wife of the man to whom she is indentured, makes her ineligible for automatic release in the seventh year, unless she is found unsatisfactory as a wife. This case may refer specifically to girls handed over as wives (not concubines), with the possibility of servitude for unmarried daughters precluded.[106] The rulings have an interest in the welfare of such a female as the secondary wife for a man or his son. In the latter instance, she has the rights of daughter (probably daughter-in-law) of the household. In the former instance, she retains full conjugal rights – food, clothing, and "marital rights" – even if the husband takes another wife. The Hebrew term translated "marital rights" is unusual; the ancient versions and most commentaries understand it to mean sexual rights but it may also designate another commodity.

Violence (homicide and assault; 21:12–32). These verses deal with a variety of crimes against persons beginning with the most serious ones, capital offenses (vv. 12–17), which are presented more forcefully than the other rulings in this first section. They have the "whoever" form and provide absolute rules for remedying situations that would rupture community stability. The method of carrying out the death penalty is not stipulated. As would be expected, the trauma involved in the taking of a human life by another person appears first (vv. 12–14), and the text is careful to distinguish between murder and unintentional homicide. (The phrase "act of God" refers to an accident and not to any kind of specific divine causality of the death.) It also provides asylum for those who inadvertently cause the death of another and who, in a kinship-based tribal society such as ancient Israel, would be vulnerable to "blood revenge."[107] The mention of a

---

[104] Timothy John Turnham, "Male and Female Slaves in the Sabbath Year Laws of Exodus 21:1–11," *SBL Seminar Papers No. 26*, ed. Kent Harold Richards (Atlanta: Scholars Press, 1987), 545–9.

[105] Carolyn Pressler, "Female (and Male) Hebrew Slaves (Exod 21:7–11, 20, 26–27; Lev 19:20; 25:6; Deut 5:14; 15:12–18; 1 Sam 8:16; Jer 34:8–16)," *WIS*, 193–4.

[106] Joseph Fleishman, "Does the Law of Exodus 21:7–11 Permit a Father to Sell His Daughter as a Slave?" *JLA* 13 (2000): 47–64.

[107] A more developed treatment of this situation appears in Numbers (35:6, 9–32) and Deuteronomy (4:41–43; 19:1–13); see Timothy M. Willis, "Homicide, Asylum, and City

place of safety for someone unintentionally taking a life is the only instance of the mention of God in the first person in the entire set of rulings and regulations in Exodus 21–23. Kidnapping, presumably with the intention of selling the victim into slavery, was apparently tantamount to taking a life and is punished similarly (v. 16).

A third capital offense concerns parent–child relationships (vv. 15, 17) and is related to the imperative in the Decalogue about honoring parents. In addition to striking one's elders, dishonoring them in any other way was considered a grave offense. NRSV "curses" in verse 17 may not be quite accurate; the Hebrew root (*qll*) is the semantic opposite of "honor" and means "to treat contemptuously." Yet it can also signify cursing in a more technical sense, that is, offering an imprecation; doing so was considered extremely serious in that curses were believed to cause harm to the person to whom they were directed. The social context for these rulings, which seem exceedingly harsh to us, involves two aspects of ancient life. First, as suggested in the discussion of Exod 20:5, the offspring here are adults, not small children; and caring for the few parents who lived into old age was the only way for the senior members of a family, no longer physically able to provide for themselves, to survive. Second, before a parent reached somewhat infirm old age, he or she would be in the position of managing a household with adult sons and their wives and would need to maintain the authority to do so.[108] Invoking the death penalty for striking or cursing one's parents indicates how serious a threat to eldercare or family stability such actions would be. The gender parity in these rulings is noteworthy, in comparison to the exclusion of the mother from a related ruling in the laws of Hammurabi (§195).

The next set of rulings deals with the infliction of assault and bodily injury. An assailant who injures someone must compensate the victim for lost time and for treatment (vv. 18–19); the liability for permanent injury is unspecified. Also unspecified is the punishment for a person who fatally strikes a slave; but injuring a slave (vv. 20–21) incurs no punishment (except of course the temporary loss or diminution of the victim's labor) unless that injury is permanent, in which case the compensation is freedom (vv. 26–27). These rulings are somewhat protective of nonfree persons in comparison with other ancient Near Eastern law corpora, which lack such provisions.

The *lex talionis* is attached to a particular instance of assault, in which a pregnant woman (vv. 22–25) is injured and miscarries. Monetary compensation is awarded for loss of the fetus, as is the case in several other Near Eastern law collections. Because the assailant is not treated as having committed homicide, the stipulation of a fine here implies that the fetus did not have the status

Elders," chapter 3 of *The Elders of the City: A Study of the Elders-Laws in Deuteronomy* (SBLMS 55; Atlanta: SBL, 2001).

[108] Carol Meyers, "Mother (or Father) Cursed or Struck by Offspring (Exod 21:15, 17; Lev 20:9)," *WIS*, 194–5.

of a viable human. Should the woman herself sustain injury or death, then appropriate punishment is mandated by the formulaic "eye for an eye..." principle. Debate over the meaning of this principle and whether it was meant literally has been extensive. Because of the lack of punitive mutilation in biblical texts (in contrast to other ancient legal materials) and because the terms of the law of retaliation do not fit this specific case, it is likely that the talion statement is one of judicial equity and not a barbaric mandate to inflict corporal punishment equivalent to the injury sustained.[109] The penalty would thus have been appropriate monetary compensation, based on the severity of bodily harm.

Remedies for injury caused by an animal also appear in this section (vv. 28–32). The owner of an animal known to be dangerous is subject to capital punishment for deaths it may cause; and the animal is also put to death, with no gain allowed from its carcass. Note that the animal, in fact, is stoned to death, a mode of execution and not of slaughter. Alternatively, perhaps because the owner did not directly inflict the mortal wound, the victim's family can be monetarily compensated at a very high rate.[110] No such choice is provided for the death of a slave; the ox, but not its owner, is put to death and the slave-owner is compensated. Even if the victim is a minor, the owner of the animal is penalized. This is an example of the principle that people cannot be punished for the misdeeds of others (cf. Deut 24:16), in contrast to Mesopotamian law, in which the child of someone who causes the death of another's child or even of another person might be put to death.[111]

Property and restitution (21:33–22:15). A number of crimes against property appear in these verses. Liability for environmental hazards involves compensating the owner of an animal that dies if one has created such a danger, but the guilty party can keep and use the dead animal (21:33–34). In another case of liability, the goring ox appears again, this time as the cause of death of an animal, classified as property, rather than a human (21:35–36). Unless the ox was known to be dangerous, in which case its owner must provide restitution (although he can keep and use the carcass), the goring of an animal is considered accidental and the owner is not liable; the owners of the gorer and its victim share the price of the dangerous animal, which must be sold, and the value of the dead one. Liability for one's livestock also means compensating the owner of fields or vineyards for damage if the animals graze on another's property (22:5). And someone who starts a fire must also make restitution for any ensuing crop damage (22:6).

---

[109] Tikva Frymer-Kensky, "Israelite Law: State and Judiciary Law," in *Encyclopedia of Religion,* ed. Mircea Eliade (16 vols.; New York: Macmillan, 1987), 7: 480; cf. N. M. Sarna, *Exodus* (1991), 125–7.

[110] A similar sequence in the Hammurabi corpus (§251, §252) stipulates thirty shekels as compensation for the fatal goring of an elite member of society, with a lesser sum (twenty shekels) imposed for the death of a slave; "Hammurabi" (*COS* 2.131), 350.

[111] E.g., Hammurabi §209–§210; §229–§230.

A more complicated kind of liability involves goods or animals given to another for safekeeping (22:7–8, 10–13). If the goods are stolen, the thief must
compensate by paying double. But if the thief cannot be found, it becomes possible that the bailee – the person safeguarding the items – may have stolen them.
This becomes a classic case of one's word against another's, and God resolves
the impasse. If an animal given for safeguarding is lost, sustains injury, or dies
and the cause of such damage is undetected, an oath before God is considered
convincing evidence of the innocence of the bailee. Producing the carcass of an
animal destroyed by predators has similar exculpatory power. Otherwise, the
animal is considered stolen and restitution must be made.

One more liability issue involves renting or borrowing an animal (22:14–15). If
harm befalls the animal such that it dies, full restitution to the owner is required
unless the owner is present when the mishap occurs, in which case no payment is
owed for a borrowed animal but the rental fee for hired animals must still be paid.

These liability rulings are accompanied by ones dealing with more explicit
instances of theft (22:1, 4, 9). Stealing livestock for slaughter or sale mandates
fivefold (for oxen) or fourfold (for sheep) restitution, with a thief unable to
pay damages being required to work off through indenture the debt thereby
incurred. Simple possession of unharmed stolen animals involves only twofold
restitution. The same compensation is stipulated in the contested ownership of
goods. When two people each claim they own something, God decides who is
the real owner; the other person thus is considered a thief and must provide
(double) compensation. Theft is combined with violence in one case, in which
the victim of a theft mortally attacks the perpetrator (22:2–3). The assailant is
guilty of murder but is given capital punishment only if the incident occurs in
the daytime, perhaps because it would difficult at night but not in daylight to
discern whether the thief was endangering life or only property.

Social and religious situations (22:16–20). These four cases are varied in their
form and content. One deals with sexuality and marriage; it follows the typical
case "when/if . . . " form and includes two conditions. The other three are rules
dealing with capital offenses, one being a direct imperative, the other two of the
"whoever . . . " variety. Some call the first one "secular" or social and the others
"religious," although such a distinction is not truly valid for this document in
its canonical context, in which all stipulations are deemed God's word.

The social regulation (vv. 16–17) involves premarital sex. There are no marriage (or divorce) regulations in Exodus, probably because the regulations or
customs governing marriage were well known and standard. This one deals with
a particular set of circumstances: a man having consensual sex with an unbetrothed young woman. The NRSV "virgin" (*bĕtûlâ*) is problematic. The Hebrew
word means a young woman of marriageable age in virtually all of the fifty-one
times it appears in the Hebrew Bible; it does not denote biological virginity,
which is typically indicated by the addition of a phrase such as "who has never
slept with a man." This text does not specify such virginity. It thus means that
a man who has sex with a marriageable woman incurs responsibility to either

marry her at the standard bride-price for marriageable women or be fined at that rate, namely the bride-price for "young women" (NRSV "virgins"), should the woman's father not agree to the marriage.[112] This ruling does not deal with the seduction of a woman who is already engaged, which is tantamount to being married, or with rape; both those situations appear in Deuteronomy (22:23–29).

The three rules invoke capital punishment and, like the capital offenses of 21:12–17, are absolute and unequivocal. The first involves sorcerers (v. 18). Sorcery is one of nine kinds of magic and divination forbidden in Deuteronomy (18:9–14); but sorcerers seem to be identified here only as females, perhaps because women dominated this particular occult art. Sorcery involved the activation or exorcism of the evil spirits thought to cause illness. The existence of such practitioners, whose work apparently was deemed efficacious, was considered by some to be especially threatening to the role of God as sole source of well-being.[113] The second (v. 19) forbids bestiality, abhorrent perhaps because of the Israelite sense of boundaries between species. Also, on a functional level, prohibiting nonprocreative sexuality makes sense in a society with sporadic demographic problems (i.e., underpopulation). The death punishment is given with a double form of the verb, thus providing an additional level of intensity suiting the abhorrence. The third (v. 20), dealing with sacrifice to other gods, can be related to the prohibitions of the second and third items of the Decalogue. The particular severity of such apostasy is indicated by the way the death penalty is imposed – devoting a person to destruction indicates total annihilation, which probably meant that the property as well as the life of the guilty person would be destroyed. This is capital punishment in its most extreme form.[114]

A CLOSER LOOK: MARRIAGE IN ANCIENT ISRAEL

In today's world, marriage is considered a personal relationship between two people, usually a woman and man, who typically cohabit, bear children, and share the responsibilities, joys, and difficulties of life. A marriage also includes certain legal rights, such as joint ownership of property. Frequently a marriage also is seen as a sacral relationship, meant to remain intact until "death do us part." Individuals usually choose their own spouses. Love is considered an important element in the forming of the marital relationship. However, for pre-modern peoples such as the ancient Israelites, most of these aspects of marriage as we know it in industrial societies would not apply. In biblical antiquity, as today, a marriage meant the beginning of a new nuclear family; but many other aspects of Israelite marriage would have differed fundamentally from contemporary practice.

---

[112] Matitiahu Tsevat, "běthûlāh," TDOT 2:338–42.
[113] Carol Meyers, "Female Sorcerer (Exod 22:18; Isa 57:3)," WIS, 197.
[114] Norbert Lohfink, "ḥāram; ḥērem," TDOT 5:187.

The legal texts of the Pentateuch provide no general regulations for marriage or divorce but contain only stipulations for certain atypical circumstances. Consequently, a reconstruction of the institution of marriage and of the relations between a conjugal pair must draw upon other biblical passages as well as information in other Near Eastern documents. Such sources indicate that marriages normally were arranged by parents as liaisons between two families, indicating that the larger kinship context was far more important in biblical antiquity than it is today. The preference for endogamous marriage, or marriage within one's own clan or tribe, similarly contributed to community bonds and the likelihood that related families would assist each other. Toward the end of the period of the Hebrew Bible, endogamy also seems to have become important as a way to maintain religious and ethnic identity in the absence of political autonomy. Still, examples of exogamous marriage, or marriage with someone outside one's group, appear throughout the Hebrew Bible, often reflecting political alliances when kings are involved.

The Hebrew Bible does not have a term for "marriage." The formation of a marital bond is usually expressed by saying that a man takes a woman. The word for woman and wife are the same in Hebrew, for the notion of a woman existing on her own without being part of a family structure was inconceivable. That a man "takes" her is a reflection of the patrilocal pattern of Israelite households; that is, a bride would usually move to the household in which the bridegroom resided with his family, thus forming an extended or compound family, although perhaps with each constituent nuclear family occupying adjacent but separate abodes.[115] The incest laws in Leviticus perhaps are constructed in order to deter problematic sexual intimacy with members of such a complex household group.

Except among the very poorest, financial arrangements accompanied marriage. So common and well-known were such matters that they receive scant attention in the Hebrew Bible. The most common economic feature of marriage was providing a dowry for the bride.[116] Usually consisting of moveable property such as clothing, jewelry, and household utensils, dowries in wealthier families might also include livestock and servants, as is clear from several of the Genesis narratives (e.g., Gen 24:59; 29:24, 29). Usually given by the bride's family, the groom or his family could supplement it (as in Gen 24:53). Although the husband as well as the wife had some access to the dowry during the duration of the marriage, it theoretically remained the possession of the wife and constituted her chief means of support if the marriage ended. Because many

---

[115] Lawrence E. Stager, "The Archaeology of the Family in Ancient Israel," *BASOR* 260 (1985): 18–19.

[116] R. Westbrook, *Property and the Family* (1991), 142–56. Dowries may be more typical of well-to-do families than those living at the subsistence level; but the other form of marital payment, the bride-price, was likely common to all.

women would have had a difficult time surviving on their own in the event of widowhood or divorce, especially if they had no sons or father, the dowry was an important institution.

Another kind of marital payment, the betrothal gift, was made by the groom's family to that of the bride. This "bride-price" (Hebrew *mōhar*; see Exod 22:17 and also Gen 34:12; 1 Sam 18:25) or marriage gift, given to the bride's family by the groom or his family upon betrothal, often has been taken to mean that a husband purchased a bride and thereafter owned her. To be sure, betrothal and marriage meant the exclusive sexual rights of a man to his fiancée or wife; but the idea that brides were purchased and wives were owned is a serious distortion of the function of a bride-price. Rather than give the bride the status of chattel, such payments served in several overlapping ways to maintain the viability of a family.[117] A bride-price might compensate the bride's family for the loss of a daughter's labor, which was important in agrarian families. In addition, providing a marriage gift served to establish and solidify alliances between a bride's natal family and her marital one.[118] Such alliances provided an avenue for aid should economic or other difficulties arise in one of the families. Also, it is not certain that the marriage gift became the permanent property of the bride's father. More affluent families sometimes simply added it to the dowry (cf. Gen 31:15). In any case, the payment of this fee legally established the marriage, although the betrothed couple might not physically actualize the marriage, through coitus and cohabitation, for some time. By linking families and providing security for women, both bride-price and dowry served important economic, social, and legal functions.

Very little is known about provisions for the dissolution of marriages. Divorce rulings appear only once: Deut 24:1–4 deals with a particular situation, in which a divorced man seeks to remarry a former wife. Although it is not a general statement about divorce, it has led to the supposition that only men could initiate divorce in ancient Israel. However, information from extrabiblical sources, as well as indirect evidence from other biblical texts, provides reason to question that notion.[119] Both the Deuteronomy case and Isa 50:1 mention a bill of divorce, and Mal 2:14 refers to a marriage contract (NRSV "covenant"). These references suggest the use of formal documents for establishing or dissolving a marriage; but it cannot be assumed that such written records were customary, let alone required, among all sectors of the population throughout the period of the Hebrew Bible.

---

[117] Edouard Lipiński, "*mōhar*," *TDOT* 8:142–4.
[118] Carol Meyers, "Everyday Life in Biblical Israel: Women's Social Networks," in *Life and Culture in the Ancient Near East*, eds. Richard E. Averbeck, Mark W. Chavalas, and David B. Weisberg (Bethesda, Md.: CDL Press, 2003), 193–4.
[119] Rhonda Burnette-Bletsch, "Woman Being Divorced (Deut 24:1–4; Isa 50:1)," *WIS*, 232–3.

Just as important as textual sources for understanding marriage in the period of the Hebrew Bible is the information gained by analyzing archaeologically retrieved data about household life in ancient Israel in light of ethnographic analogies. Most Israelites lived in agricultural villages, and the family households in which virtually everyone resided were largely self-sufficient units. Consequently, households had important economic, social, and religious functions as well as providing for reproduction and the rearing of children. Men may have paid a bride-price and also enjoyed exclusive sexual rights to their wives; but these features should not be, as they often have been, generalized into assumptions about overall male dominance in Israelite marriages and household life. With very few resources available from outside the household, the relationship between a married woman and man was one of interdependence.[120] Both men and women (and their children) provided the productive labor essential for the survival of the household. Women have considerable power under such circumstances, and the traditional notion of dependent wives under the patriarchal control of their husbands can be contested.[121]

The reproductive role of women was also vital, not only because of the labor potential of children but also because offspring were essential for the transmission of land and property across generations. Israelite society was organized patrilineally, with property transmitted through the male line. Thus men had a vested interest, which is subsumed into notions of male pride as well as in the desire for sons, in securing heirs for their family lands and possessions. Many aspects of marriage involved gender parity, but women and men are treated differently in others. The role of women as child-bearers along with patrilineal inheritance practices likely contributed to this differential treatment.

Such differences are apparent in Deut 22:13–21, in which a bridegroom claims that his bride was not a virgin. The elaborate procedures for evaluating this accusation indicate that sexual chastity was desirable for brides and that a man's honor would be diminished should lack of virginity be established. Many reasons for this have been suggested. Perhaps most compelling is that, because a man would want to be certain that his family lands and livelihood would not go to another man's child, a sexually intact woman would not present a problem with respect to the paternity of her first child. The concern for legitimate heirs is also a factor in the gender disparity in responses to adultery mentioned in

[120] Carol Meyers, "The Family in Early Israel," in *Families in Ancient Israel*, eds. Leo G. Perdue, Joseph Blenkinsopp, John J. Collins, Carol Meyers, (Louisville, Ky.: Westminster John Knox, 1997), 22–7, 32–5. This description of early Israelite families would pertain to village agrarian households throughout Israelite existence.

[121] Carol Meyers, "Material Remains and Social Relations: Women's Culture in Agrarian Households of the Iron Age," in *Symbiosis, Symbolism, and the Power of the Past: Canaan, Ancient Israel, and Their Neighbors from the Late Bronze Age through Roman Palestine*, eds. William G. Dever and Seymour Gitin (Winona Lake, Ind.: Eisenbrauns, 2003), 425–44.

the discussion of the adultery prohibition of the Decalogue (Exod 20:14). It was not considered adultery for Israelite men, presumably even if married, to have sex with unmarried and unbetrothed women; but, in legal texts, it is a capital offense for a married or engaged woman to have sex with someone other than her husband or fiancé lest she become pregnant with another man's child.

Concern for heirs surely was a factor in the existence of levirate marriage, in which a widow whose husband has died childless marries the deceased husband's brother; the first son produced by that marital link is considered the dead man's son and heir. Polygamy or, rather, polygyny (more than one wife), likewise is related to concern for the transmission of property to a man's own heirs. To be sure, monarchs often had multiple wives because of their high status and also to solidify internal or foreign political connections. Though it sometimes may be a mark of position or affluence, taking a second wife or a concubine was more likely to occur because a first wife failed to produce a suitable heir. The Genesis narratives may give the impression that having multiple wives was common; however, the reality of shorter life spans for women than men in the biblical period, as well as the fact that most people probably lived near the poverty level, would have precluded polygamy in most circumstances. Moreover, many texts – such as Gen 2:24, various passages in wisdom literature, the Song of Solomon, and even legal rulings (e.g., Exod 21:5) – give the impression of a monogamous ideal or norm.

Ethical and religious exhortations or norms (22:21–23:19). This is the second of the two main sections of legal materials in Exodus, and it differs from the first section in several ways. All of the stipulations in the second section are expressed as covenant materials – the direct address from God to the Israelites, sometimes as individuals and sometimes collectively, rather than in the casuistic "if/when ... then ... " or "whoever ... " type typical of the first section. And God is mentioned more than twice as often here as in the first section. The cases of the first section provide redress or remedy for intolerable acts, whereas the exhortations of the second constitute preventative precepts setting forth standards for ethical behavior as well as instructions for community life. This section is even more miscellaneous in character than the collection of case rulings and rules in the first.

Despite their diversity, the directives, commands, and prohibitions of the second section can be divided into four groups: 22:21–27; 22:28–31; 23:1–9; 23:10–19. Broadly speaking, the first and third groups (both of which begin by prohibiting the oppression of non-Israelites) concern interpersonal relationships and just treatment for all, whereas the second and fourth groups present obligations toward God.[122] Humanitarian and religious matters thereby are linked in

---

[122]   William Johnstone, "Exodus," in *Eerdmans Commentary to the Bible* (2003), 224.

a covenant context, in much the same way that those two concerns together constitute the precepts of the Decalogue.

Group 1: Concern for the disadvantaged (22:21–27). These exhortations show concern for four groups that are vulnerable in a society in which membership in a household ordinarily was necessary for survival: non-Israelites ("resident alien"), widows, orphans, and the poor. A motive clause in verse 21 situates compassion to non-Israelites in the remembered past of the Israelites' oppressed status as foreigners of Egypt. Failure to be sensitive to the plight of the first three of these groups is not remedied by human justice – how indeed could courts deal with slights to any of them? – but by divine punishment, ironically subjecting transgressors, at least with respect to the widow and orphan, to the same conditions. That is, God would cause the transgressors to die, leaving their families as widows and orphans. The concern for the poor involves the stipulation that interest must not be charged on loans to destitute people. The harsh realities of socioeconomic life in the highlands of Canaan meant the frequent need for farm families to borrow food or seed. No cases or exhortations deal with a commercial credit system, for Israel's economy was not one in which resources were lent for entrepreneurial ventures.[123] Subsistence loans, as well as compassionate handling of essential items taken as pawn, were meant to help people cope with extreme poverty and could not be a source of gain for the lenders.

Group 2: Responsibilities to God (22:28–31). The preceding exhortation, concerning a pawned garment, ends with the assertion of divine compassion and provides a transition to this next group, which focuses on God. The first exhortation in this group links one's way of behaving toward God with one's behavior toward human leadership, the chieftains; neither is to be cursed. The term for "revile," with respect to God, is actually the same as the Hebrew word in the prohibition against cursing one's parents (21:17). This parallel admonition thus declares the gravity of the blasphemous cursing of human, as well as divine, authority. This is not a casuistic statement, but elsewhere in the Pentateuch the death penalty is mandated for this offense (Lev 24:10–23; cf. 1 Kgs 21:1–16).

The other exhortations of this group are instructions for sacral activities: the offering of the first crops harvested and processed, firstborn animals, and firstborn sons (29–30); and the prohibition of eating carrion (31). With respect to offerings, the general principle is that human, animal, and agricultural fertility is dependent on God, whose beneficence is honored and acknowledged by "returning" to God part – the "first," which symbolizes all – of what is produced. The divine claim on firstborn humans and animals becomes embedded in the collective memories of the past in relation to the slaying of the Egyptian firstborn in 13:11–16, where, unlike in this terse passage, redemption is stipulated for

---

[123] Tikva Frymer-Kensky, "Israel," in *Security for Debt in Ancient Near Eastern Law*, eds. Raymond Westbrook and Richard Jasnow (Culture and History of the Ancient Near East 9; Leiden: Brill, 2001), 251–62.

humans. Special circumstances are mandated for animals, however: they shall not be taken as offerings for a week, perhaps until their viability is established. The sanctity of these offerings may be why the statement about the holiness of the people (cf. 19:6), which provides the rationale for eating only animals slaughtered for consumption, is attached here. Only unblemished animals are fit for consecrated use (i.e., sacrifice) and thus for consumption by consecrated people. This exhortation and the one in 23:19b are the only dietary stipulations in Exodus; Leviticus and Deuteronomy, in contrast, have extensive food regulations (Lev 11:1–47; Deut 14:3–21).

Group 3: Just and humane treatment for all (23:1–9). Nine different prohibitions (in vv. 1–3 and 6–8) meant to maintain integrity and fairness in the judicial process frame several exhortations (vv. 4–5) for humane treatment for all – noncitizens and even animals. Witnesses, litigants, and judicial officers alike are directed to be honest and impartial in the conduct of court cases. As might be expected, we see concern that the rich and powerful ("the mighty" [NRSV "a majority"]) not be favored (v. 2) and that the poor not be slighted (v. 6) in court; but it is striking to see the notion that lenience to the poor likewise might compromise judicial equity (v. 3). This group closes with an echo of the first stipulation in the first group by forbidding the oppression of non-Israelites (v. 9), with the memory of past oppression in Egypt again expressed in a motive clause; presumably the context here demands that foreigners be treated fairly in legal proceedings, as in any other matter (cf. 22:21).

Equity among all people is to obtain even in situations for which adjudication would not apply. A person hostile to another should not do anything to interfere with the livelihood of the other. Although verses 4–5 seem to be concerned with cruelty to animals, it is likely that the dominant interest is in protecting a person's economic resources. In the highlands of ancient Israel, livestock husbandry was as indispensable as agriculture to the subsistence economy and often meant the difference between starvation and survival in years of drought.[124]

Group 4: Observances relating to the agricultural calendar (23:10–19). Beneficial subsistence practices are also reflected in sacral events and observances that mark various aspects of agricultural life. This final section of the community regulations in Exodus gives instructions for the sabbatical year, the Sabbath, and the three agricultural festivals. In so doing, it also reiterates the need to obey God and not invoke the names of other deities; and it adds one dietary constraint.

The three mainstays of the Israelite agrarian economy are grain, grapes, and olives; all three are part of the sabbatical year (vv. 10–11). Allowing fields to remain fallow is important for restoring the fertility of soils, which are inevitably depleted by continuous cropping; awareness of the necessity for this measure

---

[124] David Hopkins, *The Highlands of Canaan: Agricultural Life in the Early Iron Age* (Social World of Biblical Antiquity Series 3; Sheffield: Almond Press with ASOR, 1985), 245–51.

has been known since the beginnings of agriculture.[125] Exodus mandates the practice of fallowing for the *seventh* year, perhaps for symbolic reasons – to synchronize the concept of rest for the land with the Sabbath rest for humans and animals on the *seventh* day. The motive clause adds a charitable rationale, namely making available the seventh year aftergrowth to the poor (and wild animals). However, the paucity of such a resource seems to indicate that the charitable aspect of fallowing is secondary to its value for restoring fertility.[126] Fallowing vineyards and orchards, on the other hand, would have only a humanitarian function. That function also appears in the exhortation to observe the Sabbath, which is not concerned only with free Israelites themselves; its motive clause focuses on the benefits of the day of rest to indentured servants and to non-Israelites and also to animals (v. 12). Because there is no mention, as there is in the Decalogue, of Sabbath rest mirroring God's rest at creation, this iteration of the seventh day rest is surely a prepriestly one.

Because all the stipulations in Exodus 21–23 as well as the Decalogue are presented in the context of the Sinai theophany following the deliverance from Egypt – that is, they are incorporated into the collective memory of the past – an additional statement here is striking in its opposite dynamic. The negative exhortation in 23:13 implores the people to "not remember [NRSV, invoke] the names of other gods." The use of the verb for remembering (*zkr*) is negated, suggesting an attempt at collective amnesia rather than remembrance.[127] Of course, this verse also shows the narrator's awareness of Israelite polytheism.

The presentation of the agricultural feasts in verses 14–17 begins and ends with instructions for holding festivals three times each year before God. In verse 17, however, it stipulates that only the males are to do this, a provision that differs from the directives in Deuteronomy, which include women and children (Deut 16:11, 14). It is difficult to understand the gender exclusivity of verse 17, given the general inclusion of women and children, as well as servants and non-Israelites, as celebrants in other texts describing festivals. Perhaps the practice of pilgrimage to Jerusalem for these festivals (required only of males in Deut 16:16) has influenced this text, as has the reference to the "house" of God (the Jerusalem temple) in verse 19. Be that as it may, it is important to realize that requiring this of men is not the same as denying it to women, whose household responsibilities at times may prevent them from traveling to participate in a festival.

The three festivals mentioned here are the foundational celebrations of the sacral calendar in Israelite and postbiblical Jewish tradition. The first, and arguably the oldest, is the Passover (see Exodus 12), here called the festival of

---

[125] Oded Borowski, *Agriculture in Iron Age Israel* (Winona Lake, Ind.: Eisenbrauns, 1987), 143–5.

[126] Cf. Deut 15:1–11, which mandates the release of debts in the seventh year and does not mention fallowing of land.

[127] M. S. Smith, *Memoirs of God* (2004), 250–5.

unleavened bread. There is a brief reference to its roots in Israel's past (v. 15) but no reference to the paschal lamb. A festal offering is mandated in the form of a negative exhortation, not to come "empty-handed." The second major festival, otherwise known as Shavuot or Feast of Weeks (34:22; also Lev 23:15–21; Num 28:26; Deut 16:10), is linked with agriculture; it is called a "harvest" or "first fruits" festival and involves rejoicing at the appearance of the first grain crops in the springtime. It is not directly connected to Israel's memories of the past in the Bible (cf. Deut 16:12) but does become associated with the Sinai theophany in postbiblical tradition. The third festival is designated as a celebration of "ingathering at the end of the year," that is in the fall, and elsewhere is designated Succoth or Booths (Lev 23:34; Deut 16:13; cf. Exod 34:22); it is related to the exodus narrative in Lev 23:43.

Appended to the directions for festivals are three instructions about sacrifices. Two – not mixing sacrificial blood with anything leavened (v. 18a); being sure that the fatty portions are burnt before dawn (v. 18b) – relate to the Passover offerings. The third (enjoining the people to bring only the finest agricultural yield, v. 19) pertains to the first fruits festival. A final instruction, prohibiting the cooking of a "kid in its mother's milk" (v. 19b), is not easily classified or understood. Repeated in Exod 34:26 (and Deut 14:21), it became extended and generalized in Jewish tradition as a dietary prohibition that forbids the mixing of any meat product with any dairy product. Many scholars interpret it as a polemic against a Canaanite rite, and others consider it a gesture precluding insensitivity to the relationship between an animal and its mother. Such theories, however, lack compelling evidence. A recent explanation, which considers economic reasons and takes into account the fact that it is part of directives for sacrifice, seems more plausible.[128] The consonants of the word rendered "milk" (ḥlb) also can have the meaning "fat." This verse then would be an interdiction against cooking a young animal in "it's mother's fat." In other words, it forbids slaughtering a young animal and also its mother. Doing so would remove two animals and their potential for increasing the herd at the same time, hardly a wise move for subsistence farmers dependent on livestock for many commodities and sometimes even for survival.[129]

Conclusion: Divine promises and admonitions (23:20–33). This brief epilogue to the cases and exhortations of Exodus reiterates God's promise to bring the Israelites into the land of Canaan. In a formal sense, coming at the end of the stipulations of a covenant document, they constitute the conditional "blessings" to be bestowed on those who honor the terms of the covenant, but without the "curses" for infidelity that are usually also present (as in Lev 26:14–33 and

---

[128] Jack Sasson, "Ritual Wisdom? On Seething a Kid in Its Mother's Milk," in *Kein Land für sich Allein: Studien zum Kulturkontakt in Kanaan, Israel/Palestina, und Ebināri für Manfred Weippert zum 65 Geburtstag*, eds. Ulrich Hübner and Ernst Axel Knauf (Orbis Biblicus et Orientalis 186; Freiburg: Universitätsverlag, 2002), 294–308.

[129] For a similar principle, see Deut 22:6–7.

Deut 28:15–68). The blessings typify what people need to survive – to "fulfill the number of your days" (v. 26) – in the highlands of Palestine: food and drink, good health, and successful procreation. These basic components of daily life and family continuity are not to be taken for granted; they are provided by God to those who are faithful to the covenant precepts. Another feature of treaty or covenant relationships evident in this conclusion to the "book of the covenant" is the idea that the adversaries of one party to a covenant become the adversaries of the other. The language of verse 22 ("I will be an enemy to your enemies and a foe to your foes"; cf. Gen 12:3) is strikingly similar to that of a Late Bronze Age treaty: "Whoever is My Majesty's friend should also be your friend; whoever is My Majesty's enemy should also be your enemy."[130]

The blessings are embedded in the notion of territory in that the idea of peoplehood is inextricably related to inhabiting a land. The problem for the Israelites was that they were not the sole occupants of the land they claimed as theirs through the idea of divine promise. The peoples mentioned in verses 23 and 28 become de facto enemies in this scheme, and God assures the Israelites that the indigenous peoples (cf. 3:7–8) eventually will be forced out so that a land with broad parameters (v. 31) will be theirs alone. Solving this problem for the Israelites ironically creates a moral problem for us as we look at it across the millennia. The concept of thrusting peoples from their land and even annihilating them, if that is what "blot them out" (v. 23) entails, brings us perilously close to the practice of "ethnic cleansing." Fortunately, archaeological investigations of Israel's territory and social science analyses of its national identity indicate that the indigenous occupants of the land more likely were absorbed into Israelite political and religious culture than forcibly expelled or killed. Nonetheless, texts like these remain as troubling reminders of an ideology of entitlement to the land expressed in language that is highly uncongenial to tolerance and acceptance of others. Representing the practices of others as sinful and thus as justification for their expulsion (v. 33) is especially problematic, even if it is understood to reflect Israel's own exile from its land in the sixth century BCE.

Israel's right to the land, this epilogue stresses, is contingent on obedience to God. This obedience is presented first as reverence toward the angel that will guide them and guard them by destroying their enemies as they complete their journey. A manifestation of divine presence and authority, this angel is part of a second tier of divine beings; it echoes the image of the destroyer of the Egyptian firstborns and that of the angelic leader of the journey from Egypt to the Reed Sea (12:23; 14:19; cf. 3:2). Concern for fidelity to God also appears in admonitions not to worship or enter into a covenant with any other deity (vv. 24, 32–3). These warnings echo the first stipulation of the Decalogue (20:3) and the "altar law"

---

[130] "Treaty between Šuppiluliuma and Aziru," translated by Itamar Singer (*COS* 2.17A), 94; the treaty is between Hittite and Syrian states.

(20:22–26), which includes the prohibition of idolatry. But this epilogue takes the concern for boundaries between cultures one step further – the Israelites not only are warned against worshipping other gods but also are enjoined to destroy their shrines.

MOSES ON THE MOUNTAIN (24:1–18)

Chapter 24 serves transitional purposes. It contains a response to the Decalogue and the community regulations of the preceding chapters; and it anticipates the continued revelations, setting forth the tabernacle and its service, in the chapters that follow. Like chapter 19, which precedes the Decalogue and regulations of chapters 20–23, chapter 24 contains a complex set of reports about the activities of Moses and other community leaders at the holy mountain. It contains several extraordinary features – a visual experience of God, an allusion to God's heavenly palace, a reference to God's body, and a sacral meal – that arguably make this passage one of the oldest Sinai traditions retained in Israel's collective memory.[131] Although the sequence of events is hard to follow, it is somewhat more coherent than chapter 19, at least with respect to the fact that different zones of holiness mentioned are accessible to different sectors of the people. These zones are reflected in the opening statement (vv. 1–2), which perhaps is a summary of the pretheophany materials of chapter 19: Moses alone can approach God's presence (cf. vv. 15–18; but in v. 13 with Joshua as an assistant); three priestly officials (cf. 6:23) and seventy sociopolitical leaders representing the totality of the people can come part way up the mountain (cf. v. 14; but in vv. 9–10 they too seem to be directly in God's presence); and the rest of the people are to stay behind.

More than being a transitional piece in the overall flow of Exodus, the first part of chapter 24 (vv. 3–8) depicts the culminating step in the establishment of a covenant relationship between God and the Israelites. The covenant, consisting of the "words" of God (presumably the Decalogue) and the "ordinances," is ratified in a complex ceremony involving (1) the reading of the covenant document ("book of the covenant"); (2) the affirmation of the people; (3) the construction of an altar and the erection of pillars that signify the twelve tribes; and (4) the offering of sacrifices with the blood splashed on both the altar and the people. Some of these steps are mentioned twice – in verse 3 and in verse 7, Moses tells/reads God's words, followed by the unanimous assertion by the people that they will obey – perhaps because of the blending of separate accounts of the ceremony.

The sacrifice itself involves a mysterious rite. The blood, the life substance of animals, is smeared on both parties to the covenant. (The altar, on which sacrifices were burnt so that the odor "went" to God, represents the divine

---

[131] M. S. Smith, *Memoirs of God* (2004), 236–40.

presence.) It is difficult to translate this bloody experience into language that makes sense to us today. Perhaps it is best understood as a ceremony in which the people swear unto death, symbolized by the slaughtered sacrificial animals, that they will remain faithful to the covenant bond with God. At the same time, it may be that they are joined to God as "blood brothers," united in a ceremony in which the blood symbolically connects them. The solemnity of the ceremony is marked by the stone monuments representing the traditional twelve tribes of all Israel – they are the witnesses to the establishment of the covenant. From an anthropological perspective, the ritual symbolism of this text incorporates social, sacral, and conceptual processes that would have enabled the Israelites, as a kinship-based society, to express and experience its moral relationships and its social and religious identity.[132]

A CLOSER LOOK: PILLARS (STANDING STONES)

The word used to designate the pillars, sometimes called "standing sacred stones" or "stelae," of the covenant ratification ceremony is found more than thirty times in the Hebrew Bible. The Hebrew term, *maṣṣēbâ*, simply refers to any stone erected by humans and not intended for architectural purposes. It can be correlated with a variety of pillars discovered in sacral contexts by archaeological excavations of many Syro–Palestinian sites.[133] The shape and size of these stones could vary, and some are rough field stones whereas others are well-trimmed and even decorated monuments.

The variety of stones is paralleled by their varied functions, as the biblical references indicate.[134] Witness to a covenant is certainly one such function, as Exod 24:4 indicates (cf. Gen 31:45–54; Josh 24:27; 2 Kgs 23:3). Pillars also could mark a burial site (Gen 35:20) or the place of a theophany (Gen 28:11–22; cf. 31:13; 35:14) and thus of God's presence. In the eschatological vision of Isa 19:19–20 a pillar is a boundary marker: " . . . there will be an altar to the LORD in the center of the land of Egypt, and a pillar to the LORD at its border . . . [as a] sign and a witness to the LORD." As they do in Exod 24:4, altar and pillar together signify God. A similar combination of altar and pillar, twelve pillars to be exact, appears in 1 Kgs 18:30–32. Israelites used pillars, perhaps to represent God in keeping with their aniconic tradition, as part of the cultic furnishings of the *bāmôt* or "high places" (e.g., 1 Kgs 14:23) that were accepted places of sacrifice and worship

---

[132] Ronald S. Hendel, "Sacrifice as a Cultural System: The Ritual Symbolism of Exodus 24, 3–8," *ZAW* 101 (1989): 366–90.

[133] Beth Alpert Nakhai, *Archaeology and the Religions of Canaan and Israel* (ASOR Books 7; Boston, Mass.: ASOR, 2001), ad loc.

[134] Elizabeth C. LaRocca-Pitts, *"Of Wood and Stone": The Significance of Israelite Cultic Items in the Bible and Its Early Interpreters* (HSM 61; Winona Lake, Ind.: Eisenbrauns, 2001), 205–28.

until the late monarchic period. In short, standing stones served to concretize an event (such as covenant ratification), a person, a group of people, a deity, or some combination thereof.

These prominent and positive roles for pillars, however, are complicated by the fact that Canaanites had long been using such monuments as witnesses or symbols of their own deities. Several biblical texts thus see them as an anathema to Israelite cultic practice, as indicated by the command to break down the pillars of the inhabitants of the land in Exod 23:24 and 34:13. The high places with pillars among their furnishings were denounced and destroyed in the late eighth and seventh centuries BCE as part of the royal policy to centralize worship in Jerusalem (e.g., 2 Kgs 18:4; 2 Kgs 23:8, 13–14). The Deuteronomic account of this process claims that the high places were sites of idolatrous worship and compromised fidelity to Yahweh.

The many and divergent positive uses of these pillars in addition to the putative negative ones make it impossible to characterize them in any one way. They almost certainly were not actual images of God in violation of the prohibition of idolatry. The denunciation of pillars, at least those associated with *bāmôt*, is likely the result of the complicated religious and political developments in Judah toward the end of the monarchic period and not because the pillars themselves were problematic. The rhetoric of condemnation unfortunately masks their importance as historical and religious markers in many locales throughout most of the period of the Hebrew Bible.

Although other aspects of the covenant still appear, the literary unit presenting the covenant ratification ceremony ends with the repetition in verse 9 of the movement of Moses, the priests, and the leaders up the mountain. What follows in verses 10–11 is an extraordinary and ancient recollection of theophany at Sinai. These select representatives of the people have a visual experience of God (vv. 10–11), whereas various passages elsewhere in the Hebrew Bible give us the sense that God usually could not be seen. What God looks like is not indicated, perhaps in keeping with biblical reluctance to give full corporeality to God's presence. Yet, in an unusual and ancient anthropomorphism, God's feet are mentioned in this passage; and they are resting on a heavenly blue (probably lapis lazuli) pavement, the floor of God's heavenly abode. This allusion to the architecture of God's palace is probably another very old feature of verses 10–11. Its position here anticipates the succeeding chapters, which provide detailed instructions for building the splendid earthly abode of God. Whether in human form or not, the essence of God's holy presence is fraught with danger (see A Closer Look: Holiness, pp. 152–4), but Moses and his colleagues are spared and consume a meal together. The mountain meal is likely another ancient tradition (cf. 1 Kgs 18:42) and also is associated with covenant affirmation (cf. Gen 26:28–30).

A somewhat more abstract and probably later tradition of the presence of God appears in verses 15–18, where a fiery "glory" of God is within the cloud that covers the mountain. This resonates with the priestly language of the tabernacle dedication, when the structure is covered with a cloud and filled with God's glory (40:34). In this regard, note that the verb used to describe the presence of God's "glory" on the mountain in verse 16 is "dwelled" (škn; inadequately translated "settled" by the NRSV); as a noun (miškān) it designates the tabernacle, God's earthly "dwelling" (see the discussion of 25:8–9).

Between the anthropomorphic tradition of God's presence in verses 10–11 and the more abstract notion of verses 15–18 comes one further aspect of the covenant, namely, the famous "tablets of stone" as the record of the pact between the Israelites and God. Inscribed with God's "teachings [NRSV, law] and commandments" (v. 12), these tablets will ultimately be broken and replaced (chapters 32–34). The account of that incident will reveal what is inscribed on the tablets: the "ten words" or Decalogue (34:28). Important documents were inscribed on stone tablets or monuments in the ancient Near East, and the importance of the Decalogue as a covenant with God and as the foundation of community beliefs and values surely deserved such concretization. The tablets, understood to have been written by God (v. 12), thus constitute the direct record of the relationship of the people with their God. Such a significant and holy document must be properly stored; the mention of the tablets, like the appearance of the pavement of God's heavenly abode, anticipates what follows, namely the construction of the tabernacle, which will have a repository – the ark, the very first item of the sanctuary to be described (25:10–16) – for the covenant.

Chapter 24 explicitly involves the community and its select priestly and civic leaders in the covenant ratification ceremony and even in the astonishing theophany at the mountain. Yet the centrality of Moses in this episode is unmistakable. Moses tells the people what God's words are; he, and not Aaron, is the one who smears the sacrificial blood on the altar and the people; Moses is the one whom God beckons to "come up to me on the mountain" (v. 12); and Moses is the one who enters the cloud that is God's presence and remains there for forty days and nights.

V. Commentary Part III. Sanctuary and New Covenant – Exodus 25:1–40:38

BUILDING INSTRUCTIONS – EXODUS 25:1–31:17

NRSV 25 The LORD said to Moses: ²Tell the Israelites to take for me an offering; from all whose hearts prompt them to give you shall receive the offering for me. ³This is the offering that you shall receive from them: gold, silver, and bronze, ⁴blue, purple, and crimson yarns and fine linen, goats' hair, ⁵tanned rams' skins, fine leather, acacia wood, ⁶oil for the lamps, spices for the anointing oil and for the fragrant incense, ⁷onyx stones and gems to be set in the ephod and for the breastpiece. ⁸And have them make me a sanctuary, so that I may dwell among them. ⁹In accordance with all that I show you concerning the pattern of the tabernacle and of all its furniture, so you shall make it.

10 They shall make an ark of acacia wood; it shall be two and a half cubits long, a cubit and a half wide, and a cubit and a half high. ¹¹You shall overlay it with pure gold, inside and outside you shall overlay it, and you shall make a molding of gold upon it all around. ¹²You shall cast four rings of gold for it and put them on its four feet, two rings on the one side of it, and two rings on the other side. ¹³You shall make poles of acacia wood, and overlay them with gold. ¹⁴And you shall put the poles into the rings on the sides of the ark, by which to carry the ark. ¹⁵The poles shall remain in the rings of the ark; they shall not be taken from it. ¹⁶You shall put into the ark the covenant[a] that I shall give you.

17 Then you shall make a mercy seat[b] of pure gold; two cubits and a half shall be its length, and a cubit and a half its width. ¹⁸You shall make two cherubim of gold; you shall make them of hammered work, at the two ends of the mercy seat.[b] ¹⁹Make one cherub at the one end, and one cherub at the other; of one piece with the mercy seat[b] you shall make the cherubim at its two ends. ²⁰The cherubim shall spread out their wings above, overshadowing the mercy seat[b] with their wings. They shall face one to another; the faces of the cherubim shall be turned toward the mercy seat.[b]

---

[a] Or *treaty,* or *testimony*
[b] Or *cover*

²¹You shall put the mercy seatᵃ on the top of the ark; and in the ark you shall put the covenant that I shall give you. ²²There I will meet with you, and from above the mercy seat,ᵃ from between the two cherubim that are on the ark of the covenant,ᵇ I will deliver to you all my commands for the Israelites.

23 You shall make a table of acacia wood, two cubits long, one cubit wide, and a cubit and a half high. ²⁴You shall overlay it with pure gold, and make a molding of gold around it. ²⁵You shall make around it a rim a handbreadth wide, and a molding of gold around the rim. ²⁶You shall make for it four rings of gold, and fasten the rings to the four corners at its four legs. ²⁷The rings that hold the poles used for carrying the table shall be close to the rim. ²⁸You shall make the poles of acacia wood, and overlay them with gold, and the table shall be carried with these. ²⁹You shall make its plates and dishes for incense, and its flagons and bowls with which to pour drink offerings; you shall make them of pure gold. ³⁰And you shall set the bread of the Presence on the table before me always.

31 You shall make a lampstand of pure gold. The base and the shaft of the lampstand shall be made of hammered work; its cups, its calyxes, and its petals shall be of one piece with it; ³²and there shall be six branches going out of its sides, three branches of the lampstand out of one side of it and three branches of the lampstand out of the other side of it; ³³three cups shaped like almond blossoms, each with calyx and petals, on one branch, and three cups shaped like almond blossoms, each with calyx and petals, on the other branch – so for the six branches going out of the lampstand. ³⁴On the lampstand itself there shall be four cups shaped like almond blossoms, each with its calyxes and petals. ³⁵There shall be a calyx of one piece with it under the first pair of branches, a calyx of one piece with it under the next pair of branches, and a calyx of one piece with it under the last pair of branches – so for the six branches that go out of the lampstand. ³⁶Their calyxes and their branches shall be of one piece with it, the whole of it one hammered piece of pure gold. ³⁷You shall make the seven lamps for it; and the lamps shall be set up so as to give light on the space in front of it. ³⁸Its snuffers and trays shall be of pure gold. ³⁹It, and all these utensils, shall be made from a talent of pure gold. ⁴⁰And see that you make them according to the pattern for them, which is being shown you on the mountain.

NRSV 26 Moreover you shall make the tabernacle with ten curtains of fine twisted linen, and blue, purple, and crimson yarns; you shall make them with cherubim skillfully worked into them. ²The length of each curtain shall be twenty-eight cubits, and the width of each curtain four cubits; all the curtains shall be of the same size. ³Five curtains shall be joined to one another; and the other five curtains shall be joined to one another. ⁴You shall make loops of blue on the edge of the outermost curtain in the first set; and likewise you shall make loops on the edge of the outermost curtain in the second set. ⁵You shall make fifty loops on the one

---

ᵃ Or *cover*
ᵇ Or *treaty*, or *testimony*

curtain, and you shall make fifty loops on the edge of the curtain that is in the second set; the loops shall be opposite one another. [6]You shall make fifty clasps of gold, and join the curtains to one another with the clasps, so that the tabernacle may be one whole.

7 You shall also make curtains of goats' hair for a tent over the tabernacle; you shall make eleven curtains. [8]The length of each curtain shall be thirty cubits, and the width of each curtain four cubits; the eleven curtains shall be of the same size. [9]You shall join five curtains by themselves, and six curtains by themselves, and the sixth curtain you shall double over at the front of the tent. [10]You shall make fifty loops on the edge of the curtain that is outermost in one set, and fifty loops on the edge of the curtain that is outermost in the second set.

11 You shall make fifty clasps of bronze, and put the clasps into the loops, and join the tent together, so that it may be one whole. [12]The part that remains of the curtains of the tent, the half curtain that remains, shall hang over the back of the tabernacle. [13]The cubit on the one side, and the cubit on the other side, of what remains in the length of the curtains of the tent, shall hang over the sides of the tabernacle, on this side and that side, to cover it. [14]You shall make for the tent a covering of tanned rams' skins and an outer covering of fine leather.

15 You shall make upright frames of acacia wood for the tabernacle. [16]Ten cubits shall be the length of a frame, and a cubit and a half the width of each frame. [17]There shall be two pegs in each frame to fit the frames together; you shall make these for all the frames of the tabernacle. [18]You shall make the frames for the tabernacle: twenty frames for the south side; [19]and you shall make forty bases of silver under the twenty frames, two bases under the first frame for its two pegs, and two bases under the next frame for its two pegs; [20]and for the second side of the tabernacle, on the north side twenty frames, [21]and their forty bases of silver, two bases under the first frame, and two bases under the next frame; [22]and for the rear of the tabernacle westward you shall make six frames. [23]You shall make two frames for corners of the tabernacle in the rear; [24]they shall be separate beneath, but joined at the top, at the first ring; it shall be the same with both of them; they shall form the two corners. [25]And so there shall be eight frames, with their bases of silver, sixteen bases; two bases under the first frame, and two bases under the next frame.

26 You shall make bars of acacia wood, five for the frames of the one side of the tabernacle, [27]and five bars for the frames of the other side of the tabernacle, and five bars for the frames of the side of the tabernacle at the rear westward. [28]The middle bar, halfway up the frames, shall pass through from end to end. [29]You shall overlay the frames with gold, and shall make their rings of gold to hold the bars; and you shall overlay the bars with gold. [30]Then you shall erect the tabernacle according to the plan for it that you were shown on the mountain.

31 You shall make a curtain of blue, purple, and crimson yarns, and of fine twisted linen; it shall be made with cherubim skillfully worked into it. [32]You shall hang it on four pillars of acacia overlaid with gold, which have hooks of gold and rest on four bases of silver. [33]You shall hang the curtain under the clasps, and bring the ark

of the covenant[a] in there, within the curtain; and the curtain shall separate for you the holy place from the most holy. [34]You shall put the mercy seat[b] on the ark of the covenant[a] in the most holy place. [35]You shall set the table outside the curtain, and the lampstand on the south side of the tabernacle opposite the table; and you shall put the table on the north side.

36 You shall make a screen for the entrance of the tent, of blue, purple, and crimson yarns, and of fine twisted linen, embroidered with needlework. [37]You shall make for the screen five pillars of acacia, and overlay them with gold; their hooks shall be of gold, and you shall cast five bases of bronze for them.

NRSV 27 You shall make the altar of acacia wood, five cubits long and five cubits wide; the altar shall be square, and it shall be three cubits high. [2]You shall make horns for it on its four corners; its horns shall be of one piece with it, and you shall overlay it with bronze. [3]You shall make pots for it to receive its ashes, and shovels and basins and forks and firepans; you shall make all its utensils of bronze. [4]You shall also make for it a grating, a network of bronze; and on the net you shall make four bronze rings at its four corners. [5]You shall set it under the ledge of the altar so that the net shall extend halfway down the altar. [6]You shall make poles for the altar, poles of acacia wood, and overlay them with bronze; [7]the poles shall be put through the rings, so that the poles shall be on the two sides of the altar when it is carried. [8]You shall make it hollow, with boards. They shall be made just as you were shown on the mountain.

9 You shall make the court of the tabernacle. On the south side the court shall have hangings of fine twisted linen one hundred cubits long for that side; [10]its twenty pillars and their twenty bases shall be of bronze, but the hooks of the pillars and their bands shall be of silver. [11]Likewise for its length on the north side there shall be hangings one hundred cubits long, their pillars twenty and their bases twenty, of bronze, but the hooks of the pillars and their bands shall be of silver. [12]For the width of the court on the west side there shall be fifty cubits of hangings, with ten pillars and ten bases. [13]The width of the court on the front to the east shall be fifty cubits. [14]There shall be fifteen cubits of hangings on the one side, with three pillars and three bases. [15]There shall be fifteen cubits of hangings on the other side, with three pillars and three bases. [16]For the gate of the court there shall be a screen twenty cubits long, of blue, purple, and crimson yarns, and of fine twisted linen, embroidered with needlework; it shall have four pillars and with them four bases. [17]All the pillars around the court shall be banded with silver; their hooks shall be of silver, and their bases of bronze. [18]The length of the court shall be one hundred cubits, the width fifty, and the height five cubits, with hangings of fine twisted linen and bases of bronze. [19]All the utensils of the tabernacle for every use, and all its pegs and all the pegs of the court, shall be of bronze.

[a] Or *treaty,* or *testimony*
[b] Or *cover*

20 You shall further command the Israelites to bring you pure oil of beaten olives for the light, so that a lamp may be set up to burn regularly. [21]In the tent of meeting, outside the curtain that is before the covenant,[a] Aaron and his sons shall tend it from evening to morning before the LORD. It shall be a perpetual ordinance to be observed throughout their generations by the Israelites.

NRSV 28　Then bring near to you your brother Aaron, and his sons with him, from among the Israelites, to serve me as priests – Aaron and Aaron's sons, Nadab and Abihu, Eleazar and Ithamar. [2]You shall make sacred vestments for the glorious adornment of your brother Aaron. [3]And you shall speak to all who have ability, whom I have endowed with skill, that they make Aaron's vestments to consecrate him for my priesthood. [4]These are the vestments that they shall make: a breastpiece, an ephod, a robe, a checkered tunic, a turban, and a sash. When they make these sacred vestments for your brother Aaron and his sons to serve me as priests, [5]they shall use gold, blue, purple, and crimson yarns, and fine linen.

6　They shall make the ephod of gold, of blue, purple, and crimson yarns, and of fine twisted linen, skillfully worked. [7]It shall have two shoulder-pieces attached to its two edges, so that it may be joined together. [8]The decorated band on it shall be of the same workmanship and materials, of gold, of blue, purple, and crimson yarns, and of fine twisted linen. [9]You shall take two onyx stones, and engrave on them the names of the sons of Israel, [10]six of their names on the one stone, and the names of the remaining six on the other stone, in the order of their birth. [11]As a gem-cutter engraves signets, so you shall engrave the two stones with the names of the sons of Israel; you shall mount them in settings of gold filigree. [12]You shall set the two stones on the shoulder-pieces of the ephod, as stones of remembrance for the sons of Israel; and Aaron shall bear their names before the LORD on his two shoulders for remembrance. [13]You shall make settings of gold filigree, [14]and two chains of pure gold, twisted like cords; and you shall attach the corded chains to the settings.

15　You shall make a breastpiece of judgment, in skilled work; you shall make it in the style of the ephod; of gold, of blue and purple and crimson yarns, and of fine twisted linen you shall make it. [16]It shall be square and doubled, a span in length and a span in width. [17]You shall set in it four rows of stones. A row of carnelian, chrysolite, and emerald shall be the first row; [18]and the second row a turquoise, a sapphire[b] and a moonstone; [19]and the third row a jacinth, an agate, and an amethyst; [20]and the fourth row a beryl, an onyx, and a jasper; they shall be set in gold filigree. [21]There shall be twelve stones with names corresponding to the names of the sons of Israel; they shall be like signets, each engraved with its name, for the twelve tribes. [22]You shall make for the breastpiece chains of pure gold, twisted like cords; [23]and you shall make for the breastpiece two rings of gold, and put the two

---

[a]　Or *treaty,* or *testimony*
[b]　Or *lapis lazuli*

rings on the two edges of the breastpiece. ²⁴You shall put the two cords of gold in the two rings at the edges of the breastpiece; ²⁵the two ends of the two cords you shall attach to the two settings, and so attach it in front to the shoulder-pieces of the ephod. ²⁶You shall make two rings of gold, and put them at the two ends of the breastpiece, on its inside edge next to the ephod. ²⁷You shall make two rings of gold, and attach them in front to the lower part of the two shoulder-pieces of the ephod, at its joining above the decorated band of the ephod. ²⁸The breastpiece shall be bound by its rings to the rings of the ephod with a blue cord, so that it may lie on the decorated band of the ephod, and so that the breastpiece shall not come loose from the ephod. ²⁹So Aaron shall bear the names of the sons of Israel in the breastpiece of judgment on his heart when he goes into the holy place, for a continual remembrance before the Lord. ³⁰In the breastpiece of judgment you shall put the Urim and the Thummim, and they shall be on Aaron's heart when he goes in before the Lord; thus Aaron shall bear the judgment of the Israelites on his heart before the Lord continually.

31 You shall make the robe of the ephod all of blue. ³²It shall have an opening for the head in the middle of it, with a woven binding around the opening, like the opening in a coat of mail, so that it may not be torn. ³³On its lower hem you shall make pomegranates of blue, purple, and crimson yarns, all around the lower hem, with bells of gold between them all around – ³⁴a golden bell and a pomegranate alternating all around the lower hem of the robe. ³⁵Aaron shall wear it when he ministers, and its sound shall be heard when he goes into the holy place before the Lord, and when he comes out, so that he may not die.

36 You shall make a rosette of pure gold, and engrave on it, like the engraving of a signet, "Holy to the Lord." ³⁷You shall fasten it on the turban with a blue cord; it shall be on the front of the turban. ³⁸It shall be on Aaron's forehead, and Aaron shall take on himself any guilt incurred in the holy offering that the Israelites consecrate as their sacred donations; it shall always be on his forehead, in order that they may find favor before the Lord.

39 You shall make the checkered tunic of fine linen, and you shall make a turban of fine linen, and you shall make a sash embroidered with needlework.

40 For Aaron's sons you shall make tunics and sashes and headdresses; you shall make them for their glorious adornment. ⁴¹You shall put them on your brother Aaron, and on his sons with him, and shall anoint them and ordain them and consecrate them, so that they may serve me as priests. ⁴²You shall make for them linen undergarments to cover their naked flesh; they shall reach from the hips to the thighs; ⁴³Aaron and his sons shall wear them when they go into the tent of meeting, or when they come near the altar to minister in the holy place; or they will bring guilt on themselves and die. This shall be a perpetual ordinance for him and for his descendants after him.

NRSV 29 Now this is what you shall do to them to consecrate them, so that they may serve me as priests. Take one young bull and two rams without blemish, ²and unleavened bread, unleavened cakes mixed with oil, and unleavened wafers spread with oil. You shall make them of choice wheat flour. ³You shall put them in one basket and bring them in the basket, and bring the bull and the two rams. ⁴You shall bring Aaron and his sons to the entrance of the tent of meeting, and wash them with water. ⁵Then you shall take the vestments, and put on Aaron the tunic and the robe of the ephod, and the ephod, and the breastpiece, and gird him with the decorated band of the ephod; ⁶and you shall set the turban on his head, and put the holy diadem on the turban. ⁷You shall take the anointing oil, and pour it on his head and anoint him. ⁸Then you shall bring his sons, and put tunics on them, ⁹and you shall gird them with sashes and tie headdresses on them; and the priesthood shall be theirs by a perpetual ordinance. You shall then ordain Aaron and his sons.

10 You shall bring the bull in front of the tent of meeting. Aaron and his sons shall lay their hands on the head of the bull, ¹¹and you shall slaughter the bull before the Lord, at the entrance of the tent of meeting, ¹²and shall take some of the blood of the bull and put it on the horns of the altar with your finger, and all the rest of the blood you shall pour out at the base of the altar. ¹³You shall take all the fat that covers the entrails, and the appendage of the liver, and the two kidneys with the fat that is on them, and turn them into smoke on the altar. ¹⁴But the flesh of the bull, and its skin, and its dung, you shall burn with fire outside the camp; it is a sin offering.

15 Then shall take one of the rams, and Aaron and his sons shall lay their hands on the head of the ram, ¹⁶and you shall slaughter the ram, and shall take its blood and dash it against all sides of the altar. ¹⁷Then you shall cut the ram into its parts, and wash its entrails and its legs, and put them with its parts and its head, ¹⁸and turn the whole ram into smoke on the altar; it is a burnt offering to the Lord; it is a pleasing odor, an offering by fire to the Lord.

19 You shall take the other ram; and Aaron and his sons shall lay their hands on the head of the ram, ²⁰and you shall slaughter the ram, and take some of its blood and put it on the lobe of Aaron's right ear and on the lobes of the right ears of his sons, and on the thumbs of their right hands, and on the big toes of their right feet, and dash the rest of the blood against all sides of the altar. ²¹Then you shall take some of the blood that is on the altar, and some of the anointing oil, and sprinkle it on Aaron and his vestments and on his sons and his sons' vestments with him; then he and his vestments shall be holy, as well as his sons and his sons' vestments.

22 You shall also take the fat of the ram, the fat tail, the fat that covers the entrails, the appendage of the liver, the two kidneys with the fat that is on them, and the right thigh (for it is a ram of ordination), ²³and one loaf of bread, one cake of bread made with oil, and one wafer, out of the basket of unleavened bread that is before the Lord; ²⁴and you shall place all these on the palms of Aaron and on the palms of his sons, and raise them as an elevation offering before the Lord. ²⁵Then you shall take them from their hands, and turn them into smoke on the altar on top of the burnt offering of pleasing odor before the Lord; it is an offering by fire to the Lord.

26 You shall take the breast of the ram of Aaron's ordination and raise it as an elevation offering before the Lord; and it shall be your portion. [27] You shall consecrate the breast that was raised as an elevation offering and the thigh that was raised as an elevation offering from the ram of ordination, from that which belonged to Aaron and his sons. [28] These things shall be a perpetual ordinance for Aaron and his sons from the Israelites, for this is an offering; and it shall be an offering by the Israelites from their sacrifice of offerings of well-being, their offering to the Lord.

29 The sacred vestments of Aaron shall be passed on to his sons after him; they shall be anointed in them and ordained in them. [30] The son who is priest in his place shall wear them seven days, when he comes into the tent of meeting to minister in the holy place.

31 You shall take the ram of ordination, and boil its flesh in a holy place; [32] and Aaron and his sons shall eat the flesh of the ram and the bread that is in the basket, at the entrance of the tent of meeting. [33] They themselves shall eat the food by which atonement is made, to ordain and consecrate them, but no one else shall eat of them, because they are holy. [34] If any of the flesh for the ordination, or of the bread, remains until the morning, then you shall burn the remainder with fire; it shall not be eaten, because it is holy.

35 Thus you shall do to Aaron and to his sons, just as I have commanded you; through seven days you shall ordain them. [36] Also every day you shall offer a bull as a sin offering for atonement. Also you shall offer a sin offering for the altar, when you make atonement for it, and shall anoint it, to consecrate it. [37] Seven days you shall make atonement for the altar, and consecrate it, and the altar shall be most holy; whatever touches the altar shall become holy.

38 Now this is what you shall offer on the altar: two lambs a year old regularly each day. [39] One lamb you shall offer in the morning, and the other lamb you shall offer in the evening; [40] and with the first lamb one-tenth of a measure of choice flour mixed with one-fourth of a hin of beaten oil, and one-fourth of a hin of wine for a drink offering. [41] And the other lamb you shall offer in the evening, and shall offer with it a grain offering and its drink offering, as in the morning, for a pleasing odor, an offering by fire to the Lord. [42] It shall be a regular burnt offering throughout your generations at the entrance of the tent of meeting before the Lord, where I will meet with you, to speak to you there. [43] I will meet with the Israelites there, and it shall be sanctified by my glory; [44] I will consecrate the tent of meeting and the altar; Aaron also and his sons I will consecrate, to serve me as priests. [45] I will dwell among the Israelites, and I will be their God. [46] And they shall know that I am the Lord their God, who brought them out of the land of Egypt that I might dwell among them; I am the Lord their God.

NRSV 30 You shall make an altar on which to offer incense; you shall make it of acacia wood. [2] It shall be one cubit long, and one cubit wide; it shall be square, and shall be two cubits high; its horns shall be of one piece with it. [3] You shall overlay it with pure gold, its top, and its sides all around and its horns; and you shall make for it a molding of gold all around. ⁴And you shall make two golden rings for it; under its molding on two opposite sides of it you shall make them, and they shall hold the poles with which to carry it. ⁵You shall make the poles of acacia wood, and overlay them with gold. ⁶You shall place it in front of the curtain that is above the ark of the covenant,^a in front of the mercy seat^b that is over the covenant,^a where I will meet with you. ⁷Aaron shall offer fragrant incense on it; every morning when he dresses the lamps he shall offer it, ⁸and when Aaron sets up the lamps in the evening, he shall offer it, a regular incense offering before the LORD throughout your generations. ⁹You shall not offer unholy incense on it, or a burnt offering, or a grain offering; and you shall not pour a drink offering on it. ¹⁰Once a year Aaron shall perform the rite of atonement on its horns. Throughout your generations he shall perform the atonement for it once a year with the blood of the atoning sin offering. It is most holy to the LORD.

11 The LORD spoke to Moses: ¹²When you take a census of the Israelites to register them, at registration all of them shall give a ransom for their lives to the LORD, so that no plague may come upon them for being registered. ¹³This is what each one who is registered shall give: half a shekel according to the shekel of the sanctuary (the shekel is twenty gerahs), half a shekel as an offering to the LORD. ¹⁴Each one who is registered, from twenty years old and upward, shall give the LORD's offering. ¹⁵The rich shall not give more, and the poor shall not give less, than the half shekel, when you bring this offering to the LORD to make atonement for your lives. ¹⁶You shall take the atonement money from the Israelites and shall designate it for the service of the tent of meeting; before the LORD it will be a reminder to the Israelites of the ransom given for your lives.

17 The LORD spoke to Moses: ¹⁸You shall make a bronze basin with a bronze stand for washing. You shall put it between the tent of meeting and the altar, and you shall put water in it; ¹⁹with the water Aaron and his sons shall wash their hands and their feet. ²⁰When they go into the tent of meeting, or when they come near the altar to minister, to make an offering by fire to the LORD, they shall wash with water, so that they may not die. ²¹They shall wash their hands and their feet, so that they may not die: it shall be a perpetual ordinance for them, for him and for his descendants throughout their generations.

22 The LORD spoke to Moses: ²³Take the finest spices: of liquid myrrh five hundred shekels, and of sweet-smelling cinnamon half as much, that is, two hundred fifty, and two hundred fifty of aromatic cane, ²⁴and five hundred of cassia – measured by the sanctuary shekel – and a hin of olive oil; ²⁵and you shall make of these a sacred anointing oil blended as by the perfumer; it shall be a holy anointing oil. ²⁶With it you shall anoint the tent of meeting and the ark of the covenant,^a ²⁷and the table and all its utensils, and the lampstand and its utensils, and the altar of incense,

---

^a Or *treaty*, or *testimony*
^b Or *cover*

²⁸and the altar of burnt offering with all its utensils, and the basin with its stand; ²⁹you shall consecrate them, so that they may be most holy; whatever touches them will become holy. ³⁰You shall anoint Aaron and his sons, and consecrate them, in order that they may serve me as priests. ³¹You shall say to the Israelites, "This shall be my holy anointing oil throughout your generations. ³²It shall not be used in any ordinary anointing of the body, and you shall make no other like it in composition; it is holy, and it shall be holy to you. ³³Whoever compounds any like it or whoever puts any of it on an unqualified person shall be cut off from the people."

34 The LORD said to Moses: Take sweet spices, stacte, and onycha, and galbanum, sweet spices with pure frankincense (an equal part of each), ³⁵and make an incense blended as by the perfumer, seasoned with salt, pure and holy; ³⁶and you shall beat some of it into powder, and put part of it before the covenant[a] in the tent of meeting where I shall meet with you; it shall be for you most holy. ³⁷When you make incense according to this composition, you shall not make it for yourselves; it shall be regarded by you as holy to the LORD. ³⁸Whoever makes any like it to use as perfume shall be cut off from the people.

NRSV 31 The LORD spoke to Moses: ²See, I have called by name Bezalel son of Uri son of Hur, of the tribe of Judah: ³and I have filled him with divine spirit,[b] with ability, intelligence, and knowledge in every kind of craft, ⁴to devise artistic designs, to work in gold, silver, and bronze, ⁵in cutting stones for setting, and in carving wood, in every kind of craft. ⁶Moreover, I have appointed with him Oholiab son of Ahisamach, of the tribe of Dan; and I have given skill to all the skillful, so that they may make all that I have commanded you: ⁷the tent of meeting, and the ark of the covenant,[a] and the mercy seat[c] that is on it, and all the furnishings of the tent, ⁸the table and its utensils, and the pure lampstand with all its utensils, and the altar of incense, ⁹and the altar of burnt offering with all its utensils, and the basin with its stand, ¹⁰and the finely worked vestments, the holy vestments for the priest Aaron and the vestments of his sons, for their service as priests, ¹¹and the anointing oil and the fragrant incense for the holy place. They shall do just as I have commanded you.

12 The LORD said to Moses: ¹³You yourself are to speak to the Israelites: "You shall keep my sabbaths, for this is a sign between me and you throughout your generations, given in order that you may know that I, the LORD, sanctify you. ¹⁴You shall keep the sabbath, because it is holy for you; everyone who profanes it shall be put to death; whoever does any work on it shall be cut off from among the people. ¹⁵Six days shall work be done, but the seventh day is a sabbath of solemn rest, holy to the LORD; whoever does any work on the sabbath day shall be put to death. ¹⁶Therefore the Israelites shall keep the sabbath, observing the sabbath throughout

[a] Or *treaty*, or *testimony*
[b] Or *with the spirit of God*
[c] Or *cover*

their generations, as a perpetual covenant. [17]It is a sign forever between me and the people of Israel that in six days the LORD made heaven and earth, and on the seventh day he rested, and was refreshed."

*T*he self-revelation of God to all Israel at Sinai is portrayed as a unique and momentous event, the culmination of redemption from Egypt, in the Exodus narrative. But the presence of God thereafter, beyond Sinai, is to be accomplished by constructing a dwelling place for God, a material structure assuring God's accessibility to the community. Virtually all of the rest of Exodus focuses on that portable structure, its appurtenances, and the priestly vestments. It is no wonder that the materials in this third part of Exodus are often referred to as "the tabernacle texts."

The text of Exodus actually uses several different terms – tabernacle, tent of meeting, sanctuary – for this shrine. The most common, "tabernacle," is used some fifty-eight times in Exodus; "tent of meeting" is mentioned thirty-four times, with an additional eighteen references to "tent" standing for tent of meeting; and another word for a shrine, translated "sanctuary," appears just twice.[1] An additional term, "tent of the covenant" appears several times elsewhere in the Hebrew Bible.[2]

The variation in terminology is complicated by the fact that "tent" is also used for the outer covering of the shrine, and "tabernacle" is also used for one of the inner coverings. Moreover, the fluidity of biblical terminology – with terms for portable dwellings used interchangeably, and with "house" sometimes denoting "tent" and vice versa – makes it difficult to ascertain what sort of structure or part thereof any given passage is denoting.[3] The multiplicity of terms is probably also related to the likelihood that the tabernacle texts of Exodus combine several traditions, including ones depicting the ancient pre-temple shrine at Shiloh (Josh 18:1; 1 Sam 2:22; 1 Chr 6:32), which may have eventually been located within the Jerusalem temple (2 Chr 24:6; 29:6; cf. 1 Kgs 8:4; Lam 2:6–7),[4] and others influenced by later traditions associated with the Jerusalem temple itself.

Many biblical scholars have accepted the theory, proposed already in the late nineteenth century, that the elaborate and costly tabernacle of Exodus has no historical basis. Rather than reflect an early sacred shrine, according to this theory the tabernacle is a complete invention of priestly writers of the exilic period or later who used knowledge of the Jerusalem temple and converted it

---

[1] The NRSV also uses "sanctuary" to translate a term relating to the sanctity of the tabernacle service or of the weights of some of the metal items.

[2] Num 9:15; 17:7, 8; 18:2; 2 Chr 24:6.

[3] Michael M. Homan, *To Your Tents, O Israel! The Terminology, Function, Form and Symbolism of Tents in the Hebrew Bible and the Ancient Near East* (Culture and History of the Ancient Near East 12; Leiden: Brill, 2002), 7–28.

[4] Richard Elliot Friedman, "Tabernacle," *ABD* 6:295.

into the Exodus account of a wilderness shrine built under the supervision of
Moses. However, a number of considerations, in addition to the other biblical
references to a tent shrine, support the authenticity of an early portable shrine.
It may not have been as elaborate as in the final form of the text, but nonetheless
it was likely an important part of Israel's early sacral culture.

What are the reasons for taking the tabernacle traditions seriously? For one
thing, such portable tent shrines are well known from the ancient world; one
example even has a red-leather covering (cf. 26:14), and descriptions of others
mention some of the same technical terms as in Exodus.[5] Some of these shrines
apparently were small and can be related to the tent tradition of Exod 33:7, but
there is also evidence from Mari for a monumental portable structure and from
Ugarit for a large tent shrine for the god El.[6] Also, the assumption that the
tabernacle's dimensions are in a 1:2 ratio with those of the Jerusalem temple
and that the tabernacle thus was invented as its half-size predecessor is now
known to be flawed.[7] In addition, the ritual tablets unearthed at Emar, which
were unknown to those positing an exilic date for the priestly writings, show
ritual practices from fourteenth–twelfth century Syria–Palestine that resonate
with practices mentioned in the tabernacle texts.[8] Another consideration is that
some of the elaborate technical details are unrelated to temple architecture or are
congruent with modes of construction of the Late Bronze and early Iron Ages
and would have been incomprehensible to later writers. Finally, the components
and pattern of the lengthy account are remarkably similar to temple-building
accounts known from the ancient Near East, with several segments of the biblical
narrative being especially similar to a sequence in Ugaritic literature.[9]

A CLOSER LOOK: TEMPLES AND TEMPLE SERVICE

Whether portable or permanent, sacred structures in the ancient Near East were
radically different in many ways from religious edifices familiar to us today. We
think of churches, synagogues, or mosques primarily as places of community
worship, whereas temples in the ancient Near East were considered the dwelling
places of deities. They were institutions that provided royally and amply for the

---

[5] M. M. Homan, *To Your Tents* (2002), 89–128.

[6] Daniel E. Fleming, "Mari's Large Public Tent and the Priestly Tent Sanctuary," *VT* 50
    (2000): 484–98.

[7] R. E. Friedman, "Tabernacle," *ABD* 6:295–9; Michael M. Homan, "The Divine Warrior
    in His Tent," *BR* 16 (2000): 24–6.

[8] Daniel Fleming, "Rituals from Emar: Evolution of an Indigenous Tradition in Second
    Millennium Syria," in *New Horizons in the Study of Ancient Syria*, ed. Mark W. Chavalas
    and John L. Hayes (Malibu, Calif.: Udena, 1992), 51–61.

[9] Victor (Avigdor) Hurowitz, "The Priestly Account of the Building of the Tabernacle,"
    JAOS 105 (1985): 21–30.

needs of their inhabitants, even if the earthly residence was only a pale copy of the heavenly prototype. Although it cannot be determined whether some or all of the people in Near Eastern antiquity believed in the literal residence of the deity in an earthly shrine, the conceptualization of such buildings as domiciles for gods or goddesses underlies their origin, symbolism, and associated functions. The architecture, furnishings, personnel, and service of temples in the biblical world can be reconstructed rather well on the basis of both archaeological and textual sources.[10]

The temple (or tabernacle) as an institution was inextricably intertwined with the political and economic organization of the community in which it was located. Especially in some of the larger urban centers of the ancient Near East, temples often were extremely powerful. They owned lands, controlled resources, and were staffed by elaborate bureaucracies of workers and artisans as well as cultic personnel.[11] Indeed, the very existence of a temple legitimized the existence of the political community. For the ancient Israelites, a national sanctuary no doubt functioned in similar ways – signaling to the people themselves, as well as to their enemies and to the nations with whom they had diplomatic ties, that the presence of Israel's deity supported and sustained Israel's national existence.

The belief that the numinous presence of the deity was essential for the success and prosperity of the community was manifest in the elaborate rituals that were meant to serve the deity. Strictly prescribed sets of daily rituals, patterned no doubt after the services provided for elite human leaders or royalty, involved washing and clothing the statue of the deity. Lavish banquets also were provided, in the form of the sacrificial offering of the choicest foodstuffs. For the Israelites, the daily sacrificial "service" was a form of such activity directed toward God as "lord of the manor," with many of the sacrifices meant to attract God's attention (see A Closer Look: Sacrifice, pp. 248–9) Although the aniconic principles of the Israelites precluded the existence of cult images, other artifacts provided the symbolic equivalent.

A hierarchy of priestly officials ministered to the deity by performing the temple service. Most of the work consisted of what we would consider menial labor – butchering animals, cleaning up the results of such activity, preparing food and drink. Typically, only those at the top of the priestly hierarchy had access to the innermost chamber, the holiest spot in the sacred temple precinct, in which the cult statue of the god or goddess was placed. The people in the community themselves probably were able to come no closer than the courtyard

---

[10] Carol Meyers, "Temples," *HBD*, 1106–8.
[11] John F. Robertson, "The Economic and Social Organization of the Mesopotamian Temple," in *Civilizations of the Ancient Near East*, ed. Jack M. Sasson (4 vols.; New York: Scribner, 1995), 1:443–54.

areas in which sacrifices were offered. For the Israelites too, access to the "most holy" was limited to the high priest; and the people themselves might approach the sanctity of the tabernacle or temple only at the outer zone of holiness (as at Sinai), in the court surrounding the structure itself, which is where most of the sacrificial activities took place. In any case, it is clear that a community's sacred structure was part of a three-part sacral system consisting of the building itself, the priestly bureaucracy, and the sacrificial service. The Israelite tabernacle (and temple) was similarly linked with the priesthood and a fixed set of rituals.

The different terms for the wilderness shrine provide a window into its functions. The word "tabernacle" (*miškān*) appears for the first time in 25:9. In the preceding verse (v. 8) the related verb (*škn*, "to dwell") is used for the proclamation that God will "dwell among them." This verb indicates a moving dynamic presence rather than one tied to a fixed location.[12] The English word "tabernacle," from the Latin *tabernaculum* ("tent"), thus designates a type of dwelling, one that is temporary and moveable. Like ancient Near Eastern temples, it is a place on earth in which God will be regularly accessible and from which God's protective power will emanate. Similarly, in the description in 1 Kings (e.g., 1 Kgs 6:1–2), the Jerusalem temple is usually referred to as the "house" or "palace" (i.e., residence) of God but not "temple." The structure and furnishings of the tabernacle are understood to be the sumptuous material surroundings befitting a divine residence. It is important to note, however, that the Hebrew verb translated "dwell" differs from the usual word (*yšb*) for inhabiting or living in a place. The latter term appears in texts that mention the Jerusalem temple as a permanent habitation for God. For example, the temple is called a "house to live in" in 2 Sam 7:5 and "an exalted house, a place for you to live [NRSV, dwell] in forever" in 1 Kgs 8:13. Thus, although both tabernacle and temple are understood to be earthly residences for God, the former indicates a portable and moveable abode and the latter a permanent structure.

The idea of the tabernacle as a dwelling may be more metaphoric than literal. It does not necessarily mean that God was believed to be literally or physically present in it. At the very end of Exodus, once the tabernacle has been constructed, God's glory as manifestation of the divine presence and as represented by a cloud fills the tabernacle (40:34–38). Moreover, 25:8 (and 29:45, 46) specifies that the tabernacle will facilitate God's presence "among," or "in the midst of" the people and seems to avoid language that would indicate that God is dwelling "in" the sanctuary. These subtle aspects of the language of a divine dwelling help negotiate the tension between the freedom of God to be everywhere and the need of humans to have tangible evidence of God's immanence and accessibility. The interplay between divine transcendence and immanence is

---

[12] M. Görg, "*šakan; šāken*," *TDOT* 14:696, 698.

apparent in the ongoing concern for the presence of God in Jewish and Christian tradition. The eschatological hopes of the postexilic community are expressed in an oracle proclaiming that God "will dwell in your midst" (Zech 2:10–11). The root (*škn*) for "dwell" appears in the Hebrew word *šĕkînâ*, which is found in rabbinic literature as a designation for the in-dwelling of God among the people and even as a name for God. Referring to the God available to humans as the Shekhinah preserves divine transcendence. And the language of John 1:14 – "the Word . . . lived among us, and we have seen his glory" – echoes the theme of God's glory "tenting" or tabernacling among the people. "Lived" is Greek *skēnoun*, to "pitch a tent"; and "glory," Greek *doxa*, like the Hebrew *kābôd* indicates a visible manifestation of God. The divine presence in Jesus as the incarnate Word functions, as does the tabernacle, as the tangible and dynamic manifestation of God among humans.[13]

The other term, "tent," that appears frequently in Exodus to designate God's dwelling also relates to God's presence. It is often used in the phrase "tent of meeting" (*'ōhel mô'ēd*), which first appears in 27:21 and is used exclusively for the shrine until "tabernacle" again appears in 35:10.[14] The word translated "meeting" indicates the oracular function of the structure, as a place where God's will is communicated to humans. As set forth in 33:7–11, Moses meets God and receives God's word at the entrance to the tent. In a somewhat different tradition, in 25:22 God proclaims, "I will *meet* with you [Moses]" in the tabernacle in the inner sanctum where the covenant is kept. Not only is the tent shrine the place where God meets a prophetic or priestly leader; but also it is presented as the repository of the covenant (or Decalogue), the physical record of the relationship between God and Israel, which is kept in the ark in that inner sanctum. The term "tent of the covenant" does not appear in Exodus. However, the term for "covenant" in that phrase is *'ēdût*, which is synonymous with *bĕrît*, the term for covenant found in 6:4–5, 19:5, and 24:7–8. The tabernacle texts describing the "ark of the covenant" (25:10–22) use the word *'ēdût* for "covenant," making the wilderness shrine de facto the "tent of the covenant."

Whether in the tabernacle as a dwelling or in the tent as the locale of oracles or in the "tent of the covenant" as the repository of the covenant document, God's presence is the epicenter of holiness. Another term used for the shrine is, appropriately, *miqdāš* (translated "sanctuary"), meaning a "place of holiness" and frequently used to denote the Jerusalem temple in the prophecies of Ezekiel. Although this designation appears only twice in Exodus, the word "holy" is found dozens of times in the tabernacle texts; and the concept of holiness is a central concern in the priestly perspective that dominates them.

The tabernacle texts of Exodus consist of two extended sections. This first (chaps. 25–31) contains what sometimes are called the "prescriptive" texts,

---

[13] Raymond E. Brown, *The Gospel According to John I-XII* (AB 29; Garden City, N.Y.: Doubleday, 1966), 13–14, 30–5.
[14] Ralph E. Hendrix, "A Literary Structural Overview of Exod 25–40," *AUSS* (1993): 123–38.

because they prescribe what is to be constructed. Then, following a complex narrative of apostasy and a new covenant (chaps. 32–34) and preceding a summary of the tabernacle's erection and installation (chap. 40), the second section (chaps. 35–39) contains the "descriptive" texts, recording how the prescriptions are implemented.[15] Biblical scholarship traditionally has seen the descriptive texts as a repetition, with much exact duplication, of the prescriptive ones. These two sections indeed contain much repetitive information, but the arrangement of the materials in them is strikingly different. The second group actually follows the standard arrangement known from ancient Near Eastern archival documents that record the construction of a monumental edifice: it begins with the structure itself, then moves inward toward the furnishings, and finally describes the surrounding court. The account of the construction of the Jerusalem temple in 1 Kings, where it appears as a royal rather than a priestly enterprise, has a similar logical orientation. The descriptive texts exhibit some literary dependence on the prescriptive ones, but the former exhibit more similarity to archival materials than do the latter.[16] The possibility that the descriptive texts are based on Israelite archival sources, with the prescriptive texts added and arranged to suit priestly canonical purposes, cannot be ruled out. Truth be told, the two accounts represent a complex literary tradition that cannot be fully understood.

Coupling the prescriptive chapters with the largely duplicate descriptive ones provides the priestly ideological basis for the sacred edifice. Because the tabernacle as divine dwelling is a microcosm of the universe (created in Genesis 1), it is fitting that it comes into being through a combination of command followed by implementation, just as the universe comes into existence through command and implementation in the priestly account of creation in Genesis 1. Also, it is no accident that Exodus 25–31 contains *seven* speeches or subsections, each beginning with "The LORD spoke [or said] to Moses," with the final one (31:12) containing the instructions for the Sabbath, the equivalent to the *seventh* day in the priestly scheme of creation.

The prescriptive section also serves to integrate the tabernacle texts into the overall flow of the Exodus narrative. It forms a connection to the preceding Sinai account, for its organization is dominated not by the logic of construction but by the concept of holiness. Just as Sinai has zones of holiness, so too does the tent shrine.[17] The prescriptive texts begin, appropriately, with the most holy (the ark, where God's presence rests and where the covenant document is placed) and work outward, whereas the descriptive texts move in the opposite direction. The use of materials also follows this pattern: the most precious materials are

---

[15] The chapter numbers for each section are rounded off here for simplicity. Note, however, that the prescriptive texts end in 31:17, with 31:18 assigned to the "covenant violation and renewal" section.

[16] Baruch A. Levine, "The Descriptive Tabernacle Texts of the Pentateuch," *JAOS* 85 (1965): 307–9.

[17] See the chart of zones in Richard E. Averbeck, "Tabernacle," *DOTP*, 808.

used for the most holy items, and they descend in value as they move away from the epicenter of sanctity.

In addition to the difference in organization, the prescriptive texts are more concerned with the priesthood, especially with the chief priest Aaron.[18] Extensive attention is given to his garments, with only a few verses specifying the garb of the other priests. Aaron first appears in 27:21 and dominates the rest of the prescriptive section, in which his name appears some thirty-three times, whereas it occurs only four times in the parallel descriptive account, which in turn mention Moses more often than do the prescriptive materials. Although the detailed specifications for the priestly vestments appear in both sections, there is no investiture of the priests in the descriptive section. The priestly interests in the tabernacle, which are far more prominent in the prescriptive section, complement the archival functions of the descriptive section.

The following table shows the differences in arrangement of the two sets of texts.

	PRESCRIPTIVE SECTION	DESCRIPTIVE SECTION
Tabernacle Texts		
introduction		
materials	25:1–9	35:4–29
main section		
ark – MOST HOLY	25:10–22	37:1–9
table – HOLY	25:23–30	37:10–16
lampstand – HOLY	25:31–40	37:17–24
structure – over MOST HOLY + HOLY	26:1–37	36:8–38
altar – LESS HOLY	27:1–8	38:1–7
court enclosure – around LESS HOLY	27:9–19	38:9–20
oil for light [out of place?]	27:20–21	35:8, 28
vestments for priests	28:1–43	39:1–31
inventory of work & metals	–	38:21–31
consecration of priests and structure	29:1–46	[Lev 8]
addendum		
incense altar [out of place?] – HOLY	30:1–10	37:25–28
census ritual	30:11–16	–
laver – LESS HOLY	30:17–21	38:8; 40:7, 30
anointing oil and incense	30:22–38	37:29
appointment of artisans	31:1–11	35:30–36:7
Sabbath observance	31:12–17	35:1–3
[completion	–	39:32–43]
[summary: erection and installation	–	40:1–38]

[18] By the postexilic period the Aaronides win a priestly power struggle, and their perspectives pervade their redaction of the Pentateuch.

No other structure or object receives as much attention in the Bible as does the tabernacle. The tabernacle texts include a great deal of specific information about dimensions, materials, and modes of construction. They seem to be a veritable blueprint in words. It is no wonder that there have been many attempts over the centuries to replicate, in models and diagrams, the tabernacle and its furnishings. Yet the results of such attempts diverge. Despite the incredible amount of detail, the texts at times provide only schematic renderings rather than complete verbal plans; at other times they contain technical terms, the meanings of which remain uncertain. The texts give the impression of realism; but they may well represent an amalgam of remembered and existing shrines and of archival records, arranged with the creative imagination of the mnemo-historical process. And perhaps it is just as well that this elaborate, ornate, and expensive tent shrine, with a hierarchy and service so foreign to our contemporary sensibilities, remains an ultimately unrecoverable textual construct. Yet it must be remembered that behind the mass of arcane details lies a yearning for God's presence and an attempt to establish a relationship between divine immanence and transcendence.

MATERIALS (25:1–9)

If the tabernacle as a whole signifies God's presence among the Israelites, it is not surprising that many of its features themselves have symbolic value. This is immediately apparent in the introductory unit, which enumerates the materials to be used in its construction. All together, there are *seven* categories – metals (gold, silver, and copper), yarn (wool and linen), skins (of goats and rams), wood, oil, spices, and gemstones (25:3–7) – signaling a totality of supplies. How the items in the first four categories were to be used must have been self-evident, for they are simply listed. In contrast, the uses for the other three are specified. Some of the items in these categories cannot be identified, but it is clear that they all represent the finest of their kind as befits the residence of a deity. These materials are to be provided not through coercive measures or taxation but rather through willing donations that Moses is to solicit from the people as a whole; for the sacred structure will serve the interests of the whole community.

The last two verses (8–9) in this introductory passage contain the directive from God, who provides a model, to construct the tabernacle. This directive contains important conceptual terms. The word "sanctuary," which emphasizes the sanctity of the building, is found only here in the tabernacle texts and in only one other place in Exodus – in the Song of the Sea (15:17), where it is parallel to "abode." The holiness of the tabernacle is a dominant aspect of its function in the community. So too is its role as God's earthly dwelling place, which is indicated by the term "tabernacle" and also in the use of the verbal root of tabernacle, "to dwell," which appears here in the statement that God will "dwell among them."

One other important term is "pattern" (v. 9). A noun form of the verb "to build," this word (*tabnît*) probably designates an archetypal heavenly structure that God is showing to Moses rather than what the NRSV "pattern" implies, namely, an actual plan that architects and artisans would use to construct a building and its appurtenances. This term also appears in the instructions for the lampstand (25:40), and the directions for making the tent structure (26:30) and the courtyard altar (27:8) allude to it. Human skill will be necessary for the tabernacle's fabrication, but divine creativity provides the model.

INTERIOR FURNISHINGS (25:10–40)

Construction begins not with the structure itself but with its contents, the furniture of God's dwelling. The structure, as we shall see, contains two internal spaces – a "most holy" space, sometimes called the "holy of holies," and the "holy" space (26:33), with a surrounding courtyard of less holy space. On the principle that the first in a series can signify the most important, the furnishings for the most intensely holy part of the tabernacle are presented first. They are made of the most costly materials. The precious metal used to overlay or construct these items is to be "pure gold," a term that probably indicates the absence of impurities in the metal. Because the techniques for the chemical refining of gold ores probably were not developed until the fifth century BCE, the concept of pure gold in the tabernacle texts refers to the highest grade of naturally occurring gold – that is, ores with the fewest traces of other metals. It also can include awareness of the "washing" technique necessary to separate alluvial gold, the most common source of gold in the ancient Near East, from its matrix.[19]

Ark and its cover (25:10–22; cf. 37:1–9). The ark is arguably the most important material object mentioned in the Hebrew Bible. The word "ark" (*'ărôn*) is used several hundred times, with twenty-six of them in the tabernacle texts. Although the term usually appears in sacral contexts, the few "secular" uses confirm that it denotes an object of everyday use, namely, a box or chest of some sort. The dimensions given for it (in cubits) in the tabernacle texts (v. 10) indicate that it was to be about forty-five inches long, twenty-seven inches wide, and twenty-seven inches deep. It was to be made of acacia wood and, as befits its intense holiness, overlaid with pure gold – the highest quality of the most precious of metals. It was to have four "feet" and attached rings for inserting wooden poles, also overlaid with gold, that could be used to carry it.

Chests used as containers for valuables, with similar dimensions and materials and even with poles for transport (vv. 14–15), have been recovered from ancient Egypt, from the fourteenth century BCE. Such early extrabiblical parallels, as well as strong ark traditions in the narratives about the premonarchic and early

---

[19] Carol L. Meyers, *The Tabernacle Menorah: A Synthetic Study of a Symbol from the Biblical Cult* (2nd edition; Piscataway, N.J.: Gorgias Press, 2003), 41–3.

monarchic period, point to the ark as an important community icon from Israel's earliest period. For a people reluctant to use actual images of a deity, the ark served intertwined religious and political functions. By embodying divine presence, it functions as a war palladium in the struggle with the Philistines and eventually becomes an essential symbol of divine legitimization for the new monarchy and its temple in Jerusalem.[20]

Details of the ark's description in Exodus convey its importance as a symbol of God's presence. For one thing, its placement in the holy of holies makes it the equivalent of the cult statue of a god according to the spatial vocabulary of ancient sacred architecture. In addition, it was covered by a rectangular lid (Hebrew *kappōret*, v. 17) with complementary symbolism. The NRSV translates this word with the infelicitous phrase "mercy seat," but it is better translated by the more neutral "cover." Its etymology remains uncertain. Many understand it in relationship to the verb *kpr*, "to atone." It also is possible that it is derived from an Egyptian phrase that would make it equivalent to a place for one's feet to rest,[21] a suggestion that gives it a tantalizingly close connection to the depiction of the ark in nonpriestly texts (1 Sam 4:4; Ps 99:1, 5), in which an invisible God seems to be present on a cherubim throne with a footstool. Given the stipulation that cherubim are to be placed on top of this cover, it may indeed make this "cover" the footrest for the enthroned presence of God. The cherubim themselves similarly convey the notion of divine presence. Their wings suggest a royal throne and also dynamic divine movement (as in 2 Sam 22:11 = Ps 18:10).[22] God is thus enthroned in the tabernacle and also is ever-moving. Divine immanence and transcendence merge, and are not in tension with each other, in this feature of the ark. This invisible presence of God in specific spatial confines can be called "empty space aniconism," for it rejects images of the deity but provides for the highly important sense of divine immanence, usually inherent in cult images, by creating a numinous "empty space."[23]

The final two verses (21–22) of the directions for making the ark bring together its role as covenant repository with its function as the locus of God's presence. The treaty between God and the people is to be placed in the ark, which is called "ark of the treaty" (*'ărôn hā'ēdût*; rendered "ark of the covenant" by NRSV) in all priestly texts.[24] Moreover, the ark is to be the place where God will meet Moses, as prophetic leader and conduit of God's messages to the people. The Hebrew word for "meet" is similar to the word for "treaty"; and the resulting pun connects the ark as container of what God has already revealed to Moses with the ark as site of future oracular revelations of God's will. What is not clear,

---

[20]   Choon-Leong Seow, "The Ark of the Covenant," *ABD* 1:389–91.
[21]   B. Lang,"*kipper*," *TDOT* 7:208.
[22]   David Noel Freedman and Michael Patrick O'Connor, "*kᵉrûb*," *TDOT* 7:310–15.
[23]   T. D. N. Mettinger, *No Graven Image?* (1995), 19–20, cf. 89–90.
[24]   Other biblical texts, especially Deuteronomic ones, call it "ark of the covenant (*bĕrît*)" or "ark of God" or "ark of the LORD" or similar designations.

however, is whether Moses is actually to enter the inner sanctum to stand before the ark. The ambiguity allows for multiple traditions (see chap. 33) – that he converses with God face to face, and that he is more vaguely in God's presence.

BRIDGING THE HORIZONS: THE ARK

Biblical narratives about the ark in the premonarchic and early monarchic periods abound. Its origins and early history are portrayed in elaborate and dramatic detail. Once it is deposited in the inner sanctum of the temple in Jerusalem in the days of Solomon, however, its whereabouts become shrouded in the mystery that inevitably results from the dearth of references to such an iconic object, let alone any account of its ultimate fate. It is no wonder that the notion of the "disappearance" of the ark has emerged, encouraging sporadic expeditions to recover it, to say nothing of a spectacularly successful Hollywood film based on the notion of a "lost ark."

The silence of the Bible about the fate of the ark has led to much speculation. It is not listed among the temple treasures carted away when the Babylonians destroyed the temple (2 Kgs 25:13–17). Hence some scholars suggest that it was either destroyed or plundered some time during the monarchy, as early as the raids of the Egyptian pharaoh Shishak in the tenth century BCE (1 Kgs 14:25–26) or as late as the seventh-century BCE reign of Manasseh, who may have put an image of the goddess Asherah in the temple in place of the ark (2 Kgs 21:7).[25] Postbiblical Jewish tradition features an assortment of legends about the ark's whereabouts. One talmudic text suggests that the reformer king Josiah, anticipating that the Babylonians would conquer Jerusalem, hid the ark along with other sacred utensils (*b. Yoma* 52b). Another legend has it that the prophet Jeremiah put the ark, along with the tent and incense altar, in a cave at the mountain (Nebo) from which Moses had viewed the promised land; it would remain forever hidden there until God revealed its location (2 Macc 2:4–8). We may not know what happened to the ark, but it is fairly certain that it never became part of the restored temple (Second Temple) constructed in Jerusalem in the late sixth century BCE.

The physical ark may have vanished some time during the First Temple period, but its symbolic importance for ancient Israel did not disappear. Beginning in late Second Temple times, when Jewish worship practices apart from temple ritual were emerging, Jews began the practice of reading from the Torah. The text of the Pentateuch was written at that time on scrolls – eventually on one continuous scroll – and these sacred documents were kept in a container. This receptacle is called the Aron Kodesh (*'ărôn haqqōdeš*), which means "holy ark," a designation found only once in the Hebrew Bible, in 2 Chr 35:3, where it clearly

---

[25] Menahem Haran, "The Disappearance of the Ark," *IEJ* 13 (1963): 46–58.

refers to the ark that Solomon brings into the Jerusalem temple. Thus there can be no doubt that the ark as a receptacle for the Torah – understood as a document given by God to the people, in much the same way that the covenant is conceptualized in the Hebrew Bible – was the intentional successor in Judaism to the biblical ark of the covenant. Indeed, folk etymology has it that the word "ark" is an acrostic, combining the first letters at the beginning of the Hebrew words for "holy ark."

Scholars do not agree about when Jews began to read and study the Torah in buildings – synagogues – set aside specifically for prayer and worship. The earliest known synagogue buildings recovered by archaeologists, from the last century BCE or the first century CE, do not have an identifiable receptacle for Torah scrolls. It is widely believed that portable wooden cabinets, which have not survived as archaeological remains, were the arks in which scrolls used in communal worship were stored. In some of the earliest synagogue buildings, a niche in the wall of the synagogue oriented towards Jerusalem apparently was used to hold the ark or the scrolls for the Torah-reading portion of the liturgy. The third-century CE synagogue at Dura-Europos in Syria has just such a niche. Moreover, depictions of these portable cabinets appear frequently in Jewish art of the Roman period.

At some point in that period (first–fourth centuries CE), the ark became a built-in architectural feature of synagogues, similar to the aediculae in which cult statues of deities were placed in Roman buildings of the time. This structural synagogue ark thus shared with its antecedent tabernacle and temple ark the role of signifying God's presence, or at least the presence of God's word in the scrolls contained within it, in the community. The ark itself, whether structural or free-standing, became second only to the Torah as the holiest object in a synagogue, as Talmudic regulations about the ark attest.[26] For example, a synagogue ark cannot be sold, destroyed, or used for some other purpose if a new one replaces it – once holy, always holy (the same being true for Torah scrolls). Worshipers are not to turn their backs to it, and they should rise to their feet when the doors of the ark are open and the Torah scrolls become visible. Opening the ark during certain prayers is a signal that those prayers are especially important.

The earliest known structural ark, dating to the late second century CE, was discovered in the Galilean synagogue at Nabratein.[27] Made of local limestone, it has a pediment that is arched in the center with finely carved rampant lions above it. A hole cut into the arch was meant for suspending a chain on which a lamp would have hung. It has been the tradition in synagogues since

---

[26] Rachel Wishnitzer, "Ark," *EJ* 3:457.

[27] Eric M. Meyers, James F. Strange, and Carol L. Meyers, "The Ark of Nabratein – A First Glance," *BA* 44 (1981): 237–43.

antiquity for an ever-burning light, reminiscent of the lamps (and also incense?) burning continually in front of the tabernacle ark to be suspended in front of the holy ark.

This earliest synagogue ark is fashioned according to the artistic conventions of its day, and such has been the case throughout the history of synagogue buildings. Sometimes features of the earliest known arks are maintained; rampant lions, for example, are often incorporated into the structure of the ark. But new features appear. In the eighteenth century in Europe, perhaps in response to Christian art, it became customary to represent the twin tablets of the Decalogue, sometimes supported by the traditional pair of lions, on top of the ark. Contemporary trends, in the twentieth and twenty-first centuries, involve daring new abstract forms and nontraditional materials, such as concrete, glass, and ceramic tiles. Throughout Jewish history, the artistic and creative sensibilities of Jews have found expression in the decorative attributes of this focal structure of their synagogues. Although it was often was thought that Jewish religious aniconic traditions preclude artistic productions, the existence of decorated synagogue arks (and other ritual objects) for millennia indicates a vibrant artistic tradition.[28] At the same time, the long history of synagogue arks represents continuity with the biblical notion of the centrality of God's holy word. The physical ark may be lost, but its symbolic significance has endured.

Table and lampstand (25:23–40; cf. 37:10–24). The main room of the tent shrine, the second zone of holiness, must now be furnished. A table and a lampstand are to be placed there; they provide for two essential needs of a residence – food and drink, and light. But these appurtenances are no ordinary items of furniture, and the instructions for their fabrication indicate unusual attributes and related symbolic meaning.

A third item, the incense altar, to be placed in this second zone of holiness is not mentioned in the prescriptive section until the addendum (30:1–10), although it does appear along with the lampstand and table in the descriptive texts (chap. 37).

Table. Like the ark, this rectangular structure, thirty-six inches by eighteen inches by twenty-seven inches high, is to be made of wood and covered with gold. It too will have legs with rings to insert poles for carrying it. Four kinds of golden vessels are to be made for the table: large plates; small bowls (NRSV "dishes for incense"); pitchers (NRSV "flagons"); and bowls.[29] The first item was probably for serving bread, the second for the accompanying expensive

---

[28]	Steven Fine, "Iconography: Jewish Iconography," in *Encyclopedia of Religion* (new edition, forthcoming).

[29]	James L. Kelso, *The Ceramic Vocabulary of the Old Testament* (ASOR Supplementary Studies 5–6; New Haven: ASOR, 1948), 22, 24, 31.

incense (frankincense; Lev 24:7), and the third for pouring libations into the fourth. The basic foodstuffs – bread and drink – will be served within the tent, and meat will be part of the courtyard offerings.[30]

Designated by the somewhat enigmatic term "bread of the Presence," the loaves (twelve in all, according to Lev 24:5) may correspond to the twelve tribes, for they are said to represent God's commitment to all the Israelites (Lev 24:8). Whatever their symbolic value, they are placed on the golden table, an appurtenance second only to the ark in holiness. This gives them a prominence that is similar to what we know about such offerings in other ancient cultures, where loaves – sometimes twelve or multiples of twelve – displayed before the deity were central ritual features.[31] Cultic scenes in ancient Near Eastern art frequently depict offering stands or tables laden with foodstuffs, especially loaves of bread. Bread was the basic foodstuff in the agricultural economy of the Israelites, with the Hebrew word for bread sometimes being used to indicate food more generally. Thus the centrality of bread in the offering scheme of the tabernacle acknowledges the dependence of the people on God for providing sustenance.

Lampstand. In comparison with the importance of bread (= food) and drink, a light source in the holy space in front of the ark may seem trivial. The significance of the lampstand (Hebrew *měnōrâ*) lies more in its iconic value than in its pragmatic function, as the details of its fabrication suggest. The various terms used for its constituent parts are replete with botanical imagery: calyxes, petals, branches, and almond blossoms. Indeed, its overall form – a central stand with branches extending from it, three from each side – is strikingly similar to stylized trees found in the representational art of the east Mediterranean in the Late Bronze and Iron Ages. The iconographic context of such representations indicates that these trees-of-life connote the divine power that provides the fertility of plant life.[32] When combined with the symbolism of the light provided by the lamps surmounting the lampstand, the lampstand has extraordinary iconic value. Representing both fertility and cosmic power, the lampstand contributes to the sense of divine presence in the tabernacle. In addition, because sacred trees and holy flames are part of the cosmological notion of the sacred center of the universe, the lampstand helps situate the tabernacle at this meeting place of heaven and earth.

As straightforward as the directions for the lampstand may seem, our conception of its appearance is inevitably affected by the depictions of the lampstand in late biblical or postbiblical Jewish art, in which the specified *seven* lamps are placed at the ends of the branches. The prescriptive text, however, does not give such directions; and the verses about lamp oil (27:20–21; cf. Lev 24:2) mention

---

[30] See chapter 30. However, blood from animals offered annually as a sin offering at the courtyard altar is to be brought into the tabernacle (Lev 16:14–15).

[31] J. Milgrom, *Leviticus 23–27* (2000), 2092.

[32] C. Meyers, *Tabernacle Menorah* (2003), 95–130.

only a single lamp (but cf. Lev 24:4). These divergent details likely reflect the blending of different traditions. Moreover, the size of the lampstand is not indicated, whereas the dimensions of the other furnishings are provided. Based on archaeological information about the technologies of stands and lamps, it is highly likely that the earliest tent shrine had a simple unbranched stand, flaring at the bottom, surmounted by a single lamp – but one with seven spouts – and that a branched stand with lamps at the ends of the branches reflects subsequent developments. In this respect, it is important to note that despite the convergence of many of the details of the Exodus tabernacle with the Jerusalem temple of 1 Kings, there also are differences, one being that the latter is said to have had *ten* lampstands, their form unspecified (1 Kgs 7:49).

Recovering the lampstand's form may be problematic, but there can be no doubt about the material to be used. Unlike the other holy furnishings, which are to be overlaid with gold, the menorah is apparently to be made only of gold.[33] The accompanying utensils, except perhaps for the lamps, for which the material is unspecified, also are to be made of gold. Moreover, the weight of all the gold needed for the stand with its snuffers and trays will be a talent (ca. seventy pounds). Although the descriptive texts (38:24–31) do summarize the amounts of precious metals used for the tabernacle in the aggregate, the amount of metal is provided for no other individual item in the tabernacle texts. The lampstand's prominence among the holy appurtenances therefore is signified by the attention to its gold as well as by its elaborate botanical embellishments.

BRIDGING THE HORIZONS: THE MENORAH (LAMPSTAND)

The form of the lampstand in the premonarchic tent shrine is shrouded in obscurity, and the form of the ten lampstands of the Jerusalem temple of 1 Kings likewise is unknown. What is clear is that the lampstand of the postexilic temple was a single, branched object. A handful of depictions from the end of the Second Temple period indicate that it was similar to the one in Exodus. It met its unhappy fate in the year 70 CE, when it was carried off to Rome by the conquerors of Jerusalem.

The loss of the temple lampstand, or menorah, as it is usually called, did not mean the end of its symbolic value. As a unique iconic object in the tabernacle texts of Exodus and in the sacred space of ancient Israel's religious architecture, it in many ways was an ideal symbol. Images of it began to proliferate in the Roman and Byzantine periods, after the temple was destroyed. Depictions

---

[33] Another but less likely possibility is that the term "hammered" (v. 31) indicates that sheet gold is to be worked into the desired shape over a wooden model that is not mentioned; the same would be true for the cherubim, the only other item said to be made of hammered work (25:18; but cf. 1 Kgs 6:23–28). See ibid., 31–4.

appear on a wide variety of artifacts – lamps, pottery, glass, coins, sarcophagi, tomb doors, amulets, bread stamps, mirrors, seals, and jewelry – as well as on synagogue mosaic floors, chancel screens, and wall paintings.[34] Only a few freestanding replicas are found in late antiquity, however, perhaps because of repeated rabbinic injunctions forbidding its reproduction (*b. Menaḥ* 28b; *b. 'Abod. Zar.* 43a; *b. Roš. Haš.* 24a, b).

In late antiquity, if not beyond, it was by far the most important Jewish symbol. Perhaps in response to the burgeoning use of the cross as a Christian symbol, the menorah became a marker of Jews and their spaces; or it could have been the other way around, for the menorah was well established as a Jewish symbol long before the cross became a common Christian symbol. More likely, these two powerful symbols developed in tandem in their respective communities, under similar cultural stimuli, expressing the unique religious views of each and also marking them off from each other. The menorah was even used sporadically in Christian art, based as it was on scriptural themes. Not surprisingly, it appears in illuminated manuscripts produced by both Jews and Christians in the medieval period.

The menorah as a Jewish symbol has endured to the present, but its meaning has varied over the centuries. Its early postbiblical significance probably was drawn from the lights it bore and their cosmic significance more than from its form as a sacred tree. Still, as in the biblical period, it thereby represented God's eternal presence.[35] Note that in the vision of the prophet Zechariah (chap. 4), the menorah represents God and the lamps are God's eyes. That it also represented everlasting life for many may be why it became so popular in funerary contexts. At the same time, according to discussions in Jewish texts from the rabbinic period onward, it came to signify the biblical past as a whole and even the Torah in its broadest sense. As a symbol of the biblical past, when Israel had a homeland and a temple, it also took on messianic hopes for the future.[36]

No other Jewish emblem has such instant and meaningful recognition value. The hexagram or "star of David," an ancient geometric form that emerged as a Jewish symbol only in the past few centuries, perhaps has become more widely used; but it lacks the rich historical pedigree of the menorah. Thus, although the hexagram appeared on its flag when Israel was declared a nation in 1948, the menorah became its official coat of arms, appearing on government stationery, buildings, and other formal aspects of the Jewish state. And freestanding

---

[34] Rachel Hachlili, *The Ancient Menorah, the Seven-armed Candelabrum: Origin, Form, Significance* (*JSJ* Supplements 68; Leiden: Brill, 2001).

[35] Erwin R. Goodenough, *Jewish Symbols in the Greco-Roman Period* (13 vols.; New York: Bollingen Foundation, 1953–68), 4:71–98, 12:79–83.

[36] Steven Fine, *Art and Judaism During the Greco-Roman Period: Toward a New "Jewish Archaeology"* (Cambridge: Cambridge University Press, 2005).

menorahs have become standard interior furnishings of many contemporary synagogues, echoing the sacral furniture of biblical antiquity and proclaiming the biblical heritage of Judaism.

STRUCTURE/DWELLING (26:1–37)

With directions for its interior furnishings completed, the text turns to the tabernacle structure itself. Chapter 26 gives instructions for its three components: coverings of textiles and skins; framework; and two textile partitions, one rendered "curtain" and the other "screen" in the NRSV. Perhaps no section of the tabernacle texts is so information dense as is this one. At the same time, the plethora of details, either because of omissions or unfamiliar technology, or both, precludes a clear understanding of how the framework with its coverings is to be assembled.

Coverings (26:1–14; cf. 36:8–19). Here the term "tabernacle" (vv. 1, 6, 7) refers just to the inner layer of materials, which consists of "panels" (NRSV "curtains") that are forty-two feet by six feet in size and are to be made of linen and richly colored wool fabric.[37] Three colors are specified for the yarns: blue, purple, and crimson (v. 1). Dyed wools were produced in the Near East as early as the end of the third millennium BCE.[38] The most prized dyes were self-fixing, which means they are relatively impervious to light and water and remain bright over time. Dying woolen strands with these colors was a costly enterprise because the raw materials often were rare or difficult to use. In the Near East, the durable and thus most desirable colors happen to be sea-snail purple from the murex shell, indigo blue, and a cochineal red. These are exactly the colors prescribed for the costly fabrics of the tabernacle and also for the priestly vestments, just as they were for royal and religious fabrics elsewhere in the ancient Near East.[39] In addition, this costly material is to be woven with cherubim designs.[40]

Just as the furnishings surrounded by these textiles are to be covered with gold, so too is gold, the metal for the loops and clasps that will join the fabric panels. Throughout the structure, there is a general correspondence between the zone of holiness and the costliness of the component materials. Bronze (more likely copper) and goats' hair were less precious than gold and embroidered fabrics. Thus bronze clasps are used to fasten the outer fabric layer, namely,

---

[37] This combination is forbidden elsewhere in the Pentateuch (Lev 19:9; Deut 22:11), but those texts refer only to garments.

[38] Elizabeth J. W. Barber, "Textiles of the Neolithic through Iron Ages," *OEANE* 5:192.

[39] E.g., "Dawn and Dusk," translated by Dennis Pardee (*COS* 1:87), 279.

[40] The "skillfully worked" technique may be what is called pattern or tapestry weaving, invented in the Near East to exploit the properties of fine wool; see Elizabeth Wayland Barber, *Women's Work: The First 20,000 Years – Women, Cloth, and Society in Early Times* (New York: Norton, 1994), 103–4.

eleven "curtains" measuring forty-five feet by six feet and made of goats' hair
to form a "tent" covering (v. 7). This tent then is completed with two layers of
less costly materials: tanned rams' skins, and the skins of another animal that
remains obscure. Fewer details are provided for the skins, and no measurements
are given. All together, four layers – two of fabric and two of skins – comprise
the portable shrine.

Frames (26:15–30; cf. 36:20–34). The coverings are to be stretched over gilded
acacia wood frames set on silver bases and fastened together with an intricate
array of gilded rings and bars. Although the dimensions are given for the length
(ten cubits or fifteen feet) and width (1½ cubits or twenty-seven inches) of each
of the frames, their thickness is not specified. The fact that there are to be
twenty frames on each side and six plus two corner frames at the rear of the
structure indicates its overall rectangular shape. Yet, because the thickness of the
frames and the way they are to be fitted together remains obscure, the overall
dimensions of the structure remain approximate. For two millennia, many have
tried, with little unanimity, to ascertain its size and shape. According to the most
comprehensive and sensible study to date, it probably would have been slightly
more than thirty cubits (forty-five feet) long and a bit more than ten cubits
(fifteen feet) wide.[41] Although its size is debatable, its east–west orientation,
with the inner sanctum at the west end (vv. 18, 20, 27), is clear.

Textile partitions (26:31–37; cf. 36:35–38). The interior space is to be divided
so that the ark with its cover, the holiest of the furnishings, will be secluded
in its own sacred space. That space is called "holy of holies" (NRSV "most
holy"), and the rest of the interior is designated "holy" (v. 33). The partition
between these two sections of the tabernacle's interior will consist of a linen and
wool fabric "veil" (NRSV "curtain"), richly colored and woven with cherubim
corresponding to the fabric panels of the tabernacle, and suspended on gilded,
acacia-wood posts fitted with gold hooks and set into silver bases. Its size is not
given, nor is its placement across the east–west axis specified; it seems likely to
have been situated so as to close off an inner sanctum about one-third the length
of the structure. Once the ark and its cover and then the veil are in place, the
lampstand and offering table can be put in their assigned positions in front of
the veil, on the south and north respectively (v. 35). A third piece of furniture,
the golden incense altar, also will be placed in front of the fabric partition that
hides the ark, but instructions for its placement come later (30:6).

One final piece of the structure remains to be specified, and that is its entrance.
The frames and curtains do not enclose the eastern end, which is left open. A
fabric screen will stretch across the open space. Of richly colored wool and
linen fabric like the veil, it lacks the cherubim and instead is embellished with
embroidery of unspecified design. Presumably, this treatment is somewhat less
elaborate than that of the veil because the screen borders on the court, the zone

[41] M. M. Homan, *To Your Tents* (2002), 137–85.

of least holiness. Like the veil, it is suspended on gilded acacia-wood poles. However, again because the screen marks the passage to the less holy court, the poles are set into bronze bases rather than the more costly silver ones of the holier space.

COURTYARD (27:1–19)

The instructions for the entryway screen provide a transition to the next section of the prescriptive texts, instructions for the courtyard surrounding the tabernacle. Virtually no domicile in the ancient Near East, whether a village house or an urban palace, lacked unroofed outdoor space. Given the warm dry climate for much of the year, occupants of a household often were more comfortable in shaded outdoor spaces than in roofed rooms. Moreover, certain household functions, such as keeping animals or roasting large pieces of meat, were performed more efficiently and pleasantly in open areas. Courtyards therefore were de rigueur in the architecture of dwellings, except in crowded areas where flat roofs were used for many of the activities otherwise carried out in courtyards.[42] Depending on space constraints, courtyards might be small spaces adjacent to one exterior wall or even incorporated into the building as interior space. Larger buildings or palaces frequently had extensive exterior courtyards, perhaps surrounding the entire structure. An enclosure wall, such as that described here for the tabernacle, surrounded virtually any exterior courtyard. However, following the same logic as the instructions for the tabernacle, the courtyard furnishings are specified before directions are provided for the enclosure wall.

Altar (27:1–8; cf. 38:1–7). Only one courtyard appurtenance is presented in this section. Another appears, as does the incense altar for the interior space, in the addendum in chapter 30 (vv. 17–21). Made of acacia wood and overlaid with bronze, the massive altar is to be five cubits square and three cubits high (ca. $7\frac{1}{2} \times 7\frac{1}{2} \times 4\frac{1}{2}$ feet) and have bronze rings and acacia-wood poles covered with bronze for transport. Note that the height, which would have necessitated steps, as well as the materials, set it apart from the low stone or earthen altars of 20: 24–26; details of altars from different periods or settings diverge. Note also that a wooden altar, even one covered with metal, is unlikely to have been functional – it seems that the idea of having a massive yet portable altar necessitated this kind of hypothetical structure; it is possible that altars familiar from a later period have been retrojected onto the image of the tabernacle altar.

Perhaps its most striking feature is the protrusion of "horns" from each of the corners. Their placement on the corners is not specified, but the many horned altars recovered in archaeological excavations indicate that the horns turn upward from the top of the corners. Most of the square, horned altars found in excavations are small ones, meant for incense and thus more relevant

---

[42] John S. Holladay, Jr., "Syro-Palestinian Houses," *OEANE* 3:95.

to the incense altar (see below). But two large examples from the period of the monarchy, one from Beersheba and the other from Arad, are somewhat similar in size to that of the tabernacle.[43] Those altars, however, are made of stone. No metal altar has ever been discovered – not because they were not used, but because, if destroyed or dismantled, the metal would have been taken for other purposes. The role of the horns on the altar is mentioned in the consecration text (29:12).

Just as the golden lampstand and table inside the tabernacle have utensils of the same metal (gold), this bronze courtyard installation has associated utensils of the same metal (bronze). Nothing is said here about how the altar will be used. However, 30:28 refers to it as the "altar of burnt offering"; and the consecration ceremony mentions that grain, oil, and wine, as well as animals, are to be offered on it (29:38–41). It apparently is to function as the main sacrificial altar for the Israelites. The summary statement (v. 19) at the end of the next section, giving instructions for erecting the courtyard enclosure, refers to the "service" (NRSV "use") of the tabernacle. In this instance, "tabernacle" designates the courtyard; and "service" is a technical term for the set of altar rituals.

Enclosure (27:9–19; cf. 38:9–20). Households and palaces typically were surrounded by enclosure walls in the ancient Near East. Such walls not only demarcated the limits of each residential unit; they also served pragmatic purposes, such as controlling the movement of animals or small children and protecting domestic space and its contents from intruders. Enclosure walls around shrines may have included these functions, but their most important role was to demarcate the boundary between the sacred space within and the profane world outside. The potential dangers as well as blessings represented by the intense holiness of the divine presence meant that access to the interior had to be carefully controlled, according to this mindset, for the safety of the populace.

The courtyard enclosure is to be constructed of panels of linen fabric suspended on silver hooks from posts banded with silver and set into bronze bases. Although not mentioned except in the summary at the end of this section (v. 19), bronze pegs are also part of the construction of the enclosure (cf. Exod 38:20, 29–31; 39:39–40). The material of the posts is unspecified; presumably they are to be made of acacia wood as are the posts that form the tabernacle itself. When the posts and fabrics are in place, the court will measure one hundred by fifty cubits (ca. one hundred-fifty by seventy-five feet). This "wall" is to be five cubits (7½ feet) high. This is half the height of the tabernacle, which apparently was meant to be seen by people outside the sacred compound. Courtyards in permanent structures would be entered through secured gateways; but entrance to this portable enclosure is provided by a twenty-cubit (thirty-foot) wide screen, with fabric panels stretching fifteen cubits on each side to form the eastern wall of the courtyard. The fabric for the entry screen would be more elaborate than

---

[43] Robert D. Haak, "Altar," *ABD* 1:166.

that for the enclosure panels; like the entrance to the tent itself (26:36), the screen would be made of richly colored wool and linen and would be embroidered.

Despite the abundant details for constructing the enclosure, the actual location of the tabernacle within the sacred precinct is not stipulated. Several placements are possible, if the general symmetry of the tabernacle and its enclosure is taken into account. But perhaps its location is omitted intentionally. The various components of God's earthly dwelling are described with considerable, albeit not complete, precision; the exact spot of divine immanence within the structure is better left unsaid.

OIL FOR LIGHT (27:20–21)

The oil required for the daily ritual use of the lamp (or lamps) of the lampstand is not mentioned in the section about constructing a lampstand but, rather, here, once instructions for making the entire structure and all its furnishings have been given. The details of this passage – the mention of only one lamp and the reference to the tent of meeting and the covenant (rather than the tabernacle and the ark of the covenant with its cover) – suggest that it belongs to a discrete tent-of-meeting tradition, presumably the earliest of the sacred shrine traditions brought together in the tabernacle texts.

That olive oil is the fuel for the lamp (as well as for anointing; see 30:24–25) is not surprising. The cultivation of olive trees for their fruit and oil and even their wood was a major part of the Syro–Palestinian agricultural economy as early as the fourth millennium BCE. Olive cultivation may even have originated in this area, and its quality was so high that it at times was exported to Egypt and Cyprus. Whether in the form of cured olives or pressed oil, olives provided the basic fat source for the Mediterranean diet. Olive oil also had cosmetic and medicinal uses, and it served as a relatively clean-burning lamp fuel. Because the mature olive tree is far less susceptible to the repeated droughts of the highlands of the land of Israel than are field crops, planting olive trees meant establishing a relatively reliable food source. The olive tree thus symbolizes fertility in many biblical passages. The use of olive oil for the light source of the lampstand enhances the tree-of-life symbolic value already present in the stand itself. The oil is to be of the highest quality: "clear" (*zak*; NRSV "pure"), meaning free of residues.

The nature of the lampstand ritual is now disclosed, but it is not not fully comprehensible. For one thing, it seems that Aaron and his sons are equally responsible. But 30:7–8 (and Lev 24:2–4) preserves a tradition focusing on Aaron; it has tending lamps as the responsibility of Aaron alone, without a cadre of other priests. The light is set up in the sacred area right in front of the ark; and the high sanctity of Aaron as chief priest makes him the appropriate figure, in terms of the zones of sanctity of priestly tradition, to perform this task. Also, a light is to burn "regularly" (*tāmîd*), which probably meant that it was to be kindled on a regular basis – lit every evening to burn through the night until morning. But *tāmîd* can also mean "continually," indicating an ever-burning light, which is how postbiblical Jewish tradition understands it. As described in Bridging the Horizons: The Ark (pp. 229–31), an "eternal light" recalling the regularly burning tabernacle light has been hung in front of the holy ark in synagogues since antiquity. The builders of synagogues took seriously the injunction (v. 21) that this rite be performed "for all time, throughout the ages" (NJPS). In any case, the mention of priests and the naming of Aaron for the first time in the tabernacle texts form an apt transition to the next two sections (28:1–43 and 29:1–46), which provide instructions for making the priestly vestments and then consecrating the priests (and the tabernacle).

VESTMENTS (28:1–43)

Temples in the ancient Near East consisted of personnel (and activities) as well as a structure with furnishings. Like palaces, which have coteries of servants to take care of the needs of their occupants, temples have priestly establishments, a hierarchy of officials to carry out the myriad of tasks involved in running a large household. The same was apparently true for the Israelites, although the tabernacle texts provide little information about the tasks, many of them little more than menial labor, of the lower echelons of the priesthood. Some priestly texts, such as the preceding passage about oil for the lamps, and others, mainly in Leviticus, provide hints about the rites that the highest priestly officer is to perform. This chapter focuses in great detail (vv. 2–39) on what he is to wear while carrying out his tasks, with a few additional verses (40–43) providing some information about the attire of Aaron's sons, second-tier priests. Because priestly documents from all over the ancient Near East contain information about elaborate and ornate priestly garb, the authenticity of special apparel for the Aaronides seems certain. However, as with other aspects of the tabernacle texts, there probably are layers of data, some much later than others, which no longer can be separated. Similarly, authentic traditions may be overlain with imaginative and hyperbolic expansions.

An elaborate set of apparel is to be prepared for Aaron and his sons, who serve with their father and will inherit the office from him (see 29:9). Those entrusted with making the vestments are to be especially skilled, and they are likely to have been female as well as male artisans (see 35:25–26 and 36:6). In setting the task for the artisans, the word "priest" is used for the first time in association with Aaron (v. 4); priestly office and priestly garb thus are inextricably related. Six items for Aaron's wardrobe are listed in verse 4: breastpiece, ephod, robe, tunic, turban, and sash. Instructions for making them are then provided although not in the same order as in the itemized list. Collectively these garments are called "sacred vestments," which can mean that the garments themselves are considered holy or that they are worn in entering holy space or, probably, both. In 35:19 they are called "service vestments" (NRSV "vestments for ministering"), indicating that they clothe Aaron as officiant. A cursory glance at the list shows that these are not ordinary items of clothing. Even the robe, for example, arguably is a garment of everyday use but is set apart from such garments by its sumptuous fabric and embellishments.

Two of the items, the ephod and breastpiece, are highly specialized, appearing almost exclusively in priestly contexts and probably having a specific role in ritual practice. Although very different in their construction, these two items share certain features. For one thing, their importance is signaled by the fact that directions for making them are far more extensive than for the other pieces of priestly garb. Another feature is that they are linked structurally with rings and cords. Perhaps most striking is that they are both to be adorned with gemstones engraved for "remembrance" (28:12, 29) with the names of the Israelite tribes. This feature has commemorative symbolic value, bringing all Israel into the tabernacle with Aaron as he carries out the rituals thought to help secure the well-being of the people or adjudicate their conflicts.

The gemstones themselves – the two on the ephod and the *twelve* on the breastpiece – are difficult to identify, as generally is the case for specific terms in biblical Hebrew for items of the natural world. The term for the two stones, each with six tribal names engraved on it, of the ephod is translated "onyx" in the NRSV but has also been identified as carnelian or lapis lazuli. Three of the stones (jacinth, agate, and amethyst) of the breastpiece are mentioned in the Bible only here and in the parallel descriptive verse and also are difficult to identify. Even those that appear several other times in the Bible cannot be identified with certainty, and they are translated by as many as seven or eight different English words in various translations.[44] Although their mineralogical identity is uncertain, the technology and function of such stones is well known. The engraving of precious stones with the names of their owners, and often also with a design or image, was a highly developed craft in biblical antiquity. The resulting objects served as seals or "signets" (28:21). These name-seals, hundreds of which have been discovered in excavations of Israelite sites of the Iron Age, probably were used for official legal documents.[45] Thus the presence of seals engraved with tribal names gives collective Israelite authority to the decisions rendered by the priest wearing the breastpiece.

The ephod and breastpiece are linked further in that a special fabric is to be used for both. The very nature of that fabric is an important clue to their significance in the tabernacle. Like the sumptuous textiles of the tabernacle itself, they are to be made of linen and richly colored wools. But the priestly vestments

---

[44] Possible translations are listed in Noel D. Osborn and Howard Hatton, *A Handbook on Exodus* (UBS Handbook Series; New York: United Bible Societies, 1999), 660–1.

[45] Nahman Avigad, *Corpus of West Semitic Stamp Seals* (revised and completed by Benjamin Sass; Jerusalem: Israel Academy of Sciences and Humanities, Israel Exploration Society, and Hebrew University Institute of Archaeology, 1997).

were even more ornate – gold is somehow to be incorporated into their design to great dramatic effect. Incorporation of gold into ceremonial garb is known from Mesopotamia, where garments meant for the statues of deities were elaborately decorated with gold.[46] Fabrics treated in this manner are fit only for deities or humans of the highest rank. The fabrics of these two vestments thus enhance the authoritative aura of the priesthood.

Neither of these priestly vestments can be reconstructed with confidence, but several aspects of each, apart from the other, can be discerned. Although not the first item in the introductory list, the *ephod* (28:6–14) is the first for which directions are given. Perhaps this piece comes at the beginning because of its apparent antiquity in the array of Israelite priestly apparel. In addition to the priestly texts of the Pentateuch, it appears in a handful of deuteronomic texts relating to the premonarchic and early monarchic periods; and an equivalent term appears in other ancient Semitic texts.[47] These sources contain such disparate information, however, that it is very difficult to understand what an ephod looked like or how it was used. Scholars have struggled with the ephod problem since antiquity. The appearance and use of the ephod clearly varied over the millennium or more represented by all these sources. What is constant is that the ephod always is related to ritual matters – sometimes as a ritual garment, sometimes as a divinatory device, and sometimes as both. In Exodus and other priestly texts, its details and its association with the breastpiece make it likely that it was worn by the priest and also used for oracular purposes.

Although the *breastpiece* is the second item, the passage presenting it is roughly twice as long as that for the ephod; in the NRSV, 196 words are devoted to the ephod and 400 to the breastpiece. The directions for the breastpiece also introduce the enigmatic Urim and Thummim (v. 30), which are to be inserted in the breastpiece and which indicate that the priestly vestments, at least the breastpiece and perhaps the ephod, by its connection to the breastpiece, are ritual appurtenances in themselves. The Urim and Thummim are divinatory devices relating to the oracular priestly functions; they apparently were utilized to obtain input from God in human decision-making processes (1 Sam 14:36–42). The breastpiece thus plays a role in the judicial functions of the priesthood. In verses 15, 29, and 30 the breastpiece is called the "breastpiece of judgment." In this context "judgment" refers to God's rulings about legal matters that human adjudicators cannot resolve (see the discussion of 18:15–16 and 22:7–9; cf. Ezra 2:63). The breastpiece and the Urim and Thummim were the instruments used by the priest to discern God's will.

---

[46] A. Leo Oppenheim, "The Golden Garments of the Gods," *JNES* 8 (1949): 172–93.
[47] Biblical texts include Judg 8:24–27; 1 Sam 18:1–4; 2 Kgs 8:8–14. A cognate term is found in Akkadian texts of the Old Assyrian period and in Ugaritic documents of the Late Bronze Age.

The presence of gemstones representing all the people, on both breastpiece and ephod, contributed literally and symbolically to the weightiness of the judicial functions of these items of priestly apparel. Similar evidence of the gravity of the judicial processes is that the breastpiece and the Urim and Thummim, as material conduits of God's message, were to be on Aaron's heart (vv. 29–30). In the Bible's anthropology, the heart was a person's affective and vital center, the originating point of thinking and planning, the seat of conscience and ethical judgment, and the locus of divine influence upon the individual.[48] What better place to position the breastpiece of judgment than over the priest's heart!

The next item of clothing, the *robe* ("robe of the ephod," v. 31), may not have such a direct role in what the priest does; but it contributes to the overall sacrality of the tabernacle and its rituals. Associated in biblical texts with royalty or other high officials, its distinctiveness lies in its border. Multicolored tassels in the shape of pomegranates are to be placed, alternately with golden bells, at its hem. Such elaborate decorations are well-known in iconographic representations of the garments of deities and rulers from northern Mesopotamia and Syria of the Iron Age.[49] Both woolen tassels as well as metal embellishments are depicted, although it is not clear whether any of the latter are bells. The presence of bells, whether or not uniquely Israelite, introduces the sense of sound to the array of sacral appurtenances, which, as a group, touch upon all the senses. More important, the bells are apotropaic, for sounds were believed to frighten away evil spirits and keep people from danger. Bells attached to Aaron's robe protect him as he moves toward the zone of greatest holiness (v. 35).

The three other items of apparel – tunic, turban, and sash – are mentioned briefly in verse 39. Two of them (tunic and sash) are to be worn by other priests (v. 40) as well as by Aaron. However, those made for Aaron are more elaborate. The hierarchy of expense and quality in relation to zones of holiness is also present in the priestly vestments. Aaron, who comes closest to the holiest zone of divine presence, has vestments restricted to him; and those worn in common with other priests, except for the linen undergarments (v. 42),[50] are more elaborate. His *tunic*, which was the standard garment for both women and men in the Levant in the Late Bronze and Iron Ages, is to be "checkered" or more likely "fringed" (NJPS). His *sash*, a typical ceremonial accoutrement of high officials (as Isa 22:21), is to be embroidered.

All priests wore headgear, probably turbans (NRSV "headdresses," v. 40); but Aaron's headgear, as would be expected, is more elaborate. In addition to the *turban*, a kind of head covering worn by top officials of royal or religious hierarchies, Aaron wears a crown or diadem (cf. Isa 62:3 and Zech 3:5). This is

---

48 Heinz-Josef Fabry, "*lēb*," *TDOT* 7:412–26.

49 Mary G. Houston, *Ancient Egyptian, Mesopotamian, and Persian Costume* (2nd edition; London: Adam & Charles Black, 1954), 132–59.

50 Undergarments were not part of ordinary apparel in biblical antiquity, nor were they sacral garments; they are perhaps mandated for reasons of modesty (cf. 20:24–26).

not mentioned in chapter 28 but does appear in 29:6 (and 39:30). Moreover, only Aaron's headdress is to be adorned with a gold plate, inscribed with the words "holy to the Lord" and placed over his forehead (vv. 36–38). The meaning of the inscription is uncertain. It may refer to Aaron's own sanctity, as ceremonial representative of all Israelites, who are holy (19:6; cf. Jer 2:3). At the same time, it seems to be related to a ceremonial function in which Aaron either bears or takes away – the Hebrew word can mean either – guilt, perhaps for any inadvertent infractions of established ritual procedures.[51] It also apparently is apotropaic, protecting Aaron so that he always has God's benevolent favor.[52] Indeed, the garments in the aggregate serve this protective purpose (v. 43).

The vestments for Aaron clearly are more than coverings for the body. They have oracular and divinatory functions, and they are related to the utter sanctity of the space in which the high priest alone carries out certain rituals. Just as important is the fact that their splendor and costliness connote the garb of deities and their most intimate human servants, kings or high priests. We must remember how highly symbolic clothing can be, serving since earliest times second only to language in its ability to convey important information.[53] What might that symbolic role be, other than signifying high office? Answering that question means looking at similar vestments in ancient Near Eastern sacred contexts.

Scholars long have noted that in both Egypt and Mesopotamia, images of the deities were carefully washed and elaborately clothed in ceremonies meant to imbue the lifeless statues with the vital presence of the deity.[54] Gods or goddesses were not necessarily thought to be confined to one place. Such ceremonies served to bring them "into" their images so that the priest or king could approach the image for oracles, blessings, judicial rulings, or whatever was needed from the deity represented by the image. In other words, adorning the statue with elaborate garments assured divine presence. But there is more to this role of garments for the gods. Communication between deity and human was effected, in part, by having the human arrayed in unique and splendid clothing similar to that of the deity. Godlike in their priestly garments, they were positioned to receive the divine will.

What we see in the tabernacle texts is ancient Israel's version of this dynamic. The elaborate vestments to be worn by Aaron would symbolize the unseen presence of God and also would empower him to approach God and receive God's word. The tabernacle as a dwelling for God may have signified God's presence among the Israelites and secured divine availability. But in terms of communicating God's will to the people, the glorious sanctity of the priest

[51] N. M. Sarna, *Exodus* (1991), 183–4.
[52] Martin Noth, *Exodus: A Commentary* (Philadelphia: Westminster, 1962), 225–6.
[53] E. W. Barber, *Women's Work* (1994), 283.
[54] E.g., Aylward M. Blackman, "The Rite of Opening the Mouth in Ancient Egypt and Babylonia," *JEA* 10 (1924): 47–59.

arrayed in highly ceremonial garb was the key mechanism. This may seem strange to us from our twenty-first-century vantage point; and it is radically different from the direct modes, more congenial to us, of God's communication with the prophets of the Hebrew Bible. Yet the priestly role in divine–human communication, in the Iron Age world of the Bible, arguably was no less important. It obtained divine responses to difficult political and legal problems and served the sacramental needs of the people and their leaders.

CONSECRATION OF PRIESTS (29:1–46)

Preparing appropriate garments for the priests is only part of what gives them the authority of their office and the ability to perform their functions. As for all high officials, an investment ceremony confers upon them what the symbolism of their garments represents. The installation rites, which will last *seven* days, appear in chapter 29 (vv. 1–37), along with instructions about a regular sacrifice (vv. 38–42) and a summation (vv. 43–46). Moses acts as a priest. He consumes the priestly portion (v. 26); and he is the one who performs the six specified rites: washing, dressing, and anointing the priests, followed by the offering of three sacrifices. This section of the prescriptive texts does not appear in the descriptive texts of Exodus, perhaps because the information needed to perform the requisite sacrifices is not provided until after the tabernacle is erected.[55] The first seven chapters of Leviticus outline the sacrificial system; the implementation of the investiture and consecration instructions then appears in Leviticus 8–9. Just as the stages of the wilderness journey continue into Numbers, the tabernacle account continues into Leviticus. Similarly, as we have seen, the exodus story is linked to various aspects of Genesis. All these connections make it clear that what may appear to us as individual biblical books really are part of the larger story presented in the Pentateuch as a whole.

The language of investiture involves two terms, which have already appeared in the summation of the vestment section (28:41; cf. 28:3): "consecrate" and "ordain." The former, which means "to make holy," appears *seven* times in this consecration section, thus signifying the complete transition of the priestly officials to the realm of the sacred. The latter (found in vv. 9, 29, 33, and 35) literally means "to fill the hand" and is used throughout the Bible to refer to the installation of someone into a priestly role (as in Judg 17:5 and 12, where the NRSV translates it "installed"). This phrase appears in almost exactly the same form in Akkadian sources to designate the handing of the scepter of office to a king at his induction to office.[56] "To fill the hand" thus is an idiom, meaning to be ordained into a high office even when placing a scepter was not part of the rite. (Note that we use "pass the baton" in similar ways to indicate the transfer

---

[55] Jacob Milgrom, *Leviticus 1–16* (AB 3; New York: Doubleday, 1991), 494–5.
[56] Ibid., 538–40.

of the rights and powers of a position.) A less likely possibility is that the phrase refers to the placement of offerings or payments on the "palms" (not "hands") of Aaron and his sons (v. 24).[57]

People everywhere typically mark any change of status with ritual procedures; think of the ceremonies that mark life passages such as birth, marriage, graduation, retirement, even death. Because priestly investiture in the biblical world meant not only a new status but also the transition from profane to sacred, a passage fraught with the dangers of mixing those two realms, investiture and consecration were especially critical processes. As elaborate as these rites seem to us, they are by no means extreme in relation to installation and dedication rituals known from elsewhere in the ancient Near East.[58] Washing and donning special garments is characteristic, as is anointing.

Anointing had cosmetic and even magical functions in daily life, but in the ceremonial realm it was a highly significant procedure that served to formalize an elevation in official status.[59] Symbolic unction under divine auspices was such an important part of accession to office that the term "anointed one" (*māšîaḥ*) is found in the Hebrew Bible as a designation for divinely appointed officials such as kings, prophets, and even patriarchs and foreign kings; eventually it refers to an eschatological figure or "messiah." Although only one biblical text (1 Chr 29:22) outside priestly materials refers to the anointing of priests, extrabiblical evidence of such practice indicates that anointing likely was part of the consecration of the chief priest early in Israel's history.[60] Priestly unction was a rite of passage to a new status and effected passage from the outer, profane world to the sanctity of the tabernacle precinct. In this section, only Aaron is anointed; elsewhere (28:41; 30:30) his sons receive sacral unction too. The hereditary nature of priestly service, marked by the transfer of the sacral garments to the next generation, is specified in verses 29–30.

Three animals are to be sacrificed as part of the investitures: a young bull and two rams.[61] Found widely in other cultic texts from the ancient Near East, as well as elsewhere in the Hebrew Bible, all of these sacrifices likely were part of Israelite ritual practice at an early stage. This consecration section provides an etiology for them, relating them to the Sinai revelation and the beginnings of a community shrine. All three are male animals, probably because sacrificial

[57] So M. Noth, *Exodus* (1962), 230–1.
[58] See, e.g., the instructions for a *seven*-day installation ceremony at Late Bronze Age Emar in Syria, "The Installation of the Storm God's High Priestess," translated by Daniel Fleming (*COS* 1:.222), 427–31.
[59] J. Milgrom, *Leviticus 1–16* (1991), 553–5.
[60] Daniel Fleming, "The Biblical Tradition of Anointing Priests," *JBL* 117 (1998): 401–14; "Installation" (*COS* 1.222), 427–8.
[61] See J. Milgrom, *Leviticus 1–16* (1991), for explanations of the burnt offering (172–6), the cereal offering (195–202), and the well-being offering (217–25); cf. Baruch A. Levine, *Leviticus* (JPS Torah Commentary; Philadelphia: JPS, 1989), 3–17.

systems must take into account the economic reality that prime male animals are expendable but that females must be preserved for their milk and for breeding. The slaughter of these animals involves procedures, such as rubbing some of the blood on the horns of the altar and on the selected body parts of the priests, that cannot be fully understood. Yet the overall significance of these offerings seems to be expiatory and purificatory, for the sacrificial altar itself (vv. 36–37) as well as for the priestly personnel.

The bull offering removes iniquity from the priests who are to come nearest to God. The handling of the animal's carcass reflects the special importance of some of the organs, which are burnt directly on the altar whereas the rest of the animal is burnt outside the tabernacle precinct in profane space. The first ram is called a "burnt offering" (v. 18; Hebrew *ōlâ*), a term for an offering that is completely consumed by fire, with the smoke reaching to the heavens and attracting divine attention.[62] The second ram is the "ram of ordination" (v. 22). Accompanied by grain offerings, part of it becomes the priestly share, eaten here by Moses (v. 26) but then also by the newly invested priests (vv. 31–34). This seems to be an etiology for the "well-being" sacrifices (v. 28), a term denoting animals slaughtered to provide food. The stipulation that only Aaron and his sons can consume this offering implies that otherwise the donors of "well-being" offerings would themselves also partake of its flesh and the accompanying grains. The sacrificial system reflected in the Hebrew Bible provided food for the maintenance of priestly families, which did not have their own lands and herds, as well as an occasion for the consumption of meat, which was not an everyday occurrence and generally was a ceremonial occasion for most people (cf. Exodus 12–13).

At the end of the chapter, the consecration ceremony is summarized following several additional verses about sacrifice (vv. 38–42a) – about the obligatory daily burnt offering that apparently served as the core of the tabernacle and temple ritual. In just a few verses (vv. 42b–46), the summary touches upon the major themes of the tabernacle texts. It emphasizes the oracular function of the tabernacle, here called the tent of meeting, where God will "meet" the people. It reiterates the sanctity of the structure, its altar, and its priests. It also specifies the tabernacle's function as the place where God will "dwell among" the people (cf. 25:8). In addition, it integrates the major components of Exodus by connecting the construction of the tabernacle with both the covenant and the exodus. Covenant language is found in the statement that "I will be their God" (cf. 6:7) and in the echo of the opening verse of the Decalogue (20:2), which identifies God as the one who brought the Israelites from Egypt.

---

62 Baruch A. Levine, "Ritual as Symbol: Modes of Sacrifice in Israelite Religion," in *Sacred Time, Sacred Space: Archaeology and the Religion of Israel*, ed. Barry Gittlen (Winona Lake, Ind.: Eisenbrauns, 2002), 134–5.

A CLOSER LOOK: SACRIFICE

Instructions concerning sacrifices of various kinds as well as descriptions of particular sacrificial events are found throughout the Pentateuch, and sacrifices are frequently mentioned in other parts of the Hebrew Bible. Yet, because the slaughter of animals, even more than the bringing of grains and fruits, seems so distant and even repugnant today, we often are reluctant to recognize just how important sacrifice was in ancient Israel and how pervasive it is in the Bible. Why did the Israelites engage so fully in a system that seems so primitive? Scholars long have tried to understand the origins and functions of sacrificial systems, which appear widely among traditional cultures. Social scientists have proposed a variety of theories about sacrifice.[63] None of these is entirely satisfactory in explaining sacrifice in all cultures, but collectively they help us understand the religious dynamics that have led so many people around the world to make sacrifice an integral part of their religious lives and institutions. With respect to information in the Hebrew Bible, some sacrifices can be considered gifts to God, in gratitude for a blessing received or in the hope that God will grant something in return. Others, as part of sacrificial meals, enabled people to experience communion with God; such collective sacrificial acts also reinforce group identity and solidarity. And certain sacrifices, as consecrated items, possibly helped people deal with the guilt of sinful behavior and thus reflect moral principles. In the aggregate, Israelite sacrifice constitutes a complex cultural system, incorporating and expressing ancient Israel's own religious and social values.[64]

As in the documents of other peoples of the ancient Near East, the phenomenon of sacrifice in the Bible is closely related to the nature of Israelite shrines as the dwelling place of God. Providing sacrifices was part of the effort to attend to the daily needs of the resident deity, whose presence in the material world was manifest in the temple or tabernacle. In fact, sacrifice can be considered the single most important part of these institutions because it entailed a series of regular daily activities.[65] The logic of having a deity or the deity's presence "reside" in a sacred structure meant that the deity had to be served with appropriate lavish banquets, which actualized the conceptual reality of accessibility to the divine. The anthropomorphic cast of such thinking may have been problematic to some Israelites (e.g., Ps 50:12–14), but many other biblical texts seem to consider sacrifice as food for God. What sacrifices do for God may be elusive, but their role in helping premodern people negotiate the difficulties

[63]   See B. A. Nakhai, *Archaeology and the Religions of Canaan and Israel* (2001), 20–35.
[64]   R. S. Hendel, "Sacrifice as a Cultural System," *ZAW* 101 (1989).
[65]   Gary A. Anderson, "Sacrifice and Sacrificial Offerings. Old Testament," *ABD* 5:871–3. See also the discussion in the supplementary section on A Closer Look: Temples and Temple Service.

of life is indisputable, as is their economic role in maintaining the priesthood with its multifarious functions.

References to sacrifice abound in Exodus. The Passover and other festival and Sabbath sacrifices are part of the narratives of the exodus and wilderness journey. Sacrifices appear in some of the covenant stipulations as well as in the account of the Sinai theophany. And a series of sacrifices is an integral part of the investiture of priests and of the ceremonies for dedicating the tabernacle. But the most elaborate set of instructions for the regular sacrificial offerings is Leviticus 1–7, with other directives coming elsewhere in Leviticus and also in Numbers and Deuteronomy. The number of different kinds of sacrifices perhaps is best indicated by the summary statement at the end of Leviticus 7, which lists six kinds of offerings: burnt, cereal, purification (sin), reparation (guilt), ordination, and well-being (v. 37). This list is not a satisfactory taxonomy for modern readers, however, in that the designations apparently mix the substance or mode of offering with the function; nor does it relate proportionally to the instructions of Leviticus 1–7. Also, some of the six items on the list seem to have subtypes: well-being (or peace) offerings could be thanksgiving, freewill, or vowed sacrifices. Moreover, many additional kinds of sacrifice, such as those for specific festivals or life-cycle events, appear in other passages in Leviticus. The sacrificial system was exceedingly complex, at least according to the biblical data, which combine the records of hundreds of years of divergent sacrificial traditions. Despite intense exegetical scrutiny,[66] scholars do not agree on all the details of how Israelite sacrifices were performed, let alone on the meaning or even the historical reality of the various sacrificial acts.

The apparent foreignness of sacrifice in the contemporary world has led to a tendency to denigrate its important functions for the Israelites and other ancient peoples. Prophetic texts that are critical of sacrifice – such as Isa 1:11–14, Jer 7:21–23, and Amos 5:21–23 – are typically used to support such views and to suggest that there were opponents of sacrifice already in the biblical period itself. However, prophetic diatribes are more likely to represent rhetorical or polemical flourishes focusing on the abuses of sacrifice that even the priestly writers themselves acknowledged, notably in Leviticus 26, where Israel's reckless disregard of the covenant must be punished and sacrifices are not mentioned as a means of avoiding responsibility for iniquity. As important as sacrifices may have been for many of the psychological, social, and religious needs of the ancient Israelites, it is unlikely that they ever were meant to be mechanical corrections for deeds considered antithetical to God's will or substitutions for righteous and just behavior.

---

[66]   As in J. Milgrom's AB commentaries on Leviticus and works cited in them.

ADDENDUM (30:1–31:17)

The preceding verses seem to conclude the prescriptive texts. Yet chapter 30 and most of 31 contain instructions for two more appurtenances (the incense altar and the laver) and two substances (anointing oil and incense) as well as information about a census, artisans, and Sabbath observance. Scholars typically have assumed that these are afterthoughts, inserted here on the basis of ritual practices that postdated the formation of the core of the prescriptive texts in chapters 25–28 and also inserted, in their logical place, in the descriptive texts (see table on p. 225). However, given the arcane nature of these materials, at least from our contemporary perspective, it is just as likely that another kind of logic obtains for them, individually or collectively, whether or not scholars can retrieve it. Some of the features of their organization, which mitigate the likelihood that these are random additions, will be noted.

The *incense altar* (vv. 1–10), together with the lampstand and the offering table, is one of three appurtenances in the holy area within the tabernacle. Like the other two, it is to be made of gold and equipped with rings for poles to be used in transport. Incense altars were standard items of sacral equipment in the ancient Near East; and numerous stone examples, roughly the same size as this one (ca. 1½ feet square and three feet high) and with horns projecting from the four upper corners, have been recovered from archaeological excavations of Iron Age sites in Palestine.[67] Like the larger horned courtyard altar, this type may originate in Late Bronze Age Syria. Also known as the "golden altar" (39:38; 40:5) to distinguish it from the bronze courtyard altar, the incense altar shares with the lampstand a place in the regular ritual of morning and evening procedures. Indeed, it may be the most important of the three golden furnishings. For one thing, it is to be placed centrally, directly in front of the curtain that shields the holiest object, the ark of the covenant/testimony, where God meets the chief priest. It also is called "most holy" (v. 10), a designation in 26:33 for the space in which the ark is situated. Moreover, it has a role beyond the daily service: blood from the annual purification and purgation (translated "atonement" in the NRSV) sacrifice is smeared on its horns to sanctify it (Lev 16:18: cf. Lev 4:7). The purgation ritual involves bringing blood from the less holy courtyard altar into the more holy zone within the tent. This latter circumstance, in which the incense altar is in contact with materials from outside its zone, may be why it does not appear alongside instructions for the other two furnishings of its sacred zone.[68] The prescriptive text embodies the gradations in sanctity,

[67] Seymour Gitin, "The Four-Horned Altar and Sacred Space: An Archaeological Perspective," in *Sacred Time, Sacred Space: Archaeology and the Religion of Israel*, ed. Barry Gittlen (Winona Lake, Ind.: Eisenbrauns, 2002), 95–123. Gitin suggests that the four horns are actually a vestigial architectural feature, representing a tower.

[68] Carol Meyers, "Realms of Sanctity: The Case of the 'Misplaced' Incense Altar in the Tabernacle Texts of Exodus," in *Texts, Temples, and Traditions: A Tribute to Menahem Haran*, eds. Michael V. Fox *et al.* (Winona Lake, Ind.: Eisenbrauns, 1996), 33–46.

whereas this is less so for the descriptive texts, in which the incense altar is listed right after the golden table and lampstand (37:10–28). Note also that no utensils are listed for it here or in the other passages that mention it (such as 30:27 and 31:8).

The annual expiatory and purification function of the golden altar provides a link with the ensuing instructions for a *census* (30:11–16), in which the taxed amount functions as "purgation [NRSV, atonement] money" for all the people as well as a source of funds for temple operations (v. 16). The phrase for taking a census is literally "to raise the head," that is, to take a head count. As a stage in conscription, land allotment or redistribution, or tax collecting, census-taking is characteristically a contentious operation. Ill-advised censuses were thus thought to be disastrous, hence the notion that plague could result (cf. 2 Sam 24:1–25). The payment of a half-shekel (ca. .4 oz.) by all adults thus is construed as a "ransom," paid to escape death or other harm (cf. 21:30). Everyone pays the same amount so that the total number of half-shekel pieces will be equivalent to the number of tax-paying citizens, most likely men able to bear arms. That conscription was intended is evident from the similar language in Num 1:2–3. The payment is in silver according to 38:25–26, which mentions this tax; otherwise, there is no parallel account of the census in the descriptive section. Like many other rituals in Exodus, this one is given a commemorative feature; census monies are a "reminder" that the risks inherent in a census are averted by a payment.

The addendum first presents the golden incense altar and then a silver tax. Next comes the bronze *laver* (NRSV "basin," 30:17–21) of the courtyard, which follows the logic of descending value of materials, corresponding to descending level of sanctity. Placed between the altar and the entrance to the tent, it would be filled with water so that priests entering the tent or serving at the altar could perform the purificatory and protective measure of washing their hands and feet. Yet the instructions for the laver do not appear alongside those of the altar and courtyard, perhaps because it is not a ritual object itself but only part of the preparations for ritual activity.[69] No dimensions for the laver, which consists of a basin set on a stand, are provided for this less important object. Similarly, it is funded by neither donations nor the census tax (see 38:8). The implied simplicity contrasts with the elaborate design of the ten large basins and stands of the Jerusalem temple (1 Kgs 7:27–39) and the decorated metal lavers recovered from excavations of Iron Age sites.

Perhaps because anointing follows washing in the investiture sequence, directions for preparing the *anointing oil* (30:22–33) follow instructions for the laver in the addendum. Rare and therefore expensive spices are to be combined with olive oil. The formula for the four spices used in making the unction leads thematically to the formula for the three spices to be blended with frankincense and

---

[69] Carol Meyers, "Laver," *ABD* 4:241.

salt for the *incense* (30:34–38) – providing a total of *seven* precious substances. Both the anointing oil and incense are deemed "most holy." The former is also "holy to you [the Israelites]" and confers sanctity on the tabernacle and its appurtenances as well as its personnel. And the latter is also "holy to the LORD," for it creates the cloud in which God is manifest and yet not directly visible (Lev 16:2, 12–13). The utter sanctity of these substances is clear from the repeated use – *fourteen* times in verses 22–38 – of "holy" and other terms from the same Hebrew root and from the warning that personal, nonholy use will result in ostracism from the community. This punishment, which is tantamount to a death penalty under the circumstances of ancient agrarian societies, is found in the Hebrew Bible as punishment for a wide range of serious offenses in the priestly realm (cf. 12:15).[70] In this case, the severe penalty may be a deterrent to protect the supply of highly valuable and desirable commodities. Note that spices and precious oil were as valued as silver and gold, all of which are safeguarded in the national treasury (2 Kgs 20:13).

The last set of instructions for the tabernacle concerns the *artisans* (31:1–11). The Judean Bezalel is to be in charge, with the Danite Oholiab as his assistant. God gives Bezalel a series of attributes that will enable him to oversee every kind of artistry and craftwork for constructing the tabernacle, its furnishings, the priestly vestments, and the anointing oil and incense. The many others needed for such a project are referred to collectively as "all the skillful" (v. 6). In 28:3 these artisans are said to be endowed with "skill" (Hebrew *rûaḥ*). That same word appears here as part of the phrase "divine spirit" (*rûaḥ 'ĕlōhîm*, literally, "spirit/wind of/from God," v. 3), which denotes the divinely inspired creativity of the chief artisan. This may be priestly language, for the same phrase is used for God's creative energy ("wind from God," Gen 1:2) in the priestly account of creation.

The last passage of the prescriptive texts – directions for *Sabbath observance* – also alludes to the Gen 1–2:4a creation account and, as noted at the beginning of Commentary Part III, suggests that a priestly hand has shaped these materials. For the *seventh* time in chapters 25–31, the clause "the LORD said [or spoke] to Moses" (v. 12) introduces God's instructions and thus signifies the completion of the directions for making the tabernacle. Like God's six-part (six-day) creation of the cosmos, the human creativity in constructing the tabernacle has been set forth in six directives. And, like God's *seventh*-day cessation, the tabernacle work is to culminate in the Sabbath. Also, as in the version of the Decalogue in Exod 20:11, the *seventh* day of Genesis 1 is named as the paradigm for the Israelite day of rest (v. 17). The Decalogue has no provisions for failure to keep the Sabbath, but here the penalty is death or the same potentially lethal ostracism mandated for improper use of holy oil and incense. Following the elaborate presentation of sacred space in the tabernacle instructions, the Sabbath serves

---

[70] B. A. Levine, *Leviticus* (1989), 241–2.

as a sanctification of time; observing it sanctifies the people and allows them to "know" God, the epitome of holiness.

COVENANT VIOLATION AND RENEWAL – EXODUS 31:18–34:35

NRSV 31:18 When God finished speaking with Moses on Mount Sinai, he gave him the two tablets of the covenant,[a] tablets of stone, written with the finger of God.

NRSV 32 When the people saw that Moses delayed to come down from the mountain, the people gathered around Aaron, and said to him, "Come, make gods for us, who shall go before us; as for this Moses, the man who brought us up out of the land of Egypt, we do not know what has become of him." [2]Aaron said to them, "Take off the gold rings that are on the ears of your wives, your sons, and your daughters, and bring them to me." [3]So all the people took off the gold rings from their ears, and brought them to Aaron. [4]He took the gold from them, formed it in a mold, and cast an image of a calf; and they said, "These are your gods, O Israel, who brought you up out of the land of Egypt!" [5]When Aaron saw this, he built an altar before it; and Aaron made proclamation and said, "Tomorrow shall be a festival to the LORD." [6]They rose early the next day, and offered burnt offerings and brought sacrifices of well-being; and the people sat down to eat and drink, and rose up to revel.

7 The LORD said to Moses, "Go down at once! Your people, whom you brought up out of the land of Egypt, have acted perversely; [8]they have been quick to turn aside from the way that I commanded them; they have cast for themselves an image of a calf, and have worshiped it and sacrificed to it, and said, 'These are your gods, O Israel, who brought you up out of the land of Egypt!'" [9]The LORD said to Moses, "I have seen this people, how stiff-necked they are. [10]Now let me alone, so that my wrath may burn hot against them and I may consume them; and of you I will make a great nation."

11 But Moses implored the LORD his God, and said, "O LORD, why does your wrath burn hot against your people, whom you brought out of the land of Egypt with great power and with a mighty hand? [12]Why should the Egyptians say, 'It was with evil intent that he brought them out to kill them in the mountains, and to consume them from the face of the earth'? Turn from your fierce wrath; change your mind and do not bring disaster on your people. [13]Remember Abraham, Isaac, and Israel, your servants, how you swore to them by your own self, saying to them, 'I will multiply your descendants like the stars of heaven, and all this land that I have promised I will give to your descendants, and they shall inherit it forever.'

---

[a] Or *treaty,* or *testimony*

¹⁴And the LORD changed his mind about the disaster that he planned to bring on his people.

15 Then Moses turned and went down from the mountain, carrying the two tablets of the covenant^a in his hands, tablets that were written on both sides, written on the front and on the back. ¹⁶The tablets were the work of God, and the writing was the writing of God, engraved upon the tablets. ¹⁷When Joshua heard the noise of the people as they shouted, he said to Moses, "There is a noise of war in the camp." ¹⁸But he said,

> "It is not the sound made by victors,
>   or the sound made by losers;
> it is the sound of revelers that I hear."

¹⁹As soon as he came near the camp and saw the calf and the dancing, Moses' anger burned hot, and he threw the tablets from his hands and broke them at the foot of the mountain. ²⁰He took the calf that they had made, burned it with fire, ground it to powder, scattered it on the water, and made the Israelites drink it.

21 Moses said to Aaron, "What did this people do to you that you have brought so great a sin upon them?" ²²And Aaron said, "Do not let the anger of my lord burn hot; you know the people, that they are bent on evil. ²³They said to me, 'Make us gods, who shall go before us; as for this Moses, the man who brought us up out of the land of Egypt, we do not know what has become of him.' ²⁴So I said to them, 'Whoever has gold, take it off'; so they gave it to me, and I threw it into the fire, and out came this calf!"

25 When Moses saw that the people were running wild (for Aaron had let them run wild, to the derision of their enemies), ²⁶then Moses stood in the gate of the camp, and said, "Who is on the LORD's side? Come to me!" And all the sons of Levi gathered around him. ²⁷He said to them, "Thus says the LORD, the God of Israel, 'Put your sword on your side, each of you! Go back and forth from gate to gate throughout the camp, and each of you kill your brother, your friend, and your neighbor.'" ²⁸The sons of Levi did as Moses commanded, and about three thousand of the people fell on that day. ²⁹Moses said, "Today you have ordained yourselves for the service of the LORD, each one at the cost of a son or a brother, and so have brought a blessing on yourselves this day."

30 On the next day Moses said to the people, "You have sinned a great sin. But now I will go up to the LORD; perhaps I can make atonement for your sin." ³¹So Moses returned to the LORD and said, "Alas, this people has sinned a great sin; they have made for themselves gods of gold. ³²But now, if you will only forgive their sin – but if not, blot me out of the book that you have written." ³³But the LORD said to Moses, "Whoever has sinned against me I will blot out of my book. ³⁴But now go, lead the people to the place about which I have spoken to you; see, my angel shall

---

^a Or *treaty,* or *testimony*

go in front of you. Nevertheless, when the day comes for punishment, I will punish them for their sin."

35 Then the LORD sent a plague on the people, because they made the calf – the one that Aaron made.

NRSV 33 The LORD said to Moses, "Go, leave this place, you and the people whom you have brought up out of the land of Egypt, and go to the land of which I swore to Abraham, Isaac, and Jacob, saying, 'To your descendants I will give it.' [2]I will send an angel before you, and I will drive out the Canaanites, the Amorites, the Hittites, the Perizzites, the Hivites, and the Jebusites. [3]Go up to a land flowing with milk and honey; but I will not go up among you, or I would consume you on the way, for you are a stiff-necked people."

4 When the people heard these harsh words, they mourned, and no one put on ornaments. [5]For the LORD had said to Moses, "Say to the Israelites, 'You are a stiff-necked people; if for a single moment I should go up among you, I would consume you. So now take off your ornaments, and I will decide what to do to you.'" [6]Therefore the Israelites stripped themselves of their ornaments, from Mount Horeb onward.

7 Now Moses used to take the tent and pitch it outside the camp, far off from the camp; he called it the tent of meeting. And everyone who sought the LORD would go out to the tent of meeting, which was outside the camp. [8]Whenever Moses went out to the tent, all the people would rise and stand, each of them, at the entrance of their tents and watch Moses until he had gone into the tent. [9]When Moses entered the tent, the pillar of cloud would descend and stand at the entrance of the tent, and the LORD would speak with Moses. [10]When all the people saw the pillar of cloud standing at the entrance of the tent, all the people would rise and bow down, all of them, at the entrance of their tent. [11]Thus the LORD used to speak to Moses face to face, as one speaks to a friend. Then he would return to the camp; but his young assistant, Joshua son of Nun, would not leave the tent.

12 Moses said to the LORD, "See, you have said to me, 'Bring up this people'; but you have not let me know whom you will send with me. Yet you have said, 'I know you by name, and you have also found favor in my sight.' [13]Now if I have found favor in your sight, show me your ways, so that I may know you and find favor in your sight. Consider too that this nation is your people." [14]He said, "My presence will go with you, and I will give you rest." [15]And he said to him, "If your presence will not go, do not carry us up from here. [16]For how shall it be known that I have found favor in your sight, I and your people, unless you go with us? In this way, we shall be distinct, I and your people, from every people on the face of the earth."

17 The LORD said to Moses, "I will do the very thing that you have asked; for you have found favor in my sight, and I know you by name." [18]Moses said, "Show me your glory, I pray." [19]And he said, "I will make all my goodness pass before you, and will proclaim before you the name, 'The LORD'; and I will be gracious to whom I will be gracious, and will show mercy on whom I will show mercy. [20]But," he

said, "you cannot see my face; for no one shall see me and live." [21] And the LORD continued, "See, there is a place by me where you shall stand on the rock; [22] and while my glory passes by I will put you in a cleft of the rock, and I will cover you with my hand until I have passed by; [23] then I will take away my hand, and you shall see my back; but my face shall not be seen."

NRSV 34 The LORD said to Moses, "Cut two tablets of stone like the former ones, and I will write on the tablets the words that were on the former tablets, which you broke. [2] Be ready in the morning, and come up in the morning to Mount Sinai and present yourself there to me, on the top of the mountain. [3] No one shall come up with you, and do not let anyone be seen throughout all the mountain; and do not let flocks or herds graze in front of that mountain." [4] So Moses cut two tablets of stone like the former ones; and he rose early in the morning and went up on Mount Sinai, as the LORD had commanded him, and took in his hand the two tablets of stone. [5] The LORD descended in the cloud and stood with him there, and proclaimed the name, "The LORD." [6] The LORD passed before him, and proclaimed,

"The LORD, the LORD,
a God merciful and gracious,
slow to anger,
and abounding in steadfast love and faithfulness,
[7] keeping steadfast love for the thousandth generation,
forgiving iniquity and transgression and sin,
yet by no means clearing the guilty,
but visiting the iniquity of the parents
upon the children
and the children's children,
to the third and the fourth generation."

[8] And Moses quickly bowed his head toward the earth, and worshiped. [9] He said, "If now I have found favor in your sight, O Lord, I pray, let the Lord go with us. Although this is a stiff-necked people, pardon our iniquity and our sin, and take us for your inheritance."

10 He said: I hereby make a covenant. Before all your people I will perform marvels, such as have not been performed in all the earth or in any nation; and all the people among whom you live shall see the work of the LORD; for it is an awesome thing that I will do with you.

11 Observe what I command you today. See, I will drive out before you the Amorites, the Canaanites, the Hittites, the Perizzites, the Hivites, and the Jebusites. [12] Take care not to make a covenant with the inhabitants of the land to which you are going, or it will become a snare among you. [13] You shall tear down their altars, break their pillars, and cut down their sacred poles[a] [14] (for you shall worship no other god, because the LORD, whose name is Jealous, is a jealous God). [15] You shall not make a

_____

[a] Heb *Asherim*

covenant with the inhabitants of the land, for when they prostitute themselves to their gods and sacrifice to their gods, someone among them will invite you, and you will eat of the sacrifice. ¹⁶And you will take wives from among their daughters for your sons, and their daughters who prostitute themselves to their gods will make your sons also prostitute themselves to their gods.

17 You shall not make cast idols.

18 You shall keep the festival of unleavened bread. Seven days you shall eat unleavened bread, as I commanded you, at the time appointed in the month of Abib; for in the month of Abib you came out from Egypt.

19 All that first opens the womb is mine, all your male livestock, the firstborn of cow and sheep. ²⁰The firstborn of a donkey you shall redeem with a lamb, or if you will not redeem it you shall break its neck. All the firstborn of your sons you shall redeem.

No one shall appear before me empty-handed.

21 Six days you shall work, but on the seventh day you shall rest; even in plowing time and in harvest time you shall rest. ²²You shall observe the festival of weeks, the first fruits of wheat harvest, and the festival of ingathering at the turn of the year. ²³Three times in the year all your males shall appear before the LORD God, the God of Israel. ²⁴For I will cast out nations before you, and enlarge your borders; no one shall covet your land when you go up to appear before the LORD your God three times in the year.

25 You shall not offer the blood of my sacrifice with leaven, and the sacrifice of the festival of the passover shall not be left until the morning.

26 The best of the first fruits of your ground you shall bring to the house of the LORD your God.

You shall not boil a kid in its mother's milk.

27 The LORD said to Moses: Write these words; in accordance with these words I have made a covenant with you and with Israel. ²⁸He was there with the LORD forty days and forty nights; he neither ate bread nor drank water. And he wrote on the tablets the words of the covenant, the ten commandments.[a]

29 Moses came down from Mount Sinai. As he came down from the mountain with the two tablets of the covenant[b] in his hand, Moses did not know that the skin of his face shone because he had been talking with God. ³⁰When Aaron and all the Israelites saw Moses, the skin of his face was shining, and they were afraid to come near him. ³¹But Moses called to them; and Aaron and all the leaders of the congregation returned to him, and Moses spoke with them. ³²Afterward all the Israelites came near, and he gave them in commandment all that the LORD had spoken with him on Mount Sinai. ³³When Moses had finished speaking with them, he put a veil on his face; ³⁴but whenever Moses went in before the LORD to speak with him, he would take the veil off, until he came out; and when he came out, and

[a] Heb *words*
[b] Or *treaty*, or *testimony*

told the Israelites what he had been commanded, [35] the Israelites would see the face of Moses, that the skin of his face was shining; and Moses would put the veil on his face again, until he went in to speak with him.

*W*ith the instructions for the tabernacle now complete, we might expect the implementation section to begin. Instead, three chapters describing the infamous golden calf incident and its aftermath seem to interrupt the narrative. The grandeur and holiness of the prescriptive materials give way to the dramatic account of an interlude of apostasy and renewal. Scholars have long sought to understand this apparent break in the flow of the tabernacle texts. One possibility is that the overall message that people can sin and yet have God renew the covenant with them was particularly relevant to the exilic or postexilic community in which the Torah literature was organized. According to this hypothesis, the redactors included the calf episode – perhaps based on the polemic against Jeroboam I and his golden calves in 1 Kgs 12:25–33 – to reassure the people of God's abiding pact with them despite their iniquity. At the same time, it is important to acknowledge that the genre of temple-building accounts in the ancient Near East, of which the tabernacle texts are an example, sometimes exhibits a pattern in which the god's command to build is followed by a rebellion against the builder.[71]

Although they present a fairly coherent narrative, like so much of Exodus chapters 32–34 themselves seem to be an amalgam of varying traditions. For example, they contain different views about how God's presence was manifest and about where the tabernacle/tent was located. Perhaps most striking is that the account of the covenant in chapter 34 seems to depict it as an innovation rather than the restoration of a previous covenant, although 34:11–26 is a rearranged version of 23:12–33. There also are repetitions, discrepancies, and non sequiturs similar to those of other narrative sections of Exodus. It thus seems certain that several sources, which no longer can be isolated, have been incorporated into the present narrative, probably by priestly redactors.

COVENANT VIOLATION: THE GOLDEN CALF (31:18–33:23)

The end of chapter 31 contains a brief resumptive statement, connecting this episode with the end of the covenant section in 24:18, which announces that Moses is on the mountain for forty days and nights. Then, at the beginning of chapter 32, we learn that in the interim the people become unhappy because of the absence of their leader and of visible assurance of their god's presence. This anxiety and impatience lead to Aaron's fabrication of the golden image of a

---

[71] Victor (Avigdor) Hurowitz, *I Have Built You an Exalted House: Temple Building in the Bible in Light of Mesopotamian and Northwest Semitic Writings* (JSOTS 115; Sheffield: Sheffield Academic Press, 1992), 111.

calf – actually, a young bull or ox (see Ps 106:19–20) – from jewelry donated by both men and women, and also an altar for both burnt and well-being offerings.

This shocking turn of events has aroused enormous discussion. Were the people asking literally for a god? Note that the NRSV translation of "make gods for us" in 32:1 (and v. 23) is misleading, for the Hebrew just as readily allows for the rendering "make a god for us."[72] Or, rather, did they seek something to indicate divine presence? Are they asking for a representation of Yahweh? Or do they seek an image of any god who would do what Yahweh has promised? Or, is it possible that they simply want an image of the absent Moses, God's messenger and the one who is credited in 32:1, 7–8 for bringing the Israelites out of Egypt? After all, the festival to be held at the altar is for Yahweh (32:5), so they do not seem to be rejecting Yahweh. Is the calf itself a theriomorphism (representation of a deity having the form of an animal)? Or, like the cherubim, is it a throne or pedestal on which the invisible presence of a god rests? Note that the verb "bow down" appears in both the Decalogue's stipulation about images (20:4–6) and in 32:8 (where it is translated by the NRSV "worshiped"). Can it be that God is condemning the golden calf not because it signifies the worship of other gods but because it violates the prohibition against bowing down to and serving images of living beings? None of these questions can be resolved with certainty. Whatever the meaning of the narrative, the presence of the bull as the problematic animal can be understood. The bull was a symbol of divine strength, energy, fertility, and even leadership in the biblical world. In ancient Near Eastern art, gods sometimes are depicted standing on bulls and frequently wear horned headdresses.[73]

The responses of God, Moses, and Aaron in this episode are unexpected, shifting, and disturbing. God would send a great plague upon the people to destroy them all; divine wrath burning hot and consuming them (32:10–11) is idiomatic language for feverish and fatal disease (as in 32:35; cf. Num 11:33). How could God do this? Such a question emerges if we take seriously the canonical sequence, for God has already gone to extraordinary lengths to preserve this people? God then makes a surprising request, "now let me alone" (32:10), implying that God expects arguments from Moses, which in fact happens, for Moses disregards God's request to be left alone. His response is one of protest and of appeal – in a remarkable reversal of the usual call to remember, in which the people are enjoined to recall the past or when God proclaims what has been done in the past, Moses here calls upon God to "remember" the ancestors (32:13). The implication is that the covenant with the ancestors was unconditional, unlike the Sinai one, and that God is bound to honor the promise of land and descendents.

---

72 The plural forms in 32:8, probably influenced by the allusion to Jeroboam's two calves (1 Kgs 12:28 reads "Here are your gods, O Israel, who brought you up out of the land of Egypt"), could also be rendered in the singular, "This is your god" (cf. Neh 9:18).

73 *ANEP*, figs. 486, 498, 537, 538.

Divine decisions, especially this radical resolution to destroy the people bonded to God, apparently can be revoked. God can be both punitive and merciful. If human remembrance involves activity, so too does divine recollection. God takes Moses' arguments seriously and annuls the decision to annihilate the people (32:14).

Arguing with God is not Moses' only response. He finally comes down from the mountain with the two tablets of the covenant/treaty, inscribed on both sides by God, only to see the tumultuous sacrificial celebration at the altar in front of the calf. His own anger is such that he smashes the tablets, an action tantamount to voiding the document written on them. He then destroys the golden calf by burning and pulverizing it; this language of destruction is a conventional way to describe demolition and is not a literal description of how a statue might be destroyed.[74] His anger not yet abated, Moses decries the complicity of Aaron, who in turn shifts blame to the evil intents of the people. This is hardly the kind of leadership one would expect from the exalted priest of the tabernacle texts and surely a signal that ancient Israel had divergent priestly traditions. The tale then takes an ominous turn as Moses voices yet another response, dramatically selecting a group of Levites who are loyal to God and telling them to kill their reveling kin and companions, 3,000 in all. Shocking as it may seem, the violent complicity of these men earns them a blessing as well as the role of priesthood. This outcome is difficult to comprehend except as the enigmatic and troubling remnant of an ancient struggle for the rights to the priesthood.

The narrative presents one more intercessory attempt by Moses. This time he seeks to avert disaster by making atonement to God for the sins of the people. The image of the people's sins being recorded in a divine record book is striking, as is Moses' selfless entreaty to be blotted out from that book (that is, to die) along with all the sinful people should God not forgive their sins. This is especially poignant in light of the promise to Moses – that God would make him "a great nation" (v. 10). Refusing to allow sins to go unpunished, God nonetheless instructs Moses to follow the angel who will lead the people onward, away from Sinai. Presumably the people will be spared for the time being. Yet chapter 32 ends (v. 35) with God sending a plague, in contrast to the decision reported in v. 14 not to annihilate them. There is enormous tension in this episode between the concept of punishment as the inevitable consequence of human sin and that of unconditional divine promise and redemption. And clearly Moses comes off better than God – representing mercy and forgiveness in contrast with God's unremittingly punitive stance.[75]

---

[74] Cf. 2 Kgs 23:15 and also a Ugaritic text describing the demolition of Mot, "The Ba'lu Myth," translated by Dennis Pardee (*COS* 1.86), 270.

[75] R. Norman Whybray, "The Immorality of God: Reflections on Some Passages in Genesis, Job, Exodus, and Numbers," *JSOT* 72 (1996): 12–14.

BRIDGING THE HORIZONS: HEAVENLY RECORD BOOKS

The idea of God recording the names of people in a book is part of a general Near Eastern belief in heavenly ledgers. The popular conception of such records no doubt is rooted in the practices of record keeping in the political and economic realms. Because census lists determined certain aspects, such as taxes and military service, of the fate of the individuals listed in them, they are likely to have been the models for the record books of deities, who were considered the deciders of destiny. References in cuneiform documents to celestial ledgers can be traced back to Sumerian times.[76] These documents refer variously to "tablets of life" or "tablets of destiny." One famous example comes from the Neo-Babylonian period and expresses the hope of Nebuchadnezzar II (605–562 BCE) that he be granted prosperity and a long life for having restored a temple. He appeals to the god Nabu, the god of scribal arts and the one who is in charge of the tablets of destiny: "On your heavenly writing board . . . , decree for me extreme old age. Cause my deeds to find acceptance before Marduk. . . ."[77] Similarly, another Babylonian king appeals to Nabu to "inscribe the days of his life for long duration in a tablet."[78] Mesopotamian inscriptions also mention heavenly tablets that record the misdeeds as well as the good deeds of humans.

The Hebrew Bible shares this tradition. More than a dozen texts refer to heavenly ledgers, of which there are three different kinds: a book of divine decrees, in which God records the destinies of people (e.g., Ps 139:16); a book of remembrance, which keeps track of what people do (Mal 3:16); and a book of life, or of the living.[79]

The third kind is mentioned only once, in Ps 69:28, in which the beleaguered psalmist appeals to God to deal with threatening evil-doers: "Let them be blotted out of the book of the living; let them not be enrolled among the righteous." The notion of a book – actually, in biblical times, a scroll – in which the names of righteous people are recorded that they may live is the basis of Moses' poignant appeal in Exod 32:32–33, in which sinners are erased from the record and thus fated to die.

The idea of a heavenly Book of Life (*sēper ḥayyîm*) endured in early postbiblical Jewish literature, including several apocryphal books and the Dead Sea Scrolls. In the Mishnah, Rabbi Akiva speaks in considerable detail about a divine record in which all of a person's actions are written down until the Day of Judgment (*m.'Abot* 3:17). It is also found several times in the New Testament; in Phil 4:3,

---

[76] Shalom M. Paul, "Heavenly Tablets and the Book of Life," *JANES* 5 (1973): 345–53.
[77] "Nebuchadnezzar II's Restoration of E-urimin-ankia, the Ziggurat of Borsippa," translated by Paul-Alain Beaulieu (*COS* 2.122B), 310.
[78] S. M. Paul, "Heavenly Tablets," *JANES* 5 (1973): 346.
[79] N. M. Sarna, *Exodus* (1991), 209–10.

for example, Paul speaks favorably of co-workers "whose names are in the book of life."

The ancient text that most influenced later Jewish liturgy and tradition is the discussion in the Talmud (*b. Roš. Haš.* 16b), which reflects the variety of biblical references to divine ledgers and mentions three of them: one, the Book of Life, has the names of the wholly righteous; one has a list of the completely wicked; and one records people of intermediate status. In this view, each year at the New Year holiday everyone's name is inscribed in the appropriate book. But the book is not sealed until ten days later, on the Day of Atonement. That intervening period, known as the "ten days of penitence (or repentance)," gives people the opportunity to atone for their misdeeds in the hope that they will be inscribed along with the righteous in the Book of Life. The traditional liturgy for the New Year (Rosh Ha-shanah) and the Day of Atonement (Yom Kippur) includes recurrent images of the Book of Life and expresses the hope that genuine repentance will earn a place in the ledger of life. The most common greeting among Jews during this period is "may you be inscribed for good," expressing the desire for well-being in the year to come. Very traditional Jews may understand the Book of Life literally, but most others use the ancient idea of heavenly ledgers in a more general sense as a vivid reminder to repent of wrongdoing and do better in the year ahead.

The tension continues in the next chapter (33), which begins with a repeated directive to leave Sinai and proceed to the land promised to the ancestors.[80] God refuses to stay with the people on the journey but instead will send an angel. The angel here is not a manifestation of God but a separate emissary, for God's direct presence would be lethal rather than protective! This seems to contradict the notion of the beneficence of God's presence and indicates again the tension between divine justice and unconditional blessing. Moreover, God's withdrawal seems to negate the whole set of tabernacle instructions, which are meant to secure divine presence. Understandably, the people are devastated by this turn of events and remove all ornamentation (33:6) – even though they presumably have just donated their adornments so that Aaron could make the golden calf and have just indicated their refusal (v. 4) even to don them. It is likely that variant traditions have been combined. Even so, this scene strikes a discordant note in relation to other details of the calf incident and also in relation to the tabernacle texts that precede and follow it.

The next scene (33:7–11), which seems to be an aside, is a fascinating vignette of a tent shrine far simpler than the elaborate tabernacle of chapters 25–31 and 35–39. It also contains one of the several views in this section about how God's presence was manifest to Moses. Moses is depicted as pitching the tent shrine,

---

[80] See the discussion of 23:20–26.

which he calls the "tent of meeting," by himself outside the camp. He would go there to meet with God while the people watched from the entrances of their own tents, knowing that the cloud at the entrance of God's tent signified divine presence. In other words, without the cloud, God would not be available to meet with Moses. This differs from the conception of the tabernacle as a portable structure that regularizes God's presence. It also differs in suggesting a rather simple shrine, which Moses could set up by himself, rather than the elaborate tabernacle requiring many servitors to transport it and set it up (Num 1:49). And it has the tent outside the camp rather than in the center of the camp, which is portrayed as a military formation in Numbers 2.[81] Moreover, Moses would encounter God in the most intimate way – "face to face, as one speaks to a friend" (33:11) – before returning to the people, leaving Joshua at the tent. Remarkably, in this passage, unlike others that relate Moses' direct encounters with God, a human can see God directly rather than as a presence manifest in divine glory or cloud. Finally, Joshua is Moses' assistant in this account of divine revelation at the tent; priests are not mentioned. All these divergent features contribute to our understanding of Exodus as an amalgam of collective memories and traditions.

Profound anxiety about God's presence connects this tent-of-meeting passage with what precedes it and with the ensuing extraordinary dialogue (33:12–23) between Moses and God. The people have responded with mourning to God's refusal to be present on their journey (33:4); Moses responds by again challenging a divine decision. He pleads with God to be present, directly or indirectly, and guide the people as they continue their journey. In a telling reversal of the concern early in the book of Exodus about the name of God, now it is Moses' name that is known by God (vv. 12, 17). Moses offers a brilliant argument, claiming that his special relationship with God empowers him to offer an ultimatum – the people will not continue their journey if God will not agree to be with them. But, in contrast with the Rephidim episode (17:1–13), it is not simply a matter of the power of God's presence to provide sustenance or protection. Now the issue is identity: anticipating the scope of the new/renewed covenant of 34:10, Moses asserts that God's presence among the people is what sets them apart from all others (v. 16). God yields to Moses' eloquent plea, affirming Moses' status and the intimacy of their relationship. Moses looms large and, in fact, is the dominating figure of this intense exchange.

The exchange culminates in a somewhat mystifying appearance of God to Moses (33:17–23). God puts Moses in the cleft of a rock, where he is covered by God's hand. Once God's glory passes by him, Moses sees the back but not the face of God; a frontal visual experience of God would be fatal (v. 20). This

---

[81] See Myung S. Suh, *The Tabernacle in the Narrative History of Israel from the Exodus to the Conquest* (Studies in Biblical Literature 50; New York: Lang, 2003); cf. M. M. Homan, "Divine Warrior," *BR* 16 (2000): 22–32, 55.

anthropomorphic tradition mentioning the hand, back, and face of God is intertwined with a more abstract notion of God's presence manifest in a cloud and in "goodness" (v. 19), a term denoting the manifold positive attributes of Israel's god as well as the beneficence of God as partner in a covenant relationship.[82] The account of this theophany includes God's proclamation of the divine name and thus resonates with God's first appearance to Moses in 3:14. The grammatical formation of the initial revelation of the divine name ("I AM WHO I AM") recurs in the pronouncement of God's mercy and graciousness ("I will be gracious to whom I will be gracious, and will show mercy on whom I will show mercy"), which in turn anticipates the language of 34:6 in the account of the covenant restoration in the next chapter.

COVENANT RENEWAL (34:1–36)

Moses' journeys up and down the mountain of chapter 19, anticipating the theophany and covenant of chapters 20–24, are now resumed. Moses must make one final trip to the summit of Sinai so that the words of the covenant can be inscribed on a second set of tablets that Moses himself is to prepare. Again, God proclaims the divine name and follows with a self-disclosure, perhaps construed as a response to Moses' request in 33:13 to know God's ways. The resounding catalogue in 34:6–7 of God's moral attributes of love and mercy, graciousness and forgiveness also includes God's insistence on human accountability for wrongdoing. These verses, which are known as the Thirteen Attributes of God in Jewish tradition, are repeated or quoted some fourteen times in the Hebrew Bible and also appear in part in the expansion to the stipulation against worshiping images in the Decalogue (20:4–6).[83] It is thus likely that, even before the exile, they served as a creedal statement. In the rabbinic period, if not before, they were incorporated into Jewish liturgy, where their prominence in penitential prayers suggests a belief that punishment for sin might be tempered by genuine contrition.

In (re)making the covenant (34:10), God uses the term "wonders" (NRSV "marvels"), which echoes the wonders of the exodus from Egypt and seems to anticipate what lies ahead. The depiction of the future, with the Israelites taking possession of territory belonging to others, is described in verses 11–16. These verses are a shorter version of the divine promises and admonitions that represent covenant blessings and that appear in 23:20–33 as a brief epilogue to the rulings and exhortations of Exodus. Here the emphasis is on admonitions. The people are warned against interactions with the local inhabitants. Although God claims they all will be driven out, that claim may be another example of

---

[82] Michael V. Fox, "TÔB as Covenant Terminology," *BASOR* 209 (1973): 41–2.

[83] They thus fit the current context, which is the aftermath of the image-making golden calf incident.

unpalatable hyperbole; otherwise the sharp admonitions against any contacts with them would be meaningless. What kind of contacts does God prohibit? Although the making of covenants with them is forbidden, the covenant itself is not the issue; rather, the problem lies in the interactions that being in a covenanted political relationship entails. The other peoples have their own gods, and Yahweh wants to take no chances that the Israelites will join in the religious lives of their neighbors. Such might happen if they were allied by a treaty.

Similarly, such an alliance would create opportunities for marriage between Israelites and the local peoples. Yet only liaisons between Israelite males and local females are forbidden. This asymmetrical prohibition of exogamy, which in exilic biblical passages (e.g., Ezra 9:12; Neh 10:30) includes both sexes as a way of maintaining cultural boundaries in the absence of monarchic political identity, is not in this passage an interdiction against intermarriage with women from all peoples, but only with local women; it thus may reflect concerns earlier than the exilic ones. Because it allows for Israelite marriage with peoples from distant lands and for women to marry any outsiders, particular social conditions are likely to have led to this selective prohibition. Perhaps the crucial roles of women in household life would have made it a greater risk to Israelite cultural identity if local non-Israelite women were to become wives in Yahwistic households. The religious focus of the prohibition is best understood in more general cultural terms.[84]

The critique of Canaanite practices is extended in this reprise of Exod 23:20–33 to include "sacred poles" as well as pillars and altars (v. 13). The word for these objects is 'ăšērîm and probably refers to representations of the goddess Asherah, a major Canaanite deity who was popular among Israelites until late in the monarchic period.[85] Images of her apparently were installed at high places throughout the monarchic period and even in the Jerusalem temple (2 Kgs 21:7), and inscriptional evidence suggests that some considered her Yahweh's consort.[86] How widely she was worshiped among Israelites is disputed, but it seems that she was part of the royal cult until very late in the monarchy. Groups opposed to the worship of any deity but Yahweh have influenced this passage, which seems to make it more explicit than does the Decalogue (20:3) that worship of other gods is unacceptable (v. 14).

The attention to religious life in chapter 34 is expressed in instructions for what must be done as well as for what is prohibited. One last prohibition (v. 17) forbids images and links this section to the larger golden-calf context. Then a series of directives (vv. 18–26) mandates the celebration of the Sabbath and the three major festivals (Weeks, Ingathering, and Passover) and the redemption of

---

[84] Carol Meyers, "Daughters of the Inhabitants of the Land as Marriage Partners (Exod 34:16; Gen 24:3; 27:46; 28:1, 6, 8; Deut 7:3; Josh 23:12–13; Judg 3:5–6)," *WIS,* 200–1.

[85] Susan Ackerman, "Asherah/Asherim," *WIS,* 508–11.

[86] "Kuntillet 'Ajrud: Inscribed Pithos 2," translated by P. Kyle McCarter (*COS* 2.47B), 172, and "Khirbet el-Qom," translated by P. Kyle McCarter (*COS* 2.52), 179.

the firstborn. All of these have already appeared in Exodus, although this may be their oldest iteration.[87] Except for the redemption of the firstborn, which is mentioned in 13:12–13, they are stipulated in the "first" covenant in the section on observances relating to the agricultural calendar (23:12–19), along with the appended rule about the cooking of a kid. Yet the relationship among the texts of Exodus 13, 23, and 34 is problematic. The chapter 34 version of the regulations for observances is exactly the same as in earlier chapters only in some instances; in others, it is only slightly different; and in still others, it varies considerably. The clear similarity yet unmistakable variation likely indicates the complexities in the transmission of cultural traditions.[88] Multiple festival calendars and divergent cultural memories are joined in this priestly composite.

The conclusion to the covenant renewal episode foregrounds Moses once more and provides the third account of God appearing to him in this narrative of covenant violation and renewal. As for the first covenant (24:18), Moses is on the mountain for forty days and nights. But this time Moses abstains from sustenance during that period. Probably not a literal number, forty designates the great extent of Moses' fasting, necessary for him to achieve the spiritual state that will ready him for the extraordinary experience he is about to have. He himself (34:27), and not God (as in 32:16 and 34:1), will inscribe the words of the covenant – called the "ten words" (NRSV "ten commandments") here for the first time – on the tablets he has prepared.

The episode continues with the enigmatic account of Moses' shining face, the meaning of which has evoked considerable scholarly discussion and little consensus. It begins with a narrative of what happens to Moses when he descends the mountain (34:29–33) and is followed by a statement of how that experience becomes part of ongoing ritual practice. Mosaic authority seems to be at stake. As the mediator par excellence between the divine and the human, Moses takes on a unique aura, with his face so radiant that the Israelites were afraid to approach him. Such radiance, in ancient Near Eastern imagery, is the characteristic luminosity of deities.[89] Visible on human rulers, royal effulgence is part of the poetic expression of the king's divine authority.[90] Transferred to Moses when God speaks to him directly, it reflects God's glory and signifies Moses' authority. Moses' own personality is subsumed into his role as mediator, with his social and religious authority originating from God and not in his own skills

---

[87] Ernst Haag, "*šabbāt*," *TDOT* 14:392–3.

[88] B. S. Childs, *Book of Exodus* (1974), 613–15.

[89] N. M. Sarna, *Exodus* (1991), 221, 262. Because the word for "radiance" in other contexts can mean "horn," incorrect translations of this text led to depictions (such as Michelangelo's famous statue) of a horned Moses in Christian art and to the anti-Semitic notion of horned satanic Jews.

[90] "Letter of the Ruler of Gezer (Gazaru) (EA 292)," translated by William Moran (*COS* 3.92C), 239.

or charisma.[91] It is no wonder that the root for "speak" appears *seven* times in verses 29–35. Moses is fully God's spokesman – in recording the "ten words" of the covenant and in continually "going in" to speak with God. Moses has completely entered that role, for his face remains shining, permanently signifying his role as God's authoritative mouthpiece and necessitating that he thereafter wear a veil. His identity has merged with God to the extent that, like God, he must cover his face, the locus of God's presence in him.

CONSTRUCTING THE TABERNACLE – EXODUS 35:1–40:38

NRSV 35 Moses assembled all the congregation of the Israelites and said to them: These are the things that the LORD has commanded you to do:

2 Six days shall work be done, but on the seventh day you shall have a holy sabbath of solemn rest to the LORD; whoever does any work on it shall be put to death. [3]You shall kindle no fire in all your dwellings on the sabbath day.

4 Moses said to all the congregation of the Israelites: This is the thing that the LORD has commanded: [5]Take from among you an offering to the LORD; let whoever is of a generous heart bring the LORD's offering: gold, silver, and bronze; [6]blue, purple, and crimson yarns, and fine linen; goats' hair, [7]tanned rams' skins, and fine leather; acacia wood, [8]oil for the light, spices for the anointing oil and for the fragrant incense, [9]and onyx stones and gems to be set in the ephod and the breastpiece.

10 All who are skillful among you shall come and make all that the LORD has commanded: the tabernacle, [11]its tent and its covering, its clasps and its frames, its bars, its pillars, and its bases; [12]the ark with its poles, the mercy seat,[a] and the curtain for the screen; [13]the table with its poles and all its utensils, and the bread of the Presence; [14]the lampstand also for the light, with its utensils and its lamps, and the oil for the light; [15]and the altar of incense, with its poles, and the anointing oil and the fragrant incense, and the screen for the entrance, the entrance of the tabernacle; [16]the altar of burnt offering, with its grating of bronze, its poles, and all its utensils, the basin with its stand; [17]the hangings of the court, its pillars and its bases, and the screen for the gate of the court; [18]the pegs of the tabernacle and the pegs of the court, and their cords; [19]the finely worked vestments for ministering in the holy place, the holy vestments for the priest Aaron, and the vestments of his sons, for their service as priests.

20 Then all the congregation of the Israelites withdrew from the presence of Moses. [21]And they came, everyone whose heart was stirred, and everyone whose

---

[91]　Thomas B. Dozeman, "Masking Moses and Mosaic Authority in Torah," *JBL* 119 (2000): 29–30. Dozeman (33–45) also shows that there is tension in the combination of pre-priestly, tent-of-meeting traditions with priestly ones in this pivotal episode.

[a]　Or *cover*

spirit was willing, and brought the LORD's offering to be used for the tent of meeting, and for all its service, and for the sacred vestments. [22]So they came, both men and women; all who were of a willing heart brought brooches and earrings and signet rings and pendants, all sorts of gold objects, everyone bringing an offering of gold to the LORD. [23]And everyone who possessed blue or purple or crimson yarn or fine linen or goats' hair or tanned rams' skins or fine leather, brought them. [24]Everyone who could make an offering of silver or bronze brought it as the LORD's offering; and everyone who possessed acacia wood of any use in the work, brought it. [25]All the skillful women spun with their hands, and brought what they had spun in blue and purple and crimson yarns and fine linen; [26]all the women whose hearts moved them to use their skill spun the goats' hair. [27]And the leaders brought onyx stones and gems to be set in the ephod and the breastpiece, [28]and spices and oil for the light, and for the anointing oil, and for the fragrant incense. [29]All the Israelite men and women whose hearts made them willing to bring anything for the work that the LORD had commanded by Moses to be done, brought it as a freewill offering to the LORD.

30 Then Moses said to the Israelites: See, the LORD has called by name Bezalel son of Uri son of Hur, of the tribe of Judah; [31]he has filled him with divine spirit, with skill, intelligence, and knowledge in every kind of craft, [32]to devise artistic designs, to work in gold, silver, and bronze, [33]in cutting stones for setting, and in carving wood, in every kind of craft. [34]And he has inspired him to teach, both him and Oholiab son of Ahisamach, of the tribe of Dan. [35]He has filled them with skill to do every kind of work done by an artisan or by a designer or by an embroiderer in blue, purple, and crimson yarns, and in fine linen, or by a weaver – by any sort of artisan or skilled designer.

NRSV 36 Bezalel and Oholiab and every skillful one to whom the LORD has given skill and understanding to know how to do any work in the construction of the sanctuary shall work in accordance with all that the LORD has commanded.

2 Moses then called Bezalel and Oholiab and every skillful one to whom the LORD had given skill, everyone whose heart was stirred to come to do the work; [3]and they received from Moses all the freewill offerings that the Israelites had brought for doing the work on the sanctuary. They still kept bringing him freewill offerings every morning, [4]so that all the artisans who were doing every sort of task on the sanctuary came, each from the task being performed, [5]and said to Moses, "The people are bringing much more than enough for doing the work that the LORD has commanded us to do." [6]So Moses gave command, and word was proclaimed throughout the camp: "No man or woman is to make anything else as an offering for the sanctuary." So the people were restrained from bringing; [7]for what they had already brought was more than enough to do all the work.

8 All those with skill among the workers made the tabernacle with ten curtains; they were made of fine twisted linen, and blue, purple, and crimson yarns, with cherubim skillfully worked into them. [9]The length of each curtain was twenty-eight

cubits, and the width of each curtain four cubits; all the curtains were of the same size.

10 He joined five curtains to one another, and the other five curtains he joined to one another. [11]He made loops of blue on the edge of the outermost curtain of the first set; likewise he made them on the edge of the outermost curtain of the second set; [12]he made fifty loops on the one curtain, and he made fifty loops on the edge of the curtain that was in the second set; the loops were opposite one another. [13]And he made fifty clasps of gold, and joined the curtains one to the other with clasps; so the tabernacle was one whole.

14 He also made curtains of goats' hair for a tent over the tabernacle; he made eleven curtains. [15]The length of each curtain was thirty cubits, and the width of each curtain four cubits; the eleven curtains were of the same size. [16]He joined five curtains by themselves, and six curtains by themselves. [17]He made fifty loops on the edge of the outermost curtain of the one set, and fifty loops on the edge of the other connecting curtain. [18]He made fifty clasps of bronze to join the tent together so that it might be one whole. [19]And he made for the tent a covering of tanned rams' skins and an outer covering of fine leather.

20 Then he made the upright frames for the tabernacle of acacia wood. [21]Ten cubits was the length of a frame, and a cubit and a half the width of each frame. [22]Each frame had two pegs for fitting together; he did this for all the frames of the tabernacle. [23]The frames for the tabernacle he made in this way: twenty frames for the south side; [24]and he made forty bases of silver under the twenty frames, two bases under the first frame for its two pegs, and two bases under the next frame for its two pegs. [25]For the second side of the tabernacle, on the north side, he made twenty frames [26]and their forty bases of silver, two bases under the first frame and two bases under the next frame. [27]For the rear of the tabernacle westward he made six frames. [28]He made two frames for corners of the tabernacle in the rear. [29]They were separate beneath, but joined at the top, at the first ring; he made two of them in this way, for the two corners. [30]There were eight frames with their bases of silver: sixteen bases, under every frame two bases.

31 He made bars of acacia wood, five for the frames of the one side of the tabernacle, [32]and five bars for the frames of the other side of the tabernacle, and five bars for the frames of the tabernacle at the rear westward. [33]He made the middle bar to pass through from end to end halfway up the frames. [34]And he overlaid the frames with gold, and made rings of gold for them to hold the bars, and overlaid the bars with gold.

35 He made the curtain of blue, purple, and crimson yarns, and fine twisted linen, with cherubim skillfully worked into it. [36]For it he made four pillars of acacia, and overlaid them with gold; their hooks were of gold, and he cast for them four bases of silver. [37]He also made a screen for the entrance to the tent, of blue, purple, and crimson yarns, and fine twisted linen, embroidered with needlework; [38]and its five pillars with their hooks. He overlaid their capitals and their bases with gold, but their five bases were of bronze.

NRSV 37 Bezalel made the ark of acacia wood; it was two and a half cubits long, a cubit and a half wide, and a cubit and a half high. [2]He overlaid it with pure gold inside and outside, and made a molding of gold around it. [3]He cast for it four rings of gold for its four feet, two rings on its one side and two rings on its other side. [4]He made poles of acacia wood, and overlaid them with gold, [5]and put the poles into the rings on the sides of the ark, to carry the ark. [6]He made a mercy seat[a] of pure gold; two cubits and a half was its length, and a cubit and a half its width. [7]He made two cherubim of hammered gold; at the two ends of the mercy seat[a] he made them, [8]one cherub at the one end, and one cherub at the other end; of one piece with the mercy seat[a] he made the cherubim at its two ends. [9]The cherubim spread out their wings above, overshadowing the mercy seat[a] with their wings. They faced one another; the faces of the cherubim were turned toward the mercy seat.[a]

10 He also made the table of acacia wood, two cubits long, one cubit wide, and a cubit and a half high. [11]He overlaid it with pure gold, and made a molding of gold around it. [12]He made around it a rim a handbreadth wide, and made a molding of gold around the rim. [13]He cast for it four rings of gold, and fastened the rings to the four corners at its four legs. [14]The rings that held the poles used for carrying the table were close to the rim. [15]He made the poles of acacia wood to carry the table, and overlaid them with gold. [16]And he made the vessels of pure gold that were to be on the table, its plates and dishes for incense, and its bowls and flagons with which to pour drink offerings.

17 He also made the lampstand of pure gold. The base and the shaft of the lampstand were made of hammered work; its cups, its calyxes, and its petals were of one piece with it. [18]There were six branches going out of its sides, three branches of the lampstand out of one side of it and three branches of the lampstand out of the other side of it; [19]three cups shaped like almond blossoms, each with calyx and petals, on one branch, and three cups shaped like almond blossoms, each with calyx and petals, on the other branch – so for the six branches going out of the lampstand. [20]On the lampstand itself there were four cups shaped like almond blossoms, each with its calyxes and petals. [21]There was a calyx of one piece with it under the first pair of branches, a calyx of one piece with it under the next pair of branches, and a calyx of one piece with it under the last pair of branches. [22]Their calyxes and their branches were of one piece with it, the whole of it one hammered piece of pure gold. [23]He made its seven lamps and its snuffers and its trays of pure gold. [24]He made it and all its utensils of a talent of pure gold.

25 He made the altar of incense of acacia wood, one cubit long, and one cubit wide; it was square, and was two cubits high; its horns were of one piece with it. [26]He overlaid it with pure gold, its top, and its sides all around, and its horns; and he made for it a molding of gold all around, [27]and made two golden rings for it under its molding, on two opposite sides of it, to hold the poles with which to carry it. [28]And he made the poles of acacia wood, and overlaid them with gold.

---

[a] Or *cover*

29 He made the holy anointing oil also, and the pure fragrant incense, blended as by the perfumer.

NRSV 38 He made the altar of burnt offering also of acacia wood; it was five cubits long, and five cubits wide; it was square, and three cubits high. [2]He made horns for it on its four corners; its horns were of one piece with it, and he overlaid it with bronze. [3]He made all the utensils of the altar, the pots, the shovels, the basins, the forks, and the firepans: all its utensils he made of bronze. [4]He made for the altar a grating, a network of bronze, under its ledge, extending halfway down. [5]He cast four rings on the four corners of the bronze grating to hold the poles; [6]he made the poles of acacia wood, and overlaid them with bronze. [7]And he put the poles through the rings on the sides of the altar, to carry it with them; he made it hollow, with boards.

8 He made the basin of bronze with its stand of bronze, from the mirrors of the women who served at the entrance to the tent of meeting.

9 He made the court; for the south side the hangings of the court were of fine twisted linen, one hundred cubits long; [10]its twenty pillars and their twenty bases were of bronze, but the hooks of the pillars and their bands were of silver. [11]For the north side there were hangings one hundred cubits long; its twenty pillars and their twenty bases were of bronze, but the hooks of the pillars and their bands were of silver. [12]For the west side there were hangings fifty cubits long, with ten pillars and ten bases; the hooks of the pillars and their bands were of silver. [13]And for the front to the east, fifty cubits. [14]The hangings for one side of the gate were fifteen cubits, with three pillars and three bases. [15]And so for the other side; on each side of the gate of the court were hangings of fifteen cubits, with three pillars and three bases. [16]All the hangings around the court were of fine twisted linen. [17]The bases for the pillars were of bronze, but the hooks of the pillars and their bands were of silver; the overlaying of their capitals was also of silver, and all the pillars of the court were banded with silver. [18]The screen for the entrance to the court was embroidered with needlework in blue, purple, and crimson yarns and fine twisted linen. It was twenty cubits long and, along the width of it, five cubits high, corresponding to the hangings of the court. [19]There were four pillars; their four bases were of bronze, their hooks of silver, and the overlaying of their capitals and their bands of silver. [20]All the pegs for the tabernacle and for the court all around were of bronze.

21 These are the records of the tabernacle, the tabernacle of the covenant,[a] which were drawn up at the commandment of Moses, the work of the Levites being under the direction of Ithamar son of the priest Aaron. [22]Bezalel son of Uri son of Hur, of the tribe of Judah, made all that the LORD commanded Moses; [23]and with him was Oholiab son of Ahisamach, of the tribe of Dan, engraver, designer, and embroiderer in blue, purple, and crimson yarns, and in fine linen.

24 All the gold that was used for the work, in all the construction of the sanctuary, the gold from the offering, was twenty-nine talents and seven hundred thirty

[a] Or *treaty*, or *testimony*

shekels, measured by the sanctuary shekel. [25] The silver from those of the congregation who were counted was one hundred talents and one thousand seven hundred seventy-five shekels, measured by the sanctuary shekel; [26] a beka a head (that is, half a shekel, measured by the sanctuary shekel), for everyone who was counted in the census, from twenty years old and upward, for six hundred three thousand, five hundred fifty men. [27] The hundred talents of silver were for casting the bases of the sanctuary, and the bases of the curtain; one hundred bases for the hundred talents, a talent for a base. [28] Of the thousand seven hundred seventy-five shekels he made hooks for the pillars, and overlaid their capitals and made bands for them. [29] The bronze that was contributed was seventy talents, and two thousand four hundred shekels; [30] with it he made the bases for the entrance of the tent of meeting, the bronze altar and the bronze grating for it and all the utensils of the altar, [31] the bases all around the court, and the bases of the gate of the court, all the pegs of the tabernacle, and all the pegs around the court.

NRSV 39 Of the blue, purple, and crimson yarns they made finely worked vestments, for ministering in the holy place; they made the sacred vestments for Aaron; as the LORD had commanded Moses.

2 He made the ephod of gold, of blue, purple, and crimson yarns, and of fine twisted linen. [3] Gold leaf was hammered out and cut into threads to work into the blue, purple, and crimson yarns and into the fine twisted linen, in skilled design. [4] They made for the ephod shoulder-pieces, joined to it at its two edges. [5] The decorated band on it was of the same materials and workmanship, of gold, of blue, purple, and crimson yarns, and of fine twisted linen; as the LORD had commanded Moses.

6 The onyx stones were prepared, enclosed in settings of gold filigree and engraved like the engravings of a signet, according to the names of the sons of Israel. [7] He set them on the shoulder-pieces of the ephod, to be stones of remembrance for the sons of Israel; as the LORD had commanded Moses.

8 He made the breastpiece, in skilled work, like the work of the ephod, of gold, of blue, purple, and crimson yarns, and of fine twisted linen. [9] It was square; the breastpiece was made double, a span in length and a span in width when doubled. [10] They set in it four rows of stones. A row of carnelian, chrysolite, and emerald was the first row; [11] and the second row, a turquoise, a sapphire, and a moonstone; [12] and the third row, a jacinth, an agate, and an amethyst; [13] and the fourth row, a beryl, an onyx, and a jasper; they were enclosed in settings of gold filigree. [14] There were twelve stones with names corresponding to the names of the sons of Israel; they were like signets, each engraved with its name, for the twelve tribes. [15] They made on the breastpiece chains of pure gold, twisted like cords; [16] and they made two settings of gold filigree and two gold rings, and put the two rings on the two edges of the breastpiece; [17] and they put the two cords of gold in the two rings at the edges of the breastpiece. [18] Two ends of the two cords they had attached to the two settings of filigree; in this way they attached it in front to the shoulder-pieces of the ephod. [19] Then they made two rings of gold, and put them at the two ends of the breastpiece, on its inside edge next to the ephod. [20] They made two rings of

gold, and attached them in front to the lower part of the two shoulder-pieces of the ephod, at its joining above the decorated band of the ephod. [21] They bound the breastpiece by its rings to the rings of the ephod with a blue cord, so that it should lie on the decorated band of the ephod, and that the breastpiece should not come loose from the ephod; as the LORD had commanded Moses.

22 He also made the robe of the ephod woven all of blue yarn; [23] and the opening of the robe in the middle of it was like the opening in a coat of mail, with a binding around the opening, so that it might not be torn. [24] On the lower hem of the robe they made pomegranates of blue, purple, and crimson yarns, and of fine twisted linen. [25] They also made bells of pure gold, and put the bells between the pomegranates on the lower hem of the robe all around, between the pomegranates; [26] a bell and a pomegranate, a bell and a pomegranate all around on the lower hem of the robe for ministering; as the LORD had commanded Moses.

27 They also made the tunics, woven of fine linen, for Aaron and his sons, [28] and the turban of fine linen, and the headdresses of fine linen, and the linen undergarments of fine twisted linen, [29] and the sash of fine twisted linen, and of blue, purple, and crimson yarns, embroidered with needlework; as the LORD had commanded Moses.

30 They made the rosette of the holy diadem of pure gold, and wrote on it an inscription, like the engraving of a signet, "Holy to the LORD." [31] They tied to it a blue cord, to fasten it on the turban above; as the LORD had commanded Moses.

32 In this way all the work of the tabernacle of the tent of meeting was finished; the Israelites had done everything just as the LORD had commanded Moses. [33] Then they brought the tabernacle to Moses, the tent and all its utensils, its hooks, its frames, its bars, its pillars, and its bases; [34] the covering of tanned rams' skins and the covering of fine leather, and the curtain for the screen; [35] the ark of the covenant[a] with its poles and the mercy seat;[b] [36] the table with all its utensils, and the bread of the Presence; [37] the pure lampstand with its lamps set on it and all its utensils, and the oil for the light; [38] the golden altar, the anointing oil and the fragrant incense, and the screen for the entrance of the tent; [39] the bronze altar, and its grating of bronze, its poles, and all its utensils; the basin with its stand; [40] the hangings of the court, its pillars, and its bases, and the screen for the gate of the court, its cords, and its pegs; and all the utensils for the service of the tabernacle, for the tent of meeting; [41] the finely worked vestments for ministering in the holy place, the sacred vestments for the priest Aaron, and the vestments of his sons to serve as priests. [42] The Israelites had done all of the work just as the LORD had commanded Moses. [43] When Moses saw that they had done all the work just as the LORD had commanded, he blessed them.

NRSV 40 The LORD spoke to Moses: [2] On the first day of the first month you shall set up the tabernacle of the tent of meeting. [3] You shall put in it the ark of the

---

[a]   Or *treaty*, or *testimony*
[b]   Or *cover*

covenant,[a] and you shall screen the ark with the curtain. [4]You shall bring in the table, and arrange its setting; and you shall bring in the lampstand, and set up its lamps. [5]You shall put the golden altar for incense before the ark of the covenant,[a] and set up the screen for the entrance of the tabernacle. [6]You shall set the altar of burnt offering before the entrance of the tabernacle of the tent of meeting, [7]and place the basin between the tent of meeting and the altar, and put water in it. [8]You shall set up the court all around, and hang up the screen for the gate of the court. [9]Then you shall take the anointing oil, and anoint the tabernacle and all that is in it, and consecrate it and all its furniture, so that it shall become holy. [10]You shall also anoint the altar of burnt offering and all its utensils, and consecrate the altar, so that the altar shall be most holy. [11]You shall also anoint the basin with its stand, and consecrate it. [12]Then you shall bring Aaron and his sons to the entrance of the tent of meeting, and shall wash them with water, [13]and put on Aaron the sacred vestments, and you shall anoint him and consecrate him, so that he may serve me as priest. [14]You shall bring his sons also and put tunics on them, [15]and anoint them, as you anointed their father, that they may serve me as priests: and their anointing shall admit them to a perpetual priesthood throughout all generations to come.

16 Moses did everything just as the LORD had commanded him. [17]In the first month in the second year, on the first day of the month, the tabernacle was set up. [18]Moses set up the tabernacle; he laid its bases, and set up its frames, and put in its poles, and raised up its pillars; [19]and he spread the tent over the tabernacle, and put the covering of the tent over it; as the LORD had commanded Moses. [20]He took the covenant[a] and put it into the ark, and put the poles on the ark, and set the mercy seat[b] above the ark; [21]and he brought the ark into the tabernacle, and set up the curtain for screening, and screened the ark of the covenant;[a] as the LORD had commanded Moses. [22]He put the table in the tent of meeting, on the north side of the tabernacle, outside the curtain, [23]and set the bread in order on it before the LORD; as the LORD had commanded Moses. [24]He put the lampstand in the tent of meeting, opposite the table on the south side of the tabernacle, [25]and set up the lamps before the LORD; as the LORD had commanded Moses. [26]He put the golden altar in the tent of meeting before the curtain, [27]and offered fragrant incense on it; as the LORD had commanded Moses. [28]He also put in place the screen for the entrance of the tabernacle. [29]He set the altar of burnt offering at the entrance of the tabernacle of the tent of meeting, and offered on it the burnt offering and the grain offering as the LORD had commanded Moses. [30]He set the basin between the tent of meeting and the altar, and put water in it for washing, [31]with which Moses and Aaron and his sons washed their hands and their feet. [32]When they went into the tent of meeting, and when they approached the altar, they washed; as the LORD had commanded Moses. [33]He set up the court around the tabernacle and the altar, and put up the screen at the gate of the court. So Moses finished the work.

---

[a]   Or *treaty*, or *testimony*
[b]   Or *cover*

34 Then the cloud covered the tent of meeting, and the glory of the Lord filled the tabernacle. ³⁵Moses was not able to enter the tent of meeting because the cloud settled upon it, and the glory of the Lord filled the tabernacle. ³⁶Whenever the cloud was taken up from the tabernacle, the Israelites would set out on each stage of their journey; ³⁷but if the cloud was not taken up, then they did not set out until the day that it was taken up. ³⁸For the cloud of the Lord was on the tabernacle by day, and fire was in the cloudᵃ by night, before the eyes of all the house of Israel at each stage of their journey.

The last part of Exodus contains the descriptive tabernacle texts (35:1–38:20), followed by a concluding section (38:21–40:38) that summarizes the completion of the project and then describes the dedication ceremonies. In terms of the overall flow of the Exodus narrative, the disobedience of the people evident in the preceding golden-calf episode has been resolved and now is replaced by complicity. The people carry out precisely what God has commanded. The descriptive texts, as already noted, contain materials very similar to the prescriptive texts, except that they are descriptions of what has been done instead of stipulations about what must be done. The major difference between the two sets of texts is in the order. The descriptive texts are organized according to a technological logic rather than according to degree of sanctity, with the construction of the tabernacle itself preceding the fabrication of its appurtenances and vestments. Another important difference is that the descriptive texts are somewhat briefer because they omit information about how items are to be used, indicating an interest in fabrication rather than function.

INTRODUCTORY PROCEDURES – 35:1–36:7

The descriptive texts actually begin with two directives. The first (35:2–3) is a brief passage about Sabbath observance. The prescriptive texts conclude with a somewhat longer Sabbath passage (**31:12–17**). Now Sabbath observance comes first, with the strong prohibition against work on the seventh day contrasting with the intensity of the labor that will mark the construction of the tabernacle. The second directive (35:4–19) calls for the donation of materials and is somewhat longer and more systematic than the equivalent prescriptive passage (**25:1–9**). Its opening verse (v. 4) contains a compliance formula, noting that the tabernacle project is what "the Lord has commanded." Appearing repeatedly in the descriptive texts, this phrase signifying that Moses is carrying out God's will is one of the devices for adapting archival materials into the priestly concerns of the Pentateuch.[92] Now it is accompanied by a report of how generously

---

ᵃ   Heb *it*
[92]   B. A. Levine, "Descriptive Tabernacle Texts," *JAOS* 85 (1965): 310.

the people respond (35:20–29). This extended account of the general readiness of people to offer whatever they could conveys their wholehearted support and enthusiasm. The magnanimity in providing materials recurs in 36:3–7, which reports that the collected materials exceed what was needed and that Moses must halt the flow. With the materials now in hand, Moses announces the names of the artisans God has chosen for the project and summons them to receive the materials that are pouring in (35:30–36:7). The chief artisan Bezalel dominates the descriptive texts, whereas Aaron was prominent in the prescriptive section.

The role of both women and men as donors and artisans appears at the beginning of the catalog of donations (35:22) and also at the end (35:29; cf. 36:6). This *inclusio* suggests that women, no less than men, had access to all the materials that could be contributed. In only two instances is the range of donors narrowed (35:25–28): the women who are experts in making textiles provide dyed wools, first-quality linen, and goats' hair fabrics; and the leaders give precious stones for the garments, ingredients for incense and anointing oil, and oil for the lamps (**cf. 27:20–21; 30:22–38**).

A CLOSER LOOK: WOMEN AND TEXTILES

In the gendered division of household labor that characterizes traditional cultures, spinning, weaving, and other aspects of textile production are women's crafts in almost 90% of peoples around the world.[93] As Exod 35:25–26 and other biblical texts indicate, Israelite women were part of this majority. Perhaps only a small number of them could have produced the kind of costly goods that are referred to in the tabernacle texts; and they may have worked in organized workshops, as suggested by 2 Kgs 23:7 and by information about state-sponsored textile production in Mesopotamia. But virtually every woman was likely to have had the rudimentary skills necessary to produce cloth and garments for her family in the absence of a developed market economy. Proverbs 31 is a somewhat idealized image of women's work, but it is accurate in depicting an adult woman as the producer of textiles for domestic use (vv. 13, 19) as well as for market (v. 18). Scholars have long acknowledged female dominance of textile production in ancient Israel as well as in other parts of the ancient Near East.[94] Yet they have not taken advantage of that information to assess its implications for women's lives and household dynamics.

---

[93] Carol L. Costin. "Exploring the Relationship between Gender and Crafts in Complex Societies: Methodological and Theoretical Issue of Gender Attribution," in *Gender and Archaeology*, ed. Rita P. Wright (Philadelphia: University of Pennsylvania Press, 1996), 121–3, Table 4.1
[94] E. W. Barber, *Women's Work* (1994).

Using ethnographic as well as ethnohistorical data, it is possible to ascertain what female control of an essential activity in virtually every household may have meant for the social dynamics of Israelite families.[95] Gender-associated activities signify gender-associated power in premodern societies. Women's control of tasks that produce necessary commodities, which normally cannot be obtained in any other way, typically produces several kinds of informal power. One kind is social power, made possible because women usually gather together to carry out the tedious and time-consuming processes associated with cloth production. The existence of work groups of women from neighboring households fosters the formation of networks of supra-household relationships. Such networks, in turn, enhance village solidarity and contribute in manifold and often subtle ways to the vitality and even the survival of a community. For example, women who get together for common tasks know when a family is experiencing hardship or illness and can help deploy labor or other resources as appropriate. Another kind of power is that which comes from the greater expertise of some women in the technologies of their craft. In instructing others in the intricacies of spinning or weaving, they experience the prestige and status that accompany informal mentoring. Such personal power also contributes to the gratification and valued sense of self that is a concomitant of providing essential commodities.

Not only did the textile work of Israelite women produce clothing and other fabrics; but also, along with other household tasks, it would have afforded women opportunities for meaningful social interaction and a sense of personal worth. And in a handful of elite households and urban or temple workshops, it may have contributed to economic development and religious splendor.

STRUCTURE/DWELLING – 36:8–38

The actual construction finally begins. The structure itself, with all its curtains and frames, loops and bases, and the screen covering its opening, is depicted in this section, which opens with the announcement that all the artisans began the project. The NRSV obscures the presence in verse 8 of one of the frequent references in the descriptive texts to the "work" (*mĕlā'kâ*, usually referring to skilled labor or the products of such work) entailed in this project. The artisans thus carry out the "work of the tabernacle" (NRSV "workers made the tabernacle"), that is, the project as a whole.[96] The information about the structure and its components repeats **26:1–37** almost verbatim.

95 C. Meyers, "Women's Culture," in *Symbiosis, Symbolism, and the Power of the Past* (2003), 434–7.
96 Jacob Milgrom and David P. Wright, "*mᵉlā'kâ*," *TDOT* 8:325–30.

INTERIOR FURNISHINGS – 37:1–29

Once the structure in which they are to be placed is described, the fabrication of the furnishings themselves is depicted. Although the details of each piece are virtually the same as those of the parallel texts, this section describes them in logical technical sequence, beginning with the holiest item, the ark (cf. **25:10–22**). Next come the three golden items situated in front of the veil shielding the ark: the offering table (cf. **25:23–30**); the lampstand (cf. **25:31–40**); and the incense altar (cf. **30:1–10**). Unlike its position in the prescriptive texts, the incense altar is described along with the items that flanked it. Similarly, the anointing oil and incense are mentioned in this furnishings section but elsewhere in the parallel texts (cf. **30:22–38**). The incense appears here because of its association with the incense altar, and the oil is included because of its association with the incense. The descriptive texts are somewhat briefer, in keeping with their emphasis on how things are made rather than how they are used. For example, the two verses in the instructions concerned with placing the covenant in the ark and with God's presence coming between the cherubim to meet with Moses (25:21–22) are omitted in the descriptive section.

COURTYARD – 38:1–20

Now the narrative turns toward the courtyard surrounding the structure and its appurtenances with their utensils. The descriptions themselves are similar to the information in the prescriptive texts but the order differs and is spatially more logical. The two ritual items of the court – the altar (cf. **27:1–8**) and the laver (cf. **30:17–21**) – are described sequentially here before the description of the enclosure (cf. **27:9–19**). In the prescriptive texts, the enclosure precedes the altar, and the laver appears in the addendum instead of in the section on the courtyard.

One other difference is that the laver is described much more briefly here but contains a surprising piece of information not contained in the prescriptive texts: the bronze for the laver is the special contribution of the "women who served at the entrance to the tent of meeting" (38:8; cf. 1 Sam 2:22) and who donated their mirrors for this purpose. Commentators have long puzzled over the placement of this verse, which positions women at the entrance to a structure not yet complete; a tradition of female servitors apparently has been inserted here because of the connection of their bronze mirrors to the bronze of the laver. Even more perplexing has been the role that such women may have had. Most scholars are reluctant to see them as legitimate cultic functionaries, and some even have supposed they are prostitutes. More likely, because the term used to designate them is related to a word designating Levitical servitors performing menial labor, they are part of the maintenance staff of the sanctuary. Yet their position at the entrance to the tent of meeting – a site important in Moses' oracular interactions with God (33:9–10) and not off-limits to women (Num 27:1–2) – may be the vestige of an old tradition of gender-inclusive cultic activity.[97]

A CLOSER LOOK: WOMEN AND RELIGION

The reluctance of scholars to see legitimate female participation in the tabernacle service is understandable, given the biblical assignment of priestly activity to the males of the tribe of Levi. However, the debatable role of women in the institutions of tabernacle or temple does not preclude a significant, if not central, role for them in household religious practice. That role is little recognized or understood because of the dearth – a product of the national concerns of the authors and redactors of the Hebrew Bible – of biblical texts referring to household religious practice. When family religious activity is mentioned, the tone is usually critical (as in Jer 7:18) but at least indicates the existence of such activity. Although texts are clearly important for understanding religious behaviors, they are not the only sources of information. Archaeological materials combined with ethnographic data allow us to reconstruct the religious lives of Israelite women and to appreciate the importance of their religious activities for their families and communities.[98] To do so means suspending contemporary perspectives that view magic as a marginal or deviant form of religious behavior and instead acknowledging it as a legitimate and efficacious aspect in its ancient context.

The excavation of Iron Age domestic structures on both sides of the Jordan has produced groupings of artifacts, not found in community or regional temples or shrines, that apparently were used in household religious activities. These assemblages consist of items such as miniature ceramic vessels, lamps, rattles, metal blades, jewelry, terra-cotta pillar-figurines,[99] and Bes seals or images. It is the frequent presence of the terra-cottas and the images of Bes that suggests that women in particular used these assemblages.

Bes is an Egyptian dwarf god whose ugly appearance was widely believed to scare away evil demons, particularly those who would be harmful to pregnant women or women in childbirth. Representations of Bes, including on amulets actually made in Palestine, indicate that they were not simply imported images but were widely used at Israelite sites throughout the Iron Age. Such images do not necessarily imply the worship of an Egyptian god but rather the use of a symbol believed to be apotropaic (protective). The pillar-figurines, with women

---

[97] Carol Meyers, "Women at the Entrance to the Tent of Meeting (Exod 38:8; 1 Sam 2:22)," *WIS*, 202; Janet S. Everhart, "Serving Women and Their Mirrors: A Feminist Reading of Exodus 38:8b," *CBQ* 66 (2004): 44–54.

[98] Carol Meyers, *Households and Holiness: The Religious Culture of Israelite Women* (Minneapolis: Fortress, 2005).

[99] These small figurines depict nude females, either pregnant or holding their breasts; their lower bodies are stylized in the form of a pillar, hence the designation "pillar-figurines."

holding their breasts, are likewise related to female reproductive processes. Some scholars believe they represent the goddess Asherah and are appeals to her to provide fertility or assure lactation. In the absence of divine insignia on these statuettes, it is more likely that they are votive or devotional images, hoping to secure the help of Yahweh or Asherah, or both, in the reproductive process. In any case, the presence of hundreds or even thousands of such figurines in domestic contexts, along with Bes images and other objects, suggests that these assemblages were the paraphernalia of women's household religious activities, meant to secure protection and success in bearing and nurturing children.

Among the other items in the assemblages, the miniature vessels may have been used for offerings to the deity or deities. Information from ethnography helps to identify some of the other artifacts. The customs of Middle Eastern Muslim, Christian, and Jewish women in the nineteenth and early twentieth centuries show continuity with the biblical past in the use of "magic" in association with childbirth.[100] Gynecological texts from Mesopotamia and Anatolia often provide similar information.[101] The knives and rattles, for example, are used to frighten away evil spirits from a birthing room. The same is true for lamps – light keeps demons threatening newborns at bay. Wearing shiny jewelry serves similar apotropaic purposes, keeping Lilith-like forces from drying up a mother's milk.[102]

In a premodern society such as ancient Israel, the household religious activities of women were concerned with the kind of life–death issues that today are managed by medical treatment. Their practices were believed to secure fertility, safe childbirth, and healthy neonates. Consequently, as experts in and practitioners of specialized acts understood to be essential for their own welfare and that of their families, women were major religious actors in the household setting. Such roles would have afforded them status in their households and contributed to their sense of self-worth.

INVENTORY OF WORK AND METALS – 38:21–31

The description of the courtyard is followed by eleven verses presenting a detailed "inventory" (NRSV "records") of all the metal donated for the tabernacle. The list of metals has no parallel in the prescriptive texts (except perhaps for the reference in verse 26 to the silver acquired from the census assessment of 30:11–16) and thus is one of the passages unique to the descriptive texts. It contains the unusual phrase "tabernacle of the covenant" (v. 21), a designation that situates

---

[100] Some sources are cited in C. Meyers, *Households and Holiness* (2005).

[101] M. Stol, *Birth in Babylon and the Bible* (2000); G. Beckman, *Hittite Birth Rituals* (1983).

[102] Lilith was a Mesopotamian night demon who was especially threatening to women and children and who emerges as a powerful figure in postbiblical Jewish and Islamic folklore; see Carole L. Fontaine, "Lilith," *WIS*, 531.

the ensuing data about construction within the overall purpose of the project, namely, to provide a holy space for the ark of the covenant.

In descending order beginning with the most valuable precious commodity, the amounts of donated gold, silver, and bronze (probably copper) are listed. However, the accompanying information about the purposes to which these metals are put varies. No such information is provided for the amassed gold; for the silver, only the uses of the metal provided by census, but not by donation, are specified; and for the bronze, the uses of the metal from general contributions but not from the women's mirrors are enumerated. Different traditions of record-keeping perhaps have been combined, as indicated also by the fact that the silver collected by census here is used for construction expenses whereas 30:16 designates it for operating expenses.

VESTMENTS – 39:1–31

The description of the priestly apparel is quite similar to that of the prescriptive texts (**28:1–43**), but there are some differences. In keeping with their focus on construction rather than use, this section adds some technical details and omits information about function. The description of the ephod is abbreviated, although it does supply information about the making of golden threads (v. 3) that is not in the prescriptive passage. The breastpiece is called "breastpiece of judgment," in reference to its function, several times in chapter 28, but this phrase does not appear at all in chapter 39. Similarly, the Urim and Thummim, which have a mantic function, appear in the prescriptive texts but not in the descriptive equivalent. And the verse indicating how the robe of the ephod is to be used in Aaron's ministry (28:35) is abbreviated in 39:26.

Even more striking is the nearly complete absence of Aaron. His name appears some sixteen times in chapter 28 but only twice in the descriptive equivalent: once in the introduction, which arguably is part of the preceding inventory and not part of the vestment section at all;[103] and once in reference to the garments made for Aaron and his sons. None of the items made for Aaron alone involve mention of his name; and, of course, the investiture ceremony of chapter 29, in which Aaron holds center stage, does not occur at all in the descriptive texts. In contrast, Moses' name is not found in chapter 28 but appears *seven* times in 39:1–31 as part of the summary formula, "as the LORD had commanded Moses." The prominence of Aaron in the prescriptive texts may be a function of the priestly redaction of the entire tabernacle document. However, this descriptive section of the canonical whole follows the golden-calf episode, which shows Aaron's complicity in the sinfulness of the people as well as Moses' unparalleled intimacy with God. It is fitting that Aaron's priestly prominence is absent and an exalted role for Moses dominates.

---

[103]　U. Cassuto, *Exodus* (1983), 473.

COMPLETION – 39:32–43

This section begins with the information that God's instructions to Moses have been fully implemented. In reporting that the "work ... was finished," verse 32 echoes the language of the priestly account of creation, when God "finished the work" of creating everything (Gen 2:1–3). In both texts, the word "work" indicates the artisanship rather than the actual labor required for a complex project. The tabernacle is the microcosm of the universe, and language linking the human construction of God's earthly dwelling with the divine creation of the world recurs in the completion and dedication sections that bring Exodus to a close. It is no surprise, then, that the concluding verse (v. 43) of the completion passage, which echoes the opening verse, has Moses *see* the finished project, just as God *sees* the work of six days of creation in Gen 1:31. Moreover, it has Moses offer a *blessing*, as does God in Gen 1:22, 28 and 2:3. Between verses 32 and 43 is a summary of the tabernacle's construction that lists its various components in the same order as in the immediately preceding descriptive texts.

Both this section and the dedication section that follows are unique in Exodus in referring to the project as the "tabernacle of the tent of meeting" (39:32; 40:1, 6, 29). This composite phrase represents the combined tabernacle and tent-of-meeting traditions that form the tabernacle texts.

ERECTION AND INSTALLATION – 40:1–38

Allusions to creation permeate the final chapter of Exodus, strongly indicating a priestly hand in forming the canonical book. The tabernacle is to be erected, its furnishings installed, and the whole project made operational on the first day of the first month, that is, on New Year's day (v. 2). The initiation of the tabernacle thus is keyed to the creation of the world as well as to the exodus from Egypt (v. 17; cf. 12:2). Similarly, the structure of chapter 40 – God gives instructions about what is to be done (vv. 2–15) and those instructions are then carried out (vv. 16–33) – mirrors God's day-by-day directives ("Let there be ...") and implementation in Genesis 1 and also recapitulates the overall structure of the tabernacle texts, with directives followed by implementation.

Bezalel, his assistants, and the Levitical workers have made all the components of the tabernacle; it is up to Moses alone to assemble them. He does this step-by-step at God's bidding. The formula "as the LORD had commanded Moses [or him]" appears eight times in the execution passage, once as an introductory statement (v. 16) and then following each of the *seven* units (vv. 19, 21, 23, 25, 27, 29, 32) – perhaps corresponding to the *seven* days of creation – of Moses' activity in setting up the tabernacle. The central role of Moses in this enterprise means that on this occasion he washes in the laver (v. 31), puts loaves on the offering table (v. 23), arranges the lamps (v. 25), offers incense (v. 27), and makes sacrifices (v. 29) – all acts otherwise relegated to Aaron and his sons. The consecration of the priests, which will allow them to perform these rites, is not included in Exodus (it comes in Leviticus 8). At this point only Moses is qualified, and he initiates the priestly service.

The erection of the tabernacle and the installation of all its appurtenances means that it is ready to assume the role – as the one particular place on earth in which God's presence will dwell – for which it was intended. The climax of the long and detailed tabernacle texts, and of the book of Exodus as a whole, comes in its final five verses (40:34–38), in which the cloud and fire signifying divine presence cover the structure and God's glory fills it. The cloud (and fire), sometimes as a pillar, is a recurring signal of divine presence in Exodus. It guides the people from Egypt to Sinai, where it settles on the holy mountain, and now it is transferred to the tabernacle. The word "cloud" appears in each of these last five verses; the divine presence it signifies thus serves as the leitmotif of the conclusion of Exodus. Now the tabernacle is truly God's dwelling place on earth, and the intensity of God's presence is so powerful that not even Moses can enter the tabernacle.

The promise of 29:45, that God will dwell among the people and be their deity, is realized. The verb translated "settled" in verse 35 is *škn*, which means "to dwell" and, as noted at the beginning of the commentary on Part III, is the verbal root of the Hebrew word for tabernacle. The remarkable notion of God filling an earthly space is accompanied by the observation that the cloud (and fire) is not permanently above the tabernacle. God is more likely to be imminent in the tabernacle (and temple; cf. 1 Kgs 8:10–11) than in any other place on earth; yet God is not confined to a place made by human hands. God's cloud and fire, which have led the people from the Reed Sea to Sinai and which hovered over the holy mountain, will surely continue to lead the people now that the tabernacle has been completed. The wilderness journey can resume, and the narrative describing it – in Leviticus and Numbers – can now proceed.

Biblical and Extrabiblical Texts Index

Hebrew Terms Index

Author Index

Subject Index